Liquid Gold

Also by Stephen Brook

LIQUID GOLD

Dessert Wines of the World

STEPHEN BROOK

Constable · London

First published in Great Britain 1987
by Constable and Company Limited
10 Orange Street London WC2H 7EG
Copyright © 1987 by Stephen Brook
Set in Linotron Plantin 11 pt by
Rowland Phototypesetting Limited
Bury St Edmunds, Suffolk
Printed in Great Britain by
St Edmundsbury Press Limited
Bury St Edmunds, Suffolk

British Library CIP Data
Brook, Stephen
Liquid gold: dessert wines of the world
1. Wine and wine making
I. Title
641.2′2   TP548

ISBN 0 09 466920 1

Contents

Foreword

For decades fine sweet wines have been the least appreciated and most undervalued of the world's great wines. This is a question of taste rather than cost, for while it is undoubtedly true that Yquem or a great Trockenbeerenauslese is an extremely expensive bottle of wine, that is not true of many other top Sauternes or other sweet wines. Part of the difficulty is knowing, or not knowing, when to consume such wines. Although a dessert wine provides an ideal conclusion to a meal, sipped at leisure over a bowl of nuts, we are not in the habit of opening bottles either as aperitifs or as wines to end a meal except on special occasions. It is all very well for producers of Sauternes to assert, quite rightly, that their wines are an ideal accompaniment for *foie gras*, but in my household *foie gras* does not find its way onto the menu very often. Yet it still seems remarkable that there is, to the best of my knowledge, no book that deals exclusively with a style of winemaking that has been practised continuously in some parts of the world for well over 300 years.

Dessert wines were not always held in low esteem. The Russian Czars prized the sweet Hungarian wine from Tokay so greatly that in the late eighteenth century they installed their own garrison in the region to ensure the integrity of the vineyards and their wines. When in 1847 another Russian, the Grand Duke Constantine, paid 20,000 francs for 900 litres of Ch d'Yquem, he was spending four times as much as anyone had ever handed over for an equivalent quantity of French wine. The long defunct Muscats of Constantia from South Africa were valued as highly in the early nineteenth century as any European wine. Modern communications have to some extent diminished the rarity of great wines, and now that Tokay, for instance, is readily available in many supermarkets – and at prices so low our ancestors would gasp with astonishment and envy – we probably do not treasure the wine as greatly as it deserves. German Trocken-beerenauslesen, which are produced only in the best vintages, fetch astonishing prices at auction because they are produced in minute quantities. Austrian Trockenbeerenauslesen, which are made in enormous quantities in certain vintages, are underestimated not because the best of them are greatly inferior to their German counterparts, but because they are so plentiful.

The decline in popularity of dessert wines can in part be attributed to the infrequent opportunities we have of drinking them. In Britain, which more or less invented Port and Madeira, it is almost *de rigueur* in certain circles such as Oxbridge colleges and London clubs where formal dining is a regular feature of social life to consume those wines in preference to the enormous range of other sweet wines that are available. But a large measure of blame must be laid at the door of the producers themselves. As will be explained in Chapter 5, tanker-loads of inferior and sickly sweet wines have been churned out over recent decades. Their cheapness may have found a market in the short run but probably killed it in the long run. For someone of my generation 'Sauternes' was a gummy ultra-cheap sweet white wine, usually from Spain, which one drank in bulk at college parties and often regurgitated onto the floor towards the end of the festivities. It took me a dozen years to overcome my prejudices against any wine that was white and sweet. Even today the prejudice is so alive that I have had to adopt the term 'dessert wine' in preference to 'sweet wine', which still has pejorative connotations in Britain. It must also be said that outrages such as the Austrian wine scandal of 1985, and comparable adulterations in Germany at the same time, have not exactly helped the cause.

Producers have also failed to market such wines efficiently outside the regions of production. If a tenth of the energy and budget devoted to the promotion of Beaujolais Nouveau had been lavished on the better dessert wines of, say, Monbazillac or the Loire, there might be greater public awareness of these lovely wines. Fortunately the situation is becoming more hopeful with each year that passes. With the explosion of interest in fine wine in Britain, the United States, and Australia – and other countries too – many wine merchants, and their customers, are beginning to explore the marvels of French Vouvray, Italian Recioto, Californian Late Harvest Rieslings, and many other great wines.

The book that follows is not a definitive survey of the field, but, as it were, a report from the frontier. While Sauternes or Tokay are well known and well distributed worldwide, many other wines of comparable quality rarely travel beyond their zones of production. To seek them out and to garner as much information as I could concerning those wines has been an enthralling task but an exceedingly difficult one. The writer on the wines of Bordeaux or the Rheingau can make frequent trips to the region to supplement his or her researches. But since this book embraces a world of winemaking, from traditional European sites to hillsides in the New World where vines were not even planted two decades ago, such exhaustive depth of research has not been possible. Nor has it been possible to include as much historical or anecdotal material as I should have liked in an ideal world where books could be as long and discursive as their authors wished. My first priority has been to discuss the wines themselves.

The wine itself, of course, is an elusive concept, for it does not spring into being without human intervention. It is the end result of a long and arduous collaboration between nature and human beings. There are those who assert that soil conditions and vineyard exposure are the crucial determining factors in the styles of wine, and others who maintain that methods of vinification are more important than any other factor. Such debates are futile, for the truth is simple enough: all these factors – plus many others such as grape variety, viticulture, climate – are crucial in varying degrees. You cannot make good wine from bad grapes, but you can make bad wine from good grapes. It is equally true that individual winemakers impose their styles on their wines. At every stage, from pruning the vines to bottling the wine, the winemaker must make choices, and those choices determine the style and quality of the end product. It is for this reason that I have not hesitated to write about those who make the wines as well as the wines they make.

Many of the wines discussed may be obscure to most readers, either because of scarcity or, an allied reason, because they rarely leave their region of production. Consequently I have done my best to describe how the wines actually taste. This is, I am well aware, a hazardous procedure. For a start, other people's tasting notes are rarely enthralling. Then too, a wine hurriedly sampled in a chilly cellar while spiders crawl up your legs may taste very different from the same bottle sampled at leisure after a splendid meal. In some cases I have been able to taste wines more than once, sometimes up to four or five times, but that is very much the exception. I have no doubt that I will have done an injustice to certain wines, and overpraised others. It must be recognised that tasting notes are not divinely inspired and are no substitute for going out and sampling the wines oneself. Winemakers who have generously allowed me to taste at their cellars will, I hope, be indulgent if I have done any of their wines a disservice, just as I am sure they will not rush to contradict me if I have been too fulsome in my praise. It has been especially difficult to write about wine-growing countries I have not been able to visit, such as Yugoslavia, Australia, and South Africa. I have thought it prudent to place discussions of their wines in an appendix rather than in the body of the book, since my experience of them is so incomplete. I have also omitted such major wine countries as Turkey and the USSR, simply because my knowledge of their wines is negligible. In future editions of this book, if there are any, I hope to provide a more complete survey of such countries, and of regions such as the Pacific Northwest of the United States.

I have tried not to dazzle the reader with science. On the other hand, it is important to understand how these wines are made. I originally intended to write a separate chapter on techniques involved in making sweet wines, but this intention was foiled first by the realisation that there were many varying techniques, and secondly by a suspicion that nobody would read such a chapter. Instead I have talked about vinification in the context of specific wines. The most general account of how sweet wine is made is given in Chapter 1, but supplementary accounts, related to specific wines, are given in, among other places, the sections on Hungary and northern Italy. A glossary has been provided to explain technical terms.

Notation and figuration have been a major problem in organising this book. The sugar content of grapes is measured in at least five different ways, according to the country where the grapes are grown. It made no sense to convert all these systems into a single one such as potential alcohol, so I use which ever system is employed in the country under discussion. Similarly I have used hectares in discussing the vineyards of Europe, but acreage in discussing those of

California; degrees Centigrade in Europe, degrees Fahrenheit in California. It would have been perverse to do otherwise. Since I hope many readers will be encouraged by the account that follows to visit some of the wine-growing regions under discussion, it is just as well to be familiar with the measurements employed in each. On the other hand it is important to be able to compare the analyses of wines from different countries, and the reader is referred to the table of correspondences on p. 333.

Acknowledgments

My greatest debt is to the many winemakers in Europe and the United States who tolerated my often protracted visits and incessant questioning. Most of them are mentioned by name in the text of the book.

In France I am grateful to the following individuals, who went out of their way to help me with my inquiries and to ensure that my visits to their regions were fruitful: Jean Claude and Yvette Hay of the Maison du Vin de l'Anjou; M. Bosviel of Ch Saint-Martin, Cadillac; Louis Courbin of Ch Mazarin, Loupiac; Jean Perromat of Ch Cérons, Cérons; Tom Heeter of Ch Nairac, Barsac; the Meslier family of Ch Raymond-Lafon, Sauternes; Mme Brigitte Lurton-Belondrade of Ch Climens, Barsac; M. Garat of the Comité Inter-professionel des Vins de Bergerac; Robert Latrille of Ch Jolys, Jurançon; and Christine Ontivero of the Comité Interprofessionel des Vins Doux Naturels in Perpignan.

In Germany I am most grateful to Erwein Graf Matuschka-Greiffenclau, who put me in touch with almost every important winemaker in the country. Bernhard and Heinrich Breuer of Rüdesheim were generous with time and information as well as hospitality, as was Armin Diel and his family. I am also grateful to Bernd Philippi of Weingut Koehler-Ruprecht in Kallstadt, Christoff Schultz of Weingut Oberst Schultz-Werner in Gaubischofsheim, Hans-Joachim Zilliken of Weingut Forstmeister Geltz Erben Zilliken in Saarburg, and Graf Michael Adelmann of Burg Schaubeck, Kleinbottwar, all of whom offered me hospitality.

In Austria Dipl.-Ing. Johann Traxler of the Oesterreichischer Weinwirtschaftsfonds assisted me greatly in planning my visits to the Burgenland, as did Ing. Stefan Szmolyán of the Burgenland Landwirtschaftskammer. In London Cherry Chappell, Thomas Augustin, Gerry Amdor, Simon G. Hartley, and Terence Barr provided me with invaluable introductions to Austrian winemakers. I am grateful to Ing. Strobl of the Weinbauschule at Gumpoldskirchen for offering me a great deal of information at very short notice. I am also indebted to David and Jean Bolton, my hosts in Vienna, who revived me with gallons of dry white wine as an antidote on my return from the Burgenland each evening.

My visits to Italy were enlivened by the hospitality of Roberto Anselmi, Paulo and Dina Rapuzzi, and the staff of Villa Banfi at Strevi. In London the Italian Trade Centre assisted me with tastings and correspondence, and Paul Merritt of Alivini and Mark Hughes of European Vintners made crucial appointments in Italy on my behalf. Geoff Owen of Giustivini kindly travelled hundreds of miles in order to accompany me on my visit to Giuseppe Quintarelli.

The Wine Institute of California, in the persons of John Walter in London and Danny Daniels in San Francisco, were extremely helpful, and the Institute's generosity made it possible for me to visit a large number of wineries in the state. The Quady family of Madera entertained me handsomely, as did Erik and Laura Tarloff, who put me up for the duration of my visit. The Australian Trade Commission and Ross Sheppard were most helpful in providing me with information about the sweet wines of Australia. Attila Kovacs of the Hungarian Embassy helped to organise my visit to Tokay, and John Lipitch kindly read and corrected what I had to say about Hungarian wines. I am also grateful to Connoisseur Wines, City Vintagers, and Henry C. Collison & Sons for the assistance they gave me, and to Colman's of Norwich, Renato Trestini, Geoffrey Roberts Associates, and La Vigneronne for supplying the wines photographed on the jacket.

I

Sauternes

To most people, Sauternes represents the epitome of sweet wine. The district is, compared to the Tokay region in Hungary, a new-comer to the commercial production of sweet wine. Nor are the wines of Sauternes, even Ch. d'Yquem, as costly as the greatest German Trockenbeerenauslesen. What Sauternes does offer is a consistency of style and production. For well over a century the same properties have devoted their efforts to the making of a single style of wine. We can speak of 'classic' Sauternes because we have certain expectations. The region is limited, whereas in Germany any producer can make a sweet wine if the climate obliges, and the grape varieties that may be planted are also restricted. Many French wine drinkers scorn German Trockenbeerenauslesen for their excessive sweetness, and their residual sugar levels are indeed far higher than those of most Sauternes. Flip the coin, and you will find Germans puzzling over the accolades awarded to their French counterparts, since they consider most Sauternes heavy, oily, and over-alcoholic. The simple truth is that the wines are entirely different in style: the German wine is low in alcohol but high in residual sugar and acidity; the French wine often lacks acidity but has greater power and amplitude.

While the great German sweet wines are essentially freaks of nature, those of Sauternes are a norm. The Sauternais is a region blessed with a microclimate that makes possible, more years than not, the production of magnificent sweet wines. If one imagines Bordeaux giving a thumbs-down sign, then the Sauternais lies along the nail of that thumb, the remainder of which is the sprawling Graves region. Like much of the Graves that stretches for twenty-five miles between Sauternes and Bordeaux itself, the district borders the

River Garonne. But just south of the commune of Barsac, the most northerly commune of the district, the little River Ciron trickles towards the Garonne. The Ciron is a spring-fed stream that meets the warmer, tidal Garonne, and by mid-September their confluence encourages the development of evening mists and fogs that lie thickly over the vineyards on either side of the two rivers. Then late the following morning, the bright autumn sunshine burns off the mist and shines brightly until dusk, when the fogs develop once again.

This alternation of humidity and sunshine provides ideal conditions for the activities of the fungus *Botrytis cinerea*, though if the weather is too dry or too wet, the fungus will either not develop at all or combine with other, altogether undesirable forms of rot, such as *pourriture grise* (grey rot), which often attacks the grapes when the weather is soggy by penetrating the porous grape skins and negating the beneficial effects of botrytis. Grey rot can destroy the grapes and unbalance even lightly affected grapes that, if not weeded out, can prompt troublesome volatile acidity and off flavours in the finished wine. Botrytis is unwelcome to the grower of red grapes, who sprays to prevent the botrytis spores from attacking them. But in the Sauternes attacks of *pourriture noble* (noble rot), as the French call botrytis, although disgusting to behold, are welcomed. It is perfectly possible to make good sweet wines from grapes that, through the action of prolonged sunshine, are overripe and high in sugar content. But such wines will always be insipid in comparison with wines made from botrytised grapes, for the fungus induces chemical transformations within the grape that give the final product a richness and complexity that wine made only from overripe grapes can never attain.

Nourished by the sugar and tartaric acid couched within each grape, the botrytis spores cause the grape skins, deprived of much of their contents, to shrivel and rot. Once golden grapes, round and bulging with sweet juice, turn brown and purple as their skins crinkle and fold. By this time, the spores will have consumed much of the sugar within the grape, but the alternation of sunshine and humidity will dehydrate the berries, so that half or more of the water content will also have vanished. The end result of the action of the botrytis fungus, apart from the death of the grape, is to concentrate the sugar content; among other chemical actions, the grape's tartaric acid is transformed into gluconic acid and glycerol, which will give the wine its viscosity. Wine made from botrytised grapes will often have four times as much glycerol as an 'ordinary' wine. Despite such transformations of the acids, the overall acidity of the grape is not greatly altered by the action of botrytis. Other chemical actions, including those that give botrytis wines their distinctive bouquet, are even now not fully understood.

Unfortunately, *Botrytis cinerea* is a law unto itself. It does not march in with predictable regularity. It does all it can to torment the grower and the winemaker. There are some years, such as 1972 and 1978, when botrytis scarcely puts in an appearance at all. When it does manifest itself, it does so patchily. In some years, such as 1983, the fungus was reasonably obliging and swooped into the vineyards in reasonably thorough fashion. Any winemaker who made a poor Sauternes in 1983 has no excuse. But that was an exception. Usually the fungus arrives here and there. Although the spores are carried on the breeze and can spread rapidly through the vineyards, it is quite common for some grapes on each vine to remain only mildly affected while others become entirely shrivelled. Ideally, the grape pickers should only select berries that have been fully attacked by botrytis; other grapes, still healthy or only partially afflicted, should be left on the vine until their turn has come. Some Sauternes properties do indeed pick grapes individually rather than by bunches, but this is a horrifically expensive practice that few can afford. Nevertheless, it is common for pickers to make what are known as *tries successives*: repeated forays into the same vineyards in order to pick only those grapes or bunches in optimal condition. In years when botrytis is widespread and abundant, even the most meticulous proprietors do not have to make as many *passages* through the vineyards as in other years, when as many as eleven or twelve may have to be made. In 1972 Yquem made eleven *passages* but to no avail; the wine was still not worthy of the label and it was all declassified.

Nor is the climate predictable. Spells of rain or hail can interrupt the harvest, and picking cannot resume until the dehydration process has resumed. Indeed, the conscientious proprietor in the Sauternes needs nerves of steel. By mid-September the grapes are reaching maturity, and by early October they should be in splendid condition. If the harvest begins at this point, the result will be sweet wines with scant traces of botrytis. The dutiful proprietor will wait, but the longer he waits, the greater the risk of losing the entire crop to rain or other hazards of nature.

1985 is an ideal case in point. The weather was warm and dry. While the rest of France was rejoicing at the fine weather which was ensuring another excellent vintage, the Sauternes growers were biting their nails. Humidity was lacking. Some rain in late September led to the arrival of some botrytis, but then the warm dry weather returned and its development ground to a halt. The temptation, to which many growers succumbed, was to pick in October, even though the majority of grapes were healthy. More conscientious growers and proprietors sat tight, and by late October and November they were rewarded. Botrytis dug into the overripe grapes, and the crop picked at this time was perfectly suited to the making of great Sauternes. Yquem, with its usual courage and perfectionism, continued picking until just before Christmas. This brief account of a single vintage gives some indication of the hazards involved in making Sauternes, even before the grapes have arrived at the press-house. It also illuminates the danger of talking about specific vintages in Sauternes. Most vintages in Sauternes, unlike, say, 1983, are difficult. Even in a generally good year such as 1985, hard decisions had to be made. Those who picked the majority or all of their grapes early will make a very different wine from those who bravely waited until November and December.

It will now be clear that producing top-quality Sauternes is a hazardous undertaking. In Germany, for instance, Beerenauslese or Trockenbeerenauslese is the icing on the cake; in lesser years the winemaker will have no difficulty producing a gamut of wines from ordinary Qualitätswein to Spätlese or Auslese. The Sauternes proprietor is far more dependent on a single product. It is true that some properties also make a dry white wine to mop up a surplus of sound grapes, usually Sauvignon, that are not suitable for the sweet wine; and a handful of estates, such as Guiraud, even produce a small quantity of red wine. But there are also properties, such as Climens and Nairac, that only produce the sweet wine. In middling years, conscientious proprietors have made the painful decision to market no wine at all, and to sell the entire crop to wholesalers as generic Sauternes. Even in good years, proprietors are likely to discard a percentage of their crop as unworthy of their label. In 1978, a year of virtually no botrytis, Yquem rejected 85% of their own wine.

Without ruthless selection at all stages – from pruning to harvesting to the final *assemblage* – you cannot make great Sauternes. The rigorous pursuit of quality is, evidently, enormously expensive. The extraordinary thing about Sauternes is not that it is so expensive, but that it is still so cheap.

The road south from Bordeaux to Langon brings one through Barsac, the first of the five communes that make up the Sauternais. South of Barsac lies the small town of Preignac, and then the villages of Bommes, Sauternes, and Fargues. Since 1908, only wines from these communes are entitled to be sold as Sauternes, though wine from Barsac may be sold as either Barsac or Sauternes. There are considerable variations in the soil throughout the district, so it is difficult to generalise about the characteristic soils of each commune. Barsac does differ from the other communes in having alluvial deposits and clay over a chalky base. The more southerly communes, including Sauternes itself, are composed of gravel over a subsoil of clay. Sauternes and Bommes are slightly hillier than the other communes, and the presence of gentle slopes provides various permutations of exposure to the sun and drainage. So many factors go into the production of Sauternes that it is dangerous to generalise, but Sauternes tends to be fleshier and richer than Barsac, which is often more elegant. On the other hand, there are 'light' Sauternes such as Clos Haut-Peyraguey, and weighty Barsacs, such as Nairac, so it would be a mistake to put too much emphasis on variations of soil. The presence or absence of botrytis, the rejection of grapes and casks that are not up to standard, and methods of vinification and ageing also affect the final product profoundly.

Local myth has it that the great sweet wine for which the Sauternes has become so famous was first made at Yquem in 1847. The story goes that the owner of Ch La Tour Blanche, M. Focke, travelled to Germany in the 1830s and brought back the secrets of botrytised wines, which he imparted to the Comte de Lur-Saluces at Ch d'Yquem. Every corner of Europe where such wines are produced likes to provide a date when they were first made – at Schloss Johannisberg on the Rhein the *annus mirabilis* is 1775 – but it is almost certain that botrytised wines have been made for centuries. Until quite recently wine was extremely fragile and the sophisticated vinification methods that inhibit oxidation were unknown. Wine was stored in casks that tended to encourage oxidation, and thus the life expectancy of wine was limited. Estate bottling was rare until only a few decades ago, and most wines exported from the region of production had to endure long journeys in cask. Methods of conservation were essential. Fortified wines, such as Port and Madeira and the Vins Doux Naturels of southern France, were made by adding alcohol to partially fermented musts; the alcohol preserved the wine. Sugar had the same effect, and wines made from overripe, botrytised, or sun-dried grapes were less likely to spoil than those without residual sugar. So however picturesque the legends about the 'discovery' of botrytis, they can never be more than accounts of rediscoveries. A. Jullien, in his *Topographie de Tous les Vignobles*, published in 1816, refers quite explicitly to the *très moelleux* (very sweet) style of the Sauternes wines, and mentions that the harvesting of nobly rotten grapes can take up to two months. Moreover, the cellar book at Yquem of 1810 refers specifically to *triage*.

If Yquem revived the practice of making sweet wines in the Sauternais, it was a method that caught on remarkably fast, for by 1855 the great *classement impérial* was made, establishing once and for all the pecking order. There have of course been changes since 1855. Ch Rabaud at Bommes was listed as a Premier Cru, and another property, Ch Pexoto, was listed as a Deuxième Cru. Rabaud is now divided into two Premiers Crus, Sigalas-Rabaud and Rabaud-Promis, and Pexoto was long ago incorporated into Rabaud-Promis. Yet after over 130 years the classification remains astonishingly just. Yquem was singled out as the sole Premier Cru Supérieur in Sauternes, and nobody would wish to challenge that judgement. You can argue indefinitely about whether Latour or Lafite is the finest Pauillac, but nobody disputes that Yquem is still the supreme Sauternes. Other proprietors occasionally come close to matching the marvellous concentration and breed of Yquem, but no other property has consistently and regularly produced a better wine. Were one empowered to tinker with the 1855 classification, it would be easy to make adjustments. Certain properties now glorying as Premiers Crus are not worthy of the honour, and there are Deuxièmes Crus and even unclassified properties, such as Ch de Fargues and Ch Raymond-Lafon, that make wine of Premier Cru standard.

Nineteen estates were classified originally, and after over a century of divisions and mergers, the list today now consists of twenty-four. Of the twelve Premiers Crus (including Yquem), six are in Bommes, only two each in Sauternes and Barsac, while Fargues and Preignac can only claim one estate in each (Rieussec and Suduiraut, respectively). Of the dozen Deuxième Crus, seven are in Barsac, three in Sauternes, and Fargues and Preignac are again left with one each. Of the families that originally owned the classified properties, only the Lur-Saluces of Yquem still hold the reins. Many of the great estates have changed hands just in the last two decades. Climens and Nairac were sold in the early 1970s, and more recently Guiraud, Rieussec and d'Arche came under new ownership. Inevitably, such changes bring fluctuations in quality. Guiraud and d'Arche are now making far better wine than under their previous owners, and the injection of new blood into the Sauternais has been largely beneficial.

As has already been mentioned, grapes, the primary material of winemaking, are of crucial importance when it comes to the production of Sauternes. It is not difficult to make sweet wine, especially in hot regions of the world. All you have to do is pick overripe grapes and stop the fermentation at, say, 12% alcohol. The sugar not transformed into alcohol by the yeasts remains in the wine in the form of residual sugar. *Voilà!* A sweet wine! But chances are that this wine will be insipid at best and sickening at worst. To make sweet wine is easy; to make great sweet wine is, most winemakers would agree, the most difficult undertaking of all. Great sweet wine must be balanced wine: sugar alone is cloying. In Germany, sweetness is balanced by the high acidity of the Riesling grape; in Sauternes it is countered by alcohol, since the grapes permitted in the region lack the high natural acidity of Riesling. Without balance, the wine will be heavy and cloying. The greatest test for a Sauternes is whether, after finishing one glass, the palate remains sufficiently fresh to venture on another. A clumsily made Sauternes, however rich and sweet, will fatigue the palate.

Achieving this balance is a function of the vinification, but it is essential to have raw materials of high quality. Only three grape varieties are permitted in the Sauternais, and for that matter in the other regions of Bordeaux where sweet white wine is made. These are Sémillon, Sauvignon, and Muscadelle. Sémillon, which offers the strongest resistance to unwanted diseases, is nearly always dominant, accounting for between 60% and 90% of any estate's vineyards.

Nearly all properties plant between 10% and 20% of Sauvignon, which contributes a freshness to the final blend that contrasts with the fatter flavour of Sémillon. The two varieties are pruned differently, so that yields of Sauvignon are generally rather higher than those of Sémillon. Thus the fact that a property has 10% Sauvignon planted does not necessarily mean that the final blend will contain that proportion of Sauvignon wine; the proportion will often be somewhat higher than its presence in the vineyards might suggest. The third permitted variety is Muscadelle, though some properties steer clear of this notoriously tricky variety, which is prone to disease and considered by many to be more trouble than it is worth. It rarely constitutes more than 5% of a property's plantation, and is often a mere 2%. Muscadelle is blended into the wine primarily for its aromatic qualities. That enterprising British winemaker of the Dordogne, Nick Ryman of Ch La Jaubertie, made a dry wine from 100% Muscadelle in 1985, when, atypically, his Muscadelle vines were in perfect health. It was a splendid wine with a gorgeous flowery nose, highly aromatic with overtones of Muscat and grapefruit. Tasting this wine has encouraged me to think that the much maligned Muscadelle does indeed have a contribution to make to fine Sauternes.

It is possible, by planting prolific clones and by failing to prune vigorously, to obtain very high yields on many grape varieties these days. Yields of 100 hectolitres per hectare are not unusual in Alsace, and in Italy yields of 140 hl/ha are attained without difficulty. The maximum permitted yield in Sauternes is 25 hl/ha. The best properties prune their vines severely so as to reduce the yields even further; the point of this is to concentrate the sugars and flavours of each grape, rather than to disperse the nutrients among an excessive number of bunches. Were any property in Sauternes to admit to attaining even the maximum permitted yield, its wines would immediately, and probably justly, be dismissed as second-rate. At Yquem the average yield is said to be 9 hl/ha. Life can be injected into this bare statistic by explaining that this is equivalent to each vine producing no more than a single glass of wine per year. The age of the vines is another factor relating to quality. Old vines have deeper roots and bear fruit less copiously, and there is a corresponding concentration of flavour. Yet there is little fetishism about old vines in the Sauternais: even the greatest properties do not hesitate to grub up senile vines and replant, even though they must wait up to eight years before their grapes are suitable for making Sauternes.

Yields vary from year to year, and in autumns when the microclimate behaves properly, yields will be higher without any diminution of quality. In general, the best Sauternes properties report yields of between 10 and 15 hl/ha. This is one of the reasons why proprietors do not take kindly to being told that their wines are too expensive. Given the low yields, dependence on the often elusive botrytis, and the distinct possibility of losing a large part of one's crop to the assaults of nature, the wines are fairly priced. Bear in mind, too, that the grapes must be harvested by hand by skilled pickers – no machines are permitted in the region. Then, as with the great red wines of the Médoc, the wines will sit in cask or tank for up to three years, and this too adds to production costs. Médoc growers, however, can make very great wine indeed from yields three or four times as high as those of the Sauternais. For a property such as Yquem to charge, approximately, the same as a great first growth of the Médoc for a wine of far more limited production, is eminently reasonable. The rest of the pack, including top properties whose wines sometimes rival those of Yquem, can only charge prices about one-third of those obtained by Yquem. In the seventeenth century the wines of Sauternes were the most costly in the entire Bordeaux region. Such wines are nowadays, in comparative terms, extraordinary bargains, though there are signs that Sauternes is enjoying a revival and that prices, which have already risen sharply in recent years, will continue to do so.

HOW SAUTERNES IS MADE: CH D'YQUEM

To follow the process by which Sauternes is made, let us observe Ch d'Yquem at work. This property still makes the wine in a completely traditional manner. All other approaches to vinification, many of which are entirely acceptable and capable of producing excellent wine, are departures from the classic method.

The actual harvest is protracted. At Yquem it is not unusual for the harvest to last two months, and for all of this time 150 pickers must be paid, even during the days or weeks when rain stops play. Given such laborious harvesting methods, it is never possible to press all the grapes at the same time. Indeed, each day's harvest is not only pressed separately but fermented separately. At the end of the vintage and the subsequent fermentation, there may be twenty or thirty different lots. During the *assemblage* each lot will be tasted and the final blend put together; inevitably a number of casks will be rejected as not good enough to be bottled as Yquem. The grapes are gently crushed after their arrival at the presshouse. Not all properties crush their grapes, since too forceful a pressure on the skins of botrytised grapes can release into the juice chemical substances that may later impede the clarification and stabilisation of the wine. For similar reasons, the grapes are pressed in an old-fashioned vertical press (also known as a hydraulic or basket press). These old presses are favoured at Yquem because they do not exert too heavy a pressure, and the juice extracted from the grapes is relatively free of solids. The most common presses found in Sauternes, as in other wine regions of France, are horizontal presses, also known as cylindrical presses, which are faster but less dependable in terms of their quality. These presses operate by squeezing the grapes between two metal plates, and allowing the juice to slip through slats as the press revolves. A very few properties employ a pneumatic press, which combines the gentleness of the vertical press with the efficiency of the horizontal press. Pneumatic presses, which squeeze the grapes by a gradually inflating rubber bag, are, however, very expensive. It is typical of Yquem that it owns a pneumatic press, but only uses it as a back-up should one or more of the vertical presses be put out of action. Since the vertical presses are very old, there have been problems obtaining spare parts, and it would be disastrous to have

Château d'Yquem
Lur-Saluces
—— 1975 ——

newly-picked grapes lying around for days while scouring France for an obsolete part.

The grapes are pressed three times; the third pressing, from the most shrivelled berries, give the richest juice. The juice from a single day's picking is combined in a vat and then decanted into oak barrels (*barriques*) for the fermentation. It is common at most properties for a *débourbage* to take place immediately after the pressing. This simply means that the juice is poured into a vat, lightly sulphured to prevent fermentation from beginning too soon, and allowed to settle for up to twenty-four hours; heavier solids fall to the bottom of the tank and then the clear juice is racked off. It is important to have fairly clean musts, both because it aids fermentation, and because the wine need be racked less frequently while being aged. At Yquem, the use of vertical presses usually allows the winemaker to omit the *débourbage* because the juice is already sufficiently limpid. If the weather has turned cold, and by November or December it can be chilly indeed, it may be necessary to heat the cellars to about 20 °C to keep the fermentation going steadily. It will continue for between two and six weeks; the richer the must, the longer the fermentation.

As fermentation proceeds, the winemaker must give some thought to the balance of the wine. Too much alcohol, and the wine will be overpowering and clumsy; too little, and the result is likely to be cloying and even syrupy. The first factor that must be taken into consideration is the sugar content of the must. Although the function of the yeasts is to turn sugar into alcohol, the alcohol generated by the yeasts also acts as a brake to further fermentation. Alcohol is an enemy of yeast, and when the wine reaches a fairly high degree of alcohol, fermentation is likely to stop of its own accord. Sugar too inhibits fermentation, which is why the ultra-rich German Trocken-beerenauslesen are so low in alcohol. Sauternes rarely achieves such high sugar levels, though this is certainly a factor in the chemical processes that halts fermentation at properties such as Yquem, where must weights tend to be high. Sometimes, however, the winemaker, seeking an ideal balance, will want to stop fermentation before it grinds to a halt of its own accord. To accomplish this, he must either use a very expensive piece of equipment called a centrifuge that eliminates any remaining yeasts, or he must add sulphur dioxide (SO_2) or, if the process is taking place in temperature-controlled tanks, lower the temperature sharply in order to kill off the yeasts.

The addition of SO_2 is a controversial subject. It acts as an antioxidant and antibacterial agent. Whenever the juice or wine is to be exposed to the air, a small dose of sulphur dioxide must be added to the wine or casks to deter oxidation. The trouble is that SO_2 is often detectable on the nose and the palate. Not only is it disagreeable, but heavily sulphured wines can induce headaches. Improvements in winemaking technology have meant that the doses of sulphur can be drastically reduced, but not all Sauternes winemakers are able or willing to take advantage of them. It is still all too common, even among Premiers Crus, to encounter wines that are, at least in their youth, unpleasantly sulphury. Yquem may use little or no sulphur to arrest fermentation, but even here SO_2 must be employed when the wine is racked.

At Yquem, the casks are left alone until fermentation ceases of its own accord. Some other winemakers in Sauternes, accustomed to arresting fermentation by the other two methods mentioned above, question Yquem's insistence that no SO_2 is used to stop the fermentation. The *régisseur* at Yquem, Pierre Meslier, points out that because the Yquem grapes are heavily botrytised, fermentation is also arrested by the presence of an antibiotic called botrycine, which also attacks the yeasts, thus supplementing the activities of the alcohol. At those properties where wine is made principally from overripe grapes, botrycine is not present to the same degree and thus fermentation must be stopped by other means. Because fermentation at Yquem stops naturally, the amount of residual sugar in the wine will vary according to the must weight. For this reason, Yquem is very specific about the sugar content of its grapes. Since fermentation stops at around 14% alcohol, grapes picked at 19–20% potential alcohol will leave a residual sugar level of 5–6% (85–100 grammes per litre). By picking too early, Yquem would run the risk of having low must weights that would result in an unbalanced wine. Ripe grapes with little botrytis and a potential alcohol of 17% can easily be fermented to 15% alcohol, which would dominate the wine and mask the residual sugar; such badly made wines are, sadly, all too common. In certain gloriously hot and humid years it is possible to pick grapes with potential alcohol of around 25% or even higher. At such high sugar levels, fermentation is exceedingly difficult, and often grinds to a halt at a mere 8–9%, leaving the bulk of the sugar unconverted into alcohol. This is indeed what happens in Germany, resulting in intensely sweet and rich Trockenbeerenauslesen. Wines of this kind are contrary to the Sauternes model, and though particularly rich grapes are sometimes vinified separately to form a Crème de Tête or other special bottling, it is more common for such rich wines, when they occur, to be blended into the final product.

At Yquem, which is prepared to wait until Christmas, if necessary, in order to pick its grapes at the optimal moment, low must weights are rarely a problem. They hope for, and usually get, grapes with 20–22% potential alcohol. But at other properties, especially in years with a miserable autumn, the average must weight is too low to give a final wine that will attain the legal minimum degree of alcohol (13%), and leave sufficient residual sugar to balance the wine. In such vintages, permission is granted by the authorities to chaptalise the must. Although chaptalisation is routinely practised in cooler wine regions, such as Burgundy, and is becoming increasingly common in Bordeaux as a whole, hackles still rise when the word is mentioned. Chaptalisation is, simply, the addition of a sugar solution to the must in order to increase the potential alcohol by up to two degrees. According to its advocates, this sugar is converted into alcohol and thus ensures a more balanced wine, since without it, the wine would lack sweetness and richness. Even among leading properties in Sauternes, chaptalisation is practised. But there are a few properties, and Yquem is one, where chaptalisation is scorned. Its opponents argue that not all the sugar added to the must is converted into alcohol; a proportion is bound to remain in the form of residual sugar, and this residue, being partly composed of sugar solution instead of grape sugar, can give an undesirable taste and flabbiness to the wine.

Whatever the merits of the arguments on both sides, chaptalisation is here to stay. Yquem, with its unchallenged reputation and relatively high prices, can afford to be noble-minded. Lesser properties simply cannot absorb the huge losses that would be involved if they had to discard a substantial proportion of many years' crops because the must weights were insufficient. They must chaptalise in order to survive. The danger lies in the casual acceptance of chaptalisation as a routine procedure. It should be regarded as an extreme measure to be adopted in specific circumstances, not as a simple way of boosting alcohol and sugar levels. A dependence on chaptalisation also encourages laziness among proprietors. Once chaptalisation is regarded as routine, then there is less incentive to risk disaster by waiting until late in the autumn for grapes rich in botrytis as well as sugar. It is all too tempting to go for the safe option of picking early and taking care of the sugar levels after the grapes have been pressed.

At Yquem, however, the unadulterated musts will ferment through to a balance of roughly 14% alcohol, with at least 6° Baumé as residual sugar. Until it is bottled, the wine will spend all its time in new oak barrels. With the current price of new oak casks standing at 2000 francs and more, very few properties in Sauternes can afford to follow Yquem's example. Yquem, it must be realised, currently uses 950 barrels. Nor are all wines suitable for long ageing in new wood, which imparts tannins and very distinctive flavours and aromas to the wine. A lighter Sauternes, or a more racy Barsac, might well be overpowered by so many years in new wood; there is also the danger of excessive oxidation, which can occur if the wines are not kept under rigorous surveillance. But the rich, sumptuous wine of Yquem is perfectly suited to new wood, and Yquem even ferments the wine in wood, in contrast to most properties, which ferment in steel or cement tanks, even though they may age the wine in wood. A combination of evaporation and absorption by the wood causes the level of wine in cask to drop rapidly, and at Yquem the barrels are topped up with the same wine twice weekly. It is estimated that 20% of each year's wine is lost through evaporation. This too constitutes an additional expense which many proprietors are anxious to avoid; at Filhot, for example, the wine is aged in fibre-glass vats, from which there is no such loss. The cask wine at Yquem is racked into clean barrels every three months, a standard procedure at all properties where wine is aged in wood. Racking helps to clarify the wine, a process completed by fining it before bottling. Fining agents such as egg-white or bentonite encourage the precipitation of substances that could cloud the wine after it has been bottled. Yquem, in common with a few other properties, is opposed to filtration. Guy Latrille, the *maître de chai* at Yquem, considers that filtration, which strips the wine of impurities and other solid substances, can damage the wine; in any event, the long ageing process, with up to fifteen rackings followed by fining, already leaves it sufficiently pure and limpid.

The visitor to Yquem is never permitted to taste the wine before it is bottled. At most other properties, the owner or *régisseur* delights in bounding from *barrique* to *barrique* and siphoning a small quantity of new wine into the visitor's glass for his or her appraisal. At Yquem the barrels are left undisturbed, though on emerging from the cellars with M. Latrille you may be invited into the tasting room to sample a recent vintage. Nobody spits out that precious glass of Yquem, for the wine is too glorious to be wasted. The grateful taster realises that the immense care taken at Yquem is no affectation, but a genuine and mostly successful attempt to make the finest wine possible from the finest raw materials.

On leaving the tasting room, you will probably be invited to stroll around the château and admire the view. A broad expanse of gravel separates the old fortified château from the cellars and offices. You can stroll into the courtyard without fear of disturbing the occupants, for the Lur-Saluces family now lives at Bordeaux. The family acquired the estate in 1785 through marriage into the Eyquem family that had lived here since 1592. The Lur-Saluces also used to own Ch Filhot and various other properties, and still owns the Ch de Fargues, where a superb wine is made by the same team responsible for Yquem.

Opposite the château are the broad low cellars, entered through an iron gate kept locked at all times. A lane passes between the cellars, where Guy Latrille is very much in charge, and the office buildings, which are presided over by Pierre Meslier, who has been *régisseur* since 1962. There are almost fifty full-time workers at Yquem, and at the end of the afternoon tractors rumble up the lanes that climb the hill through the vineyards as workers who have been tending the vines return to base. Yquem is not only the grandest estate in Sauternes, but one of the largest with 120 hectares of vines, of which about 90 are in production; most of the remainder are planted with young vines that will not produce suitable grapes for eight years. The *encépagement* – the varieties planted – is 80% Sémillon and 20% Sauvignon. When new plantings have matured, the proportion of Sauvignon will be increased to 27%. There is no Muscadelle at Yquem. There are fine views of the vineyards from the flattened 250-foot hilltop on which the buildings stand, for Yquem is the highest property in the Sauternais, dominating the others physically as well as in terms of quality. The site is ideal for the vines, as the drainage is first-rate and the distinct soils found in different parts of the vineyards lend the wines perceptible qualities that play their part in the final blend. The only weak element in the disposition of the vineyards used to be the drainage, but over the last century 100 kilometres of man-made channels have taken care of that problem. Pruning is as rigorous as one would expect, and only organic fertilisers are used. Yquem, in short, does not put a foot wrong. Perfectionism, in the form of low yields, declassification of lots that do not make the grade, and evaporation through long barrel-ageing, result in an average of 66,000 bottles a year, with a maximum production in abundant years of 120,000. This is considerable by Sauternes standards, but negligible in terms of the demand for the wine.

Even though Yquem is not even bottled until well over three years after the harvest, it is a crime to consume Yquem until it is at least ten years old. All well-made Sauternes of a good vintage is capable of long ageing in bottle, but Yquem positively demands it. The youngest Yquem I have tasted is the 1982, tasted in 1987. The wine was lush and concentrated, broad and luxurious, exceptionally good from an atypical vintage, if not an outstanding Yquem. The 1981, tasted at the château in 1986, was stupendous, even in its youth, rich and powerful and elegant. The colour was a rich straw-gold, but there were sumptuous honeyed oaky aromas on the nose. On the palate the wine was supple, velvety, and fruity. All the qualities one expects from Yquem – a balance of richness and finesse, great length, and above all a marvellous concentration of flavour – were present. In other words the wine has superb structure, promising glories to come, like a box of jewels that is slowly being unlocked. But at that age, or lack of it, the 1981 was not yet a wine to be *drunk*.

The 1975, tasted when it was eleven years old, was, if anything, even less developed. The nose was still muted, and it was easier to appreciate its structural qualities – its concentration, creaminess, density, and impeccable balance – rather than nuances of flavour, which were still locked in. This was the greatest Sauternes made in a very great year for Sauternes, but it still requires many more years before it starts to show at its best. Lesser vintages, such as the 1973, have a rich orangey fruitiness on the palate and are much more developed than the 1975. A bottle of 1957 Yquem, tasted in 1984, gave a better idea of how superbly the wine ages. 1957 was a good year in Sauternes, with small harvests and some lean stylish wines. The wine was lush on the nose with marked botrytis aromas, and its richness on the palate was balanced by excellent acidity; there were no signs that the wine was flagging. This, sadly, was not the case with the 1892, which was ninety years old when the cork was pulled in my presence. The old bottle had certainly seen better days, but the wine was far from undrinkable. Lightly honeyed and soft on the nose, there was still enough sweetness left on the palate to give pleasure; and the wine had surprising tenacity of flavour and length. Old Sauternes often turns a coppery-amber in colour, even brown, but the 1892 Yquem was medium gold, looking far healthier than it tasted.

Those who have had the good fortune to have tasted a wide range of vintages tend to think that the greatest Yquems of accessible years were made in 1921, 1928, 1929, 1945, 1949, 1959, 1967, and 1975. Exceptional wines were made in 1937, 1942, 1953, 1955, 1962, 1970, 1971, 1976, and 1982; and very good wines of recent vintages include the 1950, 1961, 1979, 1980, and 1981.

It is impossible not to be dazzled by Yquem, by the estate itself and by the beauty of the wine. Nevertheless, other properties in the Sauternais are capable of making wines that at least approach the sublimity of Yquem in certain years, and it is to the Premiers Crus that we shall turn next.

A NOTE ON VINTAGES

It is very difficult to make clear, unambiguous pronouncements on the merits of specific vintages. A few are consistently superb, a few consistently lousy, but the majority are less clear-cut. Sometimes early rain will encourage some growers to pick sooner than they would normally do, and the result will be dilute wine; other growers will sit tight and may be rewarded with botrytis late in the autumn and thus be in a position to make wines greatly superior to those made by growers who picked early. On the other hand, the patient growers may be rewarded by frost or hail or further rain and thus harvest no grapes at all.

Four vintages stand out in recent years: 1971, 1975, 1976, and 1983. Most properties made excellent wines. A few vintages were fairly awful, and many properties declassified or were only able to bottle a small percentage of their crop. Such vintages include 1972,

1974, 1977, and 1984. Other vintages, such as those from 1979 to 1982, resulted in some very good wines, but not from all properties. Vintages such as 1978 and 1985 were warm and sunny, but lacked the humidity needed to attract botrytis. In 1985, growers who waited patiently (sometimes into December) were rewarded with splendid fruit, but the majority of growers made do with concentrated shrivelled fruit of high sugar content but little or no botrytis. Those buying Sauternes should be aware of these variable factors, and should study available tasting notes in books on the wines of Bordeaux and consult a knowledgeable wine merchant, for even within a good vintage there can be enormous variations in quality.

2

The Premiers Crus of Sauternes

CII GUIRAUD

Apart from Yquem, the only other Premier Cru property in the commune of Sauternes itself is Guiraud. This large estate lies directly south of Yquem on flatter land. In 1855 this property was listed as Ch Bayle, but a later owner changed its name to his own. In 1935 Guiraud came into the hands of M. Paul Rival, who sold it to the young Canadian business man Hamilton Narby in 1981. Before Mr Narby took over Guiraud, the property had a reputation for good but rarely great wine, but the new proprietor is determined to improve the quality so that the wine becomes a true rival to his illustrious neighbour Yquem. To that end Mr Narby has invested heavily in Guiraud, and there is no question that in recent years the wine has improved considerably and once again fully justifies its status. The château too, a grand if four-square house, has been restored.

Guiraud is a large estate, roughly the same size as Yquem. At present 83 hectares are planted with vines, though 8 of those are planted with red grapes, a legacy from M. Rival. In five years' time there will be a total of 95 hectares under vine. Guiraud's average annual production is between 70,000 and 90,000 bottles, but this includes dry red and white wine as well as a second-label Sauternes, Dauphin de Lalague, for sweet wine not considered up to Premier Cru standard. Guiraud itself, under the regime of Narby and his recently installed *régisseur* Xavier Planty, is never chaptalised. M. Rival planted a good deal of Sauvignon, and it still occupies about 38% of the plantation. Hamilton Narby is not happy about this, and as old vines are grubbed up and replaced by new, the proportion of

Sémillon will increase from 60% to 70%. There is also 2% of Muscadelle.

As one would expect of a Premier Cru, the selection of grapes is rigorous. In 1984, for instance, the yields, which are usually between 10 and 15 hl/ha, were down to a meagre 7, because only grapes with a minimum potential alcohol of 17% were picked. The grapes are pressed in horizontal presses and after *débourbage* the must is fermented in large steel tanks at 13–21 °C. Fermentation usually takes from eight to twenty days, and is arrested by chilling to −4 °C, just above the temperature at which Sauternes freezes. The wine is aged in *barriques* for up to two and a half years. It is sometimes unwise to allow the wine to absorb too much tannin and oakiness from the wood and at Guiraud there are no fixed rules about barrel-ageing. In 1984, for example, the wine, which lacked the weight and richness of, say, the 1983, spent only eighteen months in wood. When Hamilton Narby moved into Guiraud in 1981, he found many casks that were twenty-five years old. So ancient were they that when he sold them, he could only get 30 francs for each. Nowadays one third of the casks are new oak. Guiraud does not have deep or especially cold cellars, and in summer, when the thermometer rises too dramatically, the wine is transferred to temperature-controlled tanks, and replaced in cask when the heat diminishes again. Every three months, after each racking, a measure of *assemblage* takes place, so that by the time the wine is ready for bottling, Narby and Planty will have picked out the three or four lots worthy of the Guiraud label.

The wine is filtered only once, just before bottling, and chilled to eliminate tartaric acid deposits. This procedure is technically superfluous, since tartaric crystals, which are common in most white wines, are entirely inoffensive, flavourless, and do no harm to the wine. The treatment can also lower the level of acidity in the wine, not always a desirable development. However, certain export markets, notably the United States, grow alarmed at the sight of these crystals, and importers and merchants, weary of replacing bottles with tartaric deposits, insist that the wine be treated to ensure that no crystals form in the bottle. This is achieved by chilling the wine to just above freezing level for a week or so; this encourages the formation of tartaric crystals that can then be removed, thus providing the squeaky-clean wine that Americans in particular require.

There is no evidence to show that chilling actually harms the wine, though it can disturb its balance for a while, but I instinctively agree with those who maintain that no wine should be treated more than is absolutely necessary. Moreover, such treatments cost money, and the expense is passed on to the consumer. That the knowledgeable wine drinker should have to pay for the prejudices of the ignorant is regrettable. However, since 70% of Guiraud's production is exported, Narby understandably has to note the whims of his major clients. Uncommonly among Premiers Crus, Guiraud is happy to sell its wines directly to the public and is even open to visitors on Sundays. Hamilton Narby feels that many visitors and tourists come from afar to tour the Sauternais and look at its châteaux, and it should be possible for them to taste and buy the local wine.

The oldest Guiraud I have tasted was the youthful-looking 1962, an excellent wine with a pear-like bouquet, and a richness on the palate nicely cut by a lemony tone; the wine was exceptionally long on the finish. The 1964 was better than I had anticipated, for the vintage, unlike that of 1962, was unexceptional. Yet the wine was rich and luscious, and more developed than the 1962. The 1976 is a controversial wine. The year was a difficult one, for a very hot humid summer ended in mid-September with torrential rain. Many of the grapes were damaged by the storms and were more prone to oxidation than usual. This is what may well have happened at Guiraud, for the wine, even when young, had a very deep golden colour. Colour means little in Sauternes. Soil, botrytis, and wood-ageing can all affect the colour of a wine, and richness of colour does not signify richness of flavour. It can do so, but as often as not it is a warning, at least in young wine, of advancing oxidation. The 1976 Guiraud was lovely to behold and lush and sweet on the nose; but on the palate it was overblown and the aftertaste was harsh.

I have often enjoyed the 1979, a well-balanced wine, though a touch flabby in comparison with some other Sauternes of that vintage; the wine has excellent length. The 1980, tasted shortly after bottling, seemed promising but was still very closed and hard to assess. The 1981 is rich and oaky but lively on the nose. On the palate, however, its sweet broad apricot tones are marred by a slight bitterness on the aftertaste, and there are still traces of excessive sulphur. How the wine will develop it is hard to say; its lack of charm may yet slip away. 1982 was a very tricky year in Sauternes, and rain marred the harvest. This was certainly the case at Guiraud, where 60% of the crop was lost. The wine good enough to be bottled is fruity, perhaps a touch blowsy, on the nose, and quite spicy on the palate, yet lean and lacking in generosity and finesse – well below the highest standards of which the estate is capable. It is with the 1983, admittedly a glorious vintage throughout Sauternes, that the new regime began to make its mark. The wine has everything one expects from great Sauternes: the new oak dominates both nose and palate, but the wine is sufficiently rich and creamy to absorb the toasty wood tones. When mature, this wine will have exactly the balance of richness and elegance that one looks for. Although Narby and Planty reduced the time the 1984 spent in wood, a cask sample was uncomfortably woody, and sulphury on the aftertaste. The wine seemed light and loose, but since it had just been filtered, it would be unfair to attempt a judgment. However, all seems to be well with the 1985. Guiraud prolonged its harvest so as to pick as many botrytised grapes as possible; the average potential alcohol was an ideal 19.5%. There can be little doubt that Guiraud is once again worthy of its classification and, if it stays on present form, will remain one of the very best, as well as one of the most expensive, Sauternes.

CH RIEUSSEC

Walk a few hundred metres east from Ch d'Yquem, and you will enter the commune of Fargues and approach its sole Premier Cru, Rieussec. A rather functional property sprawled along the top of a small hill, Rieussec is far from lovely to look at. The property used to belong to a religious fraternity at Langon and, until M. Albert Vuillier bought the estate in 1970, no one had ever lived there. In 1984 the ownership was transferred to a consortium, of which the largest shareholder is the Domaines Barons de Rothschild, the owners of Ch Lafite. Vuillier is still associated with Rieussec, but his influence will be diminishing. The new technical director, Charles Chevallier, imported from Lafite, has made few changes so far, and Vuillier's *régisseur*, M. Gouze, remains active. When Vuillier took over, the vineyards were in poor shape, and he greatly improved the condition of the property, replanting many rows while carefully tending the old vines still capable of producing top-quality grapes. Like its neighbours, Guiraud and Yquem, Rieussec is a large property, with 70 hectares, of which 62 are entitled to the Sauternes *appellation*; those vineyards not in the Sauternes district are mainly planted with Sauvignon that is used to make Rieussec's distinguished dry wine known simply as 'R'. Rieussec's average annual production of Sauternes is between 70,000 and 80,000 bottles. The *encépagement* is thoroughly traditional, with 80% Sémillon, 19% Sauvignon, and 1% Muscadelle. The vines, of mixed ages, are planted on soil that is very gravelly over its clay and limestone base; but, as is common in Sauternes, there are great variations in the soil from one end of the property to the other. The yields are, at 13–14 hl/ha, almost as low as those of Yquem. Four *passages* are usual here.

The grapes are pressed in horizontal presses, and chaptalisation is practised when absolutely necessary. After *débourbage* the wine is fermented in steel tanks at 20 °C. Although fermentation usually stops by itself, SO_2 is added to prevent any subsequent activity by dozy yeasts. The wine spends eighteen or twenty months in *barriques*, of which half are new, and is filtered and bottled roughly two years after the harvest. Wines not up to Rieussec's exacting standards are bottled under the second label of Clos Labère.

Rieussec is a difficult wine to assess because the style of the wine has changed in recent decades. It was reputed to be a relatively light and elegant wine, though in my experience Rieussec is one of the most lush and powerful Sauternes, full in colour and striking in its impact on the palate. There is nothing decorous or self-effacing about Rieussec. The 1959 was a great wine, copybook Sauternes, an attractive gold in colour, with a honeyed botrytis nose, and sweet and luscious on the palate, yet very well balanced so that, despite its terrific length, it never became cloying. In the great years of 1975 and 1976 Rieussec made wines that are unlikely to last as well. Opinions are divided as to which is the better. I prefer the 1975, which is full gold in colour, and exceptionally fruity on the nose, with aromas of peaches and marmalade; on the palate it was somewhat blowsy, too fat for its own good; yet it showed good acidity and length and had plenty of character. The 1976 was far more developed: the colour is an almost brownish gold and on the palate is sweet and honeyed; but acidity is lacking and the wine is shorter on the finish than the 1975. Both wines are decidedly attractive, but the 1976 in particular lacks the qualities that will give it a staying power comparable to, say, the 1959. Very good wine, again with a developed golden colour, was made in 1979, though when tasted in 1986 the wine still seemed rather raw and sulphury and not yet knit. However, it was fat and rich and had good intensity and acidity, and will surely repay keeping for another ten years. 1980 was also a success for Rieussec, luscious and well balanced and very forward; five years after the vintage the wine was already showing well. The 1982 is attractive in the usual lush creamy Rieussec style, straightforward and maturing fast. In 1983 Rieussec made a golden wine full of botrytis, one of the best wines of an exceptionally good vintage, though it is an alarmingly developed Sauternes, lush and unctuous. The 1984 is surprisingly sumptuous on the palate; however, it lacks grip and 'centre', and the impact of the wine is entirely up-front. Not, I suspect, a wine to be kept for very long. First reports of the 1985 are encouraging. The hot dry weather discouraged the development of botrytis, but Rieussec continued picking until 18 November, and made seven *passages* in all. Other good wines of recent years include the 1970, 1971, 1981, and 1982.

Whether the new regime at Rieussec will alter the style of the wine it is too early to say, and M. Chevallier seems in no hurry to make changes. The wines made by M. Vuillier are certainly immensely appealing, ideal examples of how Sauternes at its most voluptuous is supposed to taste. Yet I find most of the vintages lacking in real finesse and balance; their longevity seems in doubt, and sometimes the flavour is marred, even in the generally admirable 1979, by an excess of alcohol and volatile acidity. Perhaps these wines will settle down and cruise happily into middle age as the 1959 has done. Only time will tell. What is worrying is that the 1976 already seems at or even past its best and most other recent vintages seem to be developing at a very rapid pace.

CLOS HAUT-PEYRAGUEY

We have been east of Ch d'Yquem, south of Ch d'Yquem, and now we move west of Ch d'Yquem into the commune of Bommes. On a small hill, some 60 metres high, stands the unassuming property of Clos Haut-Peyraguey, close to the hamlet of Haut Bommes, where the owner with the largest share, Jacques Pauly, lives at Ch Haut-Bommes, a *cru bourgeois*. Clos Haut-Peyraguey was once part of Ch Lafaurie-Peyraguey, but the two properties were divided in 1879. In 1914 the estate was bought by the Pauly family. It consists of 15 hectares of vineyards (and a further 10 that belong to Ch Haut-Bommes). They are planted with 83% Sémillon, 15% Sauvignon, and 2% Muscadelle, and many of the vines are thirty to thirty-five years old. Jacques Pauly regrets that he cannot plant more Muscadelle, but finds the variety too fragile: it is hard to bring it to a sufficient degree of overmaturity and it is notoriously prone to diseases, especially *pourriture grise*.

The wine is made with care. Harvesting frequently continues until the end of November, and in 1985 Pauly made six *passages* in search of botrytised grapes. His vines yield an average of 18 hl/ha, sometimes more, as in 1981 (21 hl/ha) and sometimes less, as in 1984 (15 hl/ha). Jacques Pauly is an advocate of temperature-controlled fermentation, though with very late harvesting this is more likely to involve heating the must than cooling the cellars. The must, lightly chaptalised when necessary, ferments in cement vats for up to four weeks at 19 °C. To arrest fermentation, he adds sulphur dioxide and chills the vats. The *assemblage* takes place in February, and the wines are then aged for up to two years in *barriques*, of which 20% are new. Pauly filters his wines. There are those, such as Guy Latrille at Yquem, who argue against filtration, but the majority who, like Jacques Pauly, practise it unapologetically, argue that efficient filtration enables you to reduce the amount of SO_2 added later.

Pauly accurately describes his wines as *fin* rather than *liquoreux*, that is to say, elegant rather than lusciously sweet. Nevertheless, says Pauly, his wines are capable of prolonged ageing in bottle, though I have never tasted an old vintage from this property. Production is fairly small, never more than 40,000 bottles, much of which is sold to private customers in France. Recent vintages I have tasted have been medium sweet, appley, lean, elegant, and well made, but not enormously exciting. Those who have written about other vintages of Clos Haut-Peyraguey can rarely work up much enthusiasm for any of them, with the exception of the 1976. By all accounts, they are diligently made, quite stylish and pleasant, but rarely live up to the exceptional standards one expects of a Premier Cru.

CH LAFAURIE-PEYRAGUEY

Just north of Clos Haut-Peyraguey is the property of which it once formed a part, Ch Lafaurie-Peyraguey. This is one of the most picturesque châteaux in the Sauternais, for the ivy-covered seventeenth-century mansion is surrounded by crenellated walls that date back to the thirteenth century, and massive old trees shade the grassy courtyard. Since 1913 the estate has been owned by the Bordeaux wine merchants Cordier. The estate comprises 25 hectares of vines, which have an average age of thirty years; 12 hectares are just behind the château, and the remainder is divided into two separate parcels. Many years ago Sauvignon accounted for about 30% of the vines, but is now reduced to a mere 2%, the other 98% being Sémillon. In practice, according to the *régisseur* Michel Laporte, a considerably higher proportion of Sauvignon usually makes its way into the finished wine.

Although in 1855 the property was rated third best in the region, it has lost that splendid reputation over recent decades. Standards are now being improved, and impressively. Yields at about 13 hl/ha are lower than they once were, with only 35,000 bottles being produced each year. Rigorous *triage* (there were eight *passages* in 1985, even more than at Rieussec) seeks out only botrytised grapes with potential alcohol of 20–21%; consequently, chaptalisation, while not unknown here, is very infrequent. The grapes are pressed in old-fashioned vertical presses, as at Yquem. After *débourbage*, the wine is put into *barriques*, a substantial proportion of which are new, for fermentation, which takes about six weeks at 18–20 °C. Fermentation tends to stop by the time the alcohol content reaches 15%, but SO_2 is added just to be on the safe side. The wine is then left for a month, fined, left for another month, filtered then replaced in *barriques* and racked every two months. Roughly twenty months after the harvest, the wine is chilled to get rid of the tartaric acid crystals, filtered, and bottled. Apart from these final treatments, the vinification could hardly be more traditional.

But this has not always been the case, a fact that accounts for the somewhat dim reputation of the wine. In 1967 the property installed horizontal presses and the wine, instead of ageing in oak, was stored in large glass-lined metal tanks beneath a layer of nitrogen and given a mere four months in wood before bottling. Ten years later Cordier acknowledged that this technical sophistication had led to a decline in quality, and so they reverted in the late 1970s to an utterly traditional *élevage*.

M. Laporte says he is quite pleased with the wines made in 1967 and 1975, but considers the 1983 outstanding; they achieved relatively high yields without sacrificing quality, which was very high. It is an oaky wine, but elegant and spicy and with good acidity. Judging from a cask sample, the 1985 is also very promising, a big wine, closed on the nose at present but fat, fruity, and quite alcoholic; it has good concentration and length. In 1980 Lafaurie-Peyraguey made an attractive but unexciting Sauternes marred, for me, by excessive sulphur. The 1981 is disappointingly attenuated. 1982 was not a great year, but the estate made exceptionally good wine, lemony, oaky, and intense. An old bottle from 1913, tasted in 1982, showed that Lafaurie-Peyraguey is as capable as any Premier Cru of making great Sauternes, for the wine was still sweet and rich, with a marmalade nose, even though it was just beginning to dry out. It seems likely that, with a return to traditional methods, the wines may soon re-establish themselves as worthy of their classification. That certainly seems to be the intention of Cordier and M. Laporte. Among recent vintages, the 1975, 1976, and 1982 have been well received, though clearly the 1983 marks the turning point.

CH RAYNE-VIGNEAU

This large estate, only a few hundred metres from Lafaurie-Peyraguey, has also suffered from a declining reputation, but, as at the neighbouring property, there is a concerted effort under way to improve the quality of the wine. Rayne-Vigneau has changed hands in recent years, and is now the property of the same consortium that owns Ch Grand Puy Ducasse in Pauillac. Since the consortium acquired the estate, it has doubled the cellar space and planted many new vineyards. The production is quite high, and in 1983 100,000 bottles were filled.

The decidedly ugly nineteenth-century château, ringed by trees that separate it from the cellars, is occupied by a member of the Pontac family, which acquired the estate in 1834 but sold its interest in 1961; the château no longer has any connection with the surrounding estate. A hundred metres further along the hillside are the functional cellars. The site is a good one, for, like Yquem and Rieussec, Rayne-Vigneau sits atop a small hill. The soil is unusually stony, and over the years many precious and semi-precious gems have been unearthed. Of the 65 hectares planted with vines, not all are in production; 2 to 3 hectares are replanted each year. Grapes from young vines – a vine must be eight years old before it is suitable for making sweet wine – are used to make dry white wines. The *encépagement* is 70% Sémillon and 30% Sauvignon. In comparison with most other Premiers Crus, the yields are fairly high – on average 18 hl/ha – nor are many *passages* made through the vineyards in search of perfectly botrytised grapes. In 1983 there were five, though that was unusually many for Rayne-Vigneau. M. Eymery, the energetic *régisseur*, aims for grapes with a potential alcohol of 18–19%, significantly lower than that sought by some other properties; the result, in a good year, is a wine of 14.5% alcohol and 4.5° Baumé of residual sugar, a perfectly correct balance though somewhat lacking in richness.

The grapes are pressed in horizontal presses, and the *débourbage* takes place in 4500-litre cement tanks. The must is chaptalised when necessary and fermented slowly in stainless steel at 20–22 °C.

Fermentation is arrested with SO_2 and the wine then spends eighteen months in casks; half the 800 casks here are new. Until 1980 no new wood was used, but since that time a large amount of money has been pumped into Rayne-Vigneau, and much of it has been spent on costly new *barriques*. As the wine matures, lots not up to standard are weeded out and declassified. The wine is racked every three months, then chilled to get rid of the tartaric acid crystals. After fining, the wine receives its sole filtration just before bottling, which takes place roughly two years after the harvest.

I have not tasted this wine often enough to make an adequate judgment of its qualities, though it has never excited me. The 1981 was moderately sweet but somewhat austere and lacking in charm and elegance, but more recent vintages confirm that a genuine effort is being made to restore the reputation of Rayne-Vigneau. Certainly the 1985, tasted from cask after its second racking, was a promising mouthful with excellent fruit, and an attractive citric oaky nose; it was well balanced and is likely to mature into an appealing and sound wine. Whether Rayne-Vigneau will ever be much more than a well-made commercial wine, and whether it will begin to exhibit real flair and personality, it is too early to say.

CH LA TOUR BLANCHE

Just south of Rayne-Vigneau, at the western edge of the Bommes commune, is the Tour Blanche estate. In 1855 the wine was considered good enough to win top billing after Ch d'Yquem, though nobody would make such claims nowadays. Early this century, the owner, an umbrella manufacturer whose intriguing name of Osiris still appears on the labels, bequeathed the estate to the Ministry of Agriculture, and a college of winemaking was established here. Today the property presents a functional appearance, with the school and administration buildings slightly apart from the cellars. Although the students do participate to a limited extent in the winemaking, the production of the Premier Cru Sauternes is not an integral part of the courses here. Ch La Tour Blanche is the responsibility of the *régisseur*, M. Rebérat, not of a few dozen students in need of on-the-job training. The 28 hectares of vineyards surrounding the buildings are planted with 80% Sémillon, 15%

Sauvignon, and 5% Muscadelle. Yields are very low, 12–13 hl/ha on average, occasionally as low as 8, and never higher than 18. The aim is to pick only botrytised grapes with 19–20% potential alcohol. Five *passages* were made in 1983, but there were seven in the dry year of 1985, when botrytis appeared very late in the autumn.

The grapes are pressed in horizontal presses and the fermentation takes place in steel tanks for twelve to fifteen days at 20 °C. The Premier Cru wine is never chaptalised. As at Guiraud and various other properties, La Tour Blanche has preserved for itself a variety of options. Any juice with low must weights is either fermented through to produce a dry wine, or chaptalised and bottled under the second label Cru St Marc. Fermentation is arrested by chilling; the wine is filtered and sulphured, but the dose is far lower than formerly. The wine is usually blended before it is put into wood, where it will spend from eighteen to twenty-four months, subject to the customary rackings every three months. 30% of the *barriques* are new, and none is older than five years. The wine is filtered again before bottling, which usually takes place thirty months after the harvest.

Apart from 1962, the 1960s were dire for La Tour Blanche, and no wine at all was bottled in 1963, 1964, and 1968. Subsequent years in which M. Rebérat feels the property made successful wines include 1971, 1975, 1976, 1979, 1981, and 1983. The wine does not enjoy a high reputation, and is considered by many to be unworthy of its classification. I have not tasted the wine very often, but the 1976 was nicely made, fresh and sweet, though lacking in complexity. The 1981 is clammy and awkward, lacking richness as well as finesse. The 1983 is a grave disappointment, horribly over-sulphured, pungent and one-dimensional. There are better reports of the 1985.

CH RABAUD-PROMIS

The two remaining Premiers Crus in Bommes lie just north of Ch Lafaurie-Peyraguey. Ch Rabaud-Promis and Ch Sigalas-Rabaud were once a single estate. In 1904 this property, Ch Rabaud, was divided into two, though in 1929 they were reunited. However, a second divorce took place in 1952. By one of the quirks of arcane French wine law, Ch Rabaud-Promis managed to incorporate into its estate the vineyards of Ch Pexoto, a Deuxième Cru, without losing its Premier Cru status. Present-day Rabaud-Promis is a medium-sized property of 32 hectares, producing on average 60,000 bottles each year, most of which is sold to *négociants*; about 40% is exported. The salon windows inside the modest low-slung château look out onto the surrounding vineyards, and a visitor with longer arms than mine could probably reach out and pick some grapes straight from the vine. The vineyards are planted with 80% Sémillon, 19% Sauvignon, and 1% Muscadelle, a mixture of fairly new and very old vines. Yields are on average 18 hl/ha, but not all the grapes picked will find their way into the Premier Cru wine, though in exceptional years such as 1976 the entire crop was good enough to be bottled as Rabaud-Promis. The musts are occasionally chaptalised, especially if destined for the second label, Ch Jauga, a wine I have never seen, let alone tasted.

Rabaud-Promis probably has the worst reputation of any Premier Cru. The wines of Rayne-Vigneau or Clos Haut-Peyraguey may not be wildly exciting, but few people have ever suggested that they were not cleanly made and correct. This is not the case with the wines of Rabaud-Promis. However, as at many of the other properties reviewed in this chapter, there are signs that improvements are under way, and tastings of recent vintages would seem to confirm this. There was certainly much room for improvement. M. Philippe Dejean, who became *régisseur* in 1974, has directed the property since 1981 and is responsible for some of the changes. Yet even today the cellars do not inspire confidence. A winery charging Premier Cru prices should be able to afford to keep its cellars, if not immaculate, then in clean condition. At Rabaud-Promis, the cellars were littered with old crates and pallets, and alongside an ugly tank stood a supermarket trolley crammed with hoses. Much of the wine is stored in underground tanks. These alarm some visitors, but if properly cared for, such tanks should do their job reasonably well, keeping the wines free of oxidation, which might not be the case were the wines to be stored in wooden casks.

M. Dejean tries to make his wine from botrytised grapes. In 1984 it rained at the end of September for ten days, and he waited until botrytis attacked the grapes during October. In 1985 the first *trie* produced no botrytised grapes, but subsequent pickings did, and he continued to pick until 22 November. The grapes are pressed in horizontal presses, though some use is also made of an old vertical press. M. Dejean is not entirely happy with his horizontal presses, and in 1987 will install a pneumatic press, an expensive piece of equipment that gives very good results. Fermentation takes place in the underground tanks, which would have made an excellent home for John the Baptist. They are temperature-controlled and the fermentation takes place at 19–20 °C. M. Dejean intends to replace these vats with more modern steel tanks. After fermentation the wine is filtered before being racked into new casks for about a year; the wine is racked every four months, given further ageing in tank, and bottled roughly thirty months after the harvest.

That the property is capable of producing first-rate wine is proved by the older vintages of Ch Rabaud, produced before the property was divided for the second time. A bottle of 1948 proved truly excellent: it had a soft marmalade nose, and on the palate was rich and full and sweet, slightly past its best but still a most delicious Sauternes. M. Dejean regards his 1975 highly, but his opinion is not widely shared. Tasted in 1986, the wine was over-developed: deep orange-gold in colour and showing signs of oxidation on the nose, which had tones of barleysugar and caramel; on the palate it was spicy but rather burnt, and the finish was cloying. The wine, in short, was blowsy. Still, recent vintages seem better made. The 1983, tasted from the barrel, was firm in colour, sweet and oaky on the nose, and quite impressive on the palate: rich, rounded, and not without elegance. The 1984, sampled just before it went into wood, tasted chaptalised: sweet but quite without roundness or complexity. The second *trie* of the 1985, tasted from the vat, was intensely sweet, but also fresh and lively. I could detect little botrytis and the wine was one-dimensional, but it was clean and attractive, and it seems probable that the wines of Rabaud-Promis are improving. It is clear, at the least, that its wines should no longer be dismissed out of hand, which one would have been justified in doing only a few years ago.

CH SIGALAS-RABAUD

The other portion of the former Ch Rabaud, Ch Sigalas-Rabaud, is in every way superior to its neighbour. With only 15 hectares, it is one of the smallest Premiers Crus. The actual château and some of the cellars date from the seventeenth century, and the owner is the Marquise de Lambert des Granges. Production is limited to around 20,000 bottles a year. The vineyards, some of which contain very old vines, are planted with 90% Sémillon, and there is no Muscadelle, which the *régisseur* Jean-Louis Vimeney, finds too prone to disease. Yields average 18 hl/ha, and Vimeney has the candour to admit that while he certainly waits patiently for botrytis to attack the grapes, there does come a point when the grapes have to be picked, rot or no rot. I suspect many other Sauternes *régisseurs* and vineyard managers would go along with M. Vimeney in practice, even if they would be reluctant to say so in public.

Old hydraulic vertical presses are used here. In 1985, Vimeney told me, the first pressing had a must weight of 30° Baumé, while the second was as high as 25.6°. Chaptalisation is rare (with must weights such as the ones just cited, I can see why). Fermentation takes place in vats for two weeks, and is arrested by chilling and a dose of SO_2. Vimeney does not put all the wine into wood, and during hot summer months transfers the wine into tanks. The wine is filtered and bottled young, roughly eighteen months after the harvest. There is no second label and any wine not up to scratch is simply declassified.

M. Vimeney, it will be apparent, is no traditionalist. Those who adore the rich oaky style of traditional Sauternes may look askance at his vinification practices. Yet the wine is widely admired, and, from my admittedly limited tastings, deservedly so. It is significant that many other Sauternes proprietors speak highly of Sigalas-Rabaud, even though the wine is less well known than many other Premiers Crus. Vimeney aims for freshness and elegance rather than lusciousness. He seeks to bring out the fruitiness and the fresh aromas of the wine, which is why he bottles earlier than any other Premier Cru. Yet the wine is reputed to age well. Sigalas-Rabaud can be light, but it is also stylish and finely tuned. It is a question of style, and Sauternes enthusiasts looking for a racier, immensely elegant wine will find its highest expression here. The 1983 was delicious, quite rich and sweet but with very good length and pronounced botrytis on the nose. Even with a very young wine, such as the 1985 which I tasted in 1986, the balance was impeccable; delicious in its infancy, it appears to have the intensity and structure to assure it a splendid future. Certainly M. Vimeney thinks so, for he is immensely proud of his wines, and makes no apology for bucking the trends in Sauternes. Older wines that have met with approval include the 1975, 1976, and 1981.

CH SUDUIRAUT

A mile north of Ch d'Yquem stands one of the loveliest properties in Sauternes, Ch Suduiraut, the only Premier Cru in the commune of Preignac. A long drive leads into the park where the essentially seventeenth-century château stands. The gardens behind the château were laid out by the great landscape architect Le Nôtre, and the many magnificent cedars, a rare sight in the Sauternais, form a striking backdrop. The current owners are the descendants of Léopold Fonquernie, an industrialist who bought the estate in 1940 and made many improvements. From 1964 to 1978 the *régisseur* was a M. Bavejo, and the new winemaker is the vigorous and enthusiastic Pierre Pascaud. The entire estate consists of 200 hectares, but only about 75 are under vine, though this figure fluctuates slightly. Some of the vines are sixty years old, and Pascaud places great emphasis on the severity of pruning at Suduiraut. The varieties planted are Sémillon (85%) and Sauvignon (15%). According to the brochure distributed by the estate, the yields are 7–12 hl/ha, though Pascaud's figures are considerably higher, at 12–18 hl/ha. (Such figures should be taken with a pinch of salt, as it not always clear whether they refer to the amount of grapes harvested, or the amount of wine that ends

up in bottle. Since a large quantity of wine is often declassified, some winemakers incorporate that loss into their yield figures.) The grapes are often picked much earlier than at other leading properties. Why this should be so is not clear, even allowing for a microclimate that allegedly brings the grapes to maturity more speedily here. The consequence is that Pascaud must sometimes chaptalise by the largest permitted amount, two degrees, which is hardly desirable.

The must is fermented in 5000-litre steel tanks at 18–22 °C, then stored until it is racked in the early spring. Only then, when the wine is clear, is it transferred to *barriques*, of which a third are new. Before M. Pascaud took over the winemaking, the ageing took place in tanks rather than wood. Nowadays it is barrel-aged for eighteen to twenty-four months and bottled about thirty months after the harvest. The production is quite considerable: in 1983 180,000 bottles went through the Suduiraut bottling line, and the figure will be only slightly less for the 1985.

Suduiraut is a rich and rounded Sauternes, always golden in colour and lush on the nose. Given the harvesting methods, it is something of a mystery to me how the wine attains its excellence – for the grapes are unlikely to be as stricken by noble rot as at most other good properties – but excellent it most certainly is. In Pierre Pascaud's opinion – and most wine writers agree – the finest recent vintages at Suduiraut were 1959, 1961, 1962, 1967, 1970, 1975, 1976, 1979, 1982 and 1983. The 1975 is very good indeed, more developed in colour and bouquet than on the palate, where the wine, while soft and creamy and fat, shows all the signs of having a long life ahead of it; a trifle overblown, perhaps, but with the structure to sustain it for years to come. The 1976 was also a success, and, curiously, the 1982 is better than the 1983. Pierre Pascaud is particularly proud of having made a first-rate wine in an unpromising year. His policy of picking early seems to have paid off, for by the time the rains fell in early October, Suduiraut had already harvested most of its grapes. The 1982 is no heavyweight, but lush and elegant on the nose, and lively and well balanced in the mouth, a wine of great charm and finesse. M. Pascaud also made a *crème de tête* of 4800 bottles in 1982, with 130 g/l of residual sugar, as compared to the 80 or so normally present. Since a single bottle costs 420 francs, I shall have to take M. Pascaud's word for it that the wine is wonderful. I have been less impressed with the 1983 than other tasters. Picking continued until

10 November – late for Suduiraut – and yields, at 20 hl/ha, were high; the wine was clean, creamy, and elegant, and yet dilute and lacking in grip. A cask sample of the 1985 was also disappointing: pleasant, to be sure, but lacking in depth of flavour and with no discernible botrytis. The 1985 is a perfect example of the dangers of Suduiraut's early harvesting: good well-made wine that lacks the character and intensity one expects from a prestigious and costly growth.

CH COUTET

Winemaking is a family business in the Sauternais, as elsewhere in France, so it comes as no surprise to find that Pierre Pascaud's son is the *régisseur* of the largest Barsac vineyard, Ch Coutet. The property is an ancient one, and the château itself dates from the thirteenth century and is ranged around a pretty and well-shaded courtyard; the tiny chapel dates from the fourteenth century. The estate is owned by Marcel Baly, a business man originally from Strasbourg who describes himself as *esthète et gastronome*. Its 40 hectares of vineyards give an annual production of about 85,000 bottles. At harvest time, the 2% of Muscadelle is picked first, since it attracts the feared *pourriture grise* as well as the more desirable *pourriture noble*; the remaining rows are planted with 23% Sauvignon and 75% Semillon.

The grapes are rigorously selected; Coutet made eleven *passages* in 1983, though five are more usual. The average yields are 17–18 hl/ha. Chaptalisation is rare, but there have been some years when the must has been boosted the maximum two degrees.

The vinification is highly traditional. The grapes are pressed in hydraulic presses; since each pressing can take up to two hours, this is often a laborious process, though it does result in clear juice. The must is fermented in *barriques*. This usually takes a few weeks, though during especially severe winters Pascaud must heat the cellars to prevent the fermentation from sticking, and in such conditions it can continue for up to two months. When the yeasts are exhausted, the wine is put into tank, sulphured to ensure that they will not reactivate, then racked into clean barrels. The *barriques*, of which one sixth are new, are impressively double-stacked in the long cellars; they are regularly racked, a time-consuming task when, as at Coutet, there are 800 to look after. Some blending takes place at each racking. The wine is filtered before bottling, which takes place roughly two years after the harvest.

Pascaud does not aim for an especially rich style. Coutet rarely exceeds 13.5% alcohol and 4 degrees Baumé of residual sugar. Refinement rather than unctuousness is the hallmark of Coutet. In exceptional years such as 1971 Coutet produces a *crème de tête* called Cuvée Madame. The wine is not commercially available and opportunities to taste it are rare. Those who have done so speak of the wine in the most glowing terms. Since only about 2000 bottles are produced in any year when it is made, most Sauternes drinkers, myself included, will have to content themselves with Coutet's normal bottling. Coutet is a respected and popular wine, yet it is not a property for which I can work up much enthusiasm. The only old vintage I have drunk, the 1949, was a classic Sauternes, intense and honeyed on the nose, very sweet and rich, yet balanced by the acidity. With the exception of the 1975, I am not convinced that any of the Coutets of the 1970s that I have sampled will develop as magnificently (though Sauternes that seem weak in their youth often turn out to be a living rebuttal of their critics).

The 1973 was a very good wine in a light year, surprisingly full for the vintage, the 1971 and 1976 (which I have not tasted) are widely admired, and the still youthful 1975 marvellously combines richness with delicacy, and its lively acidity gives the wine some of the raciness typical of top Barsac. The 1979 and 1980 are good but far from exciting, harmonious without being truly stylish. The 1981 is excellent, with plenty of botrytis on the nose, and plump, supple, and forward on the palate. Not so the 1983, which lacks botrytis and, after a vigorous attack on the palate, soon fades; a lean but attractive wine, yet disappointing for the vintage. So is the 1982, which lacks concentration and vigour. Although a cask sample of the 1985, tasted in 1986, was understandably sulphurous, it was not hard to see that this would be an outstanding wine with just that element of concentration that some other Coutet vintages have lacked. In 1985 the first pickings were of very ripe grapes with little botrytis; but Coutet continued picking until 11 November and these later *passages* yielded a good crop of botrytised grapes that give the wine its richness. Given the care taken with the harvesting and vinification, Coutet ought to be an outstanding wine. Yet in my experience it is too inconsistent to deserve the highest accolades, though under M. Pascaud's care the 1980s may see a return to top form.

CH CLIMENS

As the only other Premier Cru in Barsac, Climens has long been regarded, at least in wine writers' minds, as a rival to Coutet. In my experience, there is no contest, for Climens is one of the very greatest Sauternes, where good wine is made not only in the most glorious years but in the vintages acknowledged as mediocre. The property was acquired by Lucien Lurton in 1971. M. Lurton, who owns a number of fine properties elsewhere in Bordeaux, has wisely left well alone at Climens. The *maître de chai* is Christian Broustaut, and the *régisseuse* is the formidable Mme Janin, who has taken over from her husband. The château is a rather dull building that often looks closed up; since the property is not open to visitors, there is something austere about its locked gates and shuttered windows.

The wine, however, is marvellous and utterly traditional in its vinification. There is an exceptionally high proportion of Sémillon here, for only 2% of its 25 hectares are planted with Sauvignon. The vines are not especially old, about twenty-five years on average, but the yields are low: 9.6 hl/ha in 1978 and, at the high end of the scale, 15.6 in 1981. Production is limited to about 35,000 bottles in an abundant year such as 1983. Brigitte Lurton, who oversees the property, told me that when her family bought the estate in 1971, they were widely regarded as crazy. Prices for Sauternes were low and, given all the risks involved in making the wine, it seemed a terrible way to make money. But the Lurtons are lucky enough not to have to depend on Ch Climens for their bread and butter, and they are determined to continue the tradition of making great wine here, and that means refusing to cut corners.

The grapes are rigorously selected when they arrive from the vineyards, even though the quality of the fruit is generally very high, as this is the highest property in Barsac (which is not saying much) and drainage is excellent. There is no chaptalisation and only the first two pressings – Climens employs horizontal presses – are used for the Premier Cru. Since, as at Yquem, each day's lot is put into cask separately for fermentation, by the end of the autumn there can be as many as twenty-five lots from which to make their *assemblage*. Blending usually begins as soon as fermentation is completed in January, and inadequate lots are weeded out at this stage. Selection is ruthless. In 1982, when rain stopped play during the harvest, two-thirds of the crop was rejected. Fortunately the crops in 1983 and 1985 were exemplary, and almost all the wine could be used for the Premier Cru. There is no sophisticated temperature control of the cellars at Climens; instead, temperature is altered by the simple expedient of opening the cellar windows. Since fermentation takes place in casks, where the small volume prevents the generation of excessive heat, high temperatures are rarely a problem. The wine is, of course, barrel aged, but only 30% of the *barriques* are new; an excess of new oak would mar the delicacy of the wine. The barrels are racked every two or three months, and bottling takes place roughly two years after the harvest.

Climens is, for me, the model of what Barsac should be. It is leaner than the heavyweight Sauternes of Yquem or Rieussec, but by no means lacking in flavour and concentration. Climens is, in short, stylish, with enormous class and breed. The wine can age magnificently. In the early 1980s, the 1924 and 1927 (though a poor vintage), while alarmingly brown in colour, were gorgeous wines, soft and mellow and powerful. A 1918, while beginning to dry out, still had vestiges of sweetness and richness. The 1964 was disappointing: a touch soapy on the nose, and with a flabbiness on the palate not at all characteristic of Climens. Another mediocre vintage, the 1966, was losing its fruitiness after twenty years. The 1970 is distinctly disappointing, especially for the vintage, but the 1971 is a very great wine. The 1972, oaky and concentrated, is a fine example of scrupulous winemaking in a poor vintage. The 1975 and 1976 are both among the top wines of these vintages, concentrated and elegant. The balance of the 1975 is immaculate: fruit and oak and acidity are all present and in perfect relation to each other; an immensely stylish wine with decades of life ahead of it. The 1979 is another very successful Climens, with the same qualities as the 1975 though in a more muted form, reflecting the lesser quality of the vintage. 1978 saw a good wine in a mediocre year, and the 1980 is sweet and very attractive, though somewhat light. The 1981 is splendid: rich, intense, oaky, and beautifully balanced. Brigitte Lurton is convinced that both the 1983 and the 1985 are superior to the 1976. The 1983 is indeed sensational, brilliant in every respect: creamy and oaky, wine of enormous elegance and breed. It is surely one of the great Sauternes of the last twenty years.

3

The Deuxièmes Crus of Sauternes

CII DOISY-DAËNE

The Barsac properties dominate the list of Deuxièmes Crus. I begin with Doisy-Daëne, though it is atypical. This is entirely due to the personality of its proprietor, Pierre Dubourdieu, an individualist who does things very much his own way. In 1855 Ch Doisy was a single estate, but was long ago divided into three properties, differentiated from each other by the hyphenated addition of a family name. M. Daëne, improbably, was English, but after his death in 1863 the property was acquired by a local wine merchant. Since 1924 it has been in the hands of the Dubourdieu family. Pierre Dubourdieu is the owner of 55 hectares in the region, but 23 of those

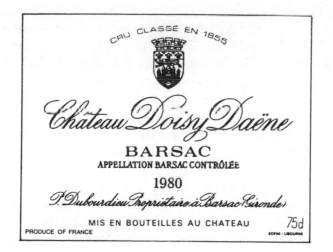

are in the Graves district, and the grapes are used to make the dry white wines and the red Graves for which M. Dubourdieu has an excellent reputation. He is also the owner of Ch Cantegril in Sauternes, and Doisy-Daëne and Cantegril have vineyards of roughly 15 hectares each. Cantegril is in effect the second label of Doisy-Daëne.

When I first approached Pierre Dubourdieu to make an appointment to visit the property, he declared, feistily: 'I'm not interested in sweet wines. I don't like them much and prefer dry wines.' Nevertheless, I pointed out, he was the proprietor of two Sauternes estates, both well regarded. He shrugged and said that he made about 250,000 bottles of dry wines, compared to only 70,000 of sweet. 'I'm interested in wines that can be drunk, not just tasted. About one glass of Yquem a year is more than enough for me – sometimes I don't even want to finish that one glass.' This spirited exercise in iconoclasm was undermined by the practical knowledge that Doisy-Daëne can be a very good wine and that M. Dubourdieu is the man who makes it. He invited me to join a party of Dutch wine merchants who were visiting the property later that day. On that occasion we sampled mostly dry wines – and very good they are too – and for some reason M. Dubourdieu kept seeking my opinion. Since my views differed from everybody else's (I like big rounded wines in defiance of the current trend favouring lean crisper wines), I expected to be thrown out on my ear. For some reason that never became clear, M. Dubourdieu not only took my comments in gracious good humour, but also invited me to return to Doisy-Daëne to taste some older vintages.

Dubourdieu is a great believer in modern methods of vinification. Hence the success of his Doisy Sec, made from macerated grapes and fermented at a very cool temperature. He employs the same degree of technical sophistication in making his sweet wine. 'I do not make Sauternes,' asserts the combative M. Dubourdieu; 'I make Doisy-Daëne.' The grapes, 100% Sémillon, are harvested by *triage*, as elsewhere, and chaptalisation is rare. Dubourdieu is quite happy with grapes of no more than 18% potential alcohol. If the wine is on the light side, that is fine with him. He wants his Sauternes to be as clean and drinkable as his dry wines. 'For me,' he asserted, ' a taste of honey in Sauternes is an abomination.' The must is fermented in steel tanks, and fermentation is arrested by chilling the wine down to 2 °C, where it remains for two or three weeks. The wine is then racked and sulphured, and, probably uniquely among Sauternes, centrifuged. Some oenologists are opposed to centrifuging because the treatment is over-brutal, rather like excessive filtrations that can rob a wine of its personality. Dubourdieu dismissed such objections: 'The only thing brutal about the centrifuge is its cost. It doesn't damage the young wine and it gives it the purity, finesse, and concentration I want.' The wine is aged in *barriques* in cellars chilled to 10–12 °C. Of the 170 barrels at Doisy-Daëne, about seventy are replaced each year. Since the style of the wine is fairly light, it rarely stays very long in wood: the 1983, for instance, spent a year in barrels and was bottled in September 1985. The wine usually receives a number of filtrations; to those who object to repeated filtrations, Dubourdieu responds that they allow him to reduce drastically the amount of SO_2 with which the wine is dosed.

Pierre Dubourdieu (in collusion with his oenologist son Denis) is an unashamed champion of reductive winemaking, that is to say, ensuring that the wine has virtually no contact with the air, thus minimising any risk of oxidation. Barrel-fermented Sauternes, such as Yquem or Coutet, invites a degree of oxidation; it is part of the style of the wine. Doisy-Daëne is at the other extreme: light, clean, very well balanced, racy, elegant. Reductive winemaking also slows the wine's evolution; it is hard to imagine a Doisy-Daëne exhibiting any blowsiness. Dubourdieu's wines retain their youthfulness for a long time, and it should not be supposed that because the wine is light in style it will fade rapidly.

The ageing potential of Doisy-Daëne is exemplified by the bottle of 1943 that I sampled in the company of M. Dubourdieu. In a sense this wine is atypical Doisy-Daëne: in 1943 grapes were picked at 21% potential alcohol, and the wine spent four years in wood. The result, not surprisingly, is a classic Barsac: a lovely medium gold in colour and with pronounced orangey botrytis on the nose, which was voluptuous and complex; in the mouth the wine was very intense, yet remarkably fresh despite indications on the finish that it was just beginning to dry out. Uncorking a bottle of his 1970, Dubourdieu muttered that this wine 'is almost too good to give a journalist'. Nevertheless, the wine flowed. The 1970 spent two years in wood and was more restrained than the 1943. The colour was gorgeous, and the bouquet ripe and peachy. The wine's distinction stemmed from its sheer vigour; while rich and concentrated, it was also lively, youthful, and very classy. The 1971 is rather peculiar; the grapes were not botrytised and the wine spent no time at all in wood. It had a curious mango-banana nose, atypical of Sauternes, and while fresh and racy on the palate, it was subtle and charming rather than rich and complex. Like most Doisy-Daëne, the 1971 had good length and a very clean finish. The 1980 is a light wine, somewhat lacking in fruit. One of the aims of reductive vinification, and of relatively early bottling, is to conserve the wine's natural aromas, and this is demonstrated by the 1982, which excels with its bouquet, which marries good fat fruitiness with a lively pineappley acidity. The 1983 has enormous charm, is concentrated and rich without being viscous or heavy. Dubourdieu thinks in time it will outstrip the 1943, with which it has much in common. The 1984 was meagre, as was the vintage, but a cask sample of the 1985 was most exciting. The grapes were still being picked in mid-November, and a proportion of botrytised grapes was used. It had real complexity and style, and should develop splendidly.

Other vintages much admired by those who have tasted them include the 1942, 1945, 1961, and 1962. No wine at all was bottled in 1956, 1963, 1965, 1968, 1974, and 1977, and hardly any in 1964 and 1967.

Pierre Dubourdieu's other Sauternes property, Ch Cantegril, was once part of the Myrat estate. Myrat is listed as a Deuxième Cru, but the vines were pulled up in 1976 and wine is no longer made at the property. The Cantegril estate was separated from Ch Myrat in 1854. The only vintages I have tasted, the 1982 and 1983, were well balanced and straightforward, and had the merit of being very reasonably priced.

CH DOISY-VÉDRINES

Since my visits to the Sauternais have always coincided with the holidays taken by the Castéja family who own Ch Doisy-Védrines, I have never visited this property. It is a fairly small estate of some 20 hectares producing about 30,000 bottles a year. It is remote from a world of centrifuges and cold fermentations, for this is a traditional Sauternes, fermented and aged in *barriques* for at least two years. Its reputation is solid without being brilliant. The 1975 is reputed to be the best vintage of recent years, followed by the 1976, 1979, and 1980. The 1982, while sweet and rich, also lacks breed.

CH DOISY-DUBROCA

This, the third part of the original Doisy estate, must be one of the tiniest properties in the Sauternais, with only 4 hectares of vineyards producing about 5000 bottles annually. The property came into the hands of the Dubroca family in the 1880s, and through a marital alliance with the Gounouilhou family that owned Ch Climens until 1971, Doisy-Dubroca came under their control. When Lucien Lurton bought Ch Climens in 1971, Doisy-Dubroca was thrown in with it. It is not a prepossessing estate, for the château is little more than a ramshackle farmhouse. The wine, however, is not without interest, for it is made by exactly the same team responsible for Climens: Christian Broustaut and Mme Janin. The vinification is identical to that at Climens – in other words, completely traditional. The wine is inevitably compared, unfavourably, with Climens, but that is to do it an injustice, for Doisy-Dubroca has never had great pretensions. As one would expect, the wine is generally lighter and less complex than Climens. Nevertheless, the 1980 was quite rich and intense, and powerfully oaky on the nose. Other vintages that have their admirers include the 1971, 1975, and 1979.

CH CAILLOU

The Caillou estate is tucked into the most westerly corner of Barsac. The toytown facade of the château, with its rather dinky turrets at either end, is unmistakable. Adjoining the living quarters are the capacious cellars, with rows of dark barrels and one of the most remarkable collections of old vintages of any property in the Sauternais. M. Bravo is the owner of Ch Caillou, and it was the father of Mme Bravo who acquired the property in 1909. The third generation is now at work here, and not surprisingly Caillou has very much the air of a family business. The elder Mme Bravo takes care of the many private clients who buy wine directly from the cellars. The 15 hectares of vineyards are planted with 90% Sémillon and 10%

Sauvignon, and produce roughly 50,000 bottles each year. The yield is often close to the legal maximum of 25 hl/ha. After the *débourbage*, fermentation takes place in cement vats and steel tanks; the wine is aged in wood, though very little new wood is employed, and racked every six months. Bottling takes place about three years after the vintage. During World War II, there was a shortage of suitable bottles, so the wine remained in cask for up to five years. Caillou is quite alcoholic, and can reach 16% in some years. Great vintages, such as 1943 and 1947, were honoured with special *crème de tête* bottlings, signifying the use of an especially high proportion of botrytised grapes.

I find it hard to admire the wines of Caillou. The old Crème de Tête wines are undoubtedly very good, but it should not be taxing to make good wine in great years. The oldest wine for sale at the cellars is the 1921 (yours for a mere 2100 francs), and Mme Bravo showed me a still intact case of the 1909 vintage from the family's reserve stock. The 1937 is also available, as are four vintages from the 1960s. The 1943 was still in excellent condition in 1984, with no browning, and an attractive soft marmalade nose; it was a very sweet intense wine, almost chewy, though it did lack depth and length. The 1947 Crème de Tête is also very fine, more oxidised in style, with those aromas of caramel and barleysugar that often develop in traditionally made older wines. The 'ordinary' bottlings are less distinguished. The 1973, while quite rich and orangey, was showing signs of a less welcome degree of oxidation, and the finish was not entirely clean. Both the 1975 and 1976 are somewhat bland and surprisingly light given the excellence of the vintages. A burnt alcoholic tone was discernible on both wines. The 1979 is sweet and soft but hollow-centred and lacking in botrytis. Caillou might be rather better if the Bravos abandoned the practice of making special *cuvées* and blended their best lots into their standard wine.

CH SUAU

This small Barsac estate of 6.5 hectares, located just south of the village, is little known outside France, where almost all the wine is sold. About 70% of the vines are Sémillon, and there is a little Muscadelle as well as Sauvignon. I have never come across the wine myself, and its reputation is fairly dim. Since 1960 the proprietor has been M. Biarnès, who also owns various other properties in the Graves region, and his Sauternes is actually made at Ch Navarro in Illats, north of Barsac. The must is fermented in concrete vats and aged in used *barriques*. Robert Parker, who has succeeded in tasting the wine, thinks well of the 1975 and 1980.

CH BROUSTET

Not far from Barsac itself is the modest Broustet estate, which is owned by Eric Fournier, who also runs the first-rate St Emilion property of Ch Canon. Broustet has been in his family for almost a century. The 16 hectares of vineyards consist of a single parcel surrounding the small château. They are planted with 63% Sémillon, 27% Sauvignon, and 10% of mostly very old Muscadelle. Like other proprietors with a fairly high proportion of Muscadelle vines, M. Fournier stresses the problems associated with this delicate variety: early ripening, and susceptibility to grey rot and rapacious insects. The yields at Broustet are quite low, from 10 to 15 hl/ha. Chaptalisation is not unknown at Broustet, but only in the weakest vintages; in 1982, 1983, and 1985 there was none.

The grapes are pressed in horizontal presses, and after the *débourbage* the must is fermented in steel tanks. Fournier has installed a number of small 2500-litre tanks, both because it is easier to control the temperature of the fermentation with small-volume tanks and because they allow him to separate different lots for subsequent *assemblage*. Each tank can contain a single day's crop. Fermentation comes to a virtual halt at 15% alcohol, at which point Fournier chills the tanks, adds a dose of SO_2, and filters the wine before placing it in *barriques*, of which a third are new each year, for about two years. The wine is filtered again before bottling. Fournier aims for a style that is quite high in alcohol and not excessively sweet. Wine not up to the Broustet standards is bottled under the second label, of Ch de Segur.

Recent vintages have been good but not exceptional. The 1975, 1979, and 1980 are well regarded. I have found that a number of the wines have a curious waxy nose and taste, and lack finesse. The 1981 is rather different from other vintages of Broustet in that at five years old the wine was still aggressively oaky on the nose and palate. The 1980 was more rounded and easygoing, while the somewhat dilute 1982 was a touch broad and flabby. The 1983 has been well received, though I have not tasted it, and since picking in 1985 continued until 23 November, there should be a good proportion of botrytised grapes in that wine. A tasting of two lots of 1985, one of Sémillon, the other of Sauvignon, was most promising.

CH NAIRAC

On the northern outskirts of Barsac stands the imposing Ch Nairac, built in the 1780s for the Nairac family, who were Bordeaux merchants. After their flight during the Revolution, the property fell into a prolonged decline, and for many decades the château stood empty. When the vineyards were reconstructed after phylloxera, red grapes were planted, though replaced in the 1950s by traditional white varieties. Any wine made at Nairac in the 1960s was sold in bulk to Bordeaux wholesalers. This all changed in the early 1970s, when Tom Heeter, a native of Ohio, relinquished his passion for racing Porsche cars and devoted himself to reviving this Deuxième Cru. He had spent some time working at Ch Giscours in the Médoc, and successfully courted the daughter of the proprietor, M. Tari. In 1972 Tom Heeter and his wife Nicole took possession of Nairac and began to restore both house and vineyards. The property is medium-

sized, with just over 15 hectares of vines, 9 behind the château, 3 along the nearby main road, and 2, recently purchased, close to Ch Climens. 90% of the vines are Sémillon, with 6% Sauvignon and 4% Muscadelle. Yields are very variable, 13–15 hl/ha on average, but ranging from zero in abysmal years to about 20 in abundant years such as 1983. Heeter tends to pick the Sauvignon grapes relatively early, before the fruit is completely shrivelled by botrytis, as he is anxious to preserve its flowery aromas.

The Fates were not kind to the new proprietors. Severe frost in 1977 badly damaged the vines, and the house and cellars were devastated in 1981 when the Garonne flooded. The vines were not damaged by the flood, which obligingly deposited a new layer of natural fertiliser on the vineyards, but Heeter lost a quarter of his wine, including the best lots of the 1981 vintage. In the early 1980s a somewhat acrimonious parting of the marital ways led to much uncertainty about the future of the property, but at the time of writing it seems likely that Nairac will remain in Tom Heeter's hands.

Heeter stresses the importance of selecting the fruit with the utmost care. Pruning is severe, and during the harvest the bunches are scrutinised to ensure that no grapes attacked by grey rot find their way into the press. It is in the difficult years that *tries successives* are essential; in 1974, for instance, the Nairac pickers went through the vineyards eleven times, and despite these efforts, the Heeters finally declassified 70% of the crop. In comparison with such vintages, years like 1982 and 1983 are straightforward. The grapes are given a gentle pressing in a hydraulic press, and the juice is left to settle overnight. At this stage, some SO_2 is added to the juice to deter oxidation and bacterial infection. Heeter also adds some Vitamin B_1, on the suggestion of his consultant oenologist, the revered Professor Peynaud of Bordeaux. B_1 is one of the natural vitamins destroyed by botrytis, and by replacing it in the must Heeter says he is able to reduce the doses of SO_2. The must is briefly aerated and settled before being racked into *barriques* for the fermentation. There is no need for temperature control, as the outdoor temperatures tend to be low at that time of year, and wine fermenting in small casks heats up less than wine fermented in large-volume tanks. Should there be an Indian summer, Heeter cools down the cellars by hosing down the walls, and the ensuing evaporation lowers the temperature. I was intrigued to find other evidence of Heeter's ingenious cellar-craft. Instead of using proper bungs to seal the barrels, he uses empty quarter-bottles of wine. 'Why not?' says Heeter, 'They work perfectly well as safety valves during fermentation, and they cost a mere 60 centimes each, far less than a bung.' The wine stays in *barrique* for up to three years. About half the casks are renewed each year. For the first three months after fermentation, there is a monthly racking; thereafter, this happens much less frequently. There is no fining, and a light filtration only just before bottling.

It will be apparent that Nairac is a wine made to exacting standards by entirely traditional methods. Tom Heeter has not hesitated to declassify wine not up to standard, and no wine was bottled in 1977, 1978, and 1984. Very good wines were made in the rather dim vintages of 1972, 1973, and 1974. The style of the wine is very oaky, as one would expect, but it never lacks elegance. There is nothing fatiguing about a glass of Nairac: its special quality is its combination of raciness with a rounded flavour of fruit and new oak. The 1975 and 1976 show Nairac at its best: pale gold in colour, and rich and oaky on the nose; then fresh and fruity on the palate, with invigorating finesse. The 1979 has some of the plumpness of the 1976, while the 1980, with its charm and delicacy and backbone, is closer in style to the 1975. The 1975 is possibly the finest Nairac Tom Heeter has made, though some prefer the richer 1976. The 1982 was still aggressively oaky in 1987, but I suspect the wine will develop well. Only the 1981 is a bit disappointing, rather hard and austere and lacking in sweetness. Cask samples of the 1983 have been lush and elegant, spicy and complex, and the wine may well combine the richness of the 1976 with the breed of the 1975 and prove to be the finest vintage of all. A cask sample of 1985, mostly Sauvignon, was lean and intense, with little obvious botrytis; the Sémillon sample, predictably, was much fatter and more complex.

CH D'ARCHE

Like so many Sauternes properties, Ch d'Arche has had a chequered history. The château itself is a modest Louis XV mansion of one storey with two courtyards, one embraced by the house, the other by the cellars. It was originally owned by the Comte d'Arche, but during the Revolution it was appropriated by the state and divided into many parcels. Various sections were reunited over the years and from the 1920s the estate was in the hands of the Bastit St Martin family. In 1981 Ch d'Arche was leased to Pierre Perromat, an eloquent and charming man who for many years had been chairman of INAO, the powerful body that regulates the system of *appellations d'origine contrôlée*. M. Perromat says that his sole purpose in taking over the winemaking at Ch d'Arche was to produce the very finest Sauternes possible. Indeed, it would be somewhat shaming should the former chairman of INAO be discovered to be a mediocre exponent of the activity he once helped to regulate.

As with all good Sauternes, the work begins in the vineyards, which are the highest in the commune of Sauternes, slightly more elevated than those of Yquem. The *encépagement* is 90% Sémillon and 10% Sauvignon, and the 30 hectares produce roughly 60,000 bottles. The grapes are picked in the classic manner, with up to ten *passages* through the vineyards, and yields are on average 15 hl/ha. Indeed, in 1983 M. Perromat waited too long, and the final *trie* had to be rejected. The grapes pass through hydraulic presses and the must is fermented in steel tanks at 18–19 °C. After the wine is racked, a preliminary selection is made and the least distinguished lots are weeded out. The final selection is made eighteen months later. 60% of the wine spends two years in new oak, and M. Perromat admits that he aims to make a wine of sufficient power to withstand long barrel-ageing. The former second label at Ch d'Arche, Ch d'Arche-Lafaurie, has been discontinued.

During the Bastit St Martin regime, the wine was widely regarded as uninspired, though a bottle of the 1936, a poor vintage, tasted almost half a century later, was remarkably good. The wines of the 1960s and 1970s have been criticised for their pedestrian respectability, correct but dull. It is already clear, however, that under Pierre Perromat's regime the wines have improved considerably. The 1982 was good if straightforward, a soft attractive wine of some richness, above average for this rained-out vintage. The 1983 was still closed in 1986 but showed enormous promise, a wine of rich concentrated fruit and great elegance. The 1980 and 1981 are said to be good, though I have not tasted them. It is instructive that properties such as Ch d'Arche and Ch Nairac that used to be more or less written off have been so successfully resuscitated. It seems to show that, despite variations in soil and microclimate, just about any property in the Sauternais district is theoretically capable of producing first-rate wine. What are required are the resources and the commitment to putting such an intention into effect.

CH LAMOTHE

This property, just south of Ch d'Arche on a neighbouring ridge once occupied by a Roman fortress, also once belonged to M. Bastit St Martin, but was sold in 1961 to M. Jean Despujols. It is a small property of only 8 hectares, planted with 70% Sémillon, 20% Sauvignon, and 10% Muscadelle, but yields are fairly high at just over 20 hl/ha. The wine is aged both in wood and in vats, and bottled about two years after the vintage. The style of the wine is light and commercial, and it has won few accolades from those who have tasted it. I was pleasantly surprised by the 1983, which was sweet and rich with crisp acidity on the finish.

Ch Lamothe should not be confused with Ch Lamothe-Guignard, an estate of 11 hectares also sold by M. Bastit St Martin in 1961. Since 1981, this property has been owned by Philippe and Jacques Guignard. To add to the confusion, this property used to be known as Ch Lamothe-Bergey. The first wines made by the Guignards have been well received.

CH FILHOT

It is hard to forget my first visit to Ch Filhot. The owner, Comte Henri de Vaucelles, greeted me warmly, then drove me to a grassy corner of the park in which the magnificent château is set. Here we stood for an hour in the December wind while he held forth on the economic history of the Sauternes region. Parenthetically, he also touched upon winemaking in ancient Russia, the influence of religious taboos on the commercial exploitation of wine, and, of course, the history of Ch Filhot. Later, after I was chilled to the bone but very well informed, M. de Vaucelles drove me to the cellars to taste the new wines. It is equally difficult to forget my next visit to Ch Filhot. Once again I was warmly greeted and whisked down to a familiar patch of lawn. Here, in an uncharacteristic July drizzle, M. de Vaucelles gave me the identical lecture, though in an expanded form. By the time we reached the cellars an hour and a half later, I was even better informed than two years before.

This property had been in existence long before the Filhot family acquired it in 1709, and it was again expanded after the estate came through marriage into the hands of the Lur-Saluces family. The Filhots had replanted the vineyards destroyed by the frost of 1705, and the property soon won a high reputation for its wines. In the 1780s Thomas Jefferson rated Filhot as the best wine after Yquem, and commented that the two wines fetched the same price. The same situation obtained in 1816, according to the wine writer A. Jullien. Under the Lur-Saluces Filhot became the largest property in the Sauternais, and it still is. The entire estate consists of 330 hectares, of which 120 used to be under vine. But as the nineteenth century wore on, the vineyards were poorly maintained, and by 1935 there were no more than 20 hectares of vineyards. Moreover, the name of Filhot disappeared altogether and the wine was sold in bulk as Ch Sauternes until 1900, when the original name was restored (though I recall tasting a 1896 wine sold as Ch Filhot). In 1935 Ch Filhot was sold by the Lur-Saluces to their relative Comte Etienne de Lacarelle. New vineyards were planted and the property restored. Comte Henri de

Vaucelles, M. de Lacarelle's nephew and an industrialist, took over the running of the estate in 1974.

He encountered severe problems at Filhot. As M. de Vaucelles is only too ready to admit, Filhot's palatial grandeur exceeds its place in the local economy. His predecessors had cooked up various schemes – tobacco growing, cattle raising – to exploit the estate, but all had floundered. Meanwhile he found himself with 2 hectares of roofs to maintain, not to mention an ill-organised agricultural estate. To survive, he has had to run a tight ship, but prudent management is not necessarily conducive to great winemaking.

At present there are 60 hectares of vineyards on sandy soil, planted with 65% Sémillon, 33% Sauvignon, and 2% Muscadelle. Yields can be quite high, as in 1983, when yields of 23 hl/ha resulted in 150,000 bottles of wine, though 100,000 is more usual. Grapes ripen more slowly at Filhot than at most other properties, because of its site as the most southerly estate in Sauternes. The harvest usually begins a week later than in Barsac, and is particularly susceptible to frosts. The pickers usually make only three or four *passages*, for M. de Vaucelles maintains that grapes picked very late are more prone to oxidation (which, even if true, is surely a routine hazard). The must is chaptalised when necessary, and fermented in fibreglass vats for about two weeks. Up to three vintages are stored in the huge cellars, mostly in fibreglass, though on my latest visit to Filhot I did see some *barriques* in place, since M. de Vaucelles intends to put the 1985 wine, which at 14.5% is slightly higher in alcohol than most Filhot wines, into wood for at least part of its ageing process.

Some years ago I was greatly impressed by the 1976, a rich, pineappley wine of considerable intensity. Few other recent vintages have been able to approach that success. The 1975 is clean but not very interesting, and the 1978, admittedly a light year, is insipid and short. The 1979 is adequate, a medium-bodied wine attractive on the palate and with a dried apricot taste on the finish. The 1980, while quite beguiling on the nose, lacks concentration. The 1981 was acceptable but bland, and the 1982, while broader, lacked structure. (1982 was a difficult year at Filhot, and after heavy rains half of the Sémillon crop had to be declassified.) A vat sample of the 1983 tasted a year after the vintage was disappointing, light in the mouth and bitter on the finish. The same wine almost two years later, again tasted from the vat, was noticeably beginning to oxidise. The 1984 simply lacked fruit, though M. de Vaucelles says there was no lack of botrytis. The 1985 is very sweet and intense, but lacks the character and amplitude of wine made from botrytised grapes. Almost all the wines are marred by a hard bitter sulphurous finish. More recent tastings of the 1976, which I enjoyed so much in its youth, have been increasingly disappointing, suggesting that the wine is falling apart. The 1971, a mildly sweet, moderately rich, lemony wine, is in much sounder condition. Filhot, sadly, lacks the consistent presence of features that mark great wines as opposed to sound ones, and on occasion even soundness is absent.

CH ROMER DU HAYOT

The Romer vineyards, the sole Deuxième Cru in Fargues, are bordered by the Autoroute that divides Barsac and most of Preignac from the rest of the Sauternais. It is a small property of 12 hectares of sandy, gravelly soil planted with 70% Sémillon, 25% Sauvignon, and 5% Muscadelle producing some 40,000 bottles each year. The principal owner, M. André du Hayot, makes the wine at Ch Guiteronde, his 14-hectare estate in Barsac. The property was known simply as Ch Romer until M. du Hayot tacked on his own name. He makes a modest fresh wine, sweet but lean, by fermenting and ageing in vats for no more than two years. In recent years, however, M. du Hayot has been putting a proportion of the wine into *barrique*. I have tasted this wine too infrequently to assess its qualities, but the 1975, 1976, 1979, 1980 and 1983 have been admired.

CH DE MALLE

On the other side of the Autoroute, in Preignac, stands the very lovely Ch de Malle, a stately home that is open to the public. The elegant seventeenth century château, beautifully furnished, and the Italian-style gardens are owned by Comte Pierre de Bournazel, who is, like Comte Henri de Vaucelles, related to the Lur-Saluces family. The cellars are tucked away in a wing to the left of the main facade. This is a medium-sized estate of about 25 hectares, planted with 73% Sémillon, 22% Sauvignon, and 3% Muscadelle. The proprietor is a trained engineer, and the winemaking here combines technological sophistication with traditional *élevage*. Both steel tanks and *barriques* are used for both fermentation and maturation and some of the barrels are renewed each year. Although my tastings of the wine, limited to the vintages of 1938, 1962, and 1979, have not impressed me greatly, it must be said that de Malle has a good reputation for elegant, charming, soundly made wine. Like other Sauternes in a lighter style, de Malle is often at its most persuasive within the first decade of its life. The 1975, 1976 and 1980 have been well received, and the 1983 is said to be exceptionally good.

4

Other Sauternes Wines

Given the antiquity of the 1855 classification, it is not surprising that some unclassified properties produce wine as good as the classed growths, and it is to some of these estates that I now turn. This is a highly selective list. While I hope to have included all the properties where outstandingly good Sauternes is made, I have no doubt that there are others that make good wine which I have overlooked. The properties are listed in alphabetical order.

DOMAINE D'ARCHE-PUGNEAU

I have a soft spot for this modest Preignac property. Although its vinification is unsophisticated, indeed rustic, the wine is enjoyable. M. Jean-Pierre Daney owns this 14-hectare estate and practises *triage*, though he is often content to pick overripe grapes rather than wait indefinitely for botrytis. Yields are quite low, between 11 and 15 hl/ha. The must is fermented and aged in old barrels for about three years, and racked every three months. The wine is only bottled in good years, and much of the crop is sold in *barriques* directly to *négociants* in Bordeaux. The 1983, while sweet and rounded and with a distinct taste of apricots, lacked complexity; I much preferred the 1982, a rounded yet spicy mouthful with a barleysugar finish indicative of the gentle oxidation that comes from long barrel-ageing. The 1985, though well balanced and charming, is not especially interesting. This pleasantly old-fashioned wine, and the warm welcome from Mme Daney, proved refreshing after visiting some of the more aloof properties in the neighbourhood.

CH BASTOR-LAMONTAGNE

This medium-sized Preignac property occupies 83 hectares of flat land on sandy, stony soil opposite Ch Suduiraut and adjoining Ch de Malle. Named after its eighteenth-century proprietor, François de Lamontagne, it frequently changed hands until in 1936 it was acquired by a bank, the Credit Foncier de France. The *régisseur* is Jean Baup. The 37 hectares of vineyards are planted with 70% Sémillon, 20% Sauvignon, and 10% Muscadelle. Baup does not conceal the fact that his pickers harvest by the bunch, even when only a proportion of the grapes on the cluster are botrytised. He aims for a potential alcohol of 18–19% and chaptalisation is rare. Yields are quite high, and sometimes nudge the legal maximum of 25 hl/ha; the maximum annual production is 120,000 bottles. Fermentation takes place in steel tanks for two weeks at 18–19 °C and is arrested with chilling and a dose of SO_2. After an *assemblage* the wine is put into *barrique* for two to three years, though in a mediocre year such as 1984 it will be bottled roughly two years after harvest. 20% of the barrels are renewed each year.

Bastor-Lamontagne is now making some very good wines, superior to some of the lesser Deuxièmes Crus. It is not fair to judge the wine by the very highest standards, for the property has no pretensions to being top-flight. But the wine is made with care, mediocre lots are declassified, and the wine is properly aged before being released. I have only tasted vintages since 1981 (excellent here, with

ample botrytis and richness) and the wine can lack concentration, no doubt because the yields are too high; it can also be sulphury. On the other hand, Bastor-Lamontagne is relatively inexpensive and offers very good value. It is a moderately rich, well-balanced wine of some style and vigour. The general view is that the best vintages of recent years are 1975, 1976, 1979, 1982, and 1983.

CH DE FARGUES

This property is tucked away not far from Langon in the furthest corner of the commune of the same name. It has been owned by the Lur-Saluces family since 1472, and though there have long been vineyards on the estate, it was only in the 1930s that the then Marquis thought of producing fine wine here. The estate is a large one, some 175 hectares in all, but only 12 are under vine. The site is spectacular, dominated by the gutted castle, visible from miles around, that rises over the vineyards. The courtyard of the gaunt ruin is filled with low buildings that accommodate the cellar and with outbuildings that service the home farm. In a few years' time the area under vine will be increased to about 14 hectares, for some red vines have been grubbed up and are being replanted. The *encépagement* is 80% Sémillon and 20% Sauvignon.

In case you suspect that this unclassified growth is a great bargain, let me point out that Ch de Fargues is, after Yquem, usually the most expensive wine of the region. Not only is it owned by the Marquis de Lur-Saluces, but the same team responsible for making Yquem also make de Fargues. The methods of vinification are much the same as at Yquem. A pneumatic press is used here instead of a hydraulic press, but, as at Yquem, there is no *débourbage* and each day's pressings are put into *barriques* each evening. Not all the barrels are new, but there are none that could be called ancient. Pierre Meslier sees the making of de Fargues as an even greater challenge than Yquem, if only because the conditions are less propitious. The microclimate here means that grapes ripen about eight days later than at Yquem, with attendant risks of damage from cold and rain during the harvest. Even in fine years this difference in microclimate can be significant. In 1983, for instance, by the end of September only 20% of the crop had been picked here, compared to 80% at

Yquem; Meslier sat tight until mid-November, by which time every other property had completed its harvest. The gamble paid off and the crop was excellent. The yields at Ch de Fargues, on average 7.5 hl/ha, are even lower than those at Yquem. The quality of the soil is not especially good, and Pierre Meslier is convinced that were it better he could make even finer wine.

The production is tiny, no more than 10,000 bottles a year, and this has given the wine a certain mystique. In comparative tastings, de Fargues has occasionally – as in 1981 – shown better than Yquem. But Pierre Meslier feels it is misleading to compare de Fargues with Yquem; to judge its true quality, it should be compared with other Sauternes. He is convinced that while de Fargues in its youth is more approachable than Yquem, it is over the long haul that Yquem shows its distinction. In time, the 1981 Yquem will outclass the de Fargues of the same vintage. M. Meslier admits that de Fargues is unlikely to age as well as Yquem, and when I asked him how long it would keep, he shrugged and said: 'Sixty years?' Vintages to which we should look forward keenly in the year 2020 include the 1967, 1971, 1975, 1976, and 1980.

CH GILETTE

This very small Preignac property is surely the most idiosyncratic in the whole Sauternais, for the wine is rarely bottled until it is at least twenty years old. The vintages currently on offer date from the 1950s. The theory here is that wine aged for decades in concrete vats evolves very slowly since it incurs the least risk of oxidation. The property is owned by René and Christian Médeville, who also own a few other vineyards in the region, including Ch Les Justices. Les Justices, with 8 hectares of vines, is 1500 metres away from the 4.5 hectares of Ch Gilette. Since the Gilette vineyards are precocious and the grapes usually ripen a week earlier than elsewhere in the Sauternais, the harvesting is usually completed by late October. The vineyards are planted with 88% Sémillon, 10% Sauvignon, and 2% Muscadelle. The spotless modern cellars are close to the Médevilles' lovely ivy-covered house behind the church at Preignac. In recent years M. Médeville has doubled the cellar capacity and also maintains a stock, dating back to the 1930s, of roughly 200,000 bottles.

Ch Les Justices is bottled young and, unlike Gilette, is occasionally chaptalised. The must is fermented in steel at 14–15 °C for up to two weeks, and when the wine has reached 14% Médeville lowers the temperature to 10 °C to retard the fermentation until an additional degree of alcohol is attained. After fermentation, the wine is racked, filtered, then simply left alone in large concrete tanks. Wines not up to standard are declassified, and Médeville only ages wines worthy of the lengthy treatment; in the 1960s many vintages were rejected altogether. Gilette is one of the few properties where degrees of sweetness are labelled. The top category is the Crème de Tête, made only from selected grapes in great years, rewarding, says Médeville, an extravagance of nature. These wines are produced in fairly small quantities from a yield of about 9 hl/ha. A more standard quality is marked Doux, and this reflects a yield of 18–19, compared to an average yield of 21–22 at Les Justices. Demi-Doux is the least sweet wine, but this category was phased out after 1958.

Because the maturing wine is sealed tight in its concrete vats for decades (the 1955 and 1959 were not bottled until June 1982!), they evolve far more slowly than they would in bottle. A vintage of Gilette is on release a mature, ready-to-drink bottle, which is not the case anywhere else in the Sauternes. Of course, long storage of a wine that is expensive to make in the first place is a costly business, and this is reflected in its price. My own view is that, despite the undoubted quality of the wine, such lengthy cellarage is perverse. Not all Sauternes ages equally well. It is hard to predict the future of any wine, but if it is purchased from the proprietor at the going rate just after it has been bottled, it can be sampled by the buyer at various stages in its life, and drunk up at the appropriate time. With Gilette, bottling takes place after the wine is mature, even when that wine has not evolved perfectly; a wine impressive in its youth can easily become shaky thirty years later.

This stricture applies more to the Doux and Demi-Doux than to the Crèmes de Tête. The 1950 Doux, while soft, honeyed and fresh on the nose, was far too alcoholic on the palate. Far more successful is the 1955 Doux, which after thirty years was still fresh, fruity, and complex. The 1958 Demi-Doux, bottled in 1978 with only about 15 g/l residual sugar, I have tasted twice, and my notes differ. One bottle was light on the nose, but had a pleasant butterscotch flavour; the second had an elegant and complex nose with undertones of mango and tobacco, but on the palate the alcohol was far too prominent, masking the fruit. The 1950 Crème de Tête, on the other hand, is magnificent: extremely rich and orangey, but with plenty of acidity to counter the sumptuousness of the wine. This is not a Sauternes for the faint-hearted. The 1953 Crème de Tête is lighter, has a soft lanolin nose, but is marred by high alcohol. M. Médeville has confirmed that some of the Gilette wines have over 16% alcohol, and such huge wines need very rich fruit if they are not to appear clumsy. I have also had the pleasure of tasting the 1955 Crème de Tête on two occasions, and it was superb both times, intensely concentrated, viscous, and voluptuous, yet a wine of great elegance. In 1959 the grapes destined for the Crème de Tête were picked at 23%, and not surprisingly the wine is creamy and rich, with honey and marmalade on the nose. It is far from subtle, but with such velvety richness in the mouth, it is churlish to complain.

Ch Les Justices is, as one would expect, lighter than Gilette. In good years such as 1976 and 1983 it is a rounded, lively, elegant wine of some distinction. But, like most vintages of Gilette locked into their time capsules, they are marred by excessive alcohol.

I suspect that the era of protracted ageing of Gilette may be drawing to a close. In 1985 M. Médeville, for the first time, has put some of the Gilette into *barrique*. He is only waggling a toe in the water, as he has purchased a mere three barrels, and the wood-ageing is by way of an experiment. While it is undoubtedly true that bottled Gilette can be a great wine, it must be equally true that, conventionally aged in oak and bottled after three years, it would attain comparable glories after fifteen years rather than thirty. While great wine should not be rushed, it does seem unnecessary to enforce a wait of over twenty-five years on the consumer. In the meantime, it is good to know that mature Sauternes from great years, and of a quality greatly superior to that of Ch Caillou, which also maintains a large bottle stock of old wines, is still available direct from the property.

CH GRAVAS

Pierre Bernard owns this small Barsac estate, which was acquired by his ancestors in 1850. The château itself is quite pretty, and living quarters seem only tentatively separated from the cellars. His 10 hectares of gravelly soil, planted with 80% Sémillon, 10% Sauvignon, and 10% Muscadelle, are located between Ch Coutet and Ch Climens. The wine is not made to the most exacting standards, since average yields, at 22–24 hl/ha, are high and chaptalisation is practised. After fermentation the wine is racked and filtered and spends six to eight months in cask before being stored in 5800-litre underground tanks. There is a second light filtration before the wine is bottled some three years after the harvest. The dullness of his 1983 was explained by the existence of a special *cuvée* of the same year. This wine had the botrytis tones lacking in the other and was generally more stylish. With a property that only produces about 30,000 bottles a year, it seems a mistake to give special treatment to 10% of the crop, since the ordinary wine is bound to suffer from the absence of the richer lots in the blend. The 1985, tasted from the vat, was surprisingly good, appley and quite lush, with some depth of flavour, and there was only the slightest hint of the high alcohol (15.5%).

CH RAYMOND-LAFON

As if Pierre Meslier did not have enough on his hands, what with making Yquem and supervising de Fargues, he is also the proprietor of Ch Raymond-Lafon, an estate of 20 hectares (18 currently in production) that borders the Yquem vineyards. Ch Raymond-Lafon

was only established in 1850, and thus its vineyards were too young to be considered for the 1855 classification. With its ivy-covered walls and steep gables, not to mention a colourful and even flashy front garden, the château resembles a Victorian country house more than a French mansion. When Pierre Meslier bought the property, only 3.5 hectares were under vine, and he has made further purchases of neighbouring vineyards. The *encépagement* is 80% Sémillon and 20% Sauvignon. He is determined to make wine by the same classic methods that prevail at the Lur-Saluces estates. Harvesting is postponed until botrytis has attacked the grapes and the potential alcohol has risen to 19–21%. In certain years there are as many as eleven *passages* through the vineyards. Yields are 9 hl/ha, as low as at Yquem, and there is no chaptalisation. The grapes are pressed three times in a vertical press, and after fermentation (which is arrested naturally by the presence of botrycine, according to Meslier, not by doses of SO_2) it stays in *barrique* for a full three years. It is Meslier's intention to use only new oak eventually, but at 2000 francs apiece, barrels have to be purchased gradually, and at present 60% of them are new. Production is small, about 25,000 bottles a year, and in recent years demand has grown rapidly.

These days Pierre Meslier merely supervises the winemaking at the cellars adjoining his home. His son Charles-Henri is the winemaker, and his other son Jean-Pierre travels the world selling the wine while Mme Francine Meslier receives visitors at the property. Jean-Pierre is proud of the fact that he now has to allocate small quantities of this unclassified wine to a handful of wine merchants and restaurateurs across the world. Jean-Pierre is quite open about his wish to push the price of their wine to about half that of Yquem. Although I find something distasteful about a marketing effort based on scarcity and snobbery as well as quality, I have to admit that Raymond-Lafon is one of the finest Sauternes, every bit as good as some of the top Premiers Crus. Before the Mesliers bought the property, the wine was far less distinguished: pre-Meslier vintages such as 1933 and 1971 were far from exciting when tasted in the 1980s. Yet the reputation of the wine was once high. Jean-Pierre showed me a wine merchant's list of 1922. 1918 Yquem and 1916 Suduiraut were priced at 15 francs, and the 1917 Raymond-Lafon was offered at 14 francs.

As at Climens, a willingness to take chances and to declassify a percentage of the crop leads to excellent results in poor years as well as good. In 1979, for instance, when rain halted the harvest in mid-November, 60% of the crop had to be rejected. What was bottled was extremely good, a classic Sauternes with fruit and oak in perfect harmony. Only in 1974 was no wine bottled at all, but another difficult vintage, the 1978, easily outclassed many of the insipid wines made at most other properties. The 1980 is a marvellous wine. The Mesliers started picking on 20 October, and by continuing into November they managed to pick such good grapes that they were able to use 80% of their crop. It is a wine of real substance, lush and chewy in the mouth yet without any traces of heaviness; its finesse and breed are typical of Raymond-Lafon. The 1981, lean and aggressive at first, is developing into a plump and stylish wine. In 1982 only 35% of the crop was usable as a result of heavy rain in October. Despite these unpromising conditions, the wine tasted excellent in 1987, oaky and lush, stylish despite a certain lack of freshness. Properties that blended in too much of the weaker wine made bland Sauternes in 1982, but at Raymond-Lafon only grapes picked before the rain found their way into bottle. 1983 was a far easier vintage; the grapes were almost perfect and 90% of the crop was used. The wine has all the Meslier hallmarks of oakiness, concentrated fruit, and finesse. In 1985, when many proprietors were content to pick overripe grapes rather than wait for botrytis, Raymond-Lafon found itself with 40% of the crop still on the vines in December. There was then a freak change in the weather and botrytis revived. Once again patience and courage seem to have been rewarded, though I have not yet tasted the wine. It is clear, from extensive tastings of Raymond-Lafon, that the standards of harvesting and winemaking are as high as at any Sauternes property. The wine is not, however, directly comparable to Yquem. It is less massive and more approachable in its youth. Whether the long maturation in all new *barriques* which Pierre Meslier is planning will change the character of the wine, possibly by giving it an excessive toughness and austerity, it is impossible to say. It will certainly be imperative for all lovers of Sauternes to watch the development of this remarkable little property, and to continue, if we can afford to do so, to taste its impeccable wines.

CH SAINT-AMAND

This immaculate little estate in Preignac deserves to be much better known. The château is a plain low building, with two long arms at right angles that contain the cellars. 11 hectares of well-groomed vineyards surround the château, and 11 more are distributed among three parcels of land two kilometres away. This is a very ancient property and there are still vestiges of the ninth-century ecclesiastical settlement that once existed on the site. The present owner is Louis Ricard. His vines are old – forty years on average – and there are variations in soil between his vineyards. Those near the château are pebbly, while his other parcels have a higher clay content. The varieties planted are 85% Sémillon and 15% Sauvignon. Yields are fairly high, 20 hl/ha on average, and while M. Ricard does wait for as long as he can for botrytis before harvesting, he rarely makes more than four *passages*. To his taste, wine made exclusively from botry-tised grapes can be too jammy, and he prefers a blend of botrytised and merely overripe grapes. The wine is occasionally chaptalised, but Ricard is not keen on the practice: 'If the wine isn't good,' he observes, 'chaptalisation won't help.' The must is fermented for two to four weeks in cement vats or steel tanks, then racked, and returned to the vat or tank until March, when it is filtered. The wine spends from three to four months in wood, and is bottled eighteen to twenty-four months after the harvest. The wine is not fined but it is chilled to stabilise it and remove tartaric acid deposits.

These methods of vinification may not be conducive to making the very greatest Sauternes, but the wines are often excellent, especially given that their price is relatively low. Some of the 60,000 bottles produced each year are sold under the name of Ch de la Chartreuse, but the wine is the same. It tastes like Barsac, and indeed the estate does border that commune. St Amand is an attractive yellow-gold in colour, and lean and elegant on the palate. The 1981 was particularly attractive, a lemony wine touched, for the moment, by sulphur. The 1982 is a slight disappointment, fat and rather cloying on the finish, but the 1983 is delicious and well balanced. M. Ricard is very proud of his 1984, which he personally prefers to the 1983, and the 1985 is, he claims, his best wine in years. Saint-Amand is not a wine of great depth or complexity, but it is well made and excellent value.

5

Other Bordeaux Wines

The Sauternais is not the only part of the Bordeaux region where sweet white wine is made; it is merely the most prestigious, its reputation aided by the formation in 1908 of a growers' association that granted the Sauternes *appellation* only to five communes. Meanwhile the communes on both sides of the Garonne that shared the same microclimate with the Sauternais continued, as they had done for decades if not centuries, to make sweet white wines that in those days matched the splendours from Sauternes. It was only in 1935 that these other districts – Cérons, Loupiac, Ste-Croix-du-Mont – were granted their own *appellations*, which they still retain. More recent legislation has differentiated the *appellation* of Cadillac from the less specific Premières Côtes de Bordeaux. In addition, some of the communes, such as Pujols and St Pierre-de-Mons, just beyond the borders of the Sauternais, make a sweet white wine sold as Graves Supérieurs.

These districts may be capable in theory of producing great sweet wines, but sadly, with very few exceptions, they no longer do so. The reasons are economic. Until very recently, even the proprietors of Premiers Crus in the Sauternais itself considered themselves hard done by, and the great growths of Sauternes were indeed undervalued. If the prestigious properties had reason to complain, so to an even greater extent did the winemakers of the neighbouring districts. For the prices their wines could command from Bordeaux *négociants* were a fraction, a third or less, of those obtained by their illustrious neighbours. As should now be obvious, to make great sweet white wine in the Bordeaux region is costly and hazardous. These low prices discouraged many growers from continuing to make classic sweet wines and they turned increasingly to two solutions. Either they grubbed up their Sémillon and Sauvignon and planted red grapes, or they made commercial sweet wines that satisfied the minimal requirements of the *appellation* but were at best undistinguished and at worst positively filthy. There are, of course, a handful of exceptions, and in the course of this chapter I shall look at the principal Bordeaux *appellations* outside the Sauternais and point to the best that they can offer.

CÉRONS

Cérons lies just immediately north of Barsac and its wines, at their best, share the firmness and finesse of its more prestigious neighbour. Some of the vineyards are very old; enclosed by walls, they originally belonged to ecclesiastical estates. The soil is stony and flat. The *appellation* includes the communes of Podensac and Illats, and there are no more than fifty proprietors in the region. Thirty years ago almost the entire production of Cérons consisted of sweet white wine. That is no longer the case, and dry wines, both red and white, are on the increase. Production of the sweet wine stood at 6000 hectolitres in 1981, and four years later had declined to 2600 hectolitres, and there are no signs that this trend will be halted, let alone reversed.

The wines can be lively and elegant and are rarely as unctuous as Sauternes. Maximum yields are 40 hl/ha, considerably higher than those of the Sauternais, and their minimum alcohol is 12.5%, compared to 13% in the Sauternais. There are two properties that produce very attractive wine: the Grand Enclos du Château de Cérons, and Ch Cérons itself, a beautiful seventeenth-century mansion that the owner, Jean Perromat (brother of Pierre Perromat of Ch d'Arche), is now restoring. The vineyards lie behind his residence a few hundred yards away in another part of the village. M. Perromat is also the mayor of Cérons. The estate is a small one, with 6 hectares of vineyards. He makes a good red Graves as well as the sweet wine. He is very anxious to make clean wines that are as free as possible from SO_2. Indeed, he told me that the 1973 Ch Cérons is entirely free of SO_2. To achieve this, he filters frequently and because of this he can leave the wine in cask for up to twelve or even fifteen months without having to rack it. 'If your wines are clean,' he says, 'then you don't need to rack very much.' It does not sound like a formula for great wine, especially since the 1973 spent five years in cask and a portion of the 1979 was still in cask in 1986, but the wines have charm and style. I suspect the sweet wine is kept so long in cask not because it is a vital part of the maturation process, but because there is little point bottling wine that is difficult to sell. The 1973 was medium-gold in colour, and had a fine nose with aromas of peaches, apricots, and tobacco; on the palate it was soft, yet quite intense and lively, and had good length. The 1979 had a more pronounced botrytis character and was fatter and more rounded, and slightly less elegant. A cask sample of the 1985, which had spent nine months in new oak, was fruity and lively, but still quite aggressive. I could detect no botrytis in the wine, and M. Perromat says that because noble rot did not develop until very late in the season, many growers chose to make good dry white wines instead. It seems probable that wine with the Cérons *appellation* will become increasingly rare.

LOUPIAC

Loupiac is situated directly opposite Barsac along the banks of the Garonne, and the AOC region stretches a few miles back into the hills. The terrain is quite varied, and the soil up on the plateau differs from that closer to the river. The slopes face south and get the benefit of sunshine as well as humidity from fogs rising from the Garonne.

The history of the *appellation* is somewhat confused, for originally Loupiac was only one of eleven communes that used its name; this list was progressively pared down after a succession of court judgments, until in 1930 it was ruled that only wines made from grapes picked in Loupiac itself were entitled to the name, and consequently in 1936 it was awarded its own AOC. As in Cérons, the maximum yield is 40 hl/ha.

The growers of Loupiac – there are sixty-six currently listed – like to claim that there were vineyards here in Roman times. One of the proprietors, M. Bernède, also owns the site of a Roman villa, which he is continuing to excavate. M. Bernède conducts visitors around the excavations, showing them the mosaics, and, on leaving, they are invited to taste his wine, Ch Portail Rouge. It is claimed that this riverside villa was owned by Ausonus, the Roman governor and poet after whom Ch Ausone at St Emilion is named. There is, however, no evidence that Ausonus lived at Ausone, let alone at Loupiac.

As for the wines, they tend to be on the light side. Prices, even from the good properties, are very depressed. At Ch Mazarin, for instance, the 1982 Loupiac was available in 1986 for 16 francs, and even the 1979 was only 22 francs. So it is not surprising that few growers are prepared to take the pains and risks necessary to make first-rate wine. Marc Ducau, who owns Ch Loupiac-Gaudet and Ch Pontac, says the economic situation is against them: they obtain almost double the yield of Sauternes and the wine fetches a third of the price. As at Cérons, production of the sweet wine has been steadily decreasing, from 10,000 hectolitres in 1981 to 6000 in 1985.

That excellent wine was once made at Loupiac became evident after a visit to Ch Mazarin, an engaging property owned by the slightly eccentric Courbin family. Louis Courbin is an extremely jovial and entirely bald seventy-five-year-old; in recent years he has handed over most of the responsibility for making the wine to his daughter Anne-Marie. One of the charms of Ch Mazarin, which is named after the statesman who once visited the château, is the small private museum, containing old casks and cooperage tools as well as family memorabilia. The casks laid out in the grand tasting room are purely decorative, for these days the wine is made in tanks. The estate consists of 23 hectares at Loupiac (as well as 6 at Cadillac and 5 at Cérons). Chaptalisation is sometimes necessary, and the wine is matured in underground vats. The Courbins do not like to treat the wine more than necessary; filtration is light and there is no chilling to get rid of tartaric acid. The 1982 Loupiac was not impressive: closed on the nose, medium sweet on the palate, and with a delicate intensity that might develop into something interesting. The 1973 was a very pretty wine, nicely balanced and stylish. The 1937, admittedly a very great vintage, was superb. The grapes were picked at 23–24% potential alcohol – and fifty years later it showed. The wine was a lovely orange-amber in colour, and ripe and orangey on the nose; in the mouth it had great concentration and a distinct barleyougar character, but it was the vigour and eleganoe that impressed me as much as the richness; it also had excellent length. I found the wine indistinguishable from Sauternes. It is hard to see the younger wines developing as well.

M. Courbin's neighbour is Marc Ducau at Ch Loupiac-Gaudet. He owns 26 hectares of south-facing vineyards along the slopes overlooking the Garonne. The property has been in his family for three generations, and Ducau looks after the whole operation himself. He does practise *triage*. The must is fermented in steel tanks and spends six months in wood if he feels the wine needs more body. The wine is aged for two to three years before bottling; sulphuring and filtration are very light. Ducau also owns a second Loupiac property, Ch Pontac. I have sampled wines from both his properties and found them adequate but not much more, but these tastings have been very limited and form no basis for a firm judgment.

Clos Jean is one of the best-known estates up on the plateau, where the soil contains much more clay than the limestone slopes. The property was once a hostel belonging to the Knights of Malta. The proprietor, Henri Bord, also owns Ch de Rondillon, an estate of 17 hectares (the same size as Clos Jean) that he bought twenty-five years ago; the two wines are vinified separately. According to M. Bord, the Rondillon wine is more rounded than Clos Jean, which is leaner and more virile. When I commented on the lack of botrytis in the Clos Jean wines I was tasting, M. Bord said that the trouble with Sauvignon is that it matures fairly early, and if you wait for noble rot, you sometimes lose the fruit. This argument presents yet another excuse for not waiting for botrytis. While one sympathises with the economic plight of proprietors, it remains true that wines not harvested by *triage* cannot have the complexity and interest of wines from botrytised grapes. Even the 1971 Clos Jean, while still youthful, seemed hard and essentially characterless, lacking the bouquet that should develop in a fifteen-year-old sweet wine of a good vintage. The problem for M. Bord and his fellow growers is that even were they to take immense trouble and produce a first-rate *liquoreux*, they still would not be offered prices substantially higher than those fetched by run-of-the-mill wines.

One of the best-known properties in Loupiac is Ch de Ricaud, a mock-Gothic extravaganza up on the plateau. Half the wine produced here is red; there are some very old vines at Ricaud, and these are used for the *liquoreux*, while grapes from young vines are used for dry white wines. At present only Sémillon and Muscadelle are used for the sweet wine, as the Sauvignon vines are still too young. This large estate has a good reputation, but it was sold recently, and this may bring some changes. Two or occasionally three *passages* are made through the vineyards, and the musts are chaptalised, when necessary, up to the maximum two degrees. The wines are fermented in steel at a cool 15 °C and fermentation is arrested by chilling. The wine remains in tank till the summer, then it is blended and put in *barriques*, of which one third are renewed each year. The wines

appear to be made with care, yet I have never been able to admire the *liquoreux*, which have struck me as pallid and sulphury.

I have tasted other Loupiacs, including some with such promising designations as Vin de Tête, but the general standard seems mediocre. There are, I am sure, conscientious efforts to make reasonable wines within the limits imposed by low prices and a shrinking market. M. Bernède told me, as did M. Palatin, the *régisseur* at Ch de Ricaud, that they rarely attain the permitted yields of 40 hl/ha, and that 30 or even less is more common. Nevertheless the problem does lie at the harvesting stage. If the grapes are not top quality – and that means low yields, *triage*, and botrytis – you simply cannot make memorable *liquoreux*. All other factors, such as varying methods of vinification, are variables, but unless you have the raw material you cannot even bring them into play. No service is done to the wines of Loupiac by the absurd claims of the local Syndicat brochure that 'each grape is picked from the bunch only when it has reached the required degree of concentration.' If there is a single grower in Loupiac who harvests grape by grape, I have yet to hear of him.

STE-CROIX-DU-MONT

Fortunately the situation is slightly less bleak at Ste Croix. Many of the best properties are situated on the limestone slopes overlooking the Garonne, and these produce well-balanced and stylish wines. It is hard to generalise, but the wines seem to have more richness and better structure than those of Loupiac, and I detect a greater pride in the wine here than in neighbouring *appellations*. The Ste Croix *appellation* was defined in 1936 and is restricted to sweet wines made from grapes grown in the commune; red wines and dry whites have to be sold as Bordeaux. There are about 500 hectares of vines, of which about 420 are planted with white grapes. Roughly 100 growers produce 15,000 hectolitres of wine each year, but only about twenty or thirty growers are full-time winemakers. Because Ste Croix is opposite Sauternes, it is marginally less prone to autumnal fogs and humidity, since it is further away from the confluence with the Ciron. The *encépagement* here is identical to that of the Sauternais, though very little Muscadelle is planted. There are some very

long-lived vines, especially of Sémillon, at Ste Croix, and I have
seen some that are eighty years old and still producing, though
reluctantly.

The soil is very varied. On the steep slopes above the river both
clay and limestone are found. Up on the plateau, the terrain consists
of silt and clay over a limestone subsoil. Elsewhere, the soil is more
gravelly. This makes a considerable difference to the wine.
Vineyards on gravelly soils are very dry in summer, and can attract
botrytis fast, and affected grapes need to be picked quite rapidly;
grapes grown on limestone subsoils are sometimes not attacked by
botrytis until later in the season. The effect on the wines is that those
from gravelly terrains have a more floral bouquet and are best drunk
relatively young, whereas those from limestone soils are more
capable of ageing. This difference was illustrated for me by M.
Tinon, who owns vineyards in both parts of the commune. His Ch La
Grave wine, grown on stony soil, was considerably coarser and less
elegant than his Ch Grand Peyrot, which is grown on limestone.
Indeed, the 1982 and 1985 Grand Peyrot had a richness and finesse I
failed to discern in most Loupiac wines. (The vines are also younger
at La Grave, which may well make a difference too.)

As at Loupiac, there are rarely more than three *passages* through
the vineyards. Consequently, average must weights are lower than in
the Sauternais. In good years such as 1983, potential alcohol ranged
from 16–18%. In a year such as 1985 when botrytis was scarce,
it averaged no more than 15%. (A few individual producers
who harvested more selectively achieved much higher readings:
M. Saint-Marc at Ch de l'Escaley claims to have had readings of 20–
21% in 1983.) It will be apparent that chaptalisation is necessary
even in years when no self-respecting Sauternes winemaker would
contemplate it.

The region is going through a bad patch. Recent prices for a
tonneau (equivalent to 1152 bottles) of generic Sauternes were 24,000
francs; for the same quantity of Ste Croix, producers were offered no
more than 6500 francs. The reputation of their wines, which had
been very high earlier in the century, plummeted after World War II,
when the demand for sweet wines escalated. Many producers,
especially on this side of the Garonne, took advantage of this and
turned out huge quantities of very poor wines. It did not take long for
Ste Croix and Loupiac to be associated with this sea of insipid

rubbish, and the bottom dropped out of the market for good-quality *liquoreux*. Growers tell me they are convinced that the market will improve – 'only we don't know the date.'

There is one estate in Ste Croix that does make wine of a very high standard, and even manages to charge fairly high prices for it. This is Ch Loubens. From the terrace of the seventeenth-century château, there are lovely views across the Garonne, with the towers of Ch d'Yquem and Ch Rayne-Vigneau along the horizon, no doubt an inspiration to the proprietor, M. de Sèze. The château rises above a cliff composed of fossilised oyster shells. This geological curiosity is quite common along the Garonne, but it is here that it can be seen at its most spectacular. Seven galleries of early nineteenth-century cellars have been tunnelled into the cliffs, but the barrels that now line the tunnels are largely unused. The 15 hectares of vineyards, planted entirely with Sémillon, are all on the limestone slopes. The harvesting is more scrupulous than at most properties here, and in 1983 M. de Sèze made six *passages*, twice the usual number. Average yields are about 30 hl/ha and Loubens has a modest annual output of 20–30,000 bottles. The grapes are pressed in hydraulic presses, chaptalised when necessary, then fermented very slowly in steel tanks for a month or more. After racking, the wine is lightly filtered; it is blended just before bottling, which takes place about thirty months after the harvest. M. de Sèze is not a great believer in long wood-ageing, as he is anxious to preserve the aromas of the wine. He aims for a balance of 14% alcohol and 4° Baumé residual sugar, giving a wine of finesse rather than power. Loubens is certainly a powerfully

1981

Château Loubens

GRAND CRU

SAINTE-CROIX-DU-MONT

APPELLATION Ste-CROIX-DU-MONT CONTROLEE

Sᵗᵉ Cᴸᵉ DU DOMᴺᴱ DU CHᴬᵁ LOUBENS

PROPᴹᴱ A SAINTE-CROIX-DU-MONT (GIRONDE) 75cl

MIS EN BOUTEILLES AU CHATEAU

PRODUIT DE FRANCE

scented wine, and on the palate it can be intense and rich, with a good depth of flavour. That M. de Sèze bottles some of his wines under a second label, Ch Terfort, is indicative of his high standards.

Another serious Ste Croix winemaker is Roland Sessacq of Ch Lousteau-Vieil. This has been a family property since 1843 and its 10 hectares are situated on the highest land in the commune at 118 metres above sea level. The varieties planted are 85% Sémillon and 15% Sauvignon, and yields vary from 30 to 35 hl/ha. The standards of winemaking are high: in 1983 four *passages* were made, chaptalisation is used as little as possible, the wine is fermented in temperature-controlled vats, and after racking and filtering spends about a year in wood. Yet I do not care for the style of the wine, which can be a bit blowsy and lacking in depth; moreover it is very peculiar on the nose, with tropical fruit aromas one does not normally associate with Sémillon. Sessacq favours an alcoholic style as he wants his wines to be capable of ageing for at least twenty years. The 1975 showed the wine at its best: still with that tropical fruit nose, but fresher and more elegant than some of the later vintages, in particular the 1976, which is already beginning to oxidise.

Another producer with high standards is Claud Armand of Ch La Rame. He expresses considerable confidence in the *appellation* by producing over 60,000 bottles a year from 25 hectares planted with 88% Sémillon and 12% Sauvignon. After fermentation the wine is

lightly filtered, then chilled to precipitate tartaric acid crystals and other impurities. It receives no other treatments and is aged in a mixture of new and old *barriques* for eight to ten months, and bottled fairly young. Musts with a potential alcohol of less than 18% are made into wine sold cheaply in litre bottles; only his best wines are bottled under the La Rame label. M. Armand favours a fairly robust style, with an ideal balance of 14.5% alcohol (13% is the minimum for the *appellation*) plus 4° Baumé of residual sugar. The wines in their youth can be rather hard and aggressive, with flavours of wood and alcohol masking the fruit, though they also have a spiciness that suggests that the wine will be complex and lively as it develops. The wines certainly age well. The 1973 is rounded, medium-bodied and ready to drink, but the 1975 has plenty of life left in it, and is deliciously balanced, a lovely light yellow-gold in colour, sweet and elegant in the mouth, and with great length of flavour.

It would be foolish to buy any Ste Croix without tasting the wine first, for variations in quality are staggering. I visited one property with vines up to sixty years old planted on good limestone soil. Yields are pushed to the very limit, fermentation takes place either in 500-litre steel tanks or in old wooden casks and is arrested with sulphur. The wine spends up to four years in cask, and sometimes wines from different years are blended. The wines were so disgusting I must refrain from naming the offender. Not a single wine, and I tasted from bottle as well as cask, was well balanced; they were flabby, hard, and sulphury. The cellars looked as if they doubled as a cowshed, which might explain why the wine tasted as it did. At the other end of the spectrum are the stylish wines of Loubens and La Rame and Grand Peyrot, and no doubt there are other good producers. Nor should the cooperative be overlooked. A 1964 produced by the Syndicat des Viticulteurs is still going strong, a rich melony wine that I found rather overpowering; the 1970, while quite austere and elegant, seemed to be nearing the end of its life.

In general the wines of Ste-Croix-du-Mont seem considerably finer than those of Loupiac. At their best they can easily stand comparison with some of the well-made lesser Sauternes. Nor should it be forgotten that the best wines of Ste-Croix-du-Mont are relatively inexpensive and considerably cheaper than mediocre Sauternes.

CADILLAC AND THE PREMIÈRES CÔTES

I shall consider these two *appellations* together because they are linked. So subtly linked that even André Vedel, the general editor of the compendious Hachette guide to French wines, gives a false account of their relation. Cadillac is one of thirty-seven communes in the Premières Côtes, a large area stretching for about forty miles along this side of the Garonne, from just north of Bordeaux to St Macaire opposite Langon. The eastern border of the *appellation* is anything from two to five miles away from the river. Naturally, all kinds of wine are made in so large a region. Since 1937 it has been accepted by the authorities that red and white wine may be made here. The region is not known for outstanding quality, and it is legal to blend wines from different communes.

For one of these communes, Cadillac, special rules apply. Only sweet white wines made from grapes gathered by *triage* may be labelled as Cadillac (mechanical harvesting is not permitted), and the yields are the same as for Loupiac or Ste-Croix-du-Mont: 40 hl/ha. Premières Côtes is permitted yields of 50 hl/ha, with an occasional addition of 20% when the harvest is particularly abundant. Moreover, AOC Cadillac can only be applied to bottled wine; wine from Cadillac sold in tank to wholesalers can only be marketed as AOC Premières Côtes. To confuse you further, a decree of 1973 establishes that it is not only wines made from Cadillac grapes that are entitled to the *appellation*. There are twenty-one other communes that may bottle their wines as Cadillac, provided the grapes come from approved vineyards and meet the conditions stated above.

In practice, it is reasonably safe to assume that any sweet wine bottled as Premières Côtes is likely to be an amorphous blend of no distinction. Cadillac is likely to be marginally better, and the best wines should, in theory, be every bit as good as the best from Loupiac or Ste-Croix-du-Mont. The production of Cadillac, in relation to Premières Côtes, is very small. There are 6000 hectares entitled to be called Premières Côtes, of which about 4000 produce wine bottled as Bordeaux (this is predominantly dry white wine); the remaining 2000 make wine bottled either as Premières Côtes (slightly more red than white) or Cadillac. The Cadillac region itself consisted in 1980 of a mere 80 hectares producing 2500 hectolitres. (In addition I should mention another amorphous region on the other side of the Garonne,

Graves Supérieurs, which produces 12–25,000 hectolitres, of which some is sweet.)

Cadillac does not differ greatly from the other wines discussed in this chapter. The *encépagement* is the same as for Sauternes, and grapes may only be picked after the authorities decree that harvesting may begin (grapes picked earlier must be sold as Vin de Table). There are only eight full-time growers in Cadillac, and nearly all make dry white and red wine as well, since prices for Cadillac are a quarter of those for Sauternes. There is supposed to be a revival of interest in these wines, but it appears to be somewhat feeble. Growers such as M. Bosviel of Ch Saint-Martin, tell me that when they mention to a *négociant* that they have *liquoreux* for sale, the dealers do not want to know.

For a conscientious winemaker such as Bosviel, this presents a problem. Unable to sell his sweet wine to dealers, he can only sell it directly from his property. Normally the wine would be bottled fairly young, about eighteen months after the harvest, but since there is little point bottling what you cannot sell, some of his wine was still in tank four years after the harvest. His sweet wines, labelled as Premières Côtes, are pleasant light aperitif wines of no complexity. He cannot afford to age the wines in wood, since barrels are costly to buy and maintain and you lose a proportion of the wine through evaporation.

The best known property in Cadillac, and the largest, is Ch Fayau, owned by the feisty ebullient Jean Médeville, who also owns properties in the Premières Côtes and Graves, as well as Ch Barbier in Sauternes. Of his vineyards 17 hectares are devoted to white wine, 10 at Cadillac and 7 at Haux. In 1945 he made only white wine; now only a quarter of his production is white. He is more fortunate than most and can ask relatively high prices for his sweet wine, which sells for more in bottle than do his red wines. M. Médeville is no sentimentalist. His *triage* is not very rigorous. Twice through the vineyards is usually sufficient for Ch Fayau, and if half the cluster is afflicted by botrytis, his pickers will cut the lot. He has no qualms about chaptalising when necessary. Fermentation takes place in large outdoor stainless steel tanks, and usually grinds to a halt when the wine has attained 14.5–15% alcohol. He likes wines high in alcohol, but since the potential alcohol rarely surpasses 18%, the wines are low in residual sugar. They spend no time in cask – M. Médeville says candidly that the barrels cost more than the wine – and are bottled eighteen months after the harvest. The wine is made in fairly large quantities, some 80,000 bottles per year. Despite the sound reputation that Ch Fayau enjoys, I do not care for these wines. The five vintages I have sampled have shared the same qualities: though medium sweet and sometimes rounded, they are unbalanced by excessive alcohol and volatile acidity and marred by off-flavours.

Not long ago I tasted a sweet wine made in 1929 at Ch de Mont Célestin, a property I had never heard of. This was a great vintage and many wines from top properties are still sound. This particular wine, almost sixty years old, was quite deep brown in colour, and though slightly oxidised on the nose, was still sweet and lively and intense, almost buttery in the mouth; moreover it had very good length and a clean finish. On a recent visit to the Bordeaux region I decided to track down this property, which is in Verdelais, near Ste-Croix-du-Mont. The proprietor is now in his nineties and no longer makes wine. Were a wine comparable to the 1929 made today, it would be sold as Cadillac. I do not believe that the magnificent 1929 was simply a freak of nature. It was made by applying the same high standards of vinification and, above all, of harvesting that still prevail at Sauternes. Differences in soil and to a lesser extent microclimate, mean that the wines from this side of the river will rarely be as fat and unctuous as Sauternes, but they are capable of coming close. Such wines are no longer made here because only a very rich proprietor could afford to do so. And were some idealistic winemaker to produce *liquoreux* with the same scrupulous care as at, say, Climens or Rieussec, it could still only be sold at a fraction of the price obtained for top Sauternes. Despite the activity of some of the skilled and conscientious winemakers mentioned in this chapter, a wine such as the 1929 Ch de Mont Célestin (which was no doubt only one of many of comparable splendour made here that year) will never be seen again. To visit today the Premières Côtes and its village *appellations* is to experience a great tradition in decay.

6

Monbazillac and Jurançon

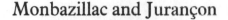

MONBAZILLAC

In Chapter 5 I mentioned that some areas of Bordeaux with very low reputations once made glorious sweet wines. Exactly the same is true of Monbazillac. I have recently had the opportunity to taste Monbazillac from 1928, 1947, and 1952, and although slightly past their best, the wines were by no means over the hill. They have the same qualities as fine old Sauternes. Although Monbazillac is some fifty miles from the Bordeaux region, the microclimatic conditions are comparable. Sémillon, Sauvignon, and Muscadelle are planted on the hills that overlook the River Dordogne as it passes Bergerac five miles away. Unusually, many of the best vineyards face north, and it is here that the fogs necessary for the development of botrytis are most frequent. The best sites are along the slopes near the communes of St Laurent-des-Vignes and Pomport. Yet, with a very few exceptions, the quality of the wine has deteriorated in recent years. Maximum permitted yields are generous: 40 hl/ha compared to 25 in the Sauternais or at Chaume and Bonnezeaux. The wines fetch fairly low prices, discouraging new investment and traditional harvesting by *triage*; the wines lack richness and seem less capable of ageing than the wines of thirty years ago.

The vineyards are very old, perhaps not quite as ancient as the local growers would have you believe, but there were major plantations in existence by the early sixteenth century. The vineyards were strictly regulated and the wines had a reputation almost as exalted as those of Bordeaux. The River Dordogne provided an ideal route for exportation, and the sweet wines of the region were popular

in northern Europe, especially in Holland, from the seventeenth century onwards. In those days, the vineyards consisted of quite substantial estates, most of which have long since been broken up, and at latest count there were 429 producers, of whom 144 belong to the Cave Coopérative. The 2500 hectares of vines are divided among five communes: Monbazillac (950), Pomport (800), Rouffignac (200), Colombier (250), and St-Laurent-des-Vignes (300). There are considerable variations in quality, since some of the vineyards, such as many of those in Colombier, are on limestone soil that gives scented wines of considerable finesse, while others are on the sandy river plain, where grapes ripen faster and achieve higher yields. The minimum alcohol requirement is lower than in Bordeaux, and wine with a minimum of 12% alcohol may be sold as Monbazillac; sweet wine with less than 12% but more than 11% must be sold as Côtes de Bergerac Moelleux. The maximum permitted chaptalisation is up to two degrees.

M. Vidal, the owner of Ch La Borderie, is a good example of a local winemaker of high standards. He also owns another property, Ch du Treuil de Nailhac, under which name his best wines are bottled, but all the vinification takes place at Ch La Borderie. Since he owns 63 hectares in all, the soil is very varied. The hillsides are composed of heavy clay and stones, which is much harder to cultivate than the sandier clay of the river plain. The plateau above the slopes is more arid and here the clay rests on a limestone base; yields are low and maturation much later than on the plain. In 1981, for instance, the yield on the slopes was 15 hl/ha with a potential alcohol of 19.5%, while down on the plain the yield was double. This is not to say that the grapes grown on the plain are necessarily inferior. M. Vidal finds that Sauvignon planted on the plain benefits from earlier maturation and is often of better quality than Sauvignon grown on the slopes. M. Vidal is atypical in that 20% of his grapes are Muscadelle (the remainder being 20% Sauvignon and 60% Sémillon) and he is tempted to plant even more.

M. Vidal explains that the difference between Monbazillac bottled as La Borderie and that bottled as Du Treuil de Nailhac is that the grapes for the former are all picked at once, while those for the latter are picked by *tries successives*. He is convinced that you cannot make good Monbazillac without botrytis, though many growers cannot be bothered to wait and simply pick overripe grapes. He is also wary of chaptalisation, though he does practise it when he feels it is necessary. On the other hand, he is not prepared to market a wine he thinks unworthy of the *appellation*, and in 1984 declassified his entire crop of Monbazillac for a trifling 1800 francs per *tonneau*. (Fortunately, like all other growers in the region, he also makes dry wines, red and white, including a delicious Bergerac Sec.) The grapes are pressed in horizontal presses, fermented in steel tanks, then filtered over the winter. The wines are matured in a combination of vats or casks. M. Vidal does not use *barriques* but 6000-litre oak *foudres*, which impart no wood flavours to the wine. The wine is bottled about three years after the vintage.

The usual balance of his Monbazillac is 14.5% alcohol plus 4° Baumé residual sugar. Occasionally he has made a much richer wine in the tradition of classic Monbazillac. In 1975, for instance, he picked on 20 November; the yield was minute, a mere 7 hl/ha, but the grapes were entirely botrytised and had a potential alcohol of over 22%. The wine took a year to ferment, and eventually emerged with 15.5% alcohol plus 7° Baumé residual sugar. This wine is superb, deep orange-gold in colour, and with a raisiny botrytis nose; on the palate it is intense and raisiny, with a trace of bitter orange on the finish, which is clean and long. The only fault one would level at the wine is its lack of freshness. At Ch Du Treuil de Nailhac in recent decades, the best vintages have been 1952, 1955 (a very great year), 1957, 1959, 1962, 1967, 1975 (also a great year), 1979, and 1981. Subsequent vintages are not yet ready to drink. M. Vidal maintains stocks of older vintages at very reasonable prices.

Clos Fontindoule, a property of 17 hectares up on the hillside not far from the splendid Ch de Monbazillac, is a far cry from the modern, well-equipped winery of M. Vidal, not to mention the large Cave Coopérative on the other side of the road from Ch La Borderie. M. Gilles Cros, the owner, is a reserved burly man of few words. He is one of the few growers who still specialises in sweet wines, which his wife sells directly from the rustic cellars behind the farmhouse. In poor years such as 1984, however, he only makes dry white wine. The *encépagement* is identical to M. Vidal's, with 20% of Muscadelle. Yields are in the region of 25–20 hl/ha up on the plateau where he has his vineyards, and he did not seem to think highly of the more copious plains vines. The grapes are harvested very late, and while M. Cros does hope for botrytised grapes, he will at a late stage in the season pick healthy shrivelled grapes as well. The must is fermented in vat, and aged in wood for eighteen to twenty-four months. He only bottles his wines in good years. He likes a high alcohol level, arguing that it helps to preserve the wine. The wine certainly keeps well, and the 1970 is still on sale at the property. According to Mme Cros, the wine is kept in cask until there is sufficient demand to justify bottling another couple of hectolitres.

The wine itself is better than it sounds. The style is very rich and raisiny; it has a taste of apricot jam and marmalade, and its long slumber in wood has slightly oxidised the wine (though not un-pleasantly), giving it overtones of caramel and barleysugar. Of the three vintages I have tasted, the 1967, 1970, and 1980, it seems evident that the wines do improve with age. The 1980 lacks fresh-ness, as indeed do the older wines, but after fifteen or more years it develops other aromas and rich flavours that make up for its heavi-ness. This is an old-fashioned style that will not appeal to all. Yet it has the unctuousness and intensity one hopes for, and too rarely finds, in good Monbazillac. Furthermore the wine is inexpensive.

It is only old and traditional proprietors such as M. Cros who can age their wines properly before releasing them. It takes decades to build up stocks of older wines, and the deplorable trend is for more and more producers to bottle their wines at the first feasible moment and then put them on sale. (I was astonished to discover at Ch Theulet, for example, that by July 1986 much of the 1985 Monbazillac had already been bottled and shipped out.) One of the few other traditional winemakers at Monbazillac is Roger Sutel of Ch La Truffière-Thibaut. Of his vineyards 13 hectares produce Monbazillac. Like M. Cros, he stresses the importance of waiting as long as possible before harvesting. He hopes for grapes with potential alcohol of 18–20%, though in some years, such as 1985, you may be stuck with no higher than 16%. To compensate, M. Sutel can look back to years such as 1918, when the potential alcohol was 24%, or to 1947, when it was 22%. He has high hopes for his 1983, for which the grapes were picked at 19.5%. To attain such high levels, *triage* is essential. Old-fashioned winemakers such as Cros and Sutel still pick by hand. When I pointed out that since the AOC regulations forbid mechanical harvesting, I assumed every grower of Monbazillac picked by hand, he shook his head. I later encountered growers who admitted that they harvested with machines. INAO, they tell me, turns a blind eye to the practice.

The vinification at La Truffière-Thibaut is fairly traditional. After *débourbage*, the must is fermented in underground tanks. A light dose of SO_2 is added to arrest fermentation completely, but Sutel does not filter. Instead, he lets the wine rest, then racks every month. The wine is aged in steel or cement tanks for at least two years before being bottled. Production is modest, no more than 30,000 bottles a year. Sutel still offers an excellent range of Monbazillacs dating back to 1918. This very old wine will set you back 800 francs, but the almost equally splendid vintages of 1943 and 1947 are available for about the same price as a Premier Cru Sauternes of 1983. I find La Truffière-Thibaut somewhat clumsy. The 1967 is comparable to that of Clos Fontindoule in style, though rather burnt in flavour. More recent vintages lack richness, though the 1975 and 1982 are, in different ways, attractive wines.

The Cave Coopérative is very powerful in Monbazillac. It was established in 1941 and only buys grapes from its members. Should the grapes not be of acceptable quality, they can be refused. The coop also makes wines from five châteaux: Ch de Monbazillac, Ch Septy,

Ch La Brie, Ch Pion, and Ch Marsalet. These five wines are vinified separately, though all the wine is made at the very modern plant along the main road to Bergerac. Roughly 18,000 hectolitres of Monbazillac is produced each year. Vinification is technologically sophisticated, and wines are pasteurized and centrifuged, and filtered three times before being bottled eighteen months after the harvest. The standard Monbazillac produced at the coop is a dull, charmless wine, but much better wines are made under the châteaux labels. Ch de Monbazillac is a splendid castle built in 1550; though moated and imposing, its air of military preparedness is somewhat bogus, since it was always intended as no more than a very grand country house. It is now owned by the Cave Coopérative and may be visited by the public. Here you can also taste and buy the wine. The 22 hectares of vineyards here give a yield of 18–19 hl/ha. The star vintage of recent years has been the outstanding 1976, a rich, chewy wine with ample botrytis and real complexity on the nose and palate. More recent vintages, while quite good, have not come close to the concentration and seductiveness of the 1976. This vintage does, however, seem to be at its peak, and while the wine should remain excellent for a few years yet, I doubt that it will ever match the

splendour and longevity of the 1929, which in 1986 was absolutely delicious and showing no signs of flagging.

The wine from Ch Septy can be good too. Its 18 hectares, planted only with Sémillon and Sauvignon, face north onto the Dordogne valley and south towards Pomport. Average yields vary from 15 to 20 hl/ha and annual production is about 50,000 bottles. The style of the wine is much lighter than that of Ch de Monbazillac, lean and lemony with some finesse. For my taste, the wine, while soundly made, is rather too lean, occasionally limp, and sulphur is often obtrusively present. The other châteaux wines made at the Cave Coopérative appeal to me even less.

Nick Ryman bought the magnificent Ch La Jaubertie in 1973 and has made wines in a variety of styles, including such experimental oddities as barrel-fermented dry Sémillon. His vineyards in the Colombier commune rarely attract botrytis, but in 1976 the grapes were attacked, and Ryman, never one to pass up an interesting opportunity, made his first Monbazillac. He freely admits he bungled the fermentation: the alcohol reached 15.5%, leaving a mere 2 g/l residual sugar. The wine is not recognisable as Monbazillac, but it was remarkably good, not unlike a through-fermented German Auslese: there was distinct botrytis on the nose, and on the palate the wine was rich but fresh and stylish. But it was not sweet. When I complimented Ryman on the unorthodox wine, he remarked: 'Keep anything for ten years, and it'll improve.' In 1986 Ryman made Monbazillac again: the best *cuvée* bottled as La Jaubertie, the remainder as Domaine de Grandchamp.

I have on occasion tasted good Monbazillac from Ch Bellevue (which produced an almost suspiciously rich wine from the mediocre 1977 vintage, as well as a full-flavoured 1976) and Domaine de Cabaroque. I see little point in listing the many properties that in my experience produce poor Monbazillac, wines that are thin, sulphury, meagre, and one-dimensional. Suffice it to say that there are all too many of them, and I fear their number will surely increase after traditional winemakers such as MM. Vidal, Cros, and Sutel retire from the field. Hand-pickers can at least be instructed to select the best bunches, if not the best individual grapes, as they move through the vineyards, but mechanical harvesters respond to no such instructions, and their increasing use in AOC Monbazillac vineyards is disgraceful. If growers are not prepared to meet the minimal conditions for making sweet wine of decent quality, then they should turn their attention to dry wines, for which mechanical harvesting can be perfectly acceptable. In the meantime, the outlook for the consumer is bleak. Monbazillac is, on French supermarket shelves, on a par with the most characterless Premières Côtes de Bordeaux, and nobody tasting such insipid wine would ever suspect that Monbazillac was once capable of rivalling the best Sauternes.

SAUSSIGNAC

This is a small *appellation* within the Bergerac region. It lies west of the Monbazillac vineyards on the south side of the River Dordogne. Twenty years ago 22,000 hectolitres were produced, but in recent years production has declined sharply, though some of the sweet white wine from the area is also bottled as Côtes de Bergerac Moelleux. Probably the best Saussignac is made at Ch Court-les-Mûts at Razac-de-Saussignac. The winemaker is Pierre-Jean Sadoux, who is also an oenologist who analyses the wines of thirty-five other producers in the area. Court-les-Mûts is best known for

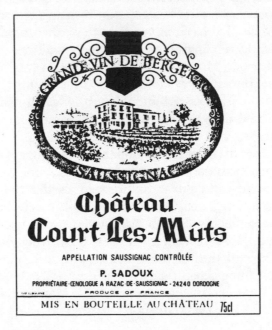

excellent red and rosé Bergerac, and Saussignac only accounts for
7–10% of its total production of 100,000 bottles. The wine is made
from overripe but healthy grapes, 70% Sémillon and 30% Sauvignon;
they are machine-harvested and average yields of 45 hl/ha are
achieved. The must is fermented in 10,000-litre vats at 19 °C, and
fermentation is arrested with a small dose of sulphur dioxide, and
filtered. M. Sadoux is very anxious to use as little SO_2 as possible, and
in tasting a wide range of his Saussignacs, I found them attractively
free of noticeable sulphur, despite the further addition of SO_2 when
racking. The wine is stabilised by chilling and bottled about eighteen
months after the harvest. Saussignac from this property will have
about 11.8% alcohol and 40 g/l residual sugar.

The appeal of the wine eludes me. High yields and machine
harvesting inevitably deprive it of richness and depth. Saussignac is
insipid and bland, mild and innocuous; because it is carefully
vinified, it is far from offensive, and can rise to a pretty melony
roundness at best. It ages gracefully, and in 1986 the 1973 was still
fresh, and had developed most in terms of its bouquet, with elegant
aromas of pears and melons. Every vintage was short on the finish, as
if the wine flees from the taste buds as soon as it slips down the throat.
It is admirable of M. Sadoux to maintain the production of this
somewhat obscure wine, but I cannot help wondering whether it is
worth the effort. Nor have examples from other properties proved
any more alluring.

HAUT-MONTRAVEL

This is another sweet white wine *appellation* within the Bergerac
region. It is made in the hills behind Ste-Foy-la-Grande and north of
Castillon, a region on the western edge of the Bergerac wine district,
and closer to some of the Bordeaux vineyards than to Bergerac itself.
Dry white wines take the Montravel *appellation*, while Haut-
Montravel is reserved for the sweet white wines from five communes.
Maximum permitted yields vary from a generous 50 to 60 hl/ha,
according to how the authorities view the vintage.

The wine suffers from the same insipidity that characterises
Saussignac. M. Banizette, proprietor of the Domaine de Libarde,
tells me that he aims for a potential alcohol of 14.5%, picks the

overripe grapes once by machine, and chaptalises up to two degrees when necessary. The *encépagement* is the same as throughout the region, but botrytis is uncommon. The wine is fermented in vats, filtered, and aged in vat for about two years before being bottled. Like Saussignac, the wine has roughly 12% alcohol and 2.5° Baumé residual sugar. M. Banizette reports that the amount of Haut-Montravel declared has dropped tenfold in the last thirty years, though he sees signs of a revival in demand. Having tasted the wine (though relatively youthful examples) I can understand the former but not the latter.

M. Barthoux, proprietor of Ch de Masburel, also produces Haut-Montravel, though he does so, he freely admits, more to keep up a local tradition than because there is any real demand for the wine. The wine only accounts for 3% of his total production. His harvesting methods match those of M. Banizette, though he achieves slightly lower yields. Unlike his neighbour, he likes to bottle the wine very young, in the spring following the vintage, so as to preserve its aromas, though he does not release the wine for sale for a further two years. His 1985 is undoubtedly attractive, fragrant on the nose, and fresh but rounded on the palate; not a wine of great character, but better than expected. Yet a wine with a few more years' bottle-age was both disjointed and flabby in the mouth. A sticky, sugary taste in all the wines was almost certainly due to liberal chaptalisation. I should stress that I have not tasted these wines, or those of Saussignac, very extensively, and it may be that there are, somewhere, examples of these *appellations* with real style and character.

JURANÇON

The small town of Jurançon is now a suburb of Pau, a popular tourist centre in the most southwesterly corner of France. Just beyond the town rise some very lovely hills, the Coteaux, which are in effect the foothills of the Pyrenees. Here lies the heart of the Jurançon *appellation*; some villages grouped around Monein constitute a larger geographical area than the Coteaux, but the quality of the wine is usually less good. It goes without saying that good and bad examples of Jurançon are found in both districts. The wines are quite distinct from those found in any other part of France because of the grape varieties used. Gros Manseng, Petit Manseng, and Courbu are all traditional varieties cultivated for centuries in this area. The reputation of Jurançon may, compared to its heyday from the fifteenth to eighteenth centuries, be in eclipse, but the region is still capable of producing excellent wines of great character.

The vineyards are very ancient, and there is evidence that vines were cultivated in the area in Gallo-Roman times. The wine acquired a lasting prestige when it became known that it was used at the christening of Henri de Navarre, later Henri IV of France. Standards of production were safeguarded by fairly rigorous local regulations. Jurançon was widely exported to Holland and Britain, but because the wine was not fortified, it was hard to maintain the quality of the wines after shipment, and the trade declined after the eighteenth century. Nevertheless, steady local demand ensured that the stony hillsides of Jurançon remained covered in vines until, in the mid-nineteenth century, a series of disasters afflicted them. First the fungus oidium ravaged the vineyards; these days spraying will prevent or discourage its pillaging, but in those days there was no known antidote. Mildew came next, followed in the 1880s by phylloxera. As was done elsewhere in France, new vines were grafted onto imported rootstocks; they were also trained high on poles or trellises to avoid frost and rot. Although the region made a recovery, there are nowadays three or four times fewer vines than in the pre-phylloxera era. Cooperatives were established after about 1950, when an end to rationing and other postwar restrictions allowed winegrowing to expand once more. Standards were not especially high, and most local winemaking was reputed to be distinctly rustic. In recent years many of the old-fashioned winemakers, for whom wine was only one product out of many in an economy of polyculture, have died off, and the introduction of more up-to-date vinification methods have led to a general increase in quality.

There are currently 500 hectares under vine, owned by 400 growers, of whom half own less than one hectare. The Cave Coopérative controls 65% of production, while 25% is divided between forty independent growers. Only the Coop and a handful of growers are large enough to export their wine, which is one reason why it remains little known. Only one third of the production is of *moelleux* (sweet) wine; the remainder is *sec* (dry), which is intended, unlike the *moelleux*, to be drunk young. The decision to make dry wine in Jurançon was deliberately undertaken after World War II, when, in the drive to improve the quality and reputation of the wine, the Cave Coopérative took the view that instead of chaptalising excessively, it was better to make a dry wine.

The *encépagement* has been simplified in recent years. In 1950 the planted varieties consisted of 50% Gros Manseng, 30% Petit Manseng, and 20% assorted grapes, including Courbu. Nowadays they are planted in the following proportions: 65% Gros Manseng, 32% Petit Manseng, 3% Courbu and other varieties. Gros Manseng, which rarely achieves potential alcohol of more than 13.5%, is the mainstay of the dry wine, and Petit Manseng, which is capable of potential alcohol of 17–19%, is the principal grape used for *moelleux*. There is also a difference in the yields, for Gros Manseng can produce over 50 hl/ha, whereas Petit Manseng, with its tiny grapes and small quantities of juice, rarely exceeds 25 hl/ha. The Manseng grapes are virtually unknown outside Jurançon, though there are occasional rows of these vines in the Gers, the *département* to the north, and in Spain. Corbu is cultivated because it gives the dry wine a certain finesse, but it contributes little to the *moelleux*.

The harvest is, on average, the latest in France. It begins in the Monein area in mid-October and in the Coteaux at the very end of the month. At this stage only grapes for the *sec* are picked. In theory the harvesting could be done by machine, but the vineyards are in many cases perilously steep, and it is simply not a practical proposition. And in a region where the holdings tend to be a hectare or less, it is clearly uneconomical to invest in mechanical harvesters. In November the Petit Manseng for the *moelleux* is picked by *tries successives*. Botrytis does not occur in Jurançon. Instead they seek a condition known as *passerillage*, which simply means letting grapes shrivel and dry so that the juice becomes more concentrated, and with it the sugar content and the acidity. The harvest usually continues until the end of November, or long after the leaves have dropped from the vine; chilly nights and even frosts, help to shrivel the grapes to the required degree. In the light of my strictures earlier in this chapter against winemakers who are too lazy to wait for botrytis, it may seem surprising that Jurançon, which is not made from botrytised grapes, should be a very fine wine. What gives it distinction is the balance between sugar and acidity. Jurançon is not unctuous, but is a wine of great finesse.

Although Petit Manseng can attain potential alcohol of up to 19%, 16% would be widely accepted as the minimum required to make good quality wine. Winemakers aim for a balance of 13% alcohol and 3° Baumé residual sugar. Any lower and chaptalisation becomes necessary. Chaptalisation rarely exceeds one degree. Fermentation is stopped with SO_2, and many winemakers chill the wine to precipitate tartaric acid crystals, and then filter. The best producers try to avoid excessive sulphur in the wine: 400 g/l is the maximum permitted in France, but good Jurançon often has less than 200. Some producers bottle the wine very young; others age the wine in wood, aiming for a rich colour and a touch of oxidation. The *moelleux* can be aged for a very long time, though most producers unload their stocks so fast that it is virtually impossible to purchase bottles of fully mature *moelleux*. Delicious in their youth, they tend to close up after a year or so in bottle, and then open up with more exotic splendour three or four years later. The best recent vintages for Jurançon *moelleux* are 1971, 1975, 1976, 1979, 1981, 1983, and 1985.

The best Jurançon I have tasted has come from Cru Lamouroux, a small property of 6 hectares set on a lovely hillside at La Chapelle-de-Rousse in the heart of the Coteaux. Some of the vines are planted in a *cirque*, a kind of natural amphitheatre in the hills that heats up splendidly. The owners, MM. Chigé and Ziemek, only produce about 18,000 bottles of *moelleux* each year. The wine is aged for eighteen months in wood. The 1983 is a superb wine, with just over 50 g/l residual sugar. The nose is surprisingly powerful, floral and spicy with just a touch of wood; on the palate the wine is full and broad and creamy, yet delightfully subtle and with a lively acidity; it is long and clean on the finish. Jurançon is quite a bracing wine, with, in good examples such as this, heady aromas of tropical fruit and spice, and comparable qualities on the palate – a lushness held together by exemplary balance between sweetness and acidity. The 1984 had similar qualities, though less marked, and this is a feature of a weaker vintage. The 1985 is quite different, since the wine only has 6–8 g/l residual sugar. Not legally marketable as a *sec*, it is not a true *moelleux* either. Since I am not an admirer of Jurançon Sec, which even in good years can be harsh and astringent, I found this wine delightful, slightly tart, vigorous, and characterful, but not in the least bit raw.

Ch Jolys is a beautiful old house set high along the ridge of the Coteaux. The owner, Robert Latrille, though Algerian-born, is a fervent promoter of the local wines and is currently head of the local Syndicat de Défense des Vins de Jurançon. I have had the pleasure of seeing him yell at a winemaker in his sonorous voice: 'Plantez des vignes, madame! Plantez des vignes!' With prices for corn and dairy products relatively depressed in this part of France, M. Latrille believes the time is ideal for wine growers to plant more vines, for, as he points out, hillsides that were covered with vines just over a century ago are now bare. The cellars at Ch Jolys are ingeniously filled with Do-It-Yourself devices he has invented. His average annual production of *moelleux* is about 80,000 bottles. The grapes are pressed in horizontal presses, then fermented in large temperature-controlled vats. The wine is filtered twice and bottled fairly young. I have only tasted his 1985 wine, for M. Latrille is typical of most producers in keeping no stocks of older wines, and though it was very fruity, sweet and enticing, with lively acidity and intensity, it was difficult to assess whether the wine would acquire more complexity as it aged. That it would age well seemed clear from its balance.

Although his cellar is modern, Robert Latrille is a traditional winemaker. More innovative is Henri Ramonteu of Domaine Cauhape at Monein. He is typical of many local producers in that he is essentially a farmer, and his cellars are surrounded by cornfields; it was only in about 1980 that he began to bottle his wines. Winemaking, however, is absorbing more and more of his energies. Under the influence of the Dubourdieu family of Ch Doisy-Daëne in Barsac, he has adopted maceration techniques, and he is one of only three producers of Jurançon who uses new wood to age his wines. In the future he intends to ferment in *barriques*; such wines will not be aged entirely in wood, but will be returned to tank for their second winter before being bottled.

In 1985 Ramonteu made wine from both principal grape varieties. He macerates the grapes overnight, and crushes them before pressing them. He had good yields from his Gros Manseng (about 50 hl/ha) and the wine is being matured in new oak; the Petit Manseng, for which the yield was only 25 hl/ha, is aged in older casks. Not surprisingly the two wines were very different, with the oak very obvious on the palate of the Gros Manseng, and the sheer intensity of fruit very marked on the Petit Manseng. No doubt both these sets of characteristics will be somewhat muted and more balanced by the time the wines are bottled. Ramonteu intends to bottle the wines separately, rather than blend them. The 1983 showed how a *moelleux* matured in new oak develops after over a year in bottle. On the nose the wine was flowery and fruity, not especially exotic, while on the palate it was surprisingly soft, notably oaky and complex, and with a lingering piquant aftertaste that gave the wine real interest. However, the ageing in new oak had given the wine a creamy complexity at the expense of its *typicité*. It was still recognisably Jurançon, but confirmed that this kind of wood-ageing must be undertaken with great care.

The Cave Coopérative at Gan has hundreds of members and is extremely influential in the district. The wines are good but not very distinctive. They have typical piquancy and liveliness, but some lacked acidity and were a trifle gummy and flabby. I found the least expensive *moelleux*, marketed as L'Aperitif d'Henry IV, better balanced and more appealing than the more costly and older Prestige wine. These wines were certainly superior to those of a well-known producer at Mournex, not far from Monein. Here the wines tasted chaptalised and they did not seem improved by a long spell in large oak casks. The wines lacked body, acidity, and structure, and were excessively sulphured. A 1975 *moelleux*, quite delicate and perfumed on the nose, proved clumsy and alcoholic in the mouth. Poor wines are still being made in Jurançon, but at their best the wines are charming and vigorous, spicy and full of interest.

7

The Loire Valley

One would imagine that the more southerly wine-growing regions would be more likely to produce great sweet wines than northerly ones. After all, sunshine is essential if the grapes are to ripen sufficiently to make rich dessert wines. Yet while Italy and Spain and other hot regions do indeed make excellent dessert wines, few of them can outclass those of Germany or the Loire, both relatively cool regions. Because, however, the climate along the banks of the Rhein, the Mosel, and the Loire is uncertain, such wines cannot be produced every year. In Vouvray, for instance, most winemakers made no sweet wine at all between 1976 and 1985, for the simple reason that the grapes did not ripen sufficiently. In the other part of the Loire Valley where sweet wines are regularly produced, the Coteaux du Layon, the peculiarities of the microclimate are more conducive both to adequate ripening of the grapes and to noble rot, but even here some years occur when the wine, if it is made at all, is somewhat feeble. Except in the very greatest of years such as 1947, the sweet wines of the Loire rarely reach the levels of alcohol and residual sugar routinely found in the wines of southern Europe.

There is more to differentiate *moelleux* wines of the Loire from other sweet wines of France than levels of richness. First, the wine is made from the versatile Chenin Blanc grape; and second, the wine is, like port, bottled young and achieves its maturation slowly in bottle rather than by long ageing in cask, as in Sauternes. Both these factors give the wine its distinctive character. The Chenin Blanc is a most extraordinary grape, with a marked acidity that explains its versatility. Much young Chenin Blanc, being grown in a cool climate, is a dry and often fiercely acidic wine that can be unpalatable in its youth. But the ferocity that makes very young Savennières or Vouvray almost undrinkable also preserves the wine long enough for that initial harshness to be transformed into something altogether rich and more opulent.

The same staying power is evident in the Coteaux du Layon. During the Renaissance and even earlier this century, the sweet wines of Anjou were spoken of in the same breath as those of Sauternes, and fetched prices almost as high. This is no longer the case, and though recent years have seen some revival in the fortunes of Coteaux du Layon, the wine remains unfashionable and distinctly undervalued. It is a most peculiar wine. In a good year, the new wine is grapy and fresh, with a pale straw-green colour, a lovely bouquet, and a lingering aftertaste. But after a year in bottle these admirable qualities begin to fade: the wine closes up, and it can take ten years before it sheds its skin and emerges in a new and far more splendid form. An old Coteaux du Layon will have deepened in colour to a medium gold, aromas of acacia, lime, or quince will swirl up from the glass, and there will be a superb balance between the fruitiness of the Chenin grape and the refreshing acidity of the wine. The *viticulteurs* of the Coteaux du Layon, and those of Vouvray too, do not claim for their wine, even at its most mature, the same qualities of richness characteristic of mature Sauternes. Instead, they point to its balance, its elegance, and its length of flavour.

The Coteaux du Layon is a complicated region. The Layon is a tributary of the Loire, which it joins near Angers. Along the slopes of the river lie about 1300 hectares of vineyards, divided between twenty-five communes. That some communes produce better wine than others is recognised by the additional AOC of Coteaux du Layon Villages. The Villages themselves are Rochefort-sur-Loire, Rablay, Faye-d'Anjou, Beaulieu, St Aubin-de-Luigné, and St Lambert-du-Lattay. In addition the hamlet of Chaume is rewarded with a superior AOC of its own: Coteaux du Layon Chaume. The matter is further complicated by the award of a separate and even more superior AOC to some fragmented vineyards within those at Chaume known as Quarts de Chaume. And finally, there is the commune of Bonne-zeaux which is also granted its own AOC status, and is generally held to be, with Quarts de Chaume, the top *cru* of the region. There are differences in soil between the various villages. The clay is thick in the Coteaux du Layon, but in Chaume and Bonnezeaux the soil also contains substantial deposits of schist, iron and other minerals, which, say the proprietors of the grander *crus*, contribute to the superior finesse of their wines. The other major difference lies in the maximum yields permitted by the authorities. In the Coteaux du Layon no more than 30 hl/ha may be harvested each year, while for Coteaux du Layon Chaume and Bonnezeaux the maximum is 25, the same as for Sauternes. For Quarts de Chaume the highest permitted yield is 22 hl/ha, the lowest of any vineyards of the Loire. In practice, yields are frequently even lower, for only grapes that are overripe or botrytised are suitable for making the wine, and yields of half the maximum are not uncommon. Some producers guard the reputation of their AOC and refuse to release wines they consider unworthy of it. Jacques Boivin, for instance, a major producer of Bonnezeaux, will only label his wine as such if he approves of the quality. Lesser wine he will release as simple Coteaux du Layon at a much lower price, even though the grapes were grown in Bonnezeaux and the wine could be sold as such quite lawfully. Other producers of Villages wines follow the same practice.

In my experience it is invariably worth digging into one's pocket for an extra few francs to buy a bottle of Villages wine. Simple Coteaux du Layon can be a perfectly good wine, but it rarely rises to great heights, and much of it is insipid and mediocre. A Coteaux du Layon Villages will cost only a little more and will almost certainly be worth it. To this rule of thumb there is one astonishing exception. The wines released by the Touchais family under the label of Moulin Touchais are technically no more than their best line of AOC Coteaux du Layon, and exported bottles of the same wine bear the even more modest label of AOC Anjou, on the dubious grounds that foreigners do not know what Coteaux du Layon is. Nevertheless they are magnificent wines. Beneath an imposing house in the sprawling little town of Doué-la-Fontaine is a labyrinth of cellars. Along these dimly lit corridors fearsome grilles screen capacious alcoves, in which are stacked thousands of bottles dating back to 1869. As an old family firm, Touchais have been willing and able to build up stocks of older wines that can scarcely be matched anywhere else along the Loire valley. Moreover, prices for Moulin Touchais, which receives at least five years' bottle-age before release, are absurdly low, reflecting the dimmed reputation of the region. Perhaps if Jean-Marie Touchais were to treble his prices overnight, he might find his wines suddenly in demand. Although Moulin Touchais can age almost indefinitely, many vintages seem at their best after twenty to thirty years in bottle. The 1969 is excellent, a surprisingly fat wine, and so is the 1964. The 1959, which was exceptionally good, is, according to Jean-Marie Touchais, just past its peak, and I was disappointed by the 1949 on the one occasion I tasted it. Nevertheless, these are in general wines that are both remarkably and reliably good, overlooked only by snobs who disdain its relatively lowly *appellation* and distrust its availability.

It is instructive to compare the wines from a property that makes both simple Coteaux du Layon and a Villages wine. The Caves de la Pierre Blanche at Champ-sur-Layon is the property of the Lecointre family, and the current winemaker is the charming and enthusiastic Vincent Lecointre. He owns about 30 hectares in the Coteaux, including 6 in Rablay. Thus he produces both wines, and one afternoon we tasted a large range of them, sampling Rablay against Coteaux du Layon of the same year. Like Boivin, Lecointre will not hesitate to declassify if he considers his Rablay is not up to standard. The difference is one of intensity and concentration, and of a more perfect matching of sweetness and acidity. Next to a Villages wine, the plain Coteaux du Layon wine from the same producer usually tastes relatively insipid. It's not that it is a poor wine;

PRODUCE OF FRANCE

Moulin Touchais

ANJOU

APPELLATION ANJOU CONTROLÉE

DOUÉ LA FONTAINE - FRANCE

J. Touchais Propriétaire

73 cl

Nº 075   MISE EN BOUTEILLES A LA PROPRIÉTÉ

rather, it possesses the qualities of the better wine to a lesser degree.

Lecointre, like all the top-quality producers of the region, practises *triage*. In the Loire, pickers will make up to four *passages*, for the grapes do not oblige the grower by ripening simultaneously. Vines closer to the river are more likely to be attacked by botrytis, which is encouraged by the mists and humidity rising from the water; other vines may be affected a week later. In some years, such as 1969 and 1985, certain vineyards escaped lavish infections of botrytis, but an exceptional September allowed the grapes to ripen and shrivel, concentrating their sugar content and intensifying their flavour. In such years the growers must pick just as these grapes reach their peak. As in the Sauternes, there is an element of risk involved. Pick too soon and the grapes may be insufficiently ripe; pick too late, and they may have been savaged by frost or rain or grey rot.

In the Coteaux du Layon (and in Vouvray) any good *viticulteur* will pick by hand. Growers who take short cuts are not going to make exceptional wine. *Triage* is not required every year, but it can be indispensable in mediocre years, when only careful selection of grapes is going to make possible the production of successful sweet wine. Lecointre made three *passages* in 1985, though only one in 1984. The number made in any one year will vary from vineyard to vineyard; what is important is that the grower is conscientious enough to practise *triage* when necessary.

Lecointre uses steel tanks to ferment his wine. There is considerable disagreement as to whether wood or tanks (be they of glass, or cement, or steel, or any other material) are more suitable for the fermentation of these sweet musts. My own view is that the skill of the winemaker is of greater importance than the material in which the wine is initially fermented. Fermentation in temperature-controlled tanks is easier to control, but wood is more likely to lend the wine character. All producers agree, however, that the wine, after racking and filtering, must be bottled no later than April. If the wine is allowed to remain either in cask or tank beyond the spring, freshness and bouquet could be lost.

There are those who ascribe particular qualities to each of the Villages, though I find it hard to offer more than the vaguest generalisations. The style of the individual winemaker seems to me as important as the qualities of soil and grape that give character to specific sites. Lecointre considers that Rablay is less powerful than some other Villages wine but has greater finesse, although some authorities define its style as powerful and rounded. At the Domaine de la Motte, André Sorin, who makes first-rate Rochefort, defined Rochefort's style as relatively dry, very long lived, and with good body even though the wine is not high in alcohol (12–12.5%). Beaulieu, on the other hand, is defined by Jean-Pierre Chéné of the Domaine d'Ambinos as being richer in acid and alcohol than most of the other Villages, though his description is at odds with those offered by other authorities.

On the basis of numerous tastings of Lecointre's wine in England and at Champ, I agree with his own assessment, and find the wines characterised by their delicate honeyed bouquet and by a moderate sweetness tempered by flavours of apple and apricot. The complex intertwining of flavours in the mouth is prolonged by the acidity, which gives the wine a clean crisp finish. The young wines are slightly bitter on the finish, with a light, not unpleasing, hint of grapefruit, but this diminishes as the wine matures. The 1976 is the most recent great year that is becoming ready to drink, though it will certainly benefit from another decade in bottle. The wine had a soft honeyed botrytis nose, considerable intensity on the palate, and remarkable freshness despite its richness. To show how superbly these wines can age, he fetched from the cellars the wine made by his great-grandfather in 1921. The colour was orange-amber, and the nose rich with aromas of marmalade and caramel; the wine itself was slightly oxidised and beginning to dry out, but it was still fruity, elegant, and complex, with a long rewarding finish.

Some producers try to sell as much of their production as they can immediately after bottling, and leave it up to the purchaser to age the wine. Others, such as Lecointre and Sorin, offer for sale wines up to fifteen years old. A very few, such as Michel Doucet, keep substantial stocks of old wine for sale and oppose the rapid sale of new wines. Doucet's property is the Ch de la Guimonière near Chaume, a property that dates back to the fifteenth century. Doucet owns 15 hectares of vineyards in Chaume, and his oldest vines are over eighty years old. He is a traditional winemaker who practises *triage* and ferments his wine in wood very slowly, usually from late October until early January. His younger wines are hard to assess because of the sulphur on the nose. As in Sauternes, SO_2 is used at various stages of vinification, but because all Coteaux du Layon is bottled young, a further dose is added at bottling to prevent any possibility of secondary fermentation. Most producers, including Doucet, say they use as little as possible, but doses vary. On a recently bottled wine the unpleasant aroma of sulphur can be not only off-putting but detract from any appreciation of the wine's other qualities. The sulphur usually fades after the bottle has been opened for some time, and it is rarely noticeable on older wines. Doucet, it should be said, does not intend his wines to be drunk during their sulphurous youth. They need many years before they harmonise, and even the older wines can seem out of balance; some leave a burnt caramel-like flavour in the mouth. On the other hand, the 1943 was absolutely superb: rich gold in colour, full on the nose; lean, refined, and elegant on the palate, with excellent length.

Despite the economic difficulties plaguing the region, there is no shortage of top-quality producers of Coteaux du Layon Villages. Excellent Beaulieu is made by Jean-Pierre Chéné of the Domaine d'Ambinos. In addition to 2 hectares of vineyards at Faye, he owns 20 at Beaulieu, divided into three *clos*: Clos du Paradis Terrestre, Clos des Mulonnières, and Clos des Ontinières. The differences between the three is, Chéné says, merely one of nuance. *Triage* is practised, though rarely more than twice. He also sells some of his wine as straightforward Beaulieu, without specifying the *clos*. Fermentation takes place in glass-lined vats for over two months, and the wine is bottled slightly later than is usual, in May or even June.

Chéné does not stock wines older than his excellent and beautifully balanced 1969 Beaulieu. The French taxation system makes maintaining a stock of old wines an expensive proposition, for profits are calculated on the basis of the opening price for the wine. Inflation has made the opening prices of older wines seem ridiculously low; so on paper the profits will seem high and thus subject to considerable taxation that does not justify the substantial cost of keeping unsold wines for decades.

One of the leading makers of Rochefort is André Sorin at Domaine de la Motte. He owns 10 hectares at Rochefort and maintains a stock of 150,000 bottles, of which the oldest offered for sale is his 1969. His wines are comparatively light, fresh and attractive rather than rich and aggressive, though they blossom after fifteen years in bottle. His

1969 has great intensity and suppleness, if not much charm. For Sorin the vintage of the century was not 1947 but 1959. This wine showed no signs of age: it was rich, soft, thick with glycerol and a flavour of dried fruits; it has fine structure and length, and although it owes its longevity to high alcohol rather than to acidity, it is so well balanced that the alcohol is not obtrusive.

Other Villages wines I have enjoyed include Yves Leduc's Ch Montbeneault at Faye, a traditionally made wine that often finds favour at competitions. Pierre and Philippe Cady make good St Aubin at the hamlet of Valette; they too practise *triage*, but ferment the wine in temperature-controlled tanks and not in wood. Other producers with good reputations whose wines I have not tasted include Paul Banchereau (St Aubin), Domaine de Pierre Bise (Beaulieu), Domaine des Maurières (St Lambert), and Domaine des Saulaies (Faye).

The wines of Chaume are exceptionally good. I have already mentioned Michel Doucet's Ch de la Guimonière. One of the most charming and skilled winemakers in the *appellation* is Dominique Jaudeau, who, unusually among *viticulteurs* of the Layon, has no family background in winemaking. He spent a year at Yquem and Coutet, a training few of his fellow growers can match, and bought the Ch de la Roulerie in 1952. Although the château and cellars are in the village of St Aubin, 7.5 of his 20 hectares are at Chaume. A most scrupulous winemaker, M. Jaudeau organised no fewer than four *passages* through his vineyards in 1985. He claims to have a minimum of three pickings each year. In 1984, he told me, the final *passage* produced such a rich crop of botrytised grapes that the must ran like oil from the press. It shows in the wine, and his 1984 Chaume is quite different from almost any other of that vintage I have tasted. Some very good Coteaux du Layon was made in 1984, and Jaudeau's is very sweet and concentrated, quite fat and opulent for such a young wine. Jaudeau is somewhat sceptical about the claims for superiority (and far higher prices) made by the proprietors of vineyards at neighbouring Quarts de Chaume. In 1952, he points out, Quarts de Chaume consisted of no more than 25 hectares, but the owners, keen to expand their production, had it extended to 45. Overnight, what had been mere Chaume was elevated to higher status.

Equally sceptical, and with an equally sound vested interest in his opinion, is Henri Rochais of Ch de Plaisance, a property he acquired in 1960. Unlike Jaudeau, who is tall and skinny with an almost scholarly air despite his blue overalls, Rochais is a burly and fast-talking man. All of his 15 hectares are in Chaume and his house is surrounded by the vineyards. Like Jaudeau, he maintains very high standards, and claims to have made no fewer than six *passages* through his vineyards one year. He prefers to ferment the wine in *cuves* so as to preserve the striking aromas of the wine, though it rests in wood after fermentation for a while; it is then racked three times and filtered. Rochais holds stock from 1964; the oldest of his wines that I have tasted, the 1976, was still quite backward and not well enough knit; another five years should take care of that, for the wine has excellent structure. In his cellars in December 1985 I compared the still fermenting wine from different *passages*; the difference was striking, and even better was the wine from the oldest vines. In a great year like 1985, it is astonishing how delicious the new wine can be. Even wines from lesser properties had enormous charm and zest, while those from the best estates had remarkable attack, concentration, and powerful fruit, followed by a sustaining acidity. If I were in the habit of drinking wine for breakfast, which I am not, this is the wine I would choose: it is as refreshing and bracing as a ripe grapefruit.

Good Chaume is also made by Jean-Paul Tijou, whose cellars are on the quayside at Rochefort but whose property is the imposing château at Bellevue, close to the slopes of Chaume, of which he owns 5 hectares. Tijou uses no wood, and perhaps this is why his wines, though crisp and elegant, strike me as somewhat lacking in character. Tijou is one of many producers who defines Chaume's special quality as *nervosité*, in the sense of its being a highly-strung, delicately balanced wine, relying on finesse rather than alcohol for its impact.

And now we climb up the final rung of the ladder of *appellations* and reach the heights of Quarts de Chaume. With only 45 hectares of vineyards in the entire district, there are few owners and the wine is much sought after. The worldly Pascal Laffourcade is fortunate enough to own two châteaux here, Suronde and L'Ercharderie, which his father acquired almost thirty years ago. Between them, the two estates include within their boundaries 19 hectares of the valuable vineyards, with vines varying from fifteen to ninety years of age. The maximum yield is 22 hl/ha, though in 1975 Laffourcade only attained 7. No wonder the wine is, relatively speaking, expensive. Vinification is overseen by a Bordeaux-trained oenologist, and the finished wine is bottled as early as possible, often in March. A comparison of young Chaume with a Quarts de Chaume of the same year was instructive, as the latter wine had not only more intensity of flavour, as one would expect, but a distinct hint of *terroir*, reflecting the conspicuous mineral content of the soil at Quarts de Chaume.

At the very foot of the hamlet, not far from the river, is the Ch de Belle Rive, a family property of 17 hectares of old vines now owned by Jacques Lalanne. The vineyards, which face south, are exceptionally sheltered. Because the wine is never heavy or cloying, the drinker is less subject to surfeit than if he or she were sipping Sauternes. Not that Quarts de Chaume is a lightweight. At Belle Rive in the great year of 1959, the potential alcohol of the first *trie* was 19.2%; the second *trie* registered 20.5%, and the third a remarkable 22.8%. Average good-quality Layon would have an alcoholic strength of 12.5–13% with perhaps 50–60 g/l residual sugar (equivalent to 3–4% potential alcohol). Since the alcoholic strength of these wines rarely reaches or exceeds 14%, the residual sugar content of the 1959 must have been unusually high. Many growers in the region reported similarly high must weights in 1985, though such claims are not reliable, since much depends on the point at which the measurement is made. It is significant that while lesser growers were speaking of potential alcohol of around 20% in 1985, the far from modest Lalanne was telling me that his best *trie* had 18.5%, with 15–16% being the average figure for the rest of the harvest. Yields average 12 hl/ha.

Lalanne is a traditionalist. The must is fermented very slowly in casks, sometimes until the end of January. Lalanne is convinced of the superiority of wood-fermented wine. None of the supposed disadvantages (such as loss of aromas) need apply, he claims, as long as the winemaker is prepared to take trouble. And fermentation in barrels does involve a good deal of labour. After fermentation Lalanne racks the wine into tanks. He then replaces the wine in cask for a month and bottles it towards the end of April. The result is certainly very fine, both elegant and complex.

Jean Baumard is a very different kind of winemaker, and his methods offer an interesting contrast to those of Lalanne. A short, dapper man, Baumard occupies a lovely house in Rochefort, which he acquired in 1955, though his family has inhabited the region for centuries. He owns 30 hectares of vineyards. 6 are in Quarts de Chaume, though at present only half are in production. He also owns a celebrated vineyard very close to the village, the Clos de Ste Catherine. Baumard insists that there is indeed a real distinction to be made between Chaume and Quarts de Chaume. His own vineyards in Quarts de Chaume have a hotter microclimate, are more prone to early botrytis, and the soil contains more substantial deposits of sandstone, schist, and granite than are found higher up the slopes. Baumard is a scrupulous winemaker. In 1985 he instructed his twenty-five pickers to make four *passages* through his vineyards, and then declassified the wine from the final *trie*. Baumard's reductive methods of vinification differ from those prevailing in the region. He says with pride that at no point does any of his wine come into contact with wood. For twenty-five years he has used steel and glass tanks. Fermentation takes place in underground vats; since Baumard is an enemy of oxidation, all contact with the air is kept to an absolute minimum. As a result, the distinctive aromas of the wine are retained. Baumard's Quarts de Chaume are undoubtedly assertive and distinctive, even though I did not always care for them. Another leading winemaker told me that Baumard's wines are so individual that in competitions some judges vote against them not because they are poor but because they are insufficiently characteristic of the *appellation*. Baumard himself describes his wines as *nerveux* and applauds their good grip; they are not conspicuously sweet and the emphasis is clearly on finesse rather than opulence. Baumard's Clos de Ste Catherine is, in my view, a less satisfactory wine than his Quarts de Chaume. Baumard himself describes it as a 'feminine' wine, lighter than the more commanding Quarts de Chaume. The vineyard, which rises up the slope behind the church at Rochefort, is north-facing, which may in part account for its crisp sweet quality, though next to Quarts de Chaume it seems to lack complexity.

Finally, we come to Bonnezeaux. Its south-facing slopes cover 130 hectares, though only about half this area is planted with vines that are used to produce the fine wine of this name. Bonnezeaux was promoted later than Quarts de Chaume, and only received its own *appellation* in 1961. The subsoil contains clay and limestone, and the wine is slightly more ample than that of Quarts de Chaume. Because the vineyards are fragmented, there are a number of growers, who make wine of varying quality. Some of the very finest wine is made by Jacques Boivin at the Ch de Fesles, which was acquired by his family in 1870. He owns 33 hectares in all, though only 14 are in Bonnezeaux. The maximum yield here is 25 hl/ha, and though Boivin usually manages to come close to this figure, in 1981, for instance, he only harvested 16. Like all the top producers, he practises *triage*. Boivin does not like excessive botrytis on his grapes, for fear that the wine will lose freshness and balance. On the other hand, the presence of good botrytis will lessen the possibility of secondary fermentation, according to Boivin, so less sulphur needs to be used when the wine is bottled. Boivin uses both wood and vats for the fermentation, which continues until Christmas.

As we sat over a glass of his excellent 1983 Bonnezeaux, we discussed the style of his wine. For Boivin, good Bonnezeaux displays *nervosité*, *finesse*, *vigueur*. That is not to say that his wines are light, as his sumptuous 1969 Bonnezeaux showed, with its lovely soft rich nose, and mouth-filling opulence beautifully countered by its finesse. For Boivin, the skill of the winemaker is paramount. 'Before the *assemblage*,' he told me, 'I stand in my cellars and have before me between six and twelve lots from different parcels of vines. I must then combine them to make the best possible wine, and the only equipment I have is the glass in my hand. Sometimes two lesser wines will combine to make a great one, and vice versa.' In 1947, which Boivin calls the greatest year of the century at Bonnezeaux, his father, contemplating the *assemblage* the following spring, admitted defeat, and bottled seven lots separately.

At this point Boivin, burly and bearded but light on his feet, disappeared to the cellars and returned with a dusty bottle. 'Talking of the 1947 . . .' It was a fitting way to take my leave of the Coteaux du Layon, for the 1947 Ch de Fesles is not only the finest sweet wine of the Loire I have ever tasted, but one of the best I have tasted from anywhere in the world. The colour was a rich amber, like polished copper, but what astonished me was its brilliance: it gleamed with health and vigour. On the nose the wine was richly aromatic, with overtones of honey, marmalade, and tobacco, a bouquet of true splendour. In the mouth it was very sweet and incredibly concentrated: the merest sip filled the mouth with layers of flavour. Yet this richness was not in the least cloying, for it was undercut by the wine's

freshness and vivacity; sweetness and acidity were in perfect equilib-
rium. The length was astonishing. Boivin told me that some of the
other lots his father had bottled almost forty years ago had been even
better, though of them nothing remains in the cellars.

The following year I returned to taste his fresh and flowery 1984,
and the magnificent 1985, delicious now and likely to be superb by
the end of the century.

VOUVRAY

The other area of the Loire valley where sweet wines are made is
Vouvray. The soil is composed of calcareous clay which, in the best
sites, is flecked with flint or limestone. The microclimate here, fifty
miles further inland from the Layon, is less conducive to the
development of botrytis, and between 1976 and 1985 virtually no
sweet wine was produced, except for one or two winemakers who
made a small quantity in 1982 and 1983. In great years, the vinification of a substantial quantity of *moelleux* is almost inevitable because
of the sheer ripeness of the grapes. Harvests tend to be later in
Vouvray than further west and in certain years some grapes are not
picked until well into November. The Chenin Blanc grape, which is
ubiquitous in Vouvray, produces three styles of wine: *sec*, *demi-sec*,
and *moelleux*. The style produced in an average year in Vouvray is the

Aigle Blanc
VOUVRAY
Appellation Vouvray Controlée
ESTATE BOTTLED BY PRINCE PONIATOWSKI
PROPRIÉTAIRE-RÉCOLTANT · Le "Clos Baudoin" VOUVRAY (I.&L.)

fruity, off-dry *demi-sec*. The other two styles are variations. *Sec* is the style winemakers are stuck with when the grapes do not ripen fully; much of this dry tart wine is used to make the *méthode champenoise* wines that comprise roughly half the annual production of Vouvray. In great years, all the grapes will have ripened to the extent that virtually no *sec* can be made. In 1976, a truly exceptional year, the leading proprietor Gaston Huet told me that 85% of his production was sweet. In 1985, however, the proportion will be between 15% and 30% throughout Vouvray.

Vouvray is a pleasant little town just east of Tours, its vineyards scattered along south-facing hillsides overlooking the Loire. Many of the leading growers own vineyards quite close to the town, but other communes entitled to the *appellation*, such as Chançay and Vernou, lie to the north and east. Although there are some cooperatives in the region, the best wines are made by individual producers, which, as in the Layon, are usually family businesses continued through many generations. One of these is Clos Naudin, owned by André Foreau and his son Philippe, who display a perfectionist attitude towards their craft. There is quite a gap between the exceptional quality of top winemakers such as the Foreaus and the often mediocre, and occasionally abysmal, quality of less fastidious growers, and Philippe was sharply critical of winemakers who do not take the pains that are commonplace at Clos Naudin. Naturally *triage* is employed here, though Philippe says the system is becoming less and less common in Vouvray, because of the cost. 'If there's no need for *triage*,' says Philippe, 'it's a sure sign that your grapes aren't ripe enough to make *moelleux*.' Maximum yields can be varied by the authorities from year to year, so yield statistics do not count for much in Vouvray. What Foreau does insist on is not simply the quality of the grapes, but the method of harvesting them. At Clos Naudin they are placed in *gueulbées*, traditional wooden containers resembling open barrels that keep the grapes intact and minimise the risk of damaging the skins or crushing the fruit.

At the cellars, the overripe grapes are pressed immediately in pneumatic presses; after a *débourbage*, the must is placed in 300-litre *fûts* of oak or chestnut. During fermentation the cellars are maintained at a constant temperature of 14–15 °C. Fermentation is prolonged and at Clos Naudin it often continues as late as mid-January. The wine is racked, fined, then bottled in April, and, as in the Coteaux du Layon, all maturation takes place in bottle. High acidity and the absence of malolactic fermentation (which is encouraged elsewhere in order to reduce acidity and soften the wine) mean that the wine is rarely drinkable until ten years old. Young Vouvray has little of the fruity charm of young Coteaux du Layon because of its higher acidity, but the best wines are almost immortal. Many old cellars contain bottles dating from the last century that are still drinkable. Because the *moelleux* wines require such lengthy maturation, only the best corks, which are as costly as an empty bottle, are used. The 1947 wines at Clos Naudin, which are maintained at a constant temperature of 13 °C, still have their original corks.

Vouvray is not high in alcohol. Even in a fine year such as 1985, when very healthy grapes had a potential alcohol of between 16–19%, fermentation would be stopped at 12–13%, leaving roughly 60 g/l residual sugar (about 3.5° Baumé). In my experience, old Vouvray is often less sweet than old Coteaux du Layon, though the high acidity in a well-made *moelleux* gives the wine its characteristic finesse and length. Young *moelleux* is interesting to sample as an experiment, though rather a waste of good wine. The 1983 Clos Naudin was a brilliant light gold, with a fresh aroma reminiscent of tropical fruit; on the palate it was intensely sweet at first, but then sharp acidity sprang up and dominated all else. The wine's structure was certainly sound and it will develop well, but in its youth it is barely drinkable. The 1976 Clos Naudin had a quite different character. Although its colour was only marginally deeper than that of the 1983, the nose was more forceful, and on the palate the wine was rich and fat, though harmonious and elegant. Sadly, the 1947 Clos Naudin I sampled was not a good bottle. Since the grapes in 1947 had had 21% potential alcohol, a bottle in top condition must be a formidable and splendid wine.

Gaston Huet is a prominent citizen of Vouvray not just because he makes wines of outstanding quality, but because he has been its mayor and a leading propagandist on behalf of its wines. A short, well-groomed man of impeccable graciousness, he owns 32 hectares of vineyards divided between three ancient properties: Le Haut Lieu (18 hectares), Clos du Bourg (6 hectares), and Le Mont (7 hectares), each of which is vinified and bottled separately. The Clos du Bourg can trace its pedigree back to the early Middle Ages, when it was an ecclesiastical holding. Clay and limestone dominate all three vineyards, though Le Mont is more stony. Huet is a traditionalist, uses no herbicides, and practises *triage* when conditions justify it. He refuses to chaptalise, so that if the grapes do not contain sufficient sugar, there is no *moelleux* that year, as was the case between 1976 and 1985. The grapes are pressed gently in horizontal presses that prevent any oxidation. Huet finds that no *débourbage* is necessary after the pressing. Fermentation takes place in casks of 220 or 600 litres at a constant temperature of 18 °C until January. The wine is bottled in April.

M. Huet characterises his wines as rich, honeyed, full-bodied, with aromas of quince and acacia. Here too 1947 was the best year of the century, and the Haut Lieu *moelleux* of that year was an exceptionally beautiful wine. Although rich in colour, aroma, and taste, there was nothing heavy about it, simply because the balance is impeccable. And despite its unusually high alcohol level of 14%, there is no hint of alcohol on the palate, for all the elements of the wine have been properly integrated by the passage of time. 1959 was another great year, and the Clos du Bourg *moelleux* was soft and rich, though with a touch of austerity that added to its elegance.

Closer to the centre of town is Clos Baudoin, a property owned by Prince Poniatowsky. His grandfather bought the Clos in 1918, but as a vineyard of a mere 3.8 hectares it was hardly a going concern. When the present Prince Poniatowsky took over in 1971, he bought additional vineyards to bring the total number of hectares to 22. The Clos itself dates from 1707, and the vines are on average forty years old. Poniatowsky vinifies and bottles the Clos wine separately, and markets the wine from his other vineyards as Aigle Blanc. Like Huet, he made no *moelleux* between 1976 and 1985. *Triage* is the custom here in appropriate years, and a further selection takes place after the pressing. The must is fermented in 600-litre *fûts* at 16 °C in the cellars adjoining the house. These cellars tunnel deep into the hillside, but that has not deterred some vine roots from burrowing their way down through forty metres of soil and rock to penetrate the cellar roof. Stacked in the cellars are numerous old bottles, beginning with wines from 1838, 1853, 1854, and the 1870s. Poniatowsky recently opened two bottles of the 1874, and assured me the wine was still exceptionally good. I had to be content with a relatively infantile Clos

Baudoin of 1964, which was a finely balanced wine that nevertheless seemed rather lean. Poniatowsky stressed the ageing potential of his wine rather than any features of its style when I asked him about its strongest characteristics. 'After thirty years, even a wine from a mediocre vintage can be transformed. One of the pleasures of wine is that it is unpredictable.' Jean-Marie Touchais made a similar observation, citing the 1958 Moulin Touchais, unexciting in its youth, that unexpectedly blossomed into magnificence.

Most producers of Vouvray specify the style of the wine on the label but this Prince Poniatowsky refuses to do. Since, he argues, there is no clear definition of the difference between, for example, *demi-sec* and *moelleux*, the category in which you place your wine remains a subjective decision. (Another winemaker of high reputation, Jean-Michel Vigneau, makes the same point in a different way: 'Sometimes the sweetest wine of one year is called *moelleux*, while the identical wine in a greater year would only be called *demi-sec*.') Moreover, Poniatowsky maintains, the wine alters as it ages, often losing some of its sweetness, and a category label attached at bottling could be quite misleading twenty years later. Poniatowsky has logic on his side, but such rigour does not help the consumer much. If you know the character of each vintage, then you can probably guess the style of the wine; but not every wine drinker is that well informed, and some guidance from the winemaker would surely be appreciated. Poniatowsky, a somewhat imperious man who dresses in what the French imagine is the habitual garb of an English country gentleman, prefers to do things his own way, but then a winemaker's foibles and strong opinions are what give wine its distinctive character.

The hills and valleys beyond Vouvray itself are dotted with the vineyards of small producers, for the AOC district includes seven other communes besides Vouvray: Rochecorbon, Chançay, Vernou, Sainte Radegonde, Noizay, Reugny and part of Parçay-Meslay. Although the riverside vineyards, with their limestone deposits, have the highest reputation, the inland communes support a number of properties of exacting standards. Their wines are less well known than those of enthusiastic exporters such as Foreau and Poniatowsky. Jean-Michel Vigneau of Chançay insists on dealing with 5000 individual customers all over Europe rather than with wholesalers. He recently turned down an impressive order from Japan. It would have simplified his life to have sold a substantial proportion of his production to a single client, but, I had the impression, he could not bear to think of his wines being downed by people with whom he had no personal connection. His methods of harvesting and vinification are the same as those practised by the other top producers. Vigneau stresses the importance of early bottling, though he admits that this often results in a pallid colour. Even his 1964 *moelleux*, a wine of depth and complexity, was only pale gold in colour and, by that criterion alone, seemed far less developed than, say, a Chaume of the same year. He does maintain stocks of older wines but does not advertise their availability, preferring to dispense them on request to some of his regular customers. His *réserve familiale* contains bottles from 1893 (Jean-Michel is the fifth generation in his family to make wine here). It is not only the great *moelleux* wines that age so superbly, according to Vigneau; a *sec* will also benefit from bottle age, though the aromas are rarely as interesting.

Vigneau took me through his cellars just as the 1985 wines were coming to the end of their fermentation period. I made a beeline for one of the casks. At my request Vigneau removed the bung and I put my ear to the hole. There are few more engaging sounds than the sizzle of fermenting wine, and few more engaging tastes than a mouthful of these newborn Chenin Blancs. Glasses in hand, we sampled new wine from half a dozen casks, remarking on their striking differences. Soil, date of picking, alcohol level, age of vines, stage of fermentation – all these factors contributed nuances that will become accentuated as the wine ages.

I repeated the experience at the *caves* of Daniel Allias, the owner of Le Petit Mont on the outskirts of Vouvray. This family property of only 10 hectares is blessed with a sizeable proportion of old vines, mostly between thirty-five and fifty years old. Cask samples confirmed the greater concentration of flavour obtained from old vines. Allias's methods of harvesting and vinification (in 250-litre *fûts*) are traditional, and his wines are very attractive. Allias was prepared to offer a definition of *demi-sec* in terms of residual sugar. While his 1976 *moelleux* had 50–65 g/l, and his 1985 is expected to have 50, his *demi-sec* wines will only contain 18–25.

Other producers of good-quality Vouvray include Gilles Champignon, Pierre Lothion, Edgar Mouzay, and Gérard Nouzillet. I have little to say about the best-known wine producer in Vouvray: Marc

Brédif of Rochecorbon. I have tasted some extremely good wines from this house in the past, but in 1980 it was bought by the distinguished Pouilly Fumé winemaker Patrick de Ladoucette. Unlike the other producers of Vouvray, Brédif also function as a wholesale wine merchant. Production amounts to some hundreds of thousands of bottles every year, so 80% of the grapes are bought in from other growers. 1985 will see the first production of *moelleux* under Ladoucette, and it will be interesting to see whether classic sweet wines in the style of their great 1947 and 1959 will continue to be made.

MONTLOUIS

On the opposite bank of the river, a few miles from Vouvray, is the town of Montlouis, which gives its name to an AOC that, until 1938, was subsumed within that of Vouvray. The honour did not compensate for the difficulty of establishing the wines under their new name, and even after half a century Montlouis is little known outside the Loire and fetches lower prices than Vouvray. Some of the best wines come from the commune of St Martin-le-Beau on the River Cher, where a small quantity of *moelleux* is made in exceptional years. One of the best winemakers here is the sophisticated Dominique Moyer. His 12 hectares at the hamlet of Husseau include some vineyards with vines up to seventy years old. Only organic fertilisers are used and *triage* is practised in exceptional years. The soil is more sandy and pebbly than at Vouvray, though the subsoil is also mostly clay. Moyer ferments in glass vats in which he seals the wine for a year before bottling. Guy Deletang, whose cellars are in the centre of St Martin-le-Beau, also makes small quantities of *moelleux*. The 1985 in cask was attractive but not exciting. Whether the sweet wines of Montlouis ever match the best of Vouvray is open to question. The wine certainly matures more rapidly.

AZAY-LE-RIDEAU

Two other *appellations* do on occasion produce sweet styles of Chenin Blanc. One of these, Coteaux de l'Aubance, flanks the Coteaux du

Layon to the east. *Moelleux* was made here in 1959, 1964, and possibly later at René Daviau's Domaine de Bablut, but commercial production of these and similar wines may have ground to a halt. Responding to changes in fashion, growers are busily deracinating their Chenin Blanc vines and replacing them with Cabernet Franc or Gamay, so as to increase their production of red Anjou. And a minute quantity of *moelleux* is occasionally made at Azay-le-Rideau, west of Tours.

The village of Saché, with its south-facing vineyards, is the spot most likely to produce grapes of sufficient ripeness. In the nearby hamlet of La Basse Chevrière, Gaston Pavy cultivates 3.5 hectares of hillside vineyards. Botrytis occasionally attacks his vines, and did so in 1985, and in such years he can make wines of considerable richness. *Triage* and methods of vinification are highly traditional; fermentation takes at least two months. Samples from seven casks of the new *moelleux* confirmed that 1985 will be as splendid a year here as in Layon and Vouvray. In a dim corner of the cool cellars, Pavy stopped and pointed at a bottle lying on its own. 'You know when that wine was made?' I shook my head. '1911. It was made by my grandfather.' I responded with appropriate astonishment.

'Why don't we taste it?' he suggested, and I did not say no. The wine was a bright medium gold, and though the nose suggested some oxidation, the taste was amazingly fresh. In style it was closer to old Vouvray than old Coteaux du Layon: only medium-sweet, elegant, with lovely balance and flavour. A lack of length suggested that from now on the wine's days might be numbered. As we were sipping this nectar, a local farmer, Gauloise in mouth and clad in the obligatory blue overalls, stumbled in for a bottle of *champenoise*. Pavy fetched a glass for his neighbour and poured him some of the golden liquid. The farmer's cries of astonishment, both on tasting the lovely wine and on being told its age (about the same as his own), were most gratifying.

Sadly, such a wine is now only a curiosity, though I dare say there are other hamlets along the Loire valley where comparable marvels await a strictly local consumption. Still, lovers of sweet wines will find their appetites can easily be assuaged in the Loire valley, which still offers a range of excellent and greatly under-valued wines. Few of them are blockbusters. Instead they have the virtues of elegance and breed that make them ideal sipping wines and aperitif wines, and, occasionally, magnificent dessert wines.

8

The Rest of France

JURA

In viticultural terms, the Jura is a most peculiar corner of France. Many of its grape varieties are unique to the region, and methods of vinification differ from those commonly found elsewhere in France. The Jura is also the only wine region of France where *vin de paille* (straw wine) is still made. Instead of picking shrivelled or botrytised grapes, growers lay healthy grapes on beds of straw or matting to dry out over a period of months. This has the effect of concentrating the sugar content. This method is common enough in Italy, where wines known as Passito are made in this way, but it has become rare in France. *Vins de paille* used to be made in the Dordogne, but on a recent visit to the region even an inquiry at the Hotel de Paille at Queyssac failed to produce a sample of the wine. If straw wine is still

made in the Dordogne, then it is only produced by small growers for personal consumption and is no longer sold commercially.

This is not the case with the straw wines of the Jura, which can be found without difficulty in the region, though since relatively little is made, it is rarely exported. A number of local grapes can be used to make *vin de paille*: Chardonnay, Savagnin (a kind of Traminer), Trousseau, and Poulsard. Dry warm weather is required before the harvest, and thus the wine cannot be made every year. The grapes, which must be healthy and untainted by rot, are either left on straw, the traditional method, or laid out on wooden trays that are often protected by metal grilles that allow air to circulate but prevent dormice from gobbling up the fruit. The bunches are left in a well ventilated area for up to three months, and then a further selection is made to ensure that no rotten grapes are pressed. The grapes are usually destalked before being pressed and fermented in cask. The wine is aged in cask for at least two years, and regularly topped up. The finished wine often has 16–17% alcohol and 40–50 g/l residual sugar – a formidable glassful. Production is, of course, very restricted: Rolet, a major producer of good quality wines, make up to 2000 litres in a suitable year, and the equally reliable Domaine de la Pinte will make between 4000 and 6000 litres.

The wines naturally differ from house to house, but they do share

common characteristics. In colour they range from orange-gold to an amber tone not unlike Amontillado; the nose is usually rich and honeyed and toffee-like; on the palate the wine is sweet, concentrated, spicy, and vigorous, and may have a caramel flavour; since the acidity is fairly high, the wine should have very good length. Most *vins de paille* from the Jura are well made and worth seeking out. They are not cheap, but cost no more than a Deuxième Cru Sauternes. Such is their intensity of flavour that I find a little goes a long way, which is probably a good thing.

BURGUNDY

Burgundy, with its uncertain weather and its reputation for producing some of the greatest dry white wines in the world, is not exactly celebrated for its sweet wine. Indeed, I have only encountered a single example, but it was of sufficient quality to merit a mention. In the village of Clessé in the Macon district, the grower and winemaker Jean Thévenet noticed that his Chardonnay grapes had been attacked by botrytis. He decided not to let the opportunity slip by, and on 30 September 1983 he picked the grapes, which had by then attained a potential alcohol of 21%. The must fermented for six weeks at 15 °C, and came to a halt at 15% alcohol and 75 g/l residual sugar. More significantly, the wine was outstanding. The botrytis was extremely obvious on the nose, which was honeyed and floral and most elegant. In the mouth the wine was sweet and spicy, somewhat appley, and, equally important, it was vigorous and persistent on the palate. Whether the wine, which costs the same as a very good Sauternes, is *sui generis* or whether M. Thévenet and the handful of other growers who duplicated his experiment are going to find themselves in the curious position of trendsetters it is too early to say.

ALSACE

Alsace is best known for its dry white wines, and in recent years inferior grape varieties have been supplanted, literally, by the handful of varieties for which the region has become celebrated: Pinot Blanc, Pinot Gris (also known as Tokay d'Alsace, though the grape is unrelated to the Hungarian grapes used to make Tokay), Sylvaner, Muscat, Riesling, and Gewürztraminer. Some of these varieties are capable of producing richer, sweeter wines, and in recent years the authorities have laid down the rules of the game. There are two categories; Vendange Tardive and Sélection de Grains Nobles. Vendange Tardive simply means late picked, and is roughly equivalent to the German term Spätlese. Fermented through, Vendange Tardive wines tend to be higher in alcohol than 'ordinary' Alsace, richer, with more amplitude and weight. Even when Vendange Tardive wines retain residual sugar, they are rarely sweet. For Riesling, the regulations require grapes to be harvested with a minimum potential alcohol of 12.9%; for Gewürztraminer and Pinot Gris the wines must have 14.3% potential alcohol, and with these varieties, unlike the Riesling, there is a possibility of finding residual sugar in the wines. In general, however, Vendange Tardive wines are noted for their alcoholic power rather than their sweetness.

This is not the case with Sélection de Grains Nobles. Only three grape varieties may be used for such wines: Gewürztraminer, Pinot Gris, and Riesling. Riesling grapes must have a potential alcohol of 15.1%; for Gewürztraminer and Pinot Gris, the grapes need 16.4%. Not surprisingly, it is only in exceptional years that such wines can be

made at all. The well-known house of Hugel pioneered the making of these wines, which were first produced in 1865 and 1921. In those days, they were identified by German categories such as Beerenauslese, and only in the last couple of decades have the French categories become mandatory. Other winemakers followed Hugel's example in 1976, and by 1983, another great year, dozens of growers were picking their grapes, many of which had been attacked by botrytis, as late as possible. According to Pamela Vandyke Price's book *Alsace Wines*, in 1983 102 growers made 7300 hectolitres of Vendange Tardive wines, and twenty-six made 750 hectolitres of Sélection de Grains Nobles. Gewürztraminer is the most common grape for these categories, and Riesling, which does not attain such high must weights as easily, the most rare.

Even for the pioneers in this field, Hugel et Fils of Riquewihr, these wines are rarities. Gewürztraminer Sélection de Grains Nobles has only been produced in 1865, 1921, 1934, 1945, 1959, 1961, 1967, 1971, 1976, 1981, and 1983. Pinot Gris Sélection de Grains Nobles has been made only in 1965, 1971, 1976, and 1983; and Riesling Sélection de Grains Nobles was only made in 1865, 1976, and 1983. In 1985 wines of Sélection de Grains Nobles standard were made by Hugel from Riesling and Gewürztraminer, but because there was very little botrytis that year, only a few hundred litres were produced. Fifteen pickers spent three days working through 4.5 hectares of vineyards; this elicited only 330 litres of Riesling, a yield of well below 1 hl/ha. The potential alcohol level for this Riesling was an extremely high 21.5%, and for the Gewürztraminer 22.2%. The sweet wines of Alsace have always been very expensive, and one dreads to think what prices these rarities will fetch if or when they reach the marketplace. The 1976 Gewürztraminer Sélection de Grains Nobles was certainly a remarkable wine, intense and concentrated, and with a lovely double-decker effect of the sweetness underpinning the inherent spiciness of the flavour; the finish was long and rich. Certainly this Gewürztraminer showed better than Muré's 1983 Sélection de Grains Nobles, which was certainly a well balanced wine but lacked real character and individuality. Muré's 1983 Pinot Gris Sélection de Grains Nobles, tasted in 1986, was less satisfactory in terms of its balance; the sweetness of the wine masked its varietal character, and the overall effect was fairly bland. Perhaps the wines will show better in a few years' time.

At present there is an element of faddishness in Alsace growers' pursuit of high must weights. As scarce luxury items, the wines have a rarity value and a snob appeal that allows winemakers to charge very high prices for them. Recent Sélection de Grains Nobles from Hugel will rival Yquem in terms of cost. Although botrytised Rieslings are the base for many of the world's greatest sweet wines in Germany, in Alsace they take on a different character. No one would want to dispute that the Hugel Sélections de Grains Nobles (and, I dare say, those from other producers such as Schlumberger) are magnificent wines, yet they seem to be something of a sideshow, rather than intrinsic to the range and style of Alsace wines. In 1985 the firm of Kientzler produced Alsace's first ice wine, and in 1986 a few other properties leapt onto the bandwagon. The results should be intriguing.

VINS DOUX NATURELS

Like May balls at Cambridge that always take place in June, Vins Doux Naturels are not what they seem. They are in fact wines fortified with alcohol, which is not my idea of 'naturel'. Moreover, although such wines are beyond the limits of this book, they deserve an extended footnote.

The term was coined in the nineteenth century, essentially as a tax avoidance scheme. When the government proposed to tax fortified wines, the winemakers of the most southerly corner of France protested that they were already penalised by the very low yields of their grapes, planted on dry rocky soils. An exemption was granted and the wines became known as Vin Doux Naturels. They have an ancient pedigree, and were allegedly invented by a celebrated medieval doctor, Arnaud da Villanova, in 1285. Such wines are found all across southern France as far as the Rhône valley, where the celebrated Muscat de Beaumes de Venise is made, but the greatest concentration of vineyards, 29,500 hectares in all, is located around the city of Perpignan, close to the Spanish border. These fortified wines of Roussillon are divided among the following *appellations*: Rivesaltes (73%), Muscat de Rivesaltes (15%), Banyuls (5%), and Maury (7%). Nearly all the Vins Doux Naturels found outside Roussillon in other parts of the Midi are Muscats, and come from

Lunel, Frontignan, Mireval, St Jean de Minervois, Beaumes de Venise, and Rasteau.

The AOC regulations are quite strict. The only permitted grape varieties are Grenache (Noir, Gris, or Blanc), Macabéo (also known as Maccabeu and unique to Roussillon), Malvoisie (now rather rare), and Muscat (either Muscat of Alexandria or Muscat Blanc à Petits Grains). The maximum permitted yield is 30 hl/ha, and grapes when harvested need to have a must weight of 252 grammes (approximately 14° Baumé). The wine does not acquire its sweetness as a result of a natural balance between sugar fermented into alcohol and sugar left residually. Instead, fermentation is arrested with a *mutage*, an addition of neutral alcohol with a strength of 96° proof. The maximum quantity of alcohol that may be added to the wine is 10%; in other words, if you have 100 hectolitres fermenting away, you may only add ten hectolitres of alcohol. If you use less than 10%, there is a danger that the yeasts may reactivate. The *mutage* will give you a wine of 15–18% alcohol and varying degrees of residual sugar. The total alcohol level (including potential alcohol remaining in the form of sugar) must be at least 21.5% after the *mutage*, so the moment at which fermentation is arrested is crucial, since it is the timing that determines the eventual sweetness of the finished wine. If the *mutage* takes place relatively early in the fermentation process, there will be a good deal of sugar remaining in the wine; if it is left until late, the fermentation will be quite advanced and the wine relatively dry. The

Domaine de Durban

Muscat de Beaumes-de-Venise

Appellation Muscat de Beaumes de Venise Contrôlée

Mis en Bouteille au Domaine 37,5 cl

LEYDIER et FILS, PROPRIETAIRES, 84190 BEAUMES-DE-VENISE
PRODUCE OF FRANCE

sweeter the finished wine, the lower the alcohol level. The following
is a rough guide to the labelling of Vins Doux Naturels: Doux (15%
alcohol and 6.5% as residual sugar); Demi-Doux (16 + 5.5); Demi-
Sec (17 + 4.5); and Sec (18 + 3).

This method of winemaking is much the same as that used for port
or other fortified wines of southern Europe, but it differs from port in
that a lesser amount of alcohol is added to the wine. A good
Rivesaltes, for instance, is likely to be a delicate wine of intense
flavour and concentration, rather than a big port-like wine of great
sweetness and pepperiness. As in any other wine region, different
producers have different styles. Some like to age the wines in large
wooden casks; others prefer the less troublesome method of ageing in
vat. There are different regulations for ageing the wine before it is
sold. Rivesaltes must be at least one year old, though many producers
age for two if not three years. Banyuls must be aged for thirty
months. The Muscats are best drunk young. Some producers, such
as Cazes Frères of Rivesaltes and Domaine du Mas Blanc of Banyuls,
are beginning to bottle some of their wines early and then giving

Grand Vin de Banyuls

DU "MAS BLANC"

Appellation Banyuls Contrôlée

mise au domaine

"Dry 1975"

S.C.A. Parcé et Fils
9, allées du Général de Gaulle
F. 66650 Banyuls-sur-Mer

PRODUCE OF FRANCE   NET CONTENTS 750 ml

them bottle-age rather than cask-ageing; in other words, they are trying to make a wine closer in style to vintage port. A more traditional method of ageing is in glass demijohns that are exposed to the air; this results in a sherry-like wine, deliberately oxidised, that is known as *rancio*. Methods of vinification differ quite widely, but the best producers give the musts a lengthy maceration in order to extract as much tannin and colour from the skins as possible. Some Rivesaltes continues to macerate for up to two weeks after the *mutage*. This is said to be the best method, but it is very expensive, since a substantial proportion of the alcohol is thrown out with the skins and pulp after the maceration is completed.

Maury is in effect a Grand Cru of Rivesaltes, and much of the wine produced there is sold to wholesalers as plain Rivesaltes because of the stringent regulations that apply to wines sold as AOC Maury. Maury must be at least two years old, and must contain at least 50% Grenache Noir (though in practice up to 80% is often used). Yields at Maury are low, about 24 hl/ha on average, since the vines often fail to flower. 1750 hectares are entitled to the *appellation*, and 80% of the production is handled by the well-run cooperative. There are also fifteen private wineries, of which Mas Amiel, with 35 hectares, is the largest. It is extremely difficult to characterise the wines because of the great variations in style that are permitted, indeed encouraged. The Cooperative produces a range of AOC Maury wines, including a Six Year Old, which is in fact a delicate combination of wood-aged wines with younger, fresher, more aromatic wines made by reductive methods (that is to say, guarded from the oxidation prompted by wood-ageing or the *rancio* method). Their best wines are given long macerations; they cannot afford to make all their wines this way, because lengthy macerations tie up vat space for up to three weeks. Their vintage wines, emulating port, are given long maceration and bottled after a year. These wines, even in their youth, have a bewildering and exciting complexity. The 1983 wine, made only on an experimental basis, was sweet and ripe on the nose with distinct aromas of cherries and Mokka; on the palate it was intense and tannic, rich but with good bite to it. The 1985, on the other hand, had aromas of mint and prunes. Maury with longer wood-ageing tends to be more delicate, less aggressive and rich, but with considerable finesse and intensity, just as tawny port usually has similar qualities not found in so marked a degree in bottle-aged vintage port.

Badly made Maury, or Rivesaltes, is cloying. The skill of the winemaker is extremely important, as there are so many variables, both in methods of vinification (especially the amount of maceration undergone by the must), the timing of the *mutage*, the methods of ageing, and the balance of the blending. I have tasted a Rivesaltes Sec from a private winery in Maury that was twenty years old, and the dryness was expressed in a smoky astringency that was distinctly unpleasant. On the other hand, the 1963 Rivesaltes Très Vieux of Cazes Frères, was lovely: deep orange-amber in colour, with a caramel aroma on the nose that hinted at oxidation without being over-oxidised, together with a knot of aromas of coffee, peaches, and honey; and on the palate the wine was soft and mellow and velvety, with all its constituents well integrated, and excellent length. It was made from Grenache Blanc and aged for twenty years before being bottled. Naturally the cost of such lengthy ageing is reflected in the price, which exceeds that of most Premier Cru Sauternes. Cazes Frères' standard Rivesaltes Vieux is made from macerated Grenache Noir and is eight years old at time of bottling; in style it is Demi-Sec, with cooked fruit on the nose, and good structure and power and elegance; slightly sweet in the mouth, it moves towards a lively peppery aftertaste.

The Vins Doux Naturels from Banyuls are reputed to be the finest in Roussillon, and that has certainly been my experience. If you travel down the coast towards Spain from Perpignan, you will pass through the four communes entitled to the *appellation*: Collioure, Port-Vendres, Cerbère, and Banyuls itself. Methods of vinification and ageing are as varied as those of Maury and Rivesaltes. Banyuls is a difficult wine to make, and the problems start in the vineyard. The soil is poor, the terrain extremely steep, and there is little rainfall and constant wind; the soil is subject to slides and terraces often need to be rebuilt. 70% of the vines, distributed over the 2000 hectares of the region, are over forty years old and have low yields. The maximum yield is 30 hl/ha, but 16 to 22 is more common. The *encépagement* differs from that of other Vins Doux Naturels. AOC Banyuls must contain 50% Grenache Noir, plus Carignan, Cinsault, Syrah, or Mourvèdre. The other permitted varieties – Malvoisie, Macabéo, and Muscat – are practically non-existent here.

Dr André Parcé, a burly authoritative man who physically resembles a more genial Revd Ian Paisley, makes classic Banyuls of the very highest quality at Domaine du Mas Blanc. Production is tiny. In 1983 his 6.5 hectares (he also owns a further 5.5 hectares planted with other grape varieties that go into the superlative dry red wine sold as AOC Collioure) yielded 9000 bottles (a yield of 10 hl/ha); in 1984 9500 bottles (a yield of 11 hl/ha). His Banyuls is made either from 90% Grenache Noir and 10% Carignan, or from 70% Grenache Noir, 20% Grenache Gris, and 10% Carignan. Maceration of partially destalked grapes continues for up to a month. The *mutage* is added to the macerating pulp, which, as explained earlier, is a costly method. Some of the wines are aged up to five years in wood; others, known as Rimage, are kept in casks or vats for an average of nine months, topped up weekly to prevent oxidation, bottled early in the style of vintage port, and stored in bottle before being released. For classic Banyuls, with longer ageing before bottling, a degree of oxidation is desirable, and the wine is less frequently topped up. Dr Parcé also makes a Rimage à Mise Tardive, which is akin to a late-bottled vintage port; this is a vintage wine topped up monthly and bottled after five years and aged for a further two before release.

Dr Parcé is a leading figure in the local community and a former mayor of Banyuls. At a private club he founded in the hills outside the village, he arranged for me to taste a full range of his wines during a long and sumptuous dinner composed of courses specially devised by celebrated chefs to accompany his wines. Since Vins Doux Naturels are beyond the scope of this book, I shall not give detailed tasting notes, although the wines – which ranged from a vigorous and delicious Sec of 1975 to a 'Hors d'Age' wine made from a solera begun in 1925, and various Rimage wines along the way, not to mention four different Collioures – were outstanding. These Banyuls are more dense than any Maury or Rivesaltes I have ever tasted. They may not have the delicacy and charm of a well-balanced wood-aged Maury, but they more than make up for it with their sheer richness and concentration of flavour. They can age superbly: a 1967 Banyuls downed in 1987 proved velvety and perfectly balanced.

I cannot respond with the same enthusiasm to the Muscats of the region. I have tasted good examples here and there, but all too often the sweet grapiness of the wine is not balanced by other qualities that would keep it from being cloying on the finish. Good Muscat needs spiciness and delicacy as well as the more easily attainable qualities of aromatic bouquet and chewy grapiness. Two varieties of Muscat are commonly planted: Muscat à Petits Grains and the larger-berried Muscat of Alexandria. The trouble with the former is that the yields are low and most growers are reluctant to plant it. It does seem to give wine of greater finesse and this may account for the success of Muscat de Beaumes de Venise. The excellent Domaine de Durban, typical of the half dozen or so first-rate producers in the region, obtains yields of no more than 30 hl/ha from its 40 hectares of Petits Grains. The vineyards are 180 metres up, close to the dramatic Dentelles de Montmirail, and the microclimate encourages the grapes to reach an advanced state of ripeness. Grapes may be picked at 14% potential alcohol but 16–16.5% is common. The *mutage* regulations and practice are the same as for all Vins Doux Naturels. At Durban, M. Leydier keeps the wine on the lees for up to three months before filtering and bottling. He recommends keeping the wine for a year, and then drinking it up. I find a flowery tangerine bouquet on the Durban wines that is pleasing, though other producers arrive at a more racy and pungent grapiness on the nose. Some wines are marred by high alcohol, since they do not have the richness and complexity of other Vins Doux Naturels and a lack of balance shows through more obviously. A well-made Muscat de Beaumes de Venise is a delicious mouthful, and is usually the most refined of the Muscats of southern France.

9

German Sweet Wines

It is impossible to come to grips with the great sweet wines of Germany unless one has a basic understanding of the complex classification system that the Germans themselves employ. They are rightly proud of the fact that they give more information on their labels than any other wine-growing nation. This is admirable but also confusing, since making sense of a German wine label can be like cracking a code: it is only logical and comprehensible once you have grasped the principles on which it has been based. German wines are classified by must weights of the grapes at picking, by grape variety, by the vineyards from which they come, and by vintage, and we shall begin by looking at each in turn.

MUST WEIGHTS

The three lowest classifications of German wines do not concern us at all. They are Deutscher Tafelwein (table wine that is entirely German in origin, comparable to a French Vin de Table); Deutscher Landwein (like Tafelwein, but with higher minimum must weights roughly equivalent in quality to a French Vin de Pays); and Qualitätswein bestimmter Anbaugebiete (abbreviated to QbA), a category restricted to grapes grown in a single one of Germany's eleven wine-growing regions. Some QbA wines can be fairly sweet, and such wines are aimed at those drinkers who like a fruity semi-sweet table wine. Liebfraumilch is the obvious example. The final category, and the one with which we are concerned, is Qualitätswein mit Prädikat (QmP). Such wines must be made from grapes grown exclusively within a single district (Bereich) within one of the 11 wine-growing regions. No inter-regional or inter-Bereich blending is permitted, and chaptalisation is also forbidden. Such wines may be sweetened after fermentation by the addition of Süssreserve, which is unfermented grape juice that must come from the same region or vineyard. Süssreserve is prevented from fermenting by cooling or sterilising or by the addition of stabilising agents, and it must be of the same quality as the grapes from which the wine itself has been made. The best producers eschew the use of Süssreserve on the grounds that it alters the character and thus diminishes the quality of their QmP wines – though wines to which Süssreserve has been added are not necessarily bad or inferior.

Within the broad QmP category, there are various divisions, each signifying a different degree of must weight (or potential alcohol). Clearly, the higher the must weight, the higher in either alcohol or residual sugar the finished wine is going to be. The lowest category, Kabinett, is usually a fairly dry wine, but with the next category, Spätlese (late-picked grapes), some residual sugar is often present. This is even more true of the next rung up the ladder, Auslese (selected grapes), which is often distinctly sweet. The regulations do not require Spätlese or Auslese wines to contain certain levels of residual sugar. Most Germans prefer their wines dry rather than sweet, and it is becoming increasingly common to encounter QmP wines that by reason of their must weight at harvest are labelled Spätlese or Auslese but taste either semi-dry or bone-dry. With the next category, Beerenauslese, the grapes are so rich in sugar that it would be impossible to through-ferment the must. Were some dogged winemaker to succeed in making a dry Beerenauslese, the result would be a wine of 16% or more of alcohol, which would almost certainly be undrinkable.

The richest musts of all are the basis of the top category, Trocken-beerenauslese (TBA). Both Beerenauslese and TBA are nearly always made from botrytised grapes. The regulations do not insist on botrytis as a precondition, presumably mindful of hot dry years such as 1934 and 1959 when excellent sweet wines were made without botrytis (though some ultra-scrupulous winemakers refused to make TBA in 1959 precisely because botrytis was lacking). For these categories harvesting is rigorous, and good TBA is made by picking grape by grape, not bunch by bunch, which is one reason why the wine is so phenomenally expensive. A final category is that of Eiswein, wine made by harvesting frozen grapes; the intense cold concentrates both sugar and acidity, giving a wine that is both luscious and very long-lived.

The ladder of categories, with a rung for each minimum must weight stipulated by law, is, unfortunately, not the same throughout the country. There are climatic variations within Germany, and grapes ripen more easily in, for example, Baden than they do in the Mosel. Grapes intended for Beerenauslese or Eiswein in the Mosel must have a minimum must weight of 110° Oechsle; in Baden the figure is 128°. A Riesling Auslese from the Nahe must be made from grapes of 85° Oechsle; in the Rheingau the same grape variety must attain a further 10° before it is entitled to be made into Auslese. Even with a single wine region, minimum must weights will vary from variety to variety. In Württemberg, for instance, a Riesling or Silvaner Spätlese must have at least 85° Oechsle, but a Kerner or Gewürztraminer Spätlese must have a minimum of 88°. (For a definition of Oechsle, see the Glossary.)

Be reassured. It is not necessary to memorise the must weights for each grape variety in each of eleven districts. The variations are not that great, except in the Mosel, where because of the climate the grapes attain lower must weights than elsewhere in Germany. In general, must weights for Spätlese vary from 85° to 92° Oechsle (76° to 83° in Mosel); for Auslese the range is 92° to 105° (83° to 110° in Mosel); for Beerenauslese and Eiswein grapes must have from 120° to 128° Oechsle (110° in Mosel), and TBA must have at least 150° to 154°. (See page 333 for a table giving the correspondence between Oechsle and potential alcohol.)

The system by which quality category is determined solely by must weight at harvest is relatively new, and only came into effect in 1971. While it seems an eminently sensible system that protects consumers from unscrupulous producers, the new law has had many critics, including some leading proprietors. Their argument is along the following lines. Before 1971, most wines at the sweet end of the scale were labelled Auslese. Labelling did not correspond to a measurable must weight but to the style of the wine. Some producers used colour-coded capsules or tags on their labels to indicate degrees of quality: thus 'Feinste Auslese' was a superior, and usually more luscious, grade to 'Feine Auslese'. Supreme quality was indicated by

price as much as by labelling. Such vaguely descriptive but subjective terms are no longer permitted under the 1971 wine law.
Consequently a Riesling Auslese from the Rheinpfalz could be made
from grapes picked at 92° Oechsle, or from grapes picked at 119°.
Those two lots are going to result in very different wines. Before 1971
a conscientious producer would have labelled the latter 'Feinste
Auslese', but this is no longer permitted.

Most of the best winemakers in Germany do not adhere strictly to
these regulations. Naturally they would not dream of labelling a
Spätlese as an Auslese, but they will often downgrade an Auslese to a
Spätlese, on the grounds that they would rather market a first-rate
Spätlese than a mediocre Auslese. Such scruples are of course
immensely beneficial to the consumer, which is why it is always
worth buying from producers of high repute – at least they have
reputations to defend. Where the regulations can work against
consumers is in the following situation. Let us imagine a Mosel
producer who picks some of his Riesling at 111° Oechsle. 'Good,' he
says, 'according to the book of rules, that's a Beerenauslese. I'll
bottle it as such and will charge twice as much as I do for the Auslese I
made from grapes picked at 100°.' This is entirely legal. The
conscientious producer will downgrade a wine he considers unworthy of Beerenauslese status; the winemaker who is greedy or
oblivious to reputation will not. Even worse, some producers will
blend their Spätlese and Auslese lots to give a wine with an average
Oechsle reading sufficient for the blend to be sold as Auslese.

This, however, is no more than a complicated way of saying that
some winemakers are more scrupulous than others. Personally, I
would rather have a strict labelling law, so that consumers are at least
aware of the boundaries. A term such as 'Feinste Auslese' was
entirely subjective and just as open to abuse as the present system.
Wine drinkers should be aware that Trockenbeerenauslese, for
example, is, or ought to be, a style of wine rather than a mathematical
calculation on the basis of must weight. There is a good deal of rather
nasty TBA on the market, and great attention must be paid not only
to the category on the label, but to the other variables of grape
variety, vineyard, and, perhaps most important of all, producer. It
must also be borne in mind that sweet wine is, or ought to be, a rarity
in Germany, since the climate is against it. The majority of German
sweet wines can only be made by the addition of Süssreserve, though

a number of winemakers refuse to follow this perfectly legal practice. The market, mostly an overseas one, for sweeter styles encouraged some unscrupulous wineries to doctor the wines or to purchase adulterated wines from Austria, though after the wine scandals of recent years one hopes that such practices are now a thing of the past. The wine scandal in Austria has been ruinous for that country's wine industry, and it has damaged the reputation of German sweet wines too. The consumption of sweeter styles has fallen in recent years by 30–35%. Some drinkers are wary of possible additives in the wine; others find the sugar content at odds with their diet programmes. Exports have also declined. Even though the general reputation of these wines may be in eclipse, they still represent, in their finest form, some of the great wines of the world, but it remains as important as it ever was to seek out trustworthy producers.

GRAPE VARIETIES

Another essential piece of information given on German wine labels is the grape variety from which the wine is made. This is extremely important, since while other Europeans often blend various grape varieties to make their wines, such blending is virtually unheard of in German QmP wines.

Riesling is the supreme grape of Germany, planted in 20% of all vineyards. In the Rheingau, it is virtually unchallenged, but elsewhere other grapes are grown in considerable quantities, and some are capable of making good sweet wines. Riesling is well suited to the northerly German climate, since it buds late, ripens late, and can withstand extremes of cold. It is usually immune from early frosts, and can benefit from prolonged autumn sunshine to ripen by late October. Yields are high and can attain 100 hl/ha without serious loss of quality, though the most conscientious growers prune for lower yields. Riesling does demand the best sites: the vines can adapt to most soils, but they require south-facing slopes that will be blessed with sunshine. Riesling is capable of making the most stylish white wine in the world. It may lack body and alcohol, but in a fine year it is wonderfully fruity, racy and aromatic on the nose, and incomparably elegant; because of its delicacy, it often reflects the nuances of soil and vineyard orientation, resulting in fascinating and complex wine.

High acidity can produce astringency in a mediocre year, but that same acidity will give Riesling superb length and breed in a good year. Other grape varieties can perform well in various parts of Germany (the Silvaner can reach great heights in Franken, for example), yet Riesling remains the greatest and most versatile German grape: it can be bracing and zesty in a young dryish wine, while rich and sumptuous and elegant in its sweeter versions. It also attracts botrytis, with spectacular results.

Müller-Thurgau was created in 1882 at the wine research institute at Geisenheim by a certain Dr Müller who came from Thurgau in Switzerland. It seems likely that the grape is a cross between Riesling and Silvaner, but no one is entirely certain, and it may well be a cross of two Riesling clones. Whereas Riesling demands good sites, Müller-Thurgau, by now the most widely planted grape in Germany, is much more easygoing, and thrives on the heavy soil of alluvial plains as well as on slopes too poor for Riesling. Although prone to rot, its very high yields have guaranteed its popularity, even in such Riesling strongholds as the Mosel. It has the additional advantage of ripening relatively early. A handy variety, but unfortunately it has low acidity and rarely makes interesting wine. In the Rheinhessen, it now accounts for 25% of plantations, compared to a trifling 5.7% of Riesling. Müller-Thurgau lacks qualities that would make it suitable for fine sweet wines.

The third grape variety in terms of quantity is *Silvaner*. Although virtually non-existent in the Mosel and Rheingau, it is widely planted in the Nahe, Rheinhessen, and Rheinpfalz, and thrives in Nierstein and Franken. In terms of its ripening, Silvaner is usually ready to be picked after Müller-Thurgau but before Riesling. Although a more interesting variety than Müller-Thurgau and capable of high acidity, it can produce characterless wines unless it is planted on very good sites. It is among the least aromatic of German grapes.

Rülander is occasionally capable of producing excellent sweet wines, though it is used more for this purpose in Austria than in Germany. This is the same variety as Pinot Gris or the Tokay d'Alsace. The grape has good yields and can be picked at roughly the same time as Silvaner. Rülander wines are more broad and ample than those from the other varieties mentioned above. The vine is very demanding, but if grown on deep fertile soils it can produce good yields of excellent grapes with high must weights. Bad fruit and poor vinification can result in flabby, heavy wine. The same is true of the other grape associated with Alsace, *Gewürztraminer*, which is also found in Germany, mostly in Baden and the Rheinpfalz, but in insignificant quantities. Usually known as Traminer, its character is milder and less spicy than that of its Alsatian cousin.

A number of cross-breeds best suited to the making of sweet wines are derived from Riesling. One of the best is *Scheurebe*, which was created in 1916 by mating Riesling with Silvaner. This variety gives high yields when planted on very good soils and ripens almost as late as Riesling. It makes a bigger wine than Riesling, with a pronounced bouquet and excellent acidity. Growers find it a moody and unpredictable variety, especially at must weights of below 100° Oechsle. Although little known outside Germany, wines made from Scheurebe are not to be despised. *Kerner* was developed by crossing Trollinger, a red grape variety, with Riesling. It too ripens late and usually attains must weights some 10–12° Oechsle higher than Riesling, though it does not have equally high acidity levels. Yields are higher than for Riesling, and Kerner's reliability, resistance to disease, adaptability to mediocre sites, and agreeable flavour have made it the fourth most popular variety in Germany. *Ehrenfelser*, first devised in 1929, is also a cross between Riesling and Silvaner. Like Scheurebe it ripens just before Riesling, but like Kerner it attains higher must weights than Riesling and comparable levels of acidity. Ehrenfelser also happens to be drought-resistant, though this is rarely an essential attribute in Germany. It has quite good acidity, and is one of the most refined of the new varieties. *Rieslaner* is another cross-breed between Riesling and Silvaner and is found in Franken, where this late-ripening variety can produce full-bodied stylish wine of high acidity and good quality. The presumptuously named *Optima* is the product of a cross between Müller-Thurgau and another cross-breed, that of Silvaner and Riesling. It ripens fairly early, and if picked late from very good sites can be suitable for sweet wines. It has been bred to attract botrytis, has reasonable acidity, but can be coarse in flavour. The same complex crossing also inspired another variety, *Bacchus*, which usefully thrives on mediocre sites and is widely planted in Rheinhessen. It ripens early but is best left on the vine for late picking, by which time it will have gained in must weight and bouquet. It can lack acidity. Analyses of must weights and acidity levels from the 1986 vintage illustrate the point. By 15

September, Riesling in the Rheinpfalz had an average must weight of 55° Oechsle and an acidity of 19.5 g/l, while in the same region Bacchus had by then attained a must weight of 68° Oechsle but had only 10.5 g/l acidity, which would decline as the grapes continued to ripen.

Kanzler is another variety that ripens early and can attain high must weights. A cross between Müller-Thurgau and Silvaner first invented in 1927, Kanzler is quite rich and full-bodied. It gives low yields and needs warm vineyards of good quality if it is to show at its best. Another grape of more obscure provenance, but quite widely planted in the Rheinpfalz and Rheinhessen, is the broad-flavoured *Huxelrebe*, a cross between Gutedel and Courtillier Musqué. This too is an early ripener and needs moderately good sites if it is to thrive. According to Bernd Philippi, an innovative winemaker from the Rheinpfalz, Huxelrebe must be pruned to assure low yields and only shows well if it has attained a must weight of at least 95° Oechsle (Auslese level). Low acidity prevents the powerfully flavoured *Siegerrebe* (Madeleine Angevine and Gewürztraminer) from ageing well, but in hot years it reaches staggering degrees of ripeness (326° Oechsle is the highest must weight ever recorded not just from Siegerrebe, but from any grape in Germany). *Ortega*, a variety obtained by crossing Müller-Thurgau and Siegerrebe, seems to have married the worst characteristics of both and is low in acidity. Although its partisans claim Ortega wines can age well, that has not been my experience.

Many of these otherwise obscure grape varieties are quite frequently encountered in Prädikatsweine. A bottle of Beerenauslese that seems to be a bargain may well be made from one of them. It need not be bad on that account, but it is important to be aware of the characteristics of these new varieties before spending a fair amount of money on a wine that may turn out to be short-lived and of disappointing quality.

VINEYARDS

The confusion mounts, for the greatest variable of all is the number of individual vineyards in Germany – 2597. There are, as has already been mentioned, eleven wine-growing districts (Anbaugebiete) in

Germany. These are divided into thirty-four Bereich, which in turn are divided into 1387 Gemeinde (villages or the equivalent of French communes). Some of these villages contain specific vineyards (Einzellagen), thus giving the total of 2597 sites divided among 100,000 growers. A larger unit is the Grosslage, which is a collective vineyard site, encompassing, for instance, all the Einzellagen of a clutch of villages. There are 152 Grosslagen in Germany. Some good quality wines may be bottled under the Grosslage name, but the top wines will almost always bear the name of an Einzellage (such as Erbacher Marcobrunn). Unfortunately there is considerable overlap between names; nor is it apparent from the label that, for instance, Forster Mariengarten is a Grosslage name, and that Forster Jesuitengarten is an Einzellage. You simply have to know the names. No wonder it is hard to sell German wines. On average, a Bereich is 3000 hectares in size, a Grosslage 600, and an Einzellage 38. The organisation is not dissimilar to that which prevails in Burgundy. Think of Côte d'Or as the Bereich, of Gevrey-Chambertin as a Gemeinde, and of Charmes-Chambertin as an Einzellage. As in Burgundy, most Einzellagen are divided between a number of proprietors, some of whom may only own a row or two of vines. The systems differ radically in one crucial respect: there is no *cru* system in Germany, and in the eyes of the law (if not the producer, the merchant, and the consumer), all vineyards are equal. Some good quality wines may be bottled under the Grosslage name (such as Erbacher Deutelsberg), but the vast majority of the best wines will bear the name of an Einzellage (such as Erbacher Marcobrunn). Thus while certain vineyards have very high reputations – such as Erbacher Marcobrunn in the Rheingau or Forster Jesuitengarten in the Rheinpfalz – it is equally important to be aware of who has grown and bottled the wine.

German wine law permits a degree of blending which goes unmentioned on the label. A grower may blend in 15% from another vintage or even another grape variety, and up to 25% of wine from another vineyard. The best producers will rarely take advantage of these lax regulations. Beerenauslesen and TBAs need contain no more than 50.1% of grapes from the vineyard specified on the label, and this too is regrettable. There is nothing wrong with judicious blending, but deceptive labelling should not be permitted.

Not all the eleven wine-growing districts are noted for their sweet wines, and we shall be paying little attention to Ahr, Mittelrhein, and the Hessische Bergstrasse. Some very good sweet wines are made in Baden and Wurttemberg, but in modest quantities. The principal regions in which such wines are made are Rheingau, Rheinpfalz, Rheinhessen, Nahe, Mosel, and Franken. On the whole I have not described the character of Einzellagen in specific detail. This is partly a question of space, but also one of taste and vintage. Some vineyards excel in hot years, others show particularly well in mediocre or wet years. Specialists in German wines do not always agree among themselves about the special qualities of specific vineyards, and I do not wish to enter into such controversies. Readers who desire more information about individual vineyards should consult Frank Schoonmaker's *The Wines of Germany* (revised by Peter Sichel) and S. F. Hallgarten's *German Wines*, and Hugh Johnson's *Atlas of German Wines*.

VINTAGE

Because Germany is a northern wine-growing area, individual vintages are of great importance. In years such as 1984, when the grapes did not ripen fully, 93% of all wine produced in Germany was either Tafelwein or QbA, leaving a mere 7% as QmP. It is commonly believed that such years are 'bad' years. This is true to the extent that there are few great sweet wines from such years, for obvious reasons. On the other hand, QbA wines can be extremely good. There are also extraordinary vintages such as 1976, when 87% of the production of all German wine was of QmP wine. Because the stylistic categories are determined by must weights, the system sorts itself out automatically. The best vintages of recent years for sweet were 1971, 1975, 1976, 1979, 1983, and 1985.

10

Rheingau: Eiswein

In the following chapters that deal with Germany, we shall look at some of the estates, many well known, others more obscure, that produce wines in the top categories. This list does not pretend to be definitive, for the range of wines of Auslese quality and above produced over the last, say, fifteen years in Germany is staggering, especially when you bear in mind the number of Einzellagen. Take, for instance, the famous Erbacher Marcobrunn, an Einzellage of only 5 hectares. Marcobrunn is parcelled out among many growers, including some of the greatest wineries in Germany. There must be dozens of different Auslesen and Beerenauslesen made since 1971 that are all entitled to be sold as Erbacher Marcobrunn. In an ideal world, I would have tasted them all and could then discuss with conviction the distinctive qualities of every Einzellage in Germany. This is hardly practical, and so I am adopting the admittedly less satisfactory approach of discussing the wines by describing those who make them, since with numerous growers sharing the same few hectares, individual styles of winemaking are extremely important.

The Rheingau is remarkably small in area, with fewer than 3000 hectares under vine, but the overall quality is among the highest in Germany. The south-facing slopes above the Rhein are sheltered to the north by the Taunus Mountains, and the region is warm but enlivened by humidity rising from the river.

SCHLOSS JOHANNISBERG

Schloss Johannisberg likes to date its existence to the early ninth century, when Charlemagne allegedly selected the hillside as ideal for vineyard plantation. In 1716 the estate was acquired by the Prince-Bishop of Fulda, who laid the foundations of the Rheingau's reputation by planting vast quantities of Riesling here. The vineyards are laid out on a steep slope predominantly of schist and quartzite overlooking the Rhein. This is the obvious estate with which to begin, because it was here that German botrytised wines were first 'discovered'. This is unlikely to be true, for wine had almost certainly been made from botrytised grapes long before the allegedly accidental discovery of their marvellous properties in 1775. The consent of the Bishop of Fulda had to be obtained before picking could commence, and that autumn, a few days before the vineyard managers proposed to start picking, a courier was dispatched, as was customary, to Fulda to seek authorisation. The journey was usually a four-day round trip, but for some reason, never explained, the courier's return was delayed for three weeks. In the meantime the grapes were attacked by botrytis, and in desperation the estate decided to pick the shrivelling berries before they succumbed entirely to the fungus. And so the first Auslese was made. So devoted are Schloss Johannisberg to this tale that they have even erected a statue to the happily tardy courier.

A corrective to such tales was provided for me by the oenologist and wine writer Bernhard Breuer, who reminded me that traditional German wine is dry. Many decades ago Auslese wines were accidents, brought about by exceptionally cold winters that impeded fermentation, by unsophisticated yeasts, and by arrested fermentations that affected barrels placed too close to the cellar doors. Auslese was a catch-all term for wines that were not fully fermented, and referred to a selection of barrels rather than to grapes that had been specifically selected in the vineyards. Nevertheless, there must be a grain of truth in the legends of Schloss Johannisberg, for in 1776 the cellarmaster here recorded his astonishment at the quality of the previous year's vintage.

What is indisputable is that Schloss Johannisberg has long made extremely good wine. In 1788 Thomas Jefferson reported that the estate's wines were 'the best made on the Rhine without comparison, and is about double the price of the oldest Hoch . . . What delicious liquor, Sir, it is!' The steep vineyards, planted solely with Riesling, are in themselves so marvellously situated that they constitute a single Ortsteil; the wines are labelled simply as Schloss Johannisberg without any additional identification of the locality. South-facing, and sloping down from a height of 180 metres to the valley floor, they are exposed to abundant sunshine and warmth; lemon trees flourish on the terraces overlooking the river, though I am reliably informed that the fruit is too bitter to be eaten. Schloss Johannisberg has become so closely identified with quintessential Riesling that some Californian wines made from authentic Riesling vines are still sold as Johannisberg Riesling. The estate was secularised in 1802 and changed hands frequently until 1816, when it was presented by Emperor Francis I of Austria to the Fürst von Metternich, whose descendants still occupy the handsome Schloss. Beneath the castle, which was reconstructed after an air raid of 1942 demolished it, are 900-year-old cellars that contain the Bibliotheca, a wonderful collection of old wines dating from 1748. Naturally these wines need to be recorked every twenty years or so. The oldest vintages are too rare for there to be enough 'extra' bottles that can be used to top up bottles with low ullages. To get round this problem, the cellarmaster raises the ullage in old bottles by dropping glass marbles into them. The principal cellars date from 1721 and enjoy a humidity level of 80%.

The vineyard is picked repeatedly to ensure that in appropriate years only botrytised grapes are selected. These are pressed in gentle pneumatic presses and the ensuing vinification is entirely traditional: fermentation as well as ageing takes place in wood. Most German casks are much larger than their French counterparts. Few winemakers wish to impart any woody tones or tannin to the delicate Riesling grape, and so they either use tanks made from a neutral material such as stainless steel or cement, or large 600- or 1200-litre casks. The sweet wines usually spend about six months in wood before being bottled, though Eiswein is usually bottled as early as possible, often just a few weeks after fermentation is completed.

The domestic market prefers dry to sweet wines, but Schloss Johannisberg continues to make most of its wines in a sweeter style to accommodate its large overseas clientele. A few decades ago Schloss Johannisberg would bottle a range of Riesling Spätlesen in appropriate years, and these lots were differentiated by colour-coded capsules. These wines were produced in such small quantities that some years ago it ceased to be feasible to continue such subtle differentiation. The only example I have tasted, a Weisslack (white label)

Spätlese from 1963, proved immensely delicate and only just past its best in 1986. The vintage was only moderately good, and Hugh Johnson, a couple of decades ago, recommended that 1963 wines be drunk by 1968. That a Spätlese from a modest vintage could still be extremely attractive twenty years later indicates how well these wines can age. Schloss Johannisberg does not make Auslese (or higher category) wines unless the grapes are botrytised. If the must weight is sufficient for Auslese but the grapes have not been attacked by botrytis, the wine will be downgraded to Spätlese. The last Auslese and Beerenauslese made here were in 1976. A 1976 Auslese, on the two occasions I tasted it, was a copybook example of the style. A brilliant light yellow-gold in colour, the honeyed botrytis nose was remarkably elegant and lively; on the palate the wine was still youthful and fresh though soft and spicy, opulent but impeccably balanced. A thousand bottles of Eiswein were made in 1985 from grapes picked at 145° Oechsle (almost TBA quality); after fermentation the wine had 138 g/l residual sugar.

German winemakers are very fond of statistical analyses, and not because of any bureaucratic obsession. Balance of sugar and acidity is crucial in German wines, since their alcohol level is so low at 8–9%. The 1976 Schloss Johannisberg Auslese is a case in point. Its 69 g/l residual sugar is equivalent to 3.8° Baumé, comparable to that of an average Sauternes. In the French wine, the sugar will be balanced by alcohol, for it is unlikely to have high acidity; in the Riesling, the sweetness is cut by the high acidity, and it is this that gives it such finesse. The acidity, rather than the alcohol, will also keep the wine fresh for a long time, and the 1976, though perfectly delicious now, will clearly keep for another decade or two. This is not the case with all 1976 QmP wines, many of which are rich and honeyed but lack acidity and will not keep as well as, say, the 1971 vintage.

A few years ago a celebrated tasting was held at the Schloss, and vintages of Ch d'Yquem were pitted against comparable vintages of Schloss Johannisberg. Because of differing climates, it would not have been fair to match each wine year for year, but sensible equivalencies were made. Judging from Michael Broadbent's tasting notes published in *Decanter*, Yquem tended to score higher marks, but that is not to say that the German wines showed poorly. If for the most part they failed to match the sheer sumptuousness and honeyed perfection of Yquem that is in part a reflection of their style. Only the richest Beerenauslesen and TBAs are truly comparable with an Yquem of a great vintage, and many of the German wines in the tasting were of Auslese quality. Bearing that in mind, these delicate old wines, one dating back to 1846, seemed to have held up very well indeed, confirming that even wines with relatively little alcohol can age marvellously.

SCHLOSS REINHARTSHAUSEN

This estate, run from a four-square yellow mansion close to the Rhein, also dates its existence back to the time of Charlemagne. It has been owned by the Prussian royal family since 1855, and the present proprietor is the great-grandson of the last Kaiser. By German standards it is an exceptionally large property, with 68 hectares, mostly in Erbach and Hattenheim. The Schloss also owns part of an island, Mariannenau, in the Rhein. There are two Einzellagen on the island, Erbacher Rheinhell and Hattenheimer Rheingarten, and the former is exclusively owned by Reinhartshausen, as is Erbacher Schlossberg. The island has its own microclimate (warm and damp) and humidity often provokes fungus attacks. Reinhartshausen also owns a substantial portion of the celebrated Erbacher Marcobrunn. Grapes with the highest must weights are usually picked from Marcobrunn and Schlossberg. Blossoming often begins seven to ten days earlier at Marcobrunn than in the other Erbach vineyards; thus the growing season is extended, encouraging the grapes to ripen thoroughly.

Grapes are pressed in pneumatic bladder presses. All fermentation takes place in tanks except for Beerenauslese and TBA, for which small casks are more practical. Only minute quantities of TBA can ever be made, and one year, having picked heavily botrytised grapes from a quarter hectare of Marcobrunn, the result was 150 litres of wine. These rich wines are also given much more cask-ageing than lighter, fresher wines. A 1976 Auslese remained in cask until 1985. Current cask capacity at Schloss Reinhartshausen is 350,000 litres, and there are a million bottles in stock, the oldest from 1863, stored at a constant temperature of 10 °C.

The 1976 Erbacher Marcobrunn Riesling Auslese illustrates perfectly the style of the best Rheingau wines. With their southern exposure and fairly rich soils, the wines have rather more weight and body than those from many other districts. (One must beware of generalisations about the German wine regions. While it remains true that, for example, the Rheinhessen is the source of a great deal of quaffable but essentially uninteresting wine, some of the best wines of Germany are also made there. And the greatest Rieslings of the Rheinpfalz can match anything produced in the Rheingau. And not every Rheingau wine is of outstanding quality. Yet all these wines are quite distinct from the leaner, lighter, racier wines of the Mosel on the one hand, and the broader, more alcoholic wines of Franken and Baden on the other.) This delicious Auslese is quite powerful and weighty, a splendid mouthful, yet there is nothing remotely heavy or cloying about it because the fairly high residual sugar (62 g/l) is balanced by acidity (7.2 g/l). The result is a wine that is fairly sweet, to be sure, but also rounded and stylish and of excellent length. With its bright medium yellow-gold colour it is a joy to look at, and the nose, with its heady ripe botrytis tones, is every bit as elegant as the taste.

The same vineyard produced a small quantity of precious TBA in that same year, 1976. It defies description. The difficulty with discussing TBAs is that their qualities do not make them sound very appetising. My tasting notes record that the wine actually made my teeth ache, albeit briefly, such was the concentration of sugar and fruit. The texture was positively syrupy, more dense than any Sauternes could ever be, yet – the crucial factor – the acidity was lively. Such a wine is in its infancy. It needs a quarter century of bottle-age before it can be considered drinkable. It is interesting to compare its components with those of the Auslese mentioned above, made from the same vineyard. The Auslese was picked at 110° Oechsle, the TBA at 180° (the minimum requirement for TBA is 150°). 110° Oechsle is equivalent to just over 15% potential alcohol; 150° would be equivalent to 21.5%; and 180° is a mind-boggling 26%. The Auslese had 64 g/l residual sugar, the TBA 154.

Even better than the 1976 Marcobrunn TBA, fabulous though that wine is, is the 1971 Erbacher Schlossberg Rülander TBA, which shows just how splendid certain other grape varieties can be in carefully chosen locations. This magnificent wine is more evolved than the 1976, but since its acidity is even higher than the Riesling (8.9 g/l as compared to 7.4), it should last almost as well. While the Riesling was bright medium-gold in colour, the Rülander was deep copper-brown, and there was a trace of oxidation on the nose. This oxidation was not a sign of decay, but probably set in while the fermentation was heaving itself into action, always a slow process with musts high in sugar. The palate made it abundantly clear that this wine would keep almost indefinitely. It was, of course, extremely sweet, and the concentration incredible. On the nose there had been aromas of tobacco and cooked fruits, and these flavours, and figs too, were also present on the palate. Every taster finds something different in these wines, so rich and complex and multi-layered are they. The length was extraordinary; a mere sip, and one could still taste the wine minutes later. This is the fascination of TBAs: they are the essence of everything that this miraculous fruit, the grape, can do, like diamonds so finely cut that they show the light in innumerable ways. Obviously they are not wines for swigging; they are to be savoured in small quantities as a feast for the senses.

Schloss Reinhartshausen made a superb Eiswein in 1984, also from the Schlossberg, but this wine, together with other Eisweine will be discussed in a separate section.

WEINGUT FREIHERR ZU KNYPHAUSEN

Another noble property is situated a few miles away near Eltville, not far from the banks of the Rhein. The estate was founded in 1141 by Cistercian monks, and in 1818 it was sold to the Knyphausen family. The current owner is Baron Gerko zu Knyphausen, who lives in a lovely early eighteenth-century mansion not far from the cellars. Most of the vineyards are in Erbach, but the estate also owns portions within Hattenheim, Kiedrich, Eltville, and Rauenthal. The property consists of 16 hectares in all, and, as at Schloss Reinhartshausen, 80% is planted with Riesling. The winery itself is modern, and most fermentation and ageing takes place in stainless steel, though smaller casks are used for the richest wines. The cellarmaster, Herr Schön, says that in 1985 they selected a few casks to be given minimal treatments. At Knyphausen it is customary to use a centrifuge, but the wine in these casks will be cleared of its lees and clarified by racking alone. I have the impression that Herr Schön does not think too much of the idea, and would rather continue to rely on efficient technology to take care of his wines.

I tasted a magnificent Eiswein at the cellars but was less impressed by a 1976 TBA from Erbacher Steinmorgen. It was made from the Ehrenfelser grape, one of the cross-breeds discussed in the previous chapter. One of the strengths of Ehrenfelser is that it is not only capable of attaining extremely high must weights (this TBA was picked at 177° Oechsle) but good acidity too (this wine has 8.0 g/l). The wine was gorgeous to look at, a deep copper-gold, and had a sumptuous cooked fruit nose of apricots and peaches. On the palate it was more disappointing: immensely sweet, of course, with an astonishing 248 g/l residual sugar (equivalent to almost 14° Baumé!), but it also tasted somewhat oily and stewed. With such high quantities of residual sugar it is very difficult for a TBA to finish clean, but the function of high acidity, apart from conserving the wine, is to prevent it from being cloying and sticky. This TBA did not quite succeed. At such high must weights the grape loses its varietal character and becomes little more than a vehicle for sugar and acidity and extract, and all these constituents, not to mention the mineral qualities extracted from the soil, need to be in perfect balance. This particular bottle seemed a near miss.

WEINGUT
FREIHERR ZU KNYPHAUSEN

KLOSTERHOF DRAIS · ELTVILLE/RHEINGAU

RHEINGAU
ERZEUGERABFÜLLUNG

1983er Erbacher Steinmorgen
Riesling — Eiswein —

33037 01384
AMTL. PRÜFUNGSNR.   Qualitätswein mit Prädikat

375 ml
W.-DEUTSCHLAND

VERITAS VINCIT

SCHLOSS VOLLRADS

This lovely castle, on the slopes a mile behind the village of Oestrich-Winkel, has for centuries been in the hands of the Greiffenclau family, and the present owner is Erwein Graf Matuschka-Greiffenclau. As the Graf is the leader of the Verband Deutscher Prädikats und Qualitätsweingüter, a growers association that includes almost all the top estates of Germany, he is a man of great influence. He has been in the forefront of the trend away from sweeter styles to Halbtrocken and Trocken wines more suitable for consumption with a meal. Nevertheless, the vineyards, planted with 98% Riesling, have produced some splendid sweet wines in the past.

The complex of cellars is grouped around a spacious courtyard, and the oldest structure at the Schloss is the fourteenth-century tower. The seventeenth century residential block is somewhat gloomy, its interior walls lined with antique Spanish leather. Upstairs in the exceedingly grand two-storey drawing room, furnished with antiques, tastings of the estate's wines take place. The 47 hectares of vineyards that adjoin the Schloss constitute an Ortsteil, and thus, like Schloss Johannisberg, Vollrads is entitled to bottle its wines under the property name alone. In 1979 Graf Matuschka leased the Fürst Löwenstein estate, a couple of miles away at Hallgarten. These wines have a different style, rather plumper and richer in bouquet than the more racy and spicy Vollrads wines. Fining often takes place before fermentation, which is mostly carried out in tanks, though the best wines are aged in wood. More than most Rheingau Rieslings, the wines of Schloss Vollrads need to be well aged before they show at their best.

The last wines of Auslese quality at Vollrads were made in 1976. Spätlese was made in 1979 and 1983, but no higher grades. The winemaker, Georg Senft, is quite pleased with the 1976. Because this very ripe vintage produced wines of relatively low acidity, it was feared that they would be less long-lived than vintages such as 1971. Yet Herr Senft has discerned little change in the wines during the last five years. They seem stable, and he thinks they will remain on this plateau for another decade, and then begin a slow decline. In 1976 Schloss Vollrads made two qualities of Auslese, differentiated by their capsules. Graf Matuschka, and other winemakers, are particularly keen on this capsule system, but I find it maddening, especially since each winery has its own variations to the system. At Schloss Vollrads, pink denotes Spätlese, but you must also memorise that a silver band through the pink capsule means the wine is dry, while a gold band through the pink signifies sweetness. There are, in appropriate years, two qualities of Auslese, denoted by a plain white capsule and by a white and gold capsule. I have tasted the Weissgold, from grapes picked at 105° Oechsle; the wine had 64 g/l residual sugar balanced by almost 10 g/l acidity. Botrytis was more apparent on the nose than on the palate, but the wine was both elegant and rounded, a beautifully balanced bottle with less sheer richness than I had anticipated from the nose.

Greater richness, as one would expect, was present in the Fürst Löwenstein wines. Two Beerenauslesen, one from 1976 and the other from 1971, showed up the considerable difference between these two excellent vintages. The 1976 (from grapes picked at 132° Oechsle, and with 109 g/l residual sugar) showed botrytis quite clearly on the nose. On the palate it was rich and intense, very ripe in flavour, but the low acidity (6.8 g/l) was detectable; the wine simply lacked the breed of the Vollrads wine. On the other hand the 1971 Beerenauslese was the essence of refinement, sweet and spicy and elegant on the nose, and richly delicious in the mouth, though the higher acidity gave the wine a lovely leanness and length on the finish. This is an example of Rheingau at its classiest. The 1976 Schloss Vollrads TBA was stupendous. The colour was one of the loveliest deep yellow-golds I have ever seen in a wine, and on the nose the aromas were of ripe peaches, tobacco, and heady botrytis. In the mouth the wine was extremely concentrated and rich, almost syrupy in texture, yet remarkably fresh. The genius of great TBA is that one does not, when sipping it, feel one is chewing on a mouthful of treacle. Freshness and vigour as well as richness and opulence are the hallmarks of first-rate TBA, and this wine had these qualities in abundance. This is a very great wine indeed. I can only hope that Schloss Vollrads will not abandon altogether this style of winemaking. Most properties that make Beerenauslesen and TBAs do so as much for prestige as for profit. Although the wines are great rarities marketed at a very high price, they are produced in such small quantities and require such devoted efforts in vineyard and winery, that many producers find them more trouble than they are worth. Those who have been privileged to taste these triumphs of the winemaker's art can only hope that estates such as Vollrads that have made some of the greatest examples in the past will continue to do so in the future, despite the vogue, encouraged by its proprietor, for drier wines.

FREIHERRLICH LANGWERTH VON SIMMERN'SCHES RENTAMT

This exceptionally fine estate has always prided itself on the costliness of its wines. Even in the sixteenth century they cost a third as much again as most other Rheingau wines. The mansion and cellars are at Eltville, grouped around a most picturesque courtyard. The principal vineyards are in Eltville, Erbach, Hattenheim, and Kiedrich, amounting to 40 hectares in all. 90% of the wines are Riesling. Average yields are about 60 hl/ha – low for Germany. According to the administrator, Helmuth Kranich, Langwerth von Simmern wines strive for longevity and good balance. Their approach is fairly conservative. Fermentation takes place in tanks, which are easier to maintain and which give more uniform results than cask fermentation. After the first racking, the wine is clarified and then aged in 1200-litre casks for between three and twenty-four months. Beerenauslese and Eiswein are still fermented in cask, not out of deliberate choice, but simply because the winery does not have small enough tanks to ferment such very limited lots of wine. I was struck by the youthfulness of the 1971 Eltviller Sonnenberg Riesling Beerenauslese. Botrytis was more evident on the nose than it had been in the case of the 1971 Fürst Löwenstein Beerenauslese. On the palate the flavour was fruity and ripe, but the acidity was very marked; even after fifteen years the wine did not seem quite knit together, and I imagine this bottle has a few more decades of life ahead of it. A 1976 Rauenthaler Baiken Riesling Auslese seemed close to perfection after ten years, ripe and concentrated, and with good acidity and length. The Eiswein from Langwerth von Simmern will be discussed later in this chapter.

There are many other properties that have made outstanding sweet wines in the Rheingau, but there is no room to discuss them all. The Domdechant Werner'sches Weingut in Hochheim is famous for a record-breaking TBA produced in 1951. The grapes were picked at

247° Oechsle, almost 100° more than the legal minimum. Eiswein and Beerenauslese were made here in 1983.

Schloss Schönborn at Hattenheim has also made some notable sweet wines in the past, though its reputation is less exalted than it once was. The Weingut Richter-Boltendahl produced a whole spate of Beerenauslesen and Eisweine in 1976, a few of which are still available. Schloss Groenesteyn is also highly regarded. The large firm of Deinhard have made a number of exquisite Auslesen and Beerenauslesen from their Oestrich vineyards.

The state wine domaine at Eltville has been the source of many remarkable sweet wines, and because the director, Dr Hans Ambrosi, is one of the pioneers of Eiswein, I shall devote much of the next section to this remarkable estate and its very distinctive wines.

EISWEIN

For many decades the Staatsweingut (state winery) at Eltville has been among the leading estates of the Rheingau; with 189 hectares of vineyards, it is also the largest wine estate in Germany. The sheer range of the wines made here is astonishing. In addition to a full gamut of Rieslings from vineyards at Eltville, Rüdesheim, Hattenheim, Rauenthal, and Hochheim, there is the superlative 32-hectare Ortsteil of Steinberg. The winery's showcase is the remarkable Cistercian monastery of Kloster Eberbach, to which many of the vineyards once belonged. In addition to the local vineyards there are red Spätburgunders from Assmanshausen, and wines from the Hessische Bergstrasse. From these varied sources the winery produces about a million litres each year, of which a third are dry wines and 10% red. Yields vary from 50 to 90 hl/ha, depending on the vintage. So many different lots are there in the tanks at Eltville that the management has installed a computer to keep track of them all. As one would expect here, the winemaking is very sophisticated. Dr Hans Ambrosi, the director here since 1966 and a man of firm opinions and sufficient willpower to combat the bureaucrats when necessary, favours reductive methods that minimise oxidation. The grapes are pressed rapidly and very few of the wines ever see wood, with the exception of some Spätlesen and Auslesen that spend six to twelve months in old casks. The public, according to Dr Ambrosi, wants fruit, freshness, and vigour. They certainly get it. The wine is usually bottled by May, but not sold immediately, and a vast warehouse stocks a million bottles on pallets of awesome height.

Romanian-born Hans Ambrosi began to develop techniques for making ice wine when he was working in South Africa. Of course ice wines have been made for decades – notably in 1875, 1880, 1890, 1902, 1908, 1912, 1949, 1950, 1961, and 1962 – but usually as an instantaneous exploitation of a freak frost. Very cold weather concentrates both sugar and acidity in the grape; the water content turns to ice; when the frozen grapes are pressed, the chips of ice fall away, leaving the intense juice. Dr Ambrosi set out to make Eiswein on a routine basis. In South Africa he was permitted to chill the grapes artificially, but this is not allowed in Germany, where the grapes must be picked frozen on the vine. One crucial difference between Eiswein and the other sweet German styles is that botrytis (*Edelfäule*) is positively unwelcome. The grapes must be entirely healthy if they are to be suitable for Eiswein.

A major difficulty in making these wines is that the grapes have to be left on the vine until very late in the season. Sometimes a sharp frost in November will oblige, but more usually the growers must wait until late December or January. Dr Ambrosi selects certain parcels of vines close to the valley floor, for it is here that frost is more likely to occur. A brief frosty spell will not suffice; under German law the temperature must drop to −8 °C, and remain that low for six to eight hours, which usually means that picking cannot begin until dawn. It is not easy to keep your grapes healthy on the vine for so many months. Storms can damage them, especially once the foliage has begun to drop off; birds feed off them; and there is always the danger of rot. Hans Ambrosi has devised a tube of plastic sheeting that covers only the grapes and is stapled to the rootstock. These sheets can only be applied after the foliage has dropped off, and they form a kind of tunnel that protects the fruit from the hazards mentioned above. The stapling is sufficiently loose to ensure that air can circulate beneath the plastic, but sufficiently tight to keep birds and other pests out. In order to provide enough room for what Dr Ambrosi refers to as his plastic 'hot pants', the grapes must be trained not to grow too close to the ground. As a result of these methods, he has only failed to make Eiswein once in twenty years (1968). Further problems can occur after the grapes have been pressed, for the must is so cold that it is hard to get fermentation going, even with the use of special yeasts.

German growers pride themselves on the ripeness of the grapes they use to make their sweet wines. The higher the Oechsle level, the greater the challenge to make a balanced wine, and the higher the prices that can be asked for the wine, especially if it is made from Riesling. In Dr Ambrosi's view, however, the ripest years are not the best for Eiswein. In years when the grapes are ripening rapidly, such as 1976 or 1983, he prefers to concentrate his efforts on Auslese and Beerenauslese, wines benefitting from botrytised grapes. Since 1982, the law requires that the grapes must have the same must weight as for Beerenauslese (125° Oechsle in the Rheingau), and this is what Dr Ambrosi aims for when picking his frozen grapes. Before 1982 it was possible to make Auslese Eiswein, but with insufficient sugar the wine could easily be unbalanced by its high acidity. The grapes will attain very high sugar levels as a result of being frozen, so Dr Ambrosi sees no point in going out of his way to pick only ultra-ripe grapes. Moreover, he cites studies by oenologists at Karlsruhe that apparently establish that the aromatic qualities of the wine diminish as the grapes ripen. In poor years, such as 1982 and 1984, Dr Ambrosi made Eisweine that he especially commends for their aromatic distinction. In mediocre years such as 1977, when Dr Ambrosi's pickers harvested frozen grapes at a modest 106° Oechsle, he adjusted the acidity to compensate for the relatively low level of residual sugar. Dr Ambrosi is perhaps most celebrated for a Hochheimer Domdechaney harvested on 6 January 1971 at −10 °C; the must weight was a dazzling 194° Oechsle, and the acidity an equally astonishing 16.2 g/l.

Eiswein tastes entirely different from Beerenauslese or TBA, despite comparable must weights. There is, of course, no trace of botrytis, but the major difference is the extraordinary acidity of the wine, which is often higher than 12 g/l (7 to 10 would normally be considered excellent for Riesling). This high acidity guarantees the wines a very long life – they should theoretically be capable of lasting a century – but it also, in my experience, makes many of the wines quite undrinkable in their youth, a youth that can last for decades. Dr Ambrosi does not agree, and maintains that his Eisweine can be drunk immediately. Perhaps so, but not with a great deal of pleasure. Eiswein is also extremely expensive, often more expensive than

Beerenauslese, but Dr Ambrosi says the State Domaine makes sufficient profits from the marketing of its Eiswein to pay for the hiring of no fewer than 300 pickers at harvesting time.

The quality of the winemaking at the Staatsweingut is indisputable. The 1983 Rauenthaler Baiken Riesling Eiswein (available at time of writing for 180 DM per bottle) is an excellent example of the style. Because of the reductive vinification, the colour is very pale, and the wine's acidity shows in its lively green-apple nose. On the palate, the fruit has enormous intensity, and the flavour of young apples is as pronounced as it was on the nose; being a young wine, the acidity is highly aggressive. As Eiswein it is a model of its kind, though still somewhat skeletal, and a few years in bottle will give more flesh to the wine. An interesting contrast is provided by the 1979 Heppenheimer Centgericht Riesling Eiswein, made from grapes grown in the unfashionable Hessische Bergstrasse to the south. This wine, which is half the price of the Rauenthaler, has all the expected Eiswein characteristics, but is much more broad; although less aggressive than the younger wine, it also lacks raciness. These relatively youthful Eisweine were showing rather better than the admittedly infantile 1985 Rüdesheimer Berg Rottland Riesling Beerenauslese. This wine seemed very closed and undeveloped in colour and bouquet, although fresh and spicy on the palate as well as

intensely sweet; what it lacked at this stage was complexity. Two Riesling Auslesen, one a 1976 Rüdesheimer Berg Rottland, the other a 1983 Hochheimer Domdechaney, were very different. The former showed botrytis on the nose, and while ripe and elegant on the palate, also seemed rather too delicate and lacking in definition and weight. It should be noted that in 1976 an astonishing 47% of all the wine made here was of Auslese standard or higher. The 1983, though without any discernible botrytis on the nose, also seemed fairly light but had a better structure and should have a good future.

Not all winemakers share Dr Ambrosi's enthusiasm for Eiswein. Herr Hupfeld, who owns the famous Königin Victoria Berg vineyard in Hochheim, was encouraged by his son Wolfram, also a winemaker, to try his hand at Eiswein. He forked out 500 DM for plastic sheets with which to make 'hot pants' and stapled them according to the Ambrosi methods. A storm whipped up one night and blew the whole lot away. He applied another set of hot pants. No storms this time around, but no frost either. Pheasants picked holes in the plastic, undermining its efficacy. By February there was still no frost and the holes were by now large enough to admit small birds that flew in and nibbled at the grapes. Herr Hupfeld gave up, claiming that making Eiswein is not a practical proposition for small estates that cannot charge high prices or absorb the costs of harvesting and production.

Other winemakers are less gloomy. Stefan Ress of the excellent Weingut Balthasar Ress of Hattenheim, made his first Eiswein on 1 January 1986. He had intended to make such a wine if the weather obliged, and had followed Dr Ambrosi's prescription by wrapping the grapes in plastic sheets. That night the temperature dropped to −11 °C. In the small hours twenty pickers, most of them friends rather than employees, rushed into the Hattenheimer Schützenhaus vineyard and spent the next three hours picking frozen grapes. After a harvest that lasted twenty-four hours, the result was 700 litres of Eiswein. The must weight measured 130° Oechsle, and yielded a wine with 10.4 g/l acidity, 10% alcohol, and 85 g/l residual sugar. The wine was bottled very young, in early March. Stefan Ress recommends opening the wine at the end of this century. In its extreme youth, it tasted like typical young Eiswein, its sweetness countered by the ferocious bite of its green-apple acidity.

Langwerth von Simmern made an Eiswein in 1978 from their Hattenheimer Nussbrunnen vineyard. The grapes were picked on 6 December and were of Beerenauslese quality. It is a striking wine, with a bracing pineapple nose, oddly mingling with a mushroom aroma; on the palate, even after seven years in bottle the acidity was so pungent it made my eyes water. On the other hand there was discernible richness and vigour in the wine, and after another twenty years or so it should make an admirable bottle. Another infant Eiswein was made in 1984 by Schloss Reinhartshausen from Erbacher Schlossberg. This wine is actually of TBA quality, since the Riesling grapes were picked at 150° Oechsle; it has 143 g/l residual sugar and 12.5 g/l acidity. The nose was somewhat curious, strangely musty, and in the mouth it was intense and lively and appley, but bony; the admirable structure of the wine was in evidence, but not the personality and character it will undoubtedly develop – in time. As fine as any Eiswein I have tasted is the 1979 Erbacher Steinmorgen Riesling from Knyphausen. Since the grapes were picked at 150° Oechsle, and 180 g/l of residual sugar remains, the wine had admirable richness as well as teeth-tingling acidity. The nose was gorgeous, like ripe pineapples, and the elegance and concentration on the palate were stunning. At 200 DM a bottle it should be good.

These wines are also made in other regions of Germany. From the Rheinpfalz comes an outstanding bottle made by Weingut Reichsrat von Buhl from the superlative Forster Jesuitengarten vineyard. Picked at 132° Oechsle, the wine retains 160 g/l residual sugar and has astonishingly high acidity at 18.0 g/l. This is beautifully constructed wine, with an aroma of fresh apples and grapes, less 'green' than many Eisweine, but showing its extreme youth on the palate: the acidity is positively searing, but lurking behind it is masses of lively fruit. When it all knits together it should be superb. Weingut Dr Bürklin-Wolf has produced a clutch of Eisweine in recent years. Their Wachenheimer Gerümpel vineyard provided frozen Riesling grapes in 1983 and 1985, though the latter were actually picked on 1 January 1986. The 1985 wine was picked at 135° Oechsle and has 109 g/l residual sugar, while the 1983 was picked at an astonishing 170° Oechsle, and has 11.4 g/l acidity (compared to 7.7 in 1985). Both wines have the intense green-apple piquancy of Eiswein, but the 1983 is far more concentrated and will in time be magnificent. It is copybook Eiswein, free from any faults, but completely unapproachable except as a tasting exercise. The other 1985 Eiswein from Bürklin-Wolf is a Scheurebe from Forster Mariengarten. This too was picked on 1 January 1986; and the grapes registered 155° Oechsle and left 215 g/l residual sugar in the finished wine. The acidity, however, is rather low at 7.2 g/l, allowing the intense sweetness and concentration of the wine to show through; consequently the Scheurebe tastes richer and broader and arguably more accessible than the two Rieslings.

That very innovative winemaker Bernd Philippi of Weingut Koehler-Ruprecht in Kallstadt in the Rheinpfalz has recently made two strongly contrasting Eisweine. Because he needs healthy grapes for Eiswein, he cannot make the wine very often. Should the grapes be sound, he will net them rather than use plastic sheeting. Philippi used to employ someone to sit with a gun to keep the birds off, but not surprisingly he found that nets were cheaper. Philippi maintains that if frost comes too late, the grapes lose acidity and are less suitable for Eiswein. In fact, he refuses to make Eiswein unless the frost attacks the grapes before 20 November. Dr Ambrosi considers such scruples unnecessary, since the ripe grapes lose acidity so slowly (about 1 g/l per month) that a delay in harvesting will make very little practical difference. Philippi's 1978 Kallstadter Steinacker Riesling TBA Eiswein is so high in acidity (14.7 g/l) that the 132 g/l residual sugar seemed scarcely noticeable. Even after eight years this wine

rcmaincd unapproachablc. Hcrr Philippi is proud of his red Eiswein, a 1983 Kallstadter Feuerberg Spätburgunder, picked at 178° Oechsle; the final wine, all 200 litres of it, has 11% alcohol and, for Philippi, quite high residual sugar at 173 g/l. In colour the wine is pale garnet, and there are light delicate strawberry aromas on the nose. This same strawberry character is present on the palate, and the wine is sufficiently sweet and viscous to stand up to the acidity (10.1 g/l). If this rounded and vigorous wine has a fault, it is that it is almost too pretty, and thus quite unlike Philippi's usual stern style. Another red Eiswein, from Trollinger grapes, has been made by Weingut Bezner-Fischer in Württemberg, but I have not tasted it. Nor have I tasted Dr Ambrosi's 1978 Spätburgunder Eiswein.

In Essingen, in the less prestigious Südliche Weinstrasse region of the Rheinpfalz, Weingut Eugen Volz has produced a number of excellent Eisweine in recent years. The most sensational was the 1983 Essinger Osterberg, made from Scheurebe picked at 186° Oechsle. With 12 g/l acidity the wine tastes extremely fresh, balancing the fat chewy sweetness on the palate.

One of the finest estates in the Nahe, the State Domaine, has recently made a number of Riesling Eisweine, though it does not go out of its way to prepare for Eiswein harvests. This very professional

winery does not bother with plastic sheeting, but trusts to luck. The 1983 Schlossböckelheimer Kupfergrube, harvested at 151° Oechsle, seems at present relatively straightforward, as does the 1985 Niederhauser Herrmannsberg. The structure of both wines is impeccable, but in this, their infancy, they seem one-dimensional. Doubtless they will grow more complex with time. On the other hand, the 1983 Niederhauser Hermannsberg is already an extraordinary wine. The grapes were picked at 180° Oechsle, and the acidity is 16.0 g/l. Entirely closed on the nose, the wine is packed with a fantastic concentration of flavour, great fruit and vigour. Even now, it has all the qualities which identify it as a great bottle. The director of the State Domaine, Dr Werner Hofäcker, says immodestly that he considers this the greatest Eiswein ever made in the Nahe, and I am quite prepared to believe him. Only 250 bottles were made, and Dr Hofäcker has priced the wine accordingly at 286 DM.

Helmuth Dönnhoff of the nearby village of Oberhausen also does not bother with plastic sheeting, though he does try to make Eiswein whenever possible. He disagrees with Dr Ambrosi's assertion that unripe grapes are perfectly suitable for Eiswein. He used unripe grapes in 1977 and did not like the result, simply because the acidity

was excessive. His 1983 Oberhäuser Brücke Riesling, harvested on 15 November at 168° Oechsle, was closed on the nose but has sumptuous pineapple fruitiness matched by intense acidity (16.0 g/l). It seemed very similar in style to the Niederhäuser Eiswein. Among other Nahe winemakers who have produced impressive Eisweine in recent years are Weingut August E. Anheuser, whose 1985 Kreuznacher Narrenknappe Riesling is delicious and already shows real class; Weingut Paul Anheuser, also of Bad Kreuznach; Weingut Zehnthof of Guldental, whose 1983 Apostelberg Riesling is vigorous and rich; and Schlossgut Diel of Burg Layen, who made a Scheurebe from their Dorsheimer Klosterpfad vineyard in 1983, a rich acidic wine of considerable power but less complexity than Riesling would offer.

Eisweine are not new, but they are very much in vogue. Dr Ambrosi points out that his Eisweine fetch higher prices at auction than his Beerenauslesen, and argues that all he is doing is responding to a public demand for these rarities. Fair enough, but I think the public's taste is questionable in this instance. There is no doubt that many of these Eisweine are great wines. But are they enjoyable wines? Even Eisweine with some bottle age are, in my view, unapproachable. It is as though the winemakers were vying with one another to produce the most statistically extraordinary wine. Schloss Reinhartshausen can pitch their Eiswein's 12.5 g/l acidity against

RHEIN PFALZ

Weingut Dr.Bürklin-Wolf

WACHENHEIM/WEINSTRASSE

Forster Kirchenstück
Riesling Trockenbeerenauslese

Erzeugerabfüllung   A. P. Nr. 5 142 043 42 77

QUALITÄTSWEIN MIT PRÄDIKAT

Ress's more modest 10.4, while Knyphausen can rout both contenders with his 14.0. In the Mosel we shall encounter other Eisweine of even higher acidity, yet to me it seems somewhat perverse to make wines that, while possibly immortal, are unlikely to give much satisfaction until after their makers are dead. However magnificent their intensity of flavour, many Eisweine strike me as over-aggressive and one-dimensional, lacking the extraordinary complexity of flavour found on a reasonably mature Beerenauslese, not to mention a TBA. This is an argument we shall find ourselves resuming when we look at the Mosel region.

11

Rheinpfalz, Rheinhessen, Nahe

RHEINPFALZ

This large wine-growing region of 23,000 hectares shows great variations in quality. The lower part, the Südliche Weinstrasse, mostly produces inexpensive wines of moderate rather than outstanding quality, but the upper part, the Mittelhaardt, is the source of some of the greatest wines of Germany. The Mittelhaardt is sheltered by the Haardt mountains, the German extension of the Vosges mountains that also provide the Alsace with an exceptionally warm dry climate. In the summer, fig and lemon and almond trees flourish here. From Ruppertsberg to the south, through Deidesheim, Forst, Wachenheim, Bad Dürkheim, and Ungstein to Kallstadt in the north, lies a ribbon of vineyards, mostly just west of the road that runs up the valley, that produce wine of unforgettable stylishness. There are certainly other corners of the Rheinpfalz that produce excellent wines, but not with the assurance and regularity of this brief string of villages. The climate (the warmest and driest in Germany) and the preponderance of Riesling result in sweet wines that equal the richness and power of the best Rheingau wines, and the basalt slopes around Forst are renowned for the sheer ripeness of the grapes that grow there. Yet fashion has swung against such wines. Indeed, some of the finest wineries, such as Weingut Acham-Magin in Forst, produce nothing but dry wines. Not even Halbtrocken. If grapes of high must weights are picked, then they are through-fermented to give Spätlese or Auslese Trocken, wines rich in flavour and high in alcohol. These wines may occasionally have as much as 6 g/l residual sugar but, against a background of high alcohol and acidity, such minimal sweetness is hardly discernible. At the very distinguished Weingut Basserman-Jordan at Deidesheim, no Beerenauslese has been made since 1976 and the current wine list does not offer a single Auslese.

For a large winery such as Weingut Reichsrat von Buhl, Beerenauslese and TBA are essentially a distraction. 70% of their wines are Trocken or Halbtrocken, in tune with the domestic market. For von Buhl it is simply more trouble than it is worth for the winemaker, Udo Loos, to expend his efforts on any wine in quantities of less than 1000 litres, and only in rare years such as 1976 will a number of vineyards each produce a sufficient number of botrytised grapes. In 1979 von Buhl only produced 370 litres of Beerenauslese, and it is unlikely that the estate will continue to make such small quantities of very sweet wine. Von Buhl aim for wines of freshness and vigour, and acidity is as important as fruit; hence they tend to pick early, in order to retain high acidity, rather than leave the grapes on the vine. The grapes, many of which come from old vines, are pressed in pneumatic presses, and fermentation and ageing take place in stainless steel tanks; the wine is filtered once fermentation ceases. An Eiswein was made in 1983 (see the preceding chapter), when an early frost attacked healthy grapes, and it seemed sensible to exploit the opportunity. Eiswein is bottled young but given two years' bottle age before being released.

Von Buhl have made some delicious Gewürztraminer Auslesen. The 1983 Forster Pechstein had remarkable freshness for Gewürztraminer, which can be broad and even clumsy on the palate. The 1976 Ruppertsberger Reiterpfad seemed almost too developed, a lovely yellow-gold in colour and with a ravishing bouquet of botrytised Gewürztraminer, ample yet delicate; but on the palate it was soft and lacking in concentration, almost lazy. An older Auslese from this estate, a 1946 Deidesheimer Leinhöhle, showed how much better Riesling can last. Bright full gold in colour, it was very delicate, almost high-strung, on the nose; on the palate it was still lively, with good extract and acidity and elegance.

Another large Rheinpfalz estate, of 110 hectares, belongs to Weingut Dr Bürklin-Wolf at Wachenheim. 70% of the grapes planted are Riesling, and the vinification is traditional, with some ageing in 1200- and 2400-litre casks. Yields for Riesling at 80–90 hl/ha are fairly high, but the variety is a productive one. Despite laws permitting

15% blending of other grape varieties, Bürklin-Wolf insist on 100% varietals. Georg Raquet, the general manager, is not convinced that yields and quality are as closely linked in the case of Riesling as they are with some of the French varieties, though he admits that with yields of over 100 hl/ha problems with quality would arise. Like von Buhl, Bürklin-Wolf imposes higher standards on itself than the law requires, and must weights are at least 5° Oechsle higher than the legal minimum. Their Auslesen have at least 100° Oechsle, and their Beerenauslesen, which are only made from botrytised grapes, at least 130°. Beerenauslesen are made in very small quantities, often no more than 300–500 litres. Bürklin-Wolf use both small steel tanks and small casks. The best wines do usually spend some time in wood, but Raquet is anxious to avoid a direct oaky flavour in the wine; he uses wood to give structure and body, not flavour. Their top-quality wines are bottled in March or April after the harvest, but spend two to three years in the cellars before being released.

Since the quantities are so minute (for a winery that produces a million litres annually), Bürklin-Wolf does not make these wines as a routine commercial activity. 'We can't live off Beerenauslese,' says Raquet; 'they are a way of showing what can be done with the grapes. We enter such wines in competitions, for the prestige of the house.' As a form of showing off, they strike me as entirely successful, to judge by two of their 1985 Riesling Beerenauslesen. One is from Ruppertsberger Geisböhl, the other from Wachenheimer Böhlig. Both sets of grapes were picked at 140° Oechsle, both have about 8 g/l acidity and about 165 g/l residual sugar. Both are full gold in colour, but while the Ruppertsberger has a fairly reserved lush botrytis nose with overtones of honey and peaches, the Wachenheimer is more earthy and smoky, and in my view marginally finer. On the palate they were comparable in terms of richness and elegance, but the Wachenheimer seemed a touch more luxurious. Still, these are early days for 1985 Beerenauslesen, and what is clear at present is that both will become magnificent wines. 1985 also yielded a Scheurebe TBA, picked at 165° Oechsle.

The final wine I tasted at Bürklin-Wolf looked most unappetizing in the glass, for it was a slightly turbid amber-brown. On the nose, however, it was quite extraordinary, very rich and fat and honeyed, almost smoky. The taste defies description, for I have rarely tasted anything so incredibly rich and concentrated, a distillation of whole

barrow-loads of fruit: pears, peaches, figs, ripe apples, all emerging
from a few intensely sweet viscous drops in the mouth. The wine, a
1967 Wachenheimer Gerümpel Riesling TBA, combined amazing
extract with vigorous acidity. Despite its aged appearance, the wine
shows no signs of flagging. Of its kind, its own rare sumptuous
ultra-luxurious kind, the wine was perfection, a miraculous trans-
formation of a modest vat of pure grape juice into an even purer
concentration of operatic complexity on the nose and palate.

   Some of the cross-bred grapes are capable of producing sweet
wines of excellent quality. Weingut Lingenfelder of Grosskarlbach
and Weingut Jakob Pfleger of Herxheim make some attractive sweet
wines from Scheurebe, showing how spicy and delicious this grape
variety can be. The Winzerverein (cooperative) at Meckenheim has
also made sweet wine from Ehrenfelser, and their 1983 TBA is
impressive. Picked at 201° Oechsle, and with an exceptional 11.7 g/l
acidity, the wine shows an attractive spiciness as well as intense
sweetness, but it will need a few years in bottle before it ceases to
make one's teeth ache. Another cooperative, the Winzergenossenschaft Vier Jahreszeiten at Bad Dürkheim made a successful 1983
Beerenauslese from Huxelbrebe, picked at 140° Oechsle from the
Feuerberg Grosslage, and an acidity of 11.8 g/l gives the wine a lively
pineapple freshness and very good length.

   South of Ruppertsberg and Neustadt runs the less prestigious
Südliche Weinstrasse. Here too a whole range of grape varieties other
than Riesling flourishes. A typical family-owned winery such as

Weingut Andreashof at Landau offers Prädikatsweine from Ortega, Kerner, Scheurebe, and Ehrenfelser as well as Riesling. The 1976 Hochstadter Trappenberg Scheurebe Beerenauslese shows quite well, with good acidity (8.7 g/l) balancing high residual sugar (123 g/l), and the result is peachy and flowery on the nose and very sweet, creamy and lively on the palate. The 1976 Essinger Trappenberg Ortega Beerenauslese looks splendid, but is unbalanced on the palate and showing traces of oxidation. The wine is not especially sweet and is slightly hot on the finish, for it is relatively high in alcohol in relation to its residual sugar content. A more successful Ortega Beerenauslese comes from Weingut Eugen Volz at Essingen. Their 1983 Essinger Osterberg, picked at 148° Oechsle and with 147 g/l residual sugar, is full-flavoured, rounded, but a touch oily. Whether it will keep any better than the 1976 Trappenberg is doubtful.

The great majority of German wine producers are thoroughly traditional. They are keen to experiment with new grape varieties, but the styles of the wines have remained traditional for decades. This is not to say they are old-fashioned. German wineries, more than their French counterparts, are well stocked with all the latest equipment: pneumatic presses, centrifuges, cold sterile bottling lines. There is nothing rustic about the vast majority of German winemaking. But it is only in recent years that the styles of German wine have begun to change. Winemakers such as Bernhard Breuer of Rüdesheim and Wolfgang Siben of Deidesheim point out that historically German wines have been dry, and that sweet wines, naturally produced, are very much the exception. Drier wines are coming increasingly into fashion, and the words Spätlese and Auslese on a label no longer automatically signify a sweet style. A number of producers are fermenting Prädikatsweine dry, giving a wine high in alcohol, a far cry indeed from the light racy Rieslings or Silvaners with 8–9% alcohol. The result is not unlike an Alsatian Vendange Tardive.

But no winemaker, to the best of my knowledge, has taken this direction as far as Bernd Philippi of Weingut Koehler-Ruprecht in Kallstadt. He relishes making wines that no one has ever made before, and he could be accused of favouring innovation for innovation's sake. Bernd Philippi took over from his father Otto as principal winemaker here in 1975, and when he is not busy inventing new styles of wine in the cellars, he is dashing around the world, to

Michigan and Portugal and China, helping to set up new wineries. The property is a modest one, a mere 8.5 hectares, planted with 65% Riesling, 15% Spätburgunder, 5% Kerner, and a host of other varieties. Philippi has no difficulty achieving high must weights. The Rheinpfalz climate is favourable, and certain grape varieties, such as Huxelrebe, attain must weights of Beerenauslese quality every year, even in the generally poor 1984. Since the wine scandals of recent years, the market for such wines has decreased, so Philippi no longer tries to make many such sweet wines, and instead will pick slightly earlier and make, say, an Auslese Trocken. He aims for high alcohol, up to 14%, and high acidity; he is less concerned about residual sugar, and feels that 80 g/l is sufficient even for Beerenauslese.

However innovative the ideas, the vinification is thoroughly traditional. The grapes come from four Kallstadt vineyards and the wine is barrel-fermented and aged in old casks of white oak. Fermentation proceeds at a leisurely pace, and the wines are bottled fairly late, with the exception of Eiswein. His Riesling Beerenauslese, for instance, spends up to two years in wood, and TBA up to four. Philippi also makes some sweet wines from red grapes, some of which he allows to oxidise in order to give them a different quality of flavour. This is no different from the standard practice in southern France for some Vins Doux Naturels, but it is a heretical deviation from German practice.

The range of Philippi's Beerenauslesen alone is staggering, and I have managed to taste a mere eight. In 1973 and 1976 Huxelrebe from the Steinacker vineyard gave a wine that was flowery on the nose but less pleasing on the palate. The 1973 has an alcoholic aftertaste and lacks acidity; the 1976 was better in those respects but was prickly on the tongue and lacked structure and complexity. Two Beerenauslesen from the chalky Saumagen vineyard were made from the Rieslaner grape, which is no longer planted. The 1965 was beginning to oxidise and has turned the colour of medium sherry; nevertheless it was still honeyed, rich, rounded, and nicely balanced, a wine that is ageing gracefully. The 1969 was slightly less impressive, mainly because it was lighter in style and without the depth of flavour of the older wine. A 1976 Saumagen Scheurebe Beerenauslese seemed less successful. It was broad and floral on the nose, but somewhat bland on the palate, lacking structure and depth. This is very much a wine in the Bernd Philippi style, with 13% alcohol and

56 g/l residual sugar, though this example was not a wine of great character. A 1976 Riesling Beerenauslese from the same vineyard had almost identical analyses, though slightly higher acidity (7.7 g/l as opposed to 6.4), but the wine struck me as unbalanced: only mildly sweet, quite spicy, but spiky and over-alcoholic, and unimpressive on the finish. The same wine from the 1953 vintage was still lovely. In colour it was a slightly cloudy coppery-whisky, but it was rich and mature on the nose, with aromas of figs and peaches; on the palate it was less grand, and though delicate and elegant, tasted just past its best. On the other hand, the same wine from 1934 (though labelled Auslese, it was almost certainly, says Philippi, of Beerenauslese quality) was exquisite: still fresh, delicate and stylish, yet full of flavour and perfectly balanced. These older wines must have been higher in residual sugar than the wines Bernd Philippi is making today, and surely this is why they have lasted so beautifully. The most bizarre of his Beerenauslesen must be the 1983 Kronenberg Spätburgunder. Other winemakers use Pinot Noir with high must weights to make Beerenauslesen, but this example has a bewildering 15% alcohol and a trifling 24 g/l residual sugar. Yet the wine works, since Philippi has encouraged oxidation by leaving it in wood for a year without topping it up, a method akin to the *rancio* method of Roussillon. In colour the wine is brick-red, with orange tones, and on the nose it resembles tawny port; it tastes dry and somewhat austere, and the high alcohol is noticeable, but the wine is also lively and has good acidity, high extract, and excellent length.

From the same vineyard Philippi made a TBA from the rosé version of Spätburgunder, known in Germany as Weissherbst. With only 90 g/l residual sugar, the wine was only medium sweet, and its 13% alcohol lent it much fierceness, happily countered by good body and extract; although this wine is not yet in balance, it may well knit together over the next decade. (In contrast, the 1983 Dürkheimer Feuerberg Spätburgunder Weissherbst TBA from the Winzergenossenschaft Vier Jahreszeiten at Bad Dürkheim, had the colour of Oloroso sherry and was very rich and honeyed on the nose. When tasted in 1986 it was so sweet and intense that it gave me instant toothache, though I dare say in a decade or two the wine will be more palatable.) Two Huxelrebe TBAs from the Steinacker vineyard showed well, though the 1973, while lighter, had a gentle raisiny intensity that I found preferable to the more chewy alcoholic style of the 1976. The 146 g/l residual sugar in the 1973 seemed to make for a more balanced TBA than the 85 g/l of the younger wine. Better than either, marginally, is the 1975 Saumagen Scheurebe TBA, which has an elegant raciness not present to the same degree in the Huxelrebe wines. Although the wine has scarcely more residual sugar than the 1976 Huxelrebe and almost as much alcohol, it seemed much better balanced, and with a good future ahead of it. (Lingenfelder's remarkable 1985 Grosskarlbacher Burgweg Scheurebe TBA, also very high in alcohol, is in a similar style.) The Eisweine, including the probably unique red Eiswein, are discussed in the previous chapter.

RHEINHESSEN

With 25,000 hectares under vine, the Rheinhessen, a large area south of the Rheingau, is the largest of the German wine regions. It is also one of the least distinguished, since its grapes often lack acidity. For some winemakers, such as Reinhard and Klaus Muth of Weingut Rappenhof at Alsheim, the 1975 vintage was superior to the 1976 precisely because the acidity was higher and the wines longer-lived. In the region as a whole, Riesling accounts for only 5% of the varieties planted, and Müller-Thurgau and Silvaner between them account for 38%. With a few exceptions, only along the banks of the Rhein is wine of outstanding quality made. The few miles from Oppenheim through Nierstein and up to Nackenheim are known as the Rheinfront and many of the best wines come from these low-yielding vineyards. Here the best Grosslagen are Rehbach overlooking the river, and Auflagen on the slopes behind Nierstein. Some of the best Einzellagen are the exceptionally steep Brudersberg, Oelberg (which gives full rich wines), Kranzberg and Pettenthal. The red hue of some of these slopes does not derive from red sandstone but from the complex mineral contents of the soil. Peter von Weymarn, owner of the Weingut Freiherr Heyl zu Herrnsheim at Nierstein, places great emphasis on the differences between the various vineyards, pointing out that, especially in poor years, certain sites are capable of producing excellent wine. This is especially true in a year such as 1984, when the grapes may have ripened much less than in 1983, but many of them were higher in acidity and extract. Such wines can be very long-lived.

Peter von Weymarn, who was president of the Verband Deutscher Prädikatsweingüter for six years and whose estate produces some of the best wines of the Rheinhessen, is one of those proprietors who laments the 1971 wine laws that codified the different categories of German wine. 'The laws put too much emphasis on must weight,' he told me. 'In 1976, even the poorest winemakers had thousands of litres of Auslese in their tanks. Most of it's undrinkable now, but people see the word Auslese on the bottle and assume it means a higher quality, not just a higher must weight. Before 1971 it was up to the discretion of the best estates whether or not to make these rich sweet wines. In 1959 we had high enough Oechsle readings for TBA, but we didn't make any because we knew the grapes didn't have enough acidity to make really great wine.'

His 28-hectare estate is planted with 60% Riesling, 20% Müller-Thurgau, and 16% Silvaner. Good Auslesen were made in 1983 from Kerner as well as Riesling, spicy, almost piquant wines that will not be ready to drink for many years. The grapes ripened late in 1983 and retained their acidity, though there was no botrytis here. A 1971 Riesling Auslese from Brudersberg was still racy and elegant, far more stylish than its rather earthy, smoky bouquet would suggest. There was a comparable elegance in the 1976 Beerenauslese from the same vineyard, though this wine, picked at 135° Oechsle and with 85 g/l residual sugar, was more rounded and weighty, slightly low in acidity (6.5 g/l), but with good definition, good length and a clean finish. Other Beerenauslesen were made in 1953, 1964, and 1971, and in 1975 a Weissburgunder Beerenauslese was made from the Hipping vineyard. One of the most curious wines made here in recent years was a 1974 Oelberg TBA. In that year Peter von Weymarn left some Silvaner grapes on the vine, intending to make Eiswein from this thick-skinned variety, but no frosts gripped the hillsides. However, by mid-January he found he still had healthy grapes on the vine, and their must weight was 216° Oechsle. He picked, and the grapes yielded 35 litres of TBA. The estate maintains good stocks of its older wines.

Another conservative winemaker in Nierstein is Friedrich Heinrich Waldeck, who for fifteen years has been the cellarmaster of Weingut Reinhold Senfter. The property went through a bad patch in recent years, but has since been sold and is being reorganised with the intention of returning to the highest standards. Herr Waldeck is not an enthusiast for the new grape varieties, preferring Riesling, Silvaner (which does well in the Rheinfront), and Scheurebe. The estate has many old vines and yields, at 40 hl/ha for Riesling and 60 hl/ha for Scheurebe, are exceptionally low. 70% of the property's 15 hectares are planted with Riesling. Herr Waldeck believes in hand cultivation (there is little choice on these steep vineyards), keeps pesticide treatments to a minimum, likes to pick as late as possible, and aims for a broad, powerful style. He is more interested in richness of fruit than any other element in the wine, though he maintains that he does not have to sacrifice good acidity levels. In 1976 he made no wine in a category lower than Auslese, and in 1979 the lowest category was Spätlese. During the last decade Beerenauslesen were made in 1976, 1979, 1983 and 1985. The 1983 Auslesen I have tasted were delicious wines, complex and elegant, vigorous and fresh. A similar freshness is present on the Niersteiner Orbel Beerenauslese made from Riesling and Silvaner in 1976, a year that produced many blowsy wines. Not this one, despite relatively low acidity (5.4 g/l). This is a lean appley wine, elegant and with good length. The last TBA to be made here was the 1976 Scheurebe, also from Orbel. Picked at 165° Oechsle, the wine has high extract and 162 g/l residual sugar; on the nose and palate it has distinctive pineapple tones, and the wine, though very good, lacks complexity. This may be because of its youth, for the Senfter cellars are dug into the hillside and the temperature never rises above 10 °C. This means that the wines mature very slowly.

Other Nierstein winemakers, such as Peter Braun of Weingut Heinrich Braun, are far less conservative, and half his production is of dry wine. He considers the Nierstein wines closer in style to those of the Rheingau than to those of the rest of the Rheinhessen. He aims for high acidity rather than must weight, and ages his Rieslings and sweet wines in wood. Herr Braun has also acquired the Gräflich Wolff Metternich estate in Nierstein, and his total holdings in Nierstein, Dienheim, and Oppenheim are 32 hectares, of which 60% is planted with Riesling and 20% with Müller-Thurgau. Braun's 1983 Riesling Auslesen struck me as good but not exceptional, somewhat broad on the palate, and lack of bite also marred his 1976 Niersteiner Rosenberg Riesling Beerenauslese, though the wine was still clean and youthful after ten years. In 1983 he made a Huxelrebe

TBA from the Schloss Hohenreschen vineyard, an intense grapy wine that should develop nicely.

In the hinterland, there are pockets of good winemaking. Weingut Schales of Florsheim-Dalsheim uses many grape varieties, including cross-breeds. I have not cared for their Auslesen from Rieslaner and Kanzler, but their 1985 Dalsheimer Steig Huxelrebe Beerenauslese is delicate and stylish despite its great sweetness on the palate. Their 1985 Dalsheimer Burgel Riesling Eiswein was less interesting. At Bingen, across the Rhein from Rüdesheim, a number of wineries produce good sweet wines. Weingut Villa Sachsen's 1979 Binger Scharlachberg Rülander Beerenauslese, for example, is a most charming and engaging wine, not perhaps with a great future ahead of it, but a most enjoyable mouthful.

One hinterland proprietor keen to make wine of better than the average standard that prevails in the Rheinhessen is Hans-Christoph Schultz of the Weingut Oberst Schultz-Werner in Gaubischofsheim. The village has 90 hectares of vineyards, but only Schultz's 13 produce wine with any pretensions to high quality. Nevertheless, Schultz reports, other growers in the village have followed his lead and planted a great deal of Riesling. In these inland hills the climate is less benign than in the river valleys; the soil takes longer to warm up and in poor years the wine is rarely of high quality. Like other good winemakers, Schultz is keen to pick grapes with high acidity levels. The estate is run along traditional lines. He uses only organic

fertilisers, prunes for low yields, and does not centrifuge his wines, relying instead on racking and filtering to eliminate the yeasts. He still has some rows planted with new grape varieties, but confesses he does not like them much. 'Their acidity is too low in relation to their sugar content. In my view they don't make typically German wines, and they lack length. It's more difficult and expensive to make wine from Riesling, you have to be more selective, but it's worth it.' Schultz bravely confirmed his view by opening a 1979 Kellersberg Ortega Beerenauslese, which was frankly nasty. Far better is his pretty 1976 Herrnberg Riesling Beerenauslese, which has a lovely racy nose, though it lacks concentration on the palate. In November 1983, when frost hit the Herrnberg, he was able to make an Eiswein. He picked the Riesling grapes at 132° Oechsle, and the wine has 141 g/l residual sugar and 10.6 g/l acidity, a delightful wine, limpid and racy, and despite its green-apple flavour, less backward than many of the intensely acidic Rheingau and Mosel Eisweine.

NAHE

This small region of 4600 hectares to the west of the Rheinhessen is still underrated, for its best wineries produce wonderfully elegant clean wines with a lively spicy flavour. Just as the Rheingau is dominated by the State Domaine at Eltville, so too in the Nahe the

Qualitätswein
mit Prädikat

Amtliche
Prüfungsnummer
4 356 065 005 84

Weingut Oberst Schultz·Werner Gau·Bischofsheim

Seit 1833 im Besitz der Familie

1983er
Gaubischofsheimer Herrnberg
Riesling Eiswein

Erzeugerabfüllung

RHEINHESSEN   0,75 L

Produce of W. Germany

pace is set by the State Domaine at Schlossböckelheim. There are many wine drinkers who think that this State Domaine is the finest in Germany, and I have certainly never drunk a disappointing wine from the estate. It was founded in 1902 by the Prussian government in a seemingly impossible site among cliffs overlooking a bend of the River Nahe. Whole cliffsides had to be rebuilt before vines could be planted. Even today the most celebrated vineyard, the Kupfergrube, adjoins a cliffside of scrub and rock, which the vineyard itself once resembled. The soil is volcanic and there is a complex mineral content, principally porphyry, which contributes to the excellence of the wine. At 90%, the proportion of Riesling planted here is the highest in the Nahe, and yields are kept to about 50 hl/ha. The only problems arise from lack of moisture in hot weather. Annual production is fairly modest, at 300,000 bottles, and vinification traditional. As at other top estates, the State Domaine has higher standards for Prädikatsweine than the law prescribes. The legal minimum for Spätlese is 78° Oechsle; the domaine insists on 86°, and Auslese must be in the high 90s. No Süssreserve is used here, so all sweet wines are naturally so. Fermentation is arrested by chilling. The director, Dr Werner Hofäcker, places great emphasis on cool fermentation and on maturing the wines in cask for six to nine months. The wines are treated as little as possible; they are fined but not chilled to precipitate tartaric acid crystals.

These are wines that require ageing, and even the dry wines benefit from a few years in bottle. In their youth, even the Auslesen hardly seem sweet at all, so marked is their acidity. It is important to note that the State Domaine is one of the wineries that in great years will bottle different lots of Auslese separately. There is no way to tell the difference except by checking the bottling number (marked AP on the label), since labelling wines as 'Feinste Auslese' or whatever is now forbidden. This presents no problem to the commercial buyer, who is told at the estate exactly which lot he is tasting. But by the time the wine is bottled and in the shops, it is virtually impossible, except by price, for the consumer to know which quality he or she is buying. Surely the well-organised German wine industry can devise some way of informing the purchaser more precisely about the quality of the wine in the bottle.

The 1983 and 1985 Auslesen are still completely closed, but after ten years in bottle a 1976 Niederhäuser Hermannsberg Beerenauslese, picked at 135° Oechsle, and with 154 g/l residual sugar and 10.5 g/l acidity, was just beginning to come round. There was rich botrytis on the nose, which was sweet and seductive, while on the palate the wine was wonderfully harmonious, with good fruit yet very fresh and delicate. Such a wine bears very little relation to some of the blowsy 1976 wines from the Rhein. It proved far more difficult to assess a TBA of the same year from the Schlossböckelheimer Kupfergrube. The grapes were picked at 174° Oechsle, yet despite the 233 g/l residual sugar, the wine is far from unctuous. It is rich and concentrated, to be sure, and quite sumptuous on the nose, but is still very fresh, and it will surely be another decade before it opens up to reveal its full fruitiness. There is ample acidity to allow the wine to develop soundly, and all the signs are that it will become a magnificent bottle. The estate's Eisweine are discussed in Chapter 10.

The neighbouring village of Oberhausen is also devoted to wine, though most of its winemakers are also farmers. Helmuth Dönnhoff is unusual in that he no longer farms, but concentrates his energies on his 7 hectares of vineyards, mostly planted with Riesling, in Oberhausen and Bad Kreuznach. As at the State Domaine, the soil is volcanic, with considerable deposits of porphyry; the surface is stony

and hard to cultivate. In hot dry years, when there can be a lack of water here, the top vineyards occasionally do less well than other vineyards where the heat is less excessive. Harvests are often delayed until mid-November, and yield about 60 hl/ha. Although the winery is equipped with a pneumatic press – virtually standard equipment in Germany – Dönnhoff prefers to use an ancient hydraulic press for sweet wines. No Süssreserve is used for these top wines, which ferment very slowly in the chilly cellars through the winter months. Fermentation takes place in 1200-litre casks, though some top wines are aged in smaller barrels. He treats the wines as little as possible and bottles in May or June. Dönnhoff makes some excellent Riesling Auslesen, including a striking 1983 Oberhäuser Brücke that was made from frozen grapes but could not be sold as Eiswein because the grapes only attained 110° Oechsle. This is a delicious wine, intensely fruity but also clean and racy. A 1985 Kreuznacher Osterhöll Scheurebe Auslese tasted very sweet but lacked complexity.

The Anheuser family has been making wine in the Bad Kreuznach area since 1627, and there are still three wineries in the town bearing their name. (These are the same Anheusers whose American relatives concocted a 'beer' called Budweiser.) Weingut Paul Anheuser is one of the largest estates in the Nahe, with 60 hectares under vine all over the region. All vinification takes place at the large well-equipped winery at Bad Kreuznach, where musts ferment in wood as slowly as possible. The present owner is Rudolf Peter Anheuser, a large, somewhat explosive man of considerable vigour. His 1976 Kreuznacher Kahlenberg Riesling Beerenauslese is a rich, well-balanced wine overshadowed by his very fine 1971 Kreuznacher Krötenpfuhl Riesling TBA, a truly luxurious wine, ripe, powerful, and honeyed on the nose, fruity and very intense on the palate, with excellent length. The wines are unquestionably well made, but seem to lack the sheer breed and finesse of the best Nahe Rieslings.

This cannot be said about the wines of the gracious Hans Crusius and his son Peter, who make beautiful Riesling at the little village of Traisen. Before visiting the cellars, Peter Crusius took me on a short hike to the top of the Rotenfels, the largest cliff face in Germany outside the Alps. At the foot of this 200-metre-high wall of rock is the Bastei, a small vineyard divided between three owners, of whom Crusius is one. These few rows of vines make some of the finest Rieslings in the Nahe, for the microclimate is so warm that the vines flower earlier than in other nearby vineyards (though this can be problematic in cold springs) and yields are pitifully low, between 12 and 14 hl/ha. The vineyard is very difficult to farm, as are many others in the region, and it is sad to see a number of plots falling into disuse. The Crusiuses have limited themselves to 10 hectares of vines that produce no more than 70,000 bottles a year. The Rieslings are fermented in wood, and bottled early, in March or April, both to preserve the youthfulness of the wines and because the demand is strong. A 1971 Traiser Rotenfelser Weissburgunder Auslese proved disappointing, too broad and lacking in piquancy, but a Bastei Riesling Auslese of the same year was absolutely superb: ravishing yellow-gold in colour, fruity and intense on the nose, and astonishingly opulent in the mouth, without being in the slightest bit cloying. This is the epitome of ripe yet fresh Auslese of the greatest finesse.

All of these winemakers have been essentially traditional. But the spirit of innovation pervades the Nahe too. In the hamlet of Burg Layen, tucked into a small valley, rises the medieval tower of the former castle, and at its foot stands the more modern house and winery of the Diel family. Dr Ingo Diel and his son Armin are the winemakers here, maintaining the highest standards and maturing all their wines in wood. Armin is also a well-known journalist and a specialist in the wines of Bordeaux, and French influences, eyed by most Germans with suspicion, have crept into his winemaking. Armin Diel is not the only winemaker to experiment with new oak in

Crusius & Sohn

NAHE

1985

Traiser Bastei

Riesling Auslese

QUALITÄTSWEIN MIT PRÄDIKAT

Erzeugerabfüllung – A.P.Nr.1 775 009 002 86

Product of Germany   750 ml

WEINGUT HANS CRUSIUS u. SOHN, TRAISEN/NAHE

Germany, but he is probably the only one to have put Riesling as well as heftier Rülander into 90% new oak. He has even adopted the French customs of bottling a few magnums and imperials and of packing bottles into wooden crates rather than cartons. That this is not mere gimmickry is confirmed not only by my own extensive tastings of Diel's wines but by the fact that in the admittedly controversial 'Classification of 1985' – an attempt to adapt the Grand Cru system of grading to German wineries – Schlossgut Diel is the only Nahe winery to be placed in the top group. I must confess to a prejudice in favour of this winery. As I drove along the Autobahn towards Burg Layen, I glimpsed the Union Jack fluttering from the flagpole over the castle tower. At first I thought it must be in celebration of the birthday of Frau Schäfer, the English wife of another Burg Layen winemaker (Alfred Schäfer, who makes attractively aromatic Auslesen from Kerner as well as Riesling) – but no, it was a blatant and wholly successful attempt to flatter me.

Armin Diel shares the current enthusiasm for dry wines. He picks for acidity rather than must weight, and many Spätlesen and Auslesen are fermented dry. In 1983 the Schlossgut made a number of Prädikatsweine, including a delicate, rather pretty Dorsheimer Goldloch Riesling Auslese and an extraordinary Beerenauslese from the same vineyard. This last wine is made from grapes picked at almost 150° Oechsle and has a remarkable 14.0 g/l acidity. At present it is positively uncomfortable to taste, so pronounced is that acidity, but the fruit is superb too, and when, after a few decades in bottle, the wine finally achieves some harmoniousness, it should be superb. For now, it is a wine to be admired extravagantly and left untouched. An equally astonishing 1983 Beerenauslese was made from the Traminer grape picked at 152° Oechsle from Burg Layer Schlossberg. The astonishment arises from the acidity, which stands at 13.0 g/l. This would be high but not unheard of for Riesling, but for Traminer it is astounding. Armin Diel admits that he did not understand how the wine achieved such high acidity and he asked the laboratory to check it again, which they did, confirming the original analysis. The nose is broad and ripe, as one would expect, with orangey overtones; on the palate that intense acidity is fighting the opulence of the Traminer flavour. At present aggressive and spicy, this wine will also need a decade or more before it settles down, but the outcome is less certain than that of the Riesling. My hunch is that it will be superb. (A 1964 Traminer 'Feine Auslese' from the same vineyard was still in excellent condition in 1986, elegant and ripe and with real depth of flavour and intensity of extract.) Perhaps the loveliest of the Schlossgut wines that have come my way is the 1971 Dorsheimer Goldloch Riesling Beerenauslese, picked at 160° Oechsle and thus technically a TBA. This beautifully balanced wine combined rich viscosity with exquisite elegance – a triumph. Almost as fine was the 1971 Dorsheimer Pittermänchen Riesling Auslese, picked at 118° Oechsle; it has comparable qualities to the Beerenauslese, but is of course lighter in style. Some of the older wines contained Süssreserve, but in recent years the Diels have put a stop to the practice. Quality is also maintained by not overcropping and yields for Riesling rarely exceed 60 hl/ha. For TBA, Armin Diel told me, their yields, at 2 hl/ha, would put even Ch d'Yquem to shame.

Nature is less generous with her favours in Nahe and Rheinhessen than in Rheingau and Rheinpfalz. Much excellent sweet wine is made in these first two regions, but they are more the result of dedicated winemaking than a gift of nature. Less prestigious than the great vineyards of the Rheingau and Rheinpfalz, these two regions can offer very good value, although the top wines, being much sought after (the Diels' entire stock of 1985 wine was sold out before the end of that year), can be as expensive as any in Germany.

12

Mosel-Saar-Ruwer

From the Vosges Mountains the River Mosel curls and meanders north-east through Luxembourg and Trier towards Koblenz on the Rhein. As the crow flies, the German section of the Mosel, which constitutes the wine region, is a distance of about eighty miles, but following the vineyards along the river, the distance is far greater. The top third of the region closest to the Rhein, the Untermosel, is of little interest to enthusiasts for fine wine. It is only at Erden and Ürzig, just after the Mittelmosel begins, that all the factors of soil and microclimate and exposure meet and marry to give that light, racy style of Riesling for which the Mosel is famous. Erden, Ürzig, Zeltingen, Wehlen, Graach, Bernkastel, Brauneberg – these are magical names to lovers of Riesling. Upstream from Brauneberg the Mosel vineyards rarely produce wines of the same outstanding quality.

Then at the village of Ruwer, a stream of the same name enters the Mosel from the south. Along the Ruwer valley are a handful of vineyards which produce a wine even more delicate and subtle than that of the Mittelmosel. Beyond the Ruwer, around the villages of Wiltingen, Ayl, Ockfen, and Serrig, and the small town of Saarburg, lie more vineyards that produce incomparable wine. In poor years Saar wine may have good acidity but insufficient fruit, but in good years, nurtured on harsh slaty soil, these are the most racy, refreshing, piquant, and elegant of all Rieslings. They are delicate yet far from fragile. Mosel wines in general, and Saar wines in particular, tend to be even lower in alcohol than those of the Rheingau and Nahe. Because the climate is so inclement the boundaries between the categories of Prädikatswein are set at lower levels in the Mosel than anywhere else. The Auslesen and other top categories can live for decades, sustained by their high natural acidity.

It is not for nothing that the wines of the Saar are described as steely, for at their best these pale, almost colourless wines with a flicker of green in the glass are firm and spicy, vivid with flavour, occasionally slightly spritzig, and have as much backbone as if they were laced with platinum thread. Here, in this somewhat chilly corner of Germany, the vines must struggle most against the elements. More often than not they lose, but when they triumphantly bring their fruit to ripeness, the results are unforgettable. Opulence is relatively easy to describe; there are plenty of synonyms to help a writer convey, however inadequately, the charms and attractions of a full, luscious wine. But the appeal of a Wehlener Sonnenuhr or a Scharzhofberger from the Saar is far harder to communicate. The exquisite is less tangible than the sensual. The best wines are expensive, in large part because of the high cost of working such steep sites. All the variables that lend subtlety and complexity (and confusion) to the other wine regions of Germany are present to an even greater extent in the Mosel. For even in the best villages, the twists and turns of the river, and the different exposures of the slopes, lead to great variations not only from vineyard to vineyard, but within vineyards as well. The unifying factor in the Mosel is the slaty soil, which both retains such heat as the sunshine provides and imparts an intense and steely tone to the wine.

55% of the almost 13,000 hectares of vines are planted with Riesling, and unless otherwise stated, all wines mentioned below are made from that grape. The properties discussed below are among the greatest in the region, but there are many others, such as the vineyard-owning seminaries and charitable institutions of Trier and other towns, that have had to be omitted. Nevertheless, I hope the style of these wines will be conveyed.

The best stretch of the Mittelmosel begins at Ürzig, situated at a bend on the river. The hills rise steeply on either side, giving a landscape that, as Hugh Johnson has observed, invites comparison with the steep vine-covered slopes of the Douro in Portugal. The most celebrated Einzellage in Ürzig is Würzgarten ('spice garden'), and the name is apt, for the slate and the loam soil beneath it give its wines a distinctive spicy quality. On the other side of the river lies

Erden, with its equally steep vineyards, of which the most famous are Prälat and Treppchen; they have somewhat lighter subsoil than Würzgarten. Wines from Erden are usually more flowery and elegant than those from Ürzig, which tend to be heavier and spicier. Local winemakers feel that Ürzig is especially fine in dry years, while Erden often shows better than its neighbour in wet ones.

There is a lovely old house in Ürzig called the Mönchhof, originally built in 1509 but much renovated since. In 1806 it was acquired by the family that still own it today. The present proprietor is the genial Robert Eymael, a burly man often rigged out in breeches and kneesocks. The winemaking is as traditional as his appearance. Weingut Mönchhof only owns 5.5 hectares, all steep sites and all planted with Riesling. Vinification takes place solely in casks, and in the cellars, also dating from 1509, there are curious wooden props between the casks and the roof that prevent the casks from floating away when the river floods. Because the harvests are late and the winters cold, fermentation proceeds slowly and stops by itself; no Süssreserve is used. 1983 was an exceptional year here, and so was 1985, though it only matched the quality of the 1983 at the very finest sites. The wines themselves are marked by their exquisite balance. A 1985 Würzgarten Auslese (Gold Capsule) was flowery and rounded on the palate, but also had an elegant flinty quality that lent it character. Acidity was high in 1985 – most Mönchhof wines have close to 9.0 g/l – and the wine has very good length. A 1957 Hochfeine Auslese from the same vineyard showed how superbly the Mosel wines can age. The 1985 was virtually colourless, but the thirty-year-old wine was a gorgeous yellow-gold, and the bouquet was also far more sumptuous, yet still delicate. On the palate the 1957 was ravishing, honeyed and with great intensity of fruit, yet entirely balanced by its fresh liveliness. The 1983 Treppchen Auslese (Gold Capsule) seemed surprisingly developed in 1986: rich, almost weighty, rounded and elegant, harmonious and satisfying. In general, Mosel Auslesen are not especially sweet, since high acidity masks the residual sugar.

A few miles further upstream lies Wehlen. Along the quay stand a number of stolid stone mansions, clearly the homes of respectable citizens and burghers. Many belong to members of the Prüm family that has dominated winemaking here for almost two centuries. Dynastic complexities make it almost impossible to work out exactly how the current Prüms are interrelated; the important thing is that they all seem to make excellent wine. On the other side of the river rises the great vineyard of Sonnenuhr, terraced around the sundial after which it is named. The best grapes grow lower down on the steepest slopes, benefiting from their sheltered position and from the moisture rising from the river. The foot of the slope is 2 °C warmer than the top, so the grapes there ripen more rapidly. Near the river the vines are often protected by fogs from the frosts that can grip the hilltops.

The best-known Prüm firm is Weingut Joh. Jos. Prüm, a 14-hectare estate inherited in 1969 by the fastidious Dr Manfred Prüm. This estate pioneered the making of Beerenauslese and TBA in the Mosel in the 1920s. The drawing rooms of the various Prüm mansions, with their heavy ugly furniture, glowering family portraits on the walls, and a sobriety enlivened only by vases bursting with fresh flowers, seem in extraordinary contrast to the finesse and beauty of their wines. In this sombre setting I tasted with Dr Prüm a range of wonderful Sonnenuhr Auslesen, including two separately bottled lots of the 1982. The Sonnenuhr wines have a particular character very difficult to define, but it shows up most strongly when tasted against the wines of the other great Mittelmosel vineyards. In their youth they have a greenish tinge, and a hint of petrol on the nose. In the mouth they are surprisingly broad and rich; their acidity and finesse are more apparent on the finish, and the wines have excellent

length. The 1982 and 1983 were still very youthful, and the harmony they would eventually attain was better indicated by the 1976 (long gold capsule, here indicating the top grade of Auslese). This wine was yellow-gold in colour (in contrast to the pale green-straw of the younger wines) and positively voluptuous, not a word one would normally associate with Mosel wines; yet there was nothing flabby or unstructured about the wine, which was elegant and clean on the finish. A 1975 Graacher Himmelreich Auslese looked and tasted at least five years younger. As with many J. J. Prüm wines, carbon dioxide, manifested by a burst of spritz on the palate, has kept it wonderfully fresh. A Beerenauslese from the exceptionally late-ripening vintage of 1970 was far from lush, though it was sweet and intense, both on the nose and especially the palate. Ripe fruit and acidity were in perfect balance. This estate's wines are renowned for their longevity.

A few doors along from Dr Prüm's home and winery is the Weingut Dr Weins-Prüm-Erben. Once again the tasting took place in a spirit-numbing drawing room lined with bad paintings, but the view across onto the Sonnenuhr made up for it. In this vineyard, as elsewhere along the Mosel, the vines are trained up eight-foot poles, their branches bent back so as to maximise their exposure to the less than ubiquitous solar rays, and in the evening sunshine the hillsides glint with the slate slabs strewn across the vineyards. Some of Dr Manfred Prüm's wines, even the Beerenauslese, had a touch of spritz, a slight prickle on the tongue that is characteristic of much Mosel wine. It is an attribute that Bert Selbach, who has made the wine at Weingut Dr Weins-Prüm-Erben since 1977, deliberately strives for. He aims for good acidity, and when the vintage and the harvest oblige, the wines can sustain high levels of residual sugar without being cloying on the finish. The vinification is up-to-date and fermentation is arrested with a centrifuge when the right balance has been achieved; no Süssreserve is used. All wines of Spätlese quality and above are matured in cask. Three Sonnenuhrs, from 1982, 1983, and 1985, were all excellent, though the 1985 was outstanding: intense, spicy, and packed with youthful fruit. The grapes were picked at 104° Oechsle (compared to 87° for the other two vintages) and the acidity was 10.0 g/l. It is worth noting that this wine was priced at 50 DM on release, making it considerably more expensive than all but the very top Premier Cru Sauternes. Top

Mosel wines do not come cheap, especially if the label bears the name Prüm. This winery also owns rows of vines in Ürzig, Erden and Graach, and the Auslese among these that seemed most striking was the 1985 Erdener Prälat, which had admirable pungency and depth of flavour, not to mention very good acidity and length.

Other Prüm wineries in Wehlen are Weingut S. A. Prüm Erben, where Raimund Prüm produces Auslesen and Beerenauslesen from Sonnenuhr of great charm and delicacy, and Weingut Maximinhof, owned by Stephen Studert-Prüm. Maximinhof own vines in many of the best sites in the Mittelmosel, including Graacher Himmelreich and Bernkasteler Graben, a neighbour of Bernkasteler Doctor, probably the most famous (and overpriced) vineyard in Germany. Connoisseurs like to speak of the qualities that differentiate the wine from these various vineyards, but even experienced tasters often find it hard to make such distinctions. True, soils vary – or at least subsoils do – but so do sites within each Einzellage, and so of course do vintages and the styles and standards of individual producers. Bernkasteler is said to be flintier than Graach, which in turn lacks the richness of Wehlen. Although there is undoubtedly some basis to these fine distinctions, such formulae should be treated with scepticism. In general, deeper soils give stronger, fuller wines, while thinner soils produce more elegant wines.

At Maximinhof the wines are mostly made from vines up to fifty years old, and all fermentation as well as maturation takes place in cask, since Studert-Prüm feels strongly that wood is essential to give the wine sound structure. It was instructive, though inconclusive, to taste 1983 Graben against 1983 Himmelreich, and 1985 Himmelreich against 1985 Sonnenuhr (all Auslesen). The 1983 Himmelreich showed much better than Graben, even though far more closed on the nose. The Himmelreich was, at this early stage in its long life, both riper and more elegant. On the other hand, the 1985 Sonnenuhr showed better than the 1985 Himmelreich, although it too was more reserved on the nose. The Sonnenuhr had a wonderful raciness combined with a good depth of flavour and extract; it also had marginally more length. 1976 Sonnenuhr Beerenauslesen from both S. A. Prüm Erben and Maximinhof were absolutely delicious: flowery, ripe, and stylish.

The Prüms are not the only dynastically intertwined winemaking family along the Mittelmosel. The Bergweilers are another, and one branch intermarried with the Prüms very thoroughly. Zacharias Bergweiler married first one Prüm daughter and then, after her death, her sister. Zacharias's daughter married a Herr Pauly, and their son Peter now owns Weingut Dr Pauly-Bergweiler in Bernkastel. Through his own marriage he has acquired further vineyards in Ürzig, though those wines are vinified and marketed separately under the name Weingut Peter Nicolay. An imposing range of wines is made at both establishments from some of the finest Mittelmosel vineyards. The Nicolay wines are prettier than the Pauly-Bergweiler range, but though more accessible when young, the latter wines, which are fermented at very cold temperatures, often appear to have better structure. Dr Pauly is very proud of his Eisweine. The 1983 Graacher Himmelreich is, or will be, superb, and may have made a stronger impression because, while far from lacking in acidity at 11.3 g/l, it does not have the still obscuring 14 g/l acidity of the 1985 Eisweine. Picked at 139° Oechsle, it retains 143 g/l residual sugar which is beautifully balanced by the pineappley acidity. The 1985 Bernkasteler Badstube Eiswein is also extremely promising: spicy, vigorous, concentrated. A 1983 Badstube Beerenauslese was sadly disappointing, loose and charmless – though it may yet pull itself together.

Just beyond Bernkastel is the hamlet of Mülheim, home of the Weingut Max Ferd. Richter, a family firm associated with the village for three centuries. The present owner is Dr Dirk Richter. In addition to his own 15 hectares of vineyards in Mülheim, Graach, Bernkastel and Brauneberg, Dr Richter buys in grapes from other growers. Vinification is traditional. Fermentation is arrested by filtration and the wines mature in oak casks. No Süssreserve is used. The estate has made something of a speciality of Eisweine in recent years. The grapes for such wines come from Mülheimer Helenenkloster, the vineyard just behind the village and easily accessible on the bitterly cold nights when the harvest must be made. Dr Richter leaves a quantity of Riesling grapes unpicked in Helenenkloster and hopes to be rewarded with sufficiently severe frosts, as he was in 1983 and 1985. The 1983 was picked at 165° Oechsle, exceptionally high for the Mosel; the 1985 registered 125° and had 11.7 g/l acidity and 120 g/l residual sugar. Both wines were copybook Eisweine, though the 1985 seemed marginally more approachable in its youth. The

Auslesen from Brauneberger Juffer-Sonnenuhr are attractive too. The estate used to make occasional straw wines, but none has been made since 1968, because the 1971 wine laws prohibited the marketing of such wines. Surviving examples in the cellars of proprietors or collectors are great rarities.

Like the Richters, the Haag family has been associated with this stretch of the river for centuries. The current winemaker at Dusemonder Hof is Fritz Haag, a great enthusiast for the wines of the region. His wines come mostly from the Juffer-Sonnenuhr vineyard in Brauneberg, a village singled out by Napoleon in 1806 when he decreed that its relatively full-bodied wine could be sold at higher prices than all other Mosel wines. Fritz Haag is the major proprietor of this vineyard. A reductive winemaker, he takes pains to ensure that the grapes and wine are as free as possible from oxidation, and as a result his wines in their youth are almost colourless. Fermentation and ageing take place in 1000-litre casks. Like many other producers, Haag bottles various lots of Auslese separately. They can be distinguished either by the AP number on the bottle or, more handily, by the capsule. A gold capsule is equivalent to what would before 1971 have been labelled Feine Auslese, while a long gold capsule is equivalent to Feinste Auslese. If you are wondering how long is a long capsule, you will have to continue in a state of puzzlement until you either learn to recognise each producer's

Weingut Dusemonder Hof - Brauneberg / Mosel

FRITZ HAAG

1985er
Brauneberger Juffer-Sonnenuhr
Riesling - Beerenauslese

Erzeugerabfüllung - Qualitätswein mit Prädikat

750 ml   A. P. Nr. 2 577 050 ● 86   Alc. 7,3 % by Vol.

capsule or until the German wine authorities devise a more straight-forward system for informing consumers about such fine but import-ant distinctions. In some years, Fritz Haag will make up to five Auslesen from the same vineyard. Thanks to Herr Haag's generos-ity, I have tasted no fewer than thirteen of his Auslesen and Beeren-auslesen, all from Juffer-Sonnenuhr, from 1985 back to 1971 and 1969. It would be tedious to describe each wine in detail. The very young wines are racy yet packed with flavour and well structured. The older wines, without exception, are superb, intensely fruity yet full of zest and finesse. Many of the top Auslesen were almost chewy with extract, yet never heavy in the mouth or lacking in acidity, length, and breed. The same is true of the 1971 Beerenauslese, which succeeded in being opulent, lively, spicy, and honeyed, all at the same time. The 1985 Beerenauslese has 171 g/l residual sugar but is so high in acidity (13.8 g/l) that the wine, while sweet, is in no way sugary. Even in years known for relatively low acidity, such as 1976 and 1982, Fritz Haag achieves about 8.0 g/l acidity in all the Auslesen, while the finer vintages such as 1971 and 1983 are still bristling with an acidity that keeps them fresh and vivid. Such wines epitomise top-quality Mittelmosel Prädikatsweine.

From Brauneberg we follow the Mosel upstream for many miles, past Piesport and Leiwen and Trittenheim. The many excellent wines made along this stretch can approach, if rarely equal, those from further downstream. This situation changes when we come to the two tributaries of the Mosel, the Ruwer and the Saar. A few miles downstream from Trier the Ruwer meets the Mosel, and a mile down the Ruwer valley stands the 33-hectare estate of Maximin Grünhaus, with its three great vineyards of Abtsberg, Bruderberg, and Herren-berg. These names reflect the history of the estate, which was given to the Benedictine monastery in Trier by Emperor Otto I in 966. The estate was secularised in 1910 and acquired by the von Schubert family in 1882. For as long as records exist, Maximin Grünhaus has been acclaimed for producing some of the finest wines in Germany, and under Dr Carl von Schubert, the present owner, the same holds true. Maximin Grünhaus has the coveted status of an Ortsteil, so fine and coherent are its wines. The manor house, which dates back to the early Middle Ages, faces the great slaty hill on which the three terraced vineyards are situated. Abtsberg, often considered the

finest, has soil mainly composed of blue slate, whereas the Herrenberg, the largest vineyard, has richer soil of softer red slate. The
Herrenberg does not warm up as rapidly as Abtsberg, but this can be
an advantage in very hot years, when the Abtsberg can suffer from
lack of moisture. The Bruderberg, exceptionally steep, excels in very
good years. The vineyards are hand-cultivated and yield about 65–70
hl/ha. Dr von Schubert pays a great deal of attention to viticulture,
and stresses that the cellarmaster, Herr Heinrich, who has been here
for over thirty years, is also the vineyard manager. Consequently,
unlike most cellarmasters, he is intimately acquainted with the
condition and quality of the grapes even before they arrive at the
presshouse. He sprays as little as possible, so as not to harm the
natural yeasts on the grapes. The harvest usually begins in mid-
October, and the pickers are equipped to select up to six different
qualities of grapes simultaneously. In very hot years, such as 1964,
1976, and 1983, the grapes may be picked early so as to ensure high
acidity in preference to, say, an additional 5° Oechsle. Eiswein was
first made here in 1965, though none was made thereafter until 1983,
an exceptionally propitious year for such wines.

   Dr von Schubert encourages natural fermentation, and is reluctant
to inoculate with yeasts, as is customary in many wineries, to get

fermentation moving, since he believes that natural yeasts produce more elegant wines. The best wines are fermented very slowly in wood in cellars where the temperature never exceeds 10 °C. The wines are treated as little as possible. When Spätlesen or Auslesen are ready, they are given a rough filtration but not sulphured. Although large tanks are used for lesser qualities, Dr von Schubert favours wood for smaller quantities of Prädikatswein. He feels that biological processes occur more swiftly in wood than in tank; sedimentation and precipitation of tartaric acid crystals are relatively rapid and you do not need to use chemical treatments to stabilise the wine. Needless to say, no Süssreserve is added at Maximin Grünhaus. Most wines are given four to five months in wood.

The soil is exceptionally poor and high must weights are not common. It is perfectly normal at Maximin Grünhaus for up to half the wine to be QbA, and their lowly status does not mean that these are mediocre wines. Indeed, I have tasted excellent QbAs from this estate. Even in a generally good year such as 1985, only 10% of the production was Spätlese or higher. Nor does Dr von Schubert adhere to the usual categories for QmP. Much of the 1983 Auslese was declassified to Spätlese. I have tasted a range of Auslesen from Abtsberg, all superb wines of incomparable breed. Cask 88 (some lots are bottled separately and are identified by their cask or AP number) of the 1983 is not high in residual sugar (50 g/l) yet has a rich soft power, and immense elegance. A special lot of the 1985, made from half-frozen grapes picked at 100° Oechsle, is atypical because of its very high acidity, yet that acidity was beautifully integrated, and richness, breadth and freshness were in perfect balance. The wine had an appley quality (probably because of higher malic acid than usual) that may be atypical. Cask 58 of the 1976 is a wine of wonderful charm and elegance, a luminous yellow-gold in colour, and ripe, spicy, and almost pretty on the palate. A 1964 Feine Auslese from the Herrenberg was quite ravishing. Again, the colour had developed to a beautiful yellow-gold; on the nose the wine was honeyed yet elegant, while on the palate it had tremendous individuality, a weighty, almost stern definition, yet completely fresh and with excellent length. A 1973 Abtsberg Spätlese was, naturally, less rich than the Auslesen, but, like the other wines, perfectly harmonious. My tasting notes grew somewhat fanciful at this point, but I recorded that rather than being positively sweet on the palate, the wine struck lovely sweet notes like a bell or a flute. Whenever I have tasted Maximin Grünhaus wines, I have been repeatedly struck by the extraordinary balance between their delicacy and their grip. There is nothing fleeting or slight about them. Although never heavy or blowsy, they are always wines to be reckoned with, to be sipped and drunk with the greatest concentration and the most satisfying pleasure.

The village of Konz marks the spot where the Mosel is joined by the Saar. The neighbouring hamlet of Filzen is the base of the Reverchon estate, founded in 1685. At first, it was little more than a hobby for the Reverchons, who were originally Huguenot bankers who came to Trier from France in the eighteenth century. Since 1954 the property has been run by Eddie Reverchon. Such is his enthusiasm for the region that he mildly flouts the wine law by underlining the word 'Saar' on his labels. The vineyards are mostly slate and schist, and the wines are aged in wood. Reverchon concentrates on making dry wines to match the German preference for the style, but on occasion he has made excellent sweeter wines. The 1983 Filzener Herrenberg Auslese (gold capsule) is impressive, and he is especially proud of his 1983 Filzener Herrenberg Eiswein, harvested at 148° Oechsle and with 160 g/l residual sugar and a terrifying 17.0 g/l acidity. Though unapproachable at present, the wine's structure and intensity are such as to suggest it will, eventually, be very fine indeed. Other delicate wines, beautifully balanced between ripe spicy fruit and vigorous acidity promising a long and gradual development, are made by Weingut Schloss Saarstein at Serrig.

A few miles up the river, in the small town of Saarburg, is the Weingut Forstmeister Geltz Zilliken, now owned by Hans-Joachim Zilliken. His winery is disguised as a perfectly ordinary, comfortable modern house, and no one would suspect from the outside that it was built above ancient cellars three storeys deep. He claims that the lowest level, which has a constant temperature of 9 °C, is the finest cellar in the Saar; the humidity is close to 100%, and, in these perfect conditions Zilliken ages 80,000 bottles of his wines. The 9 hectares of vineyards are on steep slate slopes. Saarburger Rausch has red loam, and a slate less rough and chunky than that found in his other principal holding at Ockfener Bockstein. Like Fritz Haag and Dr von Schubert, Zilliken aims for high acidity rather than high must weights. Such acidity is especially important because the wines rarely have more than 7.5% alcohol. On the other hand, that acidity must be balanced by fruit, and this is only possible in good years. The 1985 Saarburger Rausch Auslese, picked at 110° Oechsle, has 118 g/l residual sugar; with 14.0 g/l acidity the sugar is effectively disguised on the palate, though with age the fruity richness of the wine will emerge more prominently. Of two 1983 Auslesen, the Bockstein and the Rausch, I preferred the latter; it had better fruit, better balance, and great class, while the Bockstein seemed comparatively light. A 1976 Bockstein Auslese was also on the light side, very charming, but rather too pretty for my taste. Of course good Saar wines, even Auslesen, are never weighty or sappy, but what distinguishes the greatest of them is the balance between their delicacy and their fullness of flavour, a German equivalent of the French *nervosité*. To the 1976 I preferred the 1975 Rausch Auslese, light and racy on the nose, and on the palate lean, exquisite and subtle, yet with lovely fruit, a wine of effortless refinement. Zilliken's Beerenauslesen are typical of the region: they do not overwhelm with their richness, and are distinguished more by their intensity of flavour, persistence, and grapy vigour, which keeps even the 1976 Saarburger Bergschlosschen clean and youthful and very long on the finish.

Zilliken participates in the great Eiswein race. He has made Eisweine from Rausch in 1983 and 1985 and both should be classified as lethal weapons. The former, harvested at over 180° Oechsle, has 263 g/l residual sugar, and the 1985 is not far behind with 200. As both wines have over 16.0 g/l acidity, they were almost painful to sip.

When I suggested that the 1985 would take thirty years to become palatable, Zilliken did not disagree. 'Magnificent but useless' is what I wrote in my notebook at the time, and I see no reason to change that view. Winemaking should be more than an exercise in statistical outrageousness. It is all very well for wine enthusiasts to *admire* such wines, as indeed do I, lauding their structure, applauding their extremities. But wines are made to be drunk. A tannic claret may need ten or twenty years to show its true class, but at least it can be drunk at those ages with great if not complete pleasure. This is not the case with most Eisweine, and while many of them are indeed great wines, I still lament the trend to make them at the expense of Beerenauslesen and TBA, which surely are wines of greater complexity and interest. This is confirmed even by Zilliken's own TBA, such as his 1976 Bockstein. The wine is less sumptuous than the great TBAs of the Rheingau or Rheinpfalz, but that is the *typicité* of the Saar, dictated by soil and climate. On the other hand it is intense and concentrated in flavour, vigorous and stylish, and clean and pure on the finish. At present one discerns rather than tastes the layers of flavour beneath the obvious attack on the palate, and the wine will need many more years before the richness fully emerges. But the structure is excellent, and it will soon be more pleasant to drink than the Eisweine, which will still resemble a dentist's drill long after the TBA has opened up.

A few miles north of Saarburg, just outside the village of Wiltingen, stands the lovely faded-yellow manor house of the Scharzhof. Egon Müller inherited the 9-hectare estate in 1945. His ancestors acquired it when the French secularised the original monastic estate after the Revolution. The great mound of the Scharzhofberg itself, on which most of the vineyards are located, sweeps up behind the house. Schist soil dominates its steep slopes, and yields, at 55 hl/ha, are exceptionally low. Müller also owns the Le Gallais estate near Wiltingen, but the Scharzhof is superior. Indeed, many regard Müller's Scharzhofberger as Germany's finest wine. It certainly seems to fetch the highest prices at the auctions at which great estates dispose, from time to time, of their rarest and most precious wines. Any Scharzhofberger not up to Müller's exacting standards for basic Kabinett is either bottled as Le Gallais or sold as Wiltinger Scharzberg QbA. Fermentation takes places in oak casks, and Süssreserve is never used for Auslesen and higher qualities.

Egon Müller is a courtly old gentleman of military appearance, with a crisp moustache and a somewhat fierce demeanour at odds with his gentle manners. A visit to the Scharzhof – its crusty gentility manifested by wood panelling, antlers used as hatracks, and an invasion of the interior by the cool winds of the exterior – has a ritual element to it. A tasting of young vintages takes place in the sombre hall, and, if Müller is disposed to prolong the meeting, it continues in the comfort of his library, which he leaves from time to time in order to fetch increasingly more precious bottles from his cellars. He shares Peter von Weymarn's criticisms of the 1971 wine law. He particularly scorns the practice of producers who blend their casks of Spätlesen and Auslesen in order to arrive at median must weights that would entitle the whole lot to be marketed as Auslese. That is the path to mediocrity, though one does not have to share Müller's criticisms of the wine law to share his disdain for such greedy practices. The grapes are picked as late as possible at Scharzhof, and the harvest often continues into the second week of November. The exposure of the vineyards and late picking often enable higher must weights to be attained here than at other Saar estates, and Scharzhof is able to make Auslesen and even Beerenauslesen in years when other properties fail to do so. This was the case in 1979 and 1983. Nevertheless, Müller will not release a Beerenauslese unless he considers the wine actually tastes like one, whatever the Oechsle reading may have been.

The Scharzhof wines do justify their reputation. The 1985 Auslesen were far too closed on palate and nose to be properly appreciated, though their intense spicy sweetness and invigorating but not overwhelming acidity augur very well. A 1976 Auslese (AP 22) was soft and cushiony, but rather too gentle and undemanding. Müller is less than ecstatic about his 1983 Beerenauslese, but I thought it was wonderful for all its youth. Its combination of roundness and spiciness was quite bewitching. The 1976 Beerenauslese is an extraordinary wine, its character derived from the richness of the vintage, when Scharzhof grapes attained exceptionally high must weights. The wine is almost syrupy, with a whole range of fruit flavours clamouring for attention on the palate. A brilliant deep gold in colour, it is big and honeyed on the nose, though still backward. Yet despite its richness and intensity, it is also very vigorous and by no means flabby. It is hard for the more delicate 1975 Beerenauslese to show as well against so rich a wine, though it too has a fine breadth of flavour and a ripe nose of honey and peaches. Even finer than the 1975 is the 1971, probably the most elegant and perfectly balanced of the four Beerenauslesen, with aromas of honey and flavours of apples and apricots on the palate. In comparison with the younger wines, it seemed lean and lemony, but none the worse for that. It is perhaps more characteristic of Saar wines than the 1976, and remains one of the most supremely elegant Rieslings that has come my way.

TBA is rare at Scharzhof – it is surprising to note that Müller's first TBA was produced in 1959 – but Eiswein is often made. The Ambrosi method of using plastic sheeting is not employed here, but grapes are deliberately left on the vine in the hope that severe frost will work its magic. This is risky, since as the winter advances, fewer and fewer of the grapes will remain healthy. 'One year,' Müller told me, 'we had to wait until February before harvesting Eiswein grapes, and the result was a mere five litres of wine. We had the grapes, but they were empty of juice.' His first Eiswein to be marketed as such was made in 1961. Before then Eisweine had been made, as the result of freak conditions, but as late as 1950 the Scharzhof Eiswein was sold as Auslese. Now, with the vogue for Eisweine, Müller is less shy about marketing the wines, for they are prized more than Beerenauslesen. When I expressed my iconoclastic views on Eiswein to Müller, he nodded in agreement, adding that it is possible to make Eiswein from any old grapes, as long as they are healthy, but for Beerenauslese only the very best botrytised grapes will do. The 1984 Eiswein was harvested on 3 and 4 January 1985 at 124° Oechsle and 14.0 g/l acidity, an excellent wine of marked pineapple flavours and very good length. The outstanding 1971 Beereenauslese Eiswein blends grapes picked on 20 November and 8 January. Although fifteen years old when tasted, I still found the wine closed on the nose and not yet knit on the palate, where the excellent ripe fruit was overlaid with fierce acidity. However, I must record the views of Stuart Pigott, an authority on German wines who visited Scharzhof shortly before I did and tasted many of the same wines, including this one. He found the same intense richness and very fresh long acidity, but also discerned a complexity that eluded me. He concluded, in an article in *Decanter*: 'Words must fail to do justice to this amazing wine in which every element of taste is perfectly developed. Undoubtedly the finest sweet white wine I have ever tasted!' There can be no greater praise than that, and I quote it in order to make clear that my views on Eiswein are not universally shared. My reservations do not, however, detract from my admiration for these great estates of the Mosel, and their irresistible, vigorous, and harmonious wine.

13

The Rest of Germany

FRANKEN

About 150 miles east of Trier and the Mosel is the lovely city of Würzburg, the heart of Franken (Franconia), a region of northern Bavaria. Its wines are little known outside Germany but they are of exceptional quality. In style they differ greatly not only from the racy, low-alcohol wines of the Mosel, but also from the elegant fruity wines of the Rheingau. For the climate here is far more continental than those regions, with long winters and hot summers. Consequently, Riesling is ill-suited to Franken, with its frequent early frosts in autumn, and only 2% of its 5250 hectares of vineyards are planted with it. Although the most common grape is Müller-Thurgau, accounting for half the vines of Franken, Silvaner, planted in 21% of Franken vineyards, is the variety that flourishes best here. Bacchus too is a popular grape, and so are many of the other cross-breeds, such as Scheurebe, Kerner, and Ortega. With so many varieties under cultivation, all ripening at slightly different times, it is very difficult for the authorities to control the harvest. Shortly before the grapes reach their optimal point, the newspapers will publish the *Zeitpunkt* for each region, and these will vary according to grape varieties. Thus in Würzburg in 1983, Ortega and Siegerrebe were picked first, followed by Müller-Thurgau, Bacchus, and Perle; next in line were Silvaner, Kerner, Faber, Scheurebe, and Albalonga. The style of the wines is as sturdy as the traditional round Bocksbeutel flagons in which they are bottled. They are high in extract, sometimes high in alcohol, wines of great personality that age well. Greatly prized locally, Franken wines are rarely sold outside the region, let alone outside Germany. Moreover, because production is limited, the climate unreliable, and local demand so strong, prices are notably higher than for Rheingau or Mosel wines of comparable quality, and this too inhibits exportation. One of the largest producers, the Staatliche Hofkeller in Würzburg, only exports 1.5% of its wines.

About half the production is processed by cooperatives, but there are also a number of outstanding private estates, many based in Würzburg. There is a less umbilical connection between vineyard and winery in Franken than elsewhere in Germany, and the Staatliche Hofkeller owns 120 hectares dispersed all over the region. The cellars themselves, which have a capacity of two million litres, are alongside and beneath one of the wings of the Residenz, the great Baroque palace of the Prince-Bishops of Würzburg in the centre of the town. The subterranean vaults of 1721 must surely be the most spectacular in Germany, a vast tall candlelit space lined with a double stack of large oval casks, some dating from the eighteenth century and immaculately maintained. At the far end of the cellars stands a mighty wine press of about 1750. The casks, some of which hold 7000 litres, are still in use, and all wines spend a minimum of four weeks in wood, though many will stay in cask for up to a year. The Hofkeller's most famous wine was a Stein made in 1546, a year when no rain fell from April to October, and the grapes had to be picked in July. Apparently some of the wine was still in existence until quite recently, and was said to be not unlike sherry in flavour.

The Hofkeller grows all its own grapes on 170 hectares it either owns or manages. A surprisingly high proportion of Riesling is made, up to 25%, followed by 20% Müller-Thurgau and 7% Silvaner. The winery has substantial holdings in the great vineyards on the edge of the city: Stein and Innere Leiste. So celebrated is the 90 hectare Stein that Franken wine is often referred to as Steinwein, even though the term should be used only of wine from that specific vineyard. A large range of wines, reflecting all the possible permutations of vineyards, grape varieties, and QmP categories, is made, and there is very little blending. This involves extreme efficiency and dedication on the part of the director, Dr Eichelsbacher, and his staff, for some lots are made in quantities as infinitesimal as fifty litres. Such lots are fermented in very small casks or in stainless steel tanks about the size of a domestic spin-dryer. Musts with high sugar content are left to ferment unimpeded. There is no premium put on high residual sugar for its own sake. The 1983 Würzburger Stein Rieslaner Auslese, for instance, was picked at 106° Oechsle, but only had 24 g/l of residual sugar. On the other hand the acidity is fairly low, between 5 and 6 g/l, so such residual sugar as remains is noticeable. This particular wine was quite sweet and delicate, though characteristically earthy on the aftertaste. Franken wines, of which this is typical, need long ageing before they show their full quality, and many wines are bottle-aged at the Hofkeller for two to three years. Less broad than the Rieslaner was the 1983 Innere Leiste Riesling Beerenauslese, picked at 145° Oechsle and with 79 g/l residual sugar. Being made from Riesling, the wine had good lively acidity, but also that broadness on the nose common to many Franken wines.

A hundred yards from the vast palace and the Hofkeller is the Bürgerspital zum Heiligen Geist, one of the many charitable institutions that have been associated for centuries with great German winemaking. This hospital was founded in 1319 and endowed with vineyards, making it the oldest wine estate in Germany. The hospital, which now runs an old people's home, is in part supported by the revenues from the winery. Vineyards are owned not only around Würzburg but in many of the villages of Franken. With 144 hectares, of which 100 are presently under cultivation, the Bürgerspital is the fourth largest wine estate in Germany. As at the Hofkeller, much Riesling is made – roughly 20% of their annual production of about 70,000 cases – identical to the proportion of both Müller-Thurgau and Silvaner. About half the wine is stored in stainless steel, and half

in wood, but even wines kept in tank will have spent some time in wood first. On arrival at the winery, the grapes are crushed and left overnight on the skins before being pressed. Fermentation in tanks is quite slow, and it is sometimes necessary to warm the musts to keep fermentation going. After it is completed, the wines are filtered and bottled early, though bottled-aged before release.

The vast majority of Franken wines are dry. Auslese must have a minimum Oechsle reading of 100°, and Beerenauslese of 125°, but the Bürgerspital is rarely satisfied with minimal grades and only makes such wines if the Oechsle readings are considerably higher. Auslesen are infrequent in Franken, and Beerenauslesen very rare. The Bürgerspital made such wines in 1971, 1975 (minute quantities), 1976 (a great year here as elsewhere), and 1979, but the quantities are trifling, from thirty to 500 litres. As at the Hofkeller, the style tends to be high in alcohol and low in residual sugar, sometimes as low as 45–50 g/l even for Beerenauslese. This does not, as in other parts of Germany where such styles are attempted (as by Bernd Philippi in Kallstadt), result in unbalanced wines, for Franken wines are invariably high in extract, with great depth of flavour. Two 1983 Auslesen from the Stein vineyard provided a fascinating contrast. A Gewürztraminer, picked at 112° Oechsle, and with only 27g/l residual sugar but a startling 13.8% alcohol, was characteristic of the grape variety, soft and broad, but it did not have enough acidity to prevent the wine

from being somewhat awkward, and the alcohol was certainly noticeable on the palate. The Riesling – high in must weight, residual sugar
(54 g/l), and acidity (9.0 g/l), but lower in alcohol (12.9%) – was much
better balanced: elegantly fruity on the nose, and a rounded wine of
good weight, vigour, and concentration on the palate, with a lovely
spicy finish and good length. It bears no resemblance to a Rhein
Riesling, but is certainly a wine of wonderful individuality and
character. Sadly, a mere 160 bottles were made, so the chances of
finding any are remote.

Two Beerenauslesen also offered a contrast between Riesling and
a variety of lesser reputation. The 1982 Gössenheimer Homburg
Bacchus was a great surprise. Gössenheim has a very special microclimate that even orchids find congenial, and Bacchus does well here.
These grapes were picked at 135° Oechsle, and the wine has 76 g/l
residual sugar, 9.5 g/l acidity, and 13.2% alcohol. Thus it resembles
analytically the Riesling Auslese. Yet the wine has an entirely
different character: lovely pale yellow-gold in colour, it has a rich soft
botrytis nose and considerable sweetness on the palate, followed by a
fresh, spicy, almost tart aftertaste and good length. When mature,
this wine will have a definition and character as precise and strong as
that of the Riesling. A 1976 Würzburger Abtsleite Riesling Beerenauslese shows how splendidly these wines can age. Picked at 140°
Oechsle, it only has 61 g/l residual sugar. Although it is danger-
ously high in alcohol at 14.9% (even great Sauternes is rarely that
alcoholic), there is sufficient acidity (9.3 g/l) to keep the wine
balanced. Very lush on the nose, with aromas of honey, peaches, and
apples, the wine is soft and rounded on the palate, but intensely
concentrated and packed with flavour; it is also very lively and
spicy, almost racy despite the alcohol, and has very good length
and a clean finish. This bottle clearly demonstrated how superb
these top Franken wines can be, but they are very rare and very
expensive.

The third great Würzburg winery supports another hospital, the
Juliusspital. The magnificent long arcaded hospital buildings of
1720, and the exquisite chapel and rococo Apotheke (pharmacy)
tucked among them, are very much a going concern. Founded in
1576, the hospital still runs a large old people's home. The cellars,
some 250 metres long, are lined with 280 casks, many of them
magnificently carved. Fermentation still takes place in wood, though

wines are now stored in tanks before being bottled. Its vineyards, dotted around Franken, amount to 156 hectares, of which 90 are presently under cultivation. Müller-Thurgau and Silvaner occupy a quarter each of the vineyards, and the 8% presently planted with Riesling is being expanded to 12–15%. Although I have tasted many of the good dry wines from the Juliusspital, I have not sampled the rare sweeter styles. The reputation of the winery is good, but of lesser renown than the two other Würzburg wineries already discussed.

Many notable wineries flourish outside the city, for the region is a large one. Weingut Schloss Sommerhaus produced a rich spicy 1976 Sommerhäuser Reisenstein Scheurebe Beerenauslese, but that was exceptional. The grandest estate outside the city is the Fürstlich Castell'sches Domänenamt, owned by the princely family of Castell. This is a unique property, for the family control the entire village huddled beneath the Schlossberg, on which the medieval castle once stood, the palace itself, and a bank, not to mention the eight vineyards they own exclusively, a rarity in Germany. The whole place is a throwback to the days when Germany was a collection of tiny principalities. Until 1806 Castell was an independent state of 20,000 inhabitants occupying 500 square kilometres, which it defended with its own army. Some years ago a Castell daughter married Prince Michael zu Salm, owner of the Prinz zu Salm-Dalberg'sches Weingut, the oldest private estate in the Nahe. Prince Michael is now the administrator of Castell too and takes a keen interest in the management of the vineyards as well as the marketing of the wine.

Castell's 58 hectares are the most easterly vineyards in Germany, and the climate is formidable, with hot summers, cold winters, and autumnal fogs. Most of the vineyards are between 320 and 380 metres above sea level, and some, such as the Schlossberg, are exceedingly steep. The vines are all hand-cultivated, even those on flatter ground. The soil is heavy, with marl, loam, clay, gypsum, and a high mineral content. This soil structure gives the wine an earthy quality even more distinctive than that of the Würzburg wines; they also tend to be highly aromatic. Yields are fairly low, averaging about 65 hl/ha, with only 40–45 for Rieslaner. Despite the charm of the landscape, there is a primitive and raw atmosphere to this part of Germany, quite unlike the demure, profoundly settled Rhein or Mosel regions. It seemed appropriate that while gunning through the vineyards at high speed with Prince Michael in his battered orange Volkswagen we encountered a large buzzard breakfasting off a freshly impaled young hare. At Castell almost 7 hectares are planted with Rieslaner, accounting for a full 10% of the total German production of this variety. Many other grapes are planted, and thus quantities and yields vary enormously from year to year. Large estates in the other wine regions can guarantee a fairly constant supply to wholesalers, except in the very worst vintages, but in Franken even the largest properties cannot guarantee a consistent supply of the same wines, and this, as well as high cost, inhibits export.

Since early frosts are common in Franken, especially in easterly Castell, it should be relatively easy to make Eisweine here, but the fad has not spread as widely in Franken as in the Rheingau or Mosel. Castell did produce Eiswein in 1983 or 1985, when the grapes were picked at 143° and 186° Oechsle. The 1983 Casteller Schlossberg Silvaner Eiswein, of which about 3000 litres were made, was very good, high in extract, and with admirable balance between the earthy breadth of flavour and a lively elegant acidity. Grapes need 130° Oechsle to qualify as Beerenauslese in Franken, but Castell upgrades its wines and would not market a wine with a must weight of less than 150° as Beerenauslese, but would sell it as Auslese instead. Production of such wines is limited, and ranges from 200 to 2000 bottles. TBA is even more rare. Vinification varies according to the style of the wine. High-acidity white grapes such as Rieslaner are fermented in cask, but Eisweine ferment for up to three weeks in small 300- to

600-litre steel tanks. TBA, however, has been known to continue fermenting until the summer. The wines are bottled early, especially Beerenauslesen and Eisweine, but the bottles are stored for years before release. The 1979 Beerenauslese was still not released for sale by 1986. An example of the style is demonstrated by the 1976 Casteller Schlossberg Silvaner, picked at 150° Oechsle, and with 162 g/l residual sugar. The wine looked beautiful, a deep amber-gold colour, and it was very honeyed on the nose. On the palate, however, it lacked vigour and acidity, and there was a touch of caramel, as there had been on the nose, suggesting some oxidation had taken place. The wine was broad, almost chewy, with plenty of extract, but it lacked charm and vitality. In general, though, Silvaner makes some of the most reliable and long-lived wines, sweet as well as dry, in Franken.

BADEN

The Baden vineyards begin just south of the Rheinpfalz and continue all the way down to the Swiss border at Basel. As the most southerly of the German wine regions, its climate is warmer than that of the other regions and it is the only one classified by the EEC as Zone B, and is thus on a par with Alsace. The majority of the wines are made by cooperatives for local consumption. Very little is exported. The wines from a leading private estate with which I am familiar have been very rich in sugar, in contrast to those of Franken, and show a good intensity of flavour and rich, even syrupy texture. Grape varieties such as Gewürztraminer and Scheurebe are popular, and one of the better wines I have tasted was, of all things, a Müller-Thurgau Beerenauslese. In general Baden wines have the lowest acidity of any German wines, and one should not expect them to age well.

WÜRTTEMBERG

South of Franken is the geographically large region of Württemberg, which stretches to Stuttgart and beyond. Despite its size, only 9000 hectares are under vine. As in Franken and Baden, the climate seems to favour the production of sweet wines, but although the autumns are long and warm, they also tend to be very dry, and this inhibits the development of botrytis. Moreover, as in Baden, grapes tend to be low in acidity. Württemberg is also the source of much of Germany's indigenous red wine. One of the few estates that does occasionally produce sweet styles is Burg Schaubeck, a charming castle dating from the thirteenth century and set among formal gardens. Its 15 hectares of vineyards (planted with slightly more red grapes than white) are mostly located on steep slopes in the adjacent hamlet of Kleinbottwar north of Stuttgart. The owner is Graf Adelmann, whose family inherited the estate in 1914. The vintage is late and grapes are often still being picked in mid-November. Once every two or three years Burg Schaubeck will produce sweet wines. Juice with very high must weights is simply left to get on with its fermentation, which may have to be aided with inoculated yeasts and can take, in the case of TBA, up to four weeks. Sometimes the fermentation continues long enough to give a dry Auslese, but often it stops, leaving residual sugar. Exceedingly small quantities have to be fermented in 25-litre glass demijohns. Wines are bottled roughly nine months after the harvest. In recent years some Eisweine have been produced here.

Of a whole range of Auslesen made from Kerner, Traminer, and Clevner (an early-ripening mutation of Pinot Noir), the Traminers were the best. A 1975 Rülander Beerenauslese was a disappointment, limp in the mouth, while a rich succulent 1971 Riesling Beerenauslese was beginning to dry out, as was a 1979 Traminer TBA. The Eisweine were better, especially the 1985 Riesling, picked at 189° Oechsle, and with 150 g/l residual sugar and a fine 13.0 g/l acidity. The young wine was surprisingly hefty on the nose, with piercing pineapple aromas, and on the palate it was rich but racy, beautifully balanced, and though one-dimensional at present, very promising. However, only eighty litres of this wine were made, and many of the sweet wines from Burg Schaubeck are clearly made solely for family consumption. It is only fair to say that Burg Schaubeck makes no claims to be a major producer of top-quality sweet wines – its very high reputation rests on its wide range of dry and red wines – and is mentioned here simply to give an indication, however sketchy, of the style of Württemberg sweet wines, and to suggest why they are not in the top rank. Another Württemberg estate, Weingut Graf von Neipperg at Schwaigern, also produces the occasional Eiswein and rich, mouth-filling Traminer Auslesen.

14

Austria

It is tempting to think of Austrian wine as a lesser species of German wine. The similarities are, however, fairly superficial, even though the Austrian wine law of 1972 introduced a system of categories (Spätlese, Beerenauslese, etc.) based on the German model. Yet there are significant differences between the wines of the two countries. For a start, the grape varieties, although overlapping, are mostly distinct. Moreover, in Austria's more southerly climate, grapes ripen more rapidly and the minimum must weights prescribed by law within each category are slightly higher than in Germany. German Trockenbeerenauslese must be picked at a minimum of 150° Oechsle, while in Austria grapes for TBA must register 156°. And whereas wines of Beerenauslese and TBA quality are a prized and pricy rarity in Germany, comparably sweet Austrian wines are so abundant that their sheer quantity can prove an embarrassment. Many a producer in Burgenland has thousands of litres of 1981 TBA sitting in tank while the company patiently waits for its current stock of the bottled wine to be sold (and after the wine scandal of 1985, of which more later, that could be a long wait).

A further difference, minor but irksome, between German and Austrian sweet wine production is in the systems used to measure must weight. Germany uses the Oechsle system, while Austria has adopted a measurement known as Klosterneuburger Mostwaage, mercifully abbreviated to KMW. This device is an aerometer that measures the must's specific gravity as determined by its sugar content, and this sugar content is expressed in KMW as a percentage of the must weight. As a rough rule of thumb, you multiply KMW by five to find the equivalent Oechsle measurement. The minimum

KMW readings for each category of Prädikatswein are as follows: Spätlese 19 (94° Oechsle); Auslese 21 (105° Oechsle); Eiswein and Beerenauslese 25 (127° Oechsle); Ausbruch 27 (138° Oechsle); and TBA 30 (156° Oechsle).

Large areas of eastern Austria are covered with vineyards. Along the Danube stretches the Wachau, the region around the city of Krems. To the north and east, as far as the Czech border, lies the Weinviertel. South of Graz, near the Yugoslav border, are the vineyards of Steiermark (Styria). Just south of Vienna itself are Gumpoldskirchen and Vöslau, and southeast of the capital lies the Burgenland, with over 20,000 hectares under vine. Austrians themselves prefer dry wines, both white and red; their own consumption of their splendid dessert wines is minimal. In any event, the climate of the Wachau and Steiermark is rarely conducive to the cultivation of overripe or botrytised grapes. The Burgenland, however, has a microclimate that attracts botrytis the way honey attracts flies. Although not abundant every year – in 1985, for instance, the autumn was too warm and dry for much botrytis to take hold – when noble rot does attack the grapes, it tends to do so on an apocalyptic scale, producing enormous harvests. In Gumpoldskirchen too, high sugar content is routinely attained.

Before looking at these regions in greater detail, it is worth knowing something about Austrian grape varieties, for while certain of them – such as Riesling, Müller-Thurgau, Gewürztraminer, and Rülander – will be familiar to drinkers of German wines, there are other varieties found exclusively or predominantly in Austria. Few of the classic grapes are widely grown here. By far the most popular variety is *Grüner Veltliner*, which makes lively and spicy white wines, but this grape is rarely suitable for sweet wine; Grüner Veltliner Spätlesen are common enough, but the higher sugar content is reflected in greater fullness rather than sweetness. A variety greatly valued in Austria, especially in the Burgenland, is *Weissburgunder* (Pinot Blanc), from which much of the best Beerenauslese and TBA is made. If it achieves the necessarily high KMW readings, Weissburgunder can usually be relied on to have sufficiently high acidity to balance the sugar. This is not always the case with other varieties.

Welschriesling (the same as Laski Riesling in Yugoslavia and Riesling Italico) is almost as highly regarded for the making of sweet wines. Many people look down their noses at this variety. Vinified dry, it usually lacks the bouquet, elegance and breed of the true German Riesling, to which it is unrelated except by name. But when the grapes are packed with sugar, Welschriesling, like Weissburgunder, often has sufficient acidity to balance the sweetness. The true Riesling, known in Austria as *Rheinriesling*, is rarely used to make sweet wines. According to the distinguished winemaker Johannes Holler, Rheinriesling tends to contract botrytis too early and there can be a slight bitterness in the resulting wine. Moreover, Rheinriesling, like Jubiläum and Müller-Thurgau, is easily blown from the vine when in a shrivelled, nobly rotten condition; and strong winds are common in the Burgenland. *Rülander* (Pinot Gris), which gives dry wines in Alsace and northern Italy, shows at its best in Austria at Spätlese levels and above. Many distinguished Beerenauslesen and Ausbruch wines are made from Rülander.

Jubiläum is a new grape, a crossing of Blaufränkisch and Blauer Portugieser. Although these are red varieties, Jubiläum itself is a white grape. It ripens early and frequently attains high sugar levels, so it is better suited to sweet wines than to dry ones. *Neuburger*, a crossing of Weissburgunder and Silvaner, is an Austrian speciality, widely grown and made in all styles. This variety can give uneven yields and lack acidity, but it is certainly capable of making full-bodied Spätlesen and impressive TBAs. Another early-maturing grape ideal for Prädikatswein is *Bouvier*, a native variety; its principal drawbacks are low yields and occasionally weak acidity. Unlike Neuburger, Bouvier sometimes lacks distinctive varietal character; nevertheless its small, botrytised grapes can make outstanding sweet wines. Austrian *Traminer* rarely has the aromatic power of Alsatian Gewürztraminer, but the Austrian variety has the same instantly recognisable aromatic spicy bouquet. At high must weights, individual varietal character is often lost; but the Traminer grape can retain its identity even in a very sweet wine. The same is true of the *Muskat-Ottonel*. This widely planted variety has been losing popularity in recent years; but like *Müller-Thurgau* it can be impressive when sugar levels are sufficiently high. Two Austrian varieties are specialities of the Gumpoldskirchen district: *Zierfandler* (also known as Spätrot) and *Rotgipfler*. They are usually blended to produce a fat and full-flavoured wine, at its best rich and heady, at its worst blowsy and overblown. And finally, there is the red grape variety *Zweigelt* (a crossing of Blaufränkisch with St Laurent), from which wines up to Ausbruch standard are occasionally made.

The categories of Prädikatswein are identical to the German categories (and as in Germany, Prädikatsweine may not be chaptalised) and include Eiswein and a few additional categories. In some parts of the Burgenland Strohwein is produced, in the same manner as French *vin de paille* or Italian *passito*, namely, from grapes left to dry out over a period of months. You will also find the term Ausbruch on some wine labels. 'Ausbruch' used to refer not to a category of sweetness but to a method of winemaking similar to that still employed to make Tokay Aszú in Hungary. This method, however, is no longer followed in Austria, and 'Ausbruch' simply means that the grapes had dried out naturally on the vine and attained at least 27 KMW. It is permitted to enrich Ausbruch wine with fresh must or wine from the same vineyard to assist the winemaking process, which can be strenuously difficult with desiccated grapes. Austrian wine law prescribes that Beerenauslese must be made from grapes of a minimum of 25 KMW; and TBA must be picked at no less than 30 KMW. Ausbruch, then, is a wine in the upper portion of the Beerenauslese bracket. Many producers dispense with the category altogether, recognising that Austrian wine labels present quite enough complexities as it is, and sell their Ausbruch as Beerenauslese. Finally, there is Essenz. This too echoes the Tokay method, in which the sheer weight of the botrytis-shrivelled grapes in the baskets in which they are gathered causes some highly concentrated juice to seep down to the bottom, where it is collected and fermented separately. This must has such extraordinarily high sugar content that it rarely ferments to more than a few degrees of alcohol. On the other hand it can attain a residual sugar content of over 300 g/l. Some Burgenland producers make small quantities of Essenz in exceptional years.

The Burgenland, easily the most important region for the production of sweet wines, is less than an hour's drive from Vienna. As soon as you leave the city limits heading south you are surrounded by vineyards. To the west the hills of Gumpoldskirchen rise hazily against the sky, while straight ahead are the flat vineyards of Tattendorf and innumerable other villages. A band of low hills, the Leitha Gebirge, separate the Burgenland from the Vienna plains. The River

Leitha, indeed, forms the border. On the far slopes of the Leitha hills are the vineyards that overlook the villages of St Georgen, Donnerskirchen and Purbach, and the handsome little town of Eisenstadt. East of these villages lies the Neusiedler See, visible across a shallow flat shelf, most of which is an area of swamps and reeds unsuitable for cultivation and inhabited by abundant wildfowl. The vineyards stretch all the way round the lake from the west to the east, surrounding the villages of Neusiedl, Gols, and Halbturn. (The southern shores of the Neusiedler See are also under vine, but this area is Hungarian territory and mostly planted with red grapes.) The Burgenland's specialisation in sweet styles is a comparatively recent development. Viticulture has been practised here since Roman times, and sweet wines have been recorded here since the sixteenth century, though not in the vast quantities of recent decades. Until 1921, indeed, the entire Burgenland was part of Hungary, and even now there are many inhabitants of Hungarian or Croatian descent. Once the Burgenland became Austrian territory, the dire economic conditions of the 1920s and 1930s inhibited the development of the wine industry. After World War II, the Burgenland was within the Russian zone, and once again there was virtually no fresh investment in the industry. Only when the Russians withdrew in 1956 did such investment take place. Even in the 1950s and 1960s, while fine sweet wines were made when climatic conditions were appropriate, no special effort was made to produce them.

This changed in 1969, when botrytis was so widespread that most

growers found the majority of their grapes qualifying as Prädikatswein. Hans Achs of Gols recalled that when he began his harvest, his
grapes registered readings of, on average, 23 KMW, so he assumed
his instruments were broken. He went next door to borrow his
neighbour's, but the neighbour regretfully said that his were not
functioning either. The instruments, however, were completely
accurate, and growers found themselves with casks and tanks full of
splendidly rich sweet wines for which there was scant demand in
Austria itself. Some dismayed producers took to blending tanks full
of Beerenauslese with their least sugary wines in an attempt to
concoct something more commercially acceptable.

The Germans, on the other hand, were delighted. Merchants
discovered vast stocks of high-quality Prädikatswein at, by German
standards, extremely low prices. The Burgenlanders, anxious to
exploit an assured export market for their sweet wines, began to
specialise in them. In 1969 Austrian winemakers, mostly in the
Burgenland, produced an astonishing 12,225 hectolitres of Beerenauslese and 3500 hectolitres of TBA. But these figures were sur-
passed in 1973 and 1976, and more than doubled in 1981. Some firms
exported up to 90% of their production to Germany and to other
European nations with a taste for sweet wines at bargain prices. Yet
the Austrians were never able to convince the world that their sweet
wines were comparable to the best of France and Germany. Their
very cheapness probably suggested to consumers that the wines were
somehow lacking. It must also be said that the best Austrian wines
were not easy to find outside Austria and Germany. Whether the
Prädikatsweine of the Burgenland failed to establish a high international reputation because they were hard to find, or whether they
were hard to find because importers ignored wines with no international reputation is, of course, a chicken-and-egg argument: both
were true.

Then in 1985 the glycol scandal erupted. Certain producers,
mostly wholesalers who bought grapes or wine from smaller growers,
were discovered to have doctored the wines with diethylene glycol in
order to sweeten them. The results were catastrophic. Consumers
were rightly appalled by the adulteration. The Austrian authorities
were slow to react, and this bureaucratic sloth did little to reassure
the consumer. When the authorities did react, they did so not only by
placing the offenders behind bars but by promulgating new wine

laws said to be the most stringent in Europe. Some of the regulations, while they will undoubtedly reassure the consumer in the long term, will hit the wine industry hard. For instance, it is now forbidden to export Prädikatswein in bulk; all such wine must be exported in bottle. This will eliminate a sizeable proportion of export sales to Germany, a country which used to accept 60% or more of all Austrian wine exports.

However rigorous the new wine law, it came too late for many. The damage has been done. Austria's largest private winemaker, Lenz Moser, a pioneering firm of impeccable reputation, declared bankruptcy in March 1986. The Unger family, highly-reputed Burgenland producers and wholesalers, told me how over twenty-five years they had built up a business and exported almost half their production. Then overnight that export market vanished. In the aftermath of the scandal the innocent are as severely punished as the guilty. The culprits are of course in jail and their cellars closed up, but the merchants and consumers of Europe and the United States make few distinctions between guilty and innocent. The scandal inevitably altered patterns of wine production. Growers and merchants with large stocks of unsold and unsalable Prädikatswein from the abundant 1981 vintage are turning their attentions to drier styles. The microclimate of the region will ensure that very sweet wines will continue to be produced, but they are sure to be played down for at least the next decade.

On the edge of Eisenstadt stands a large mustard-coloured palace, its tall wings shading a central courtyard and a park at the rear. This Schloss is one of many built by the Esterhazy family, who once owned a further 98 such residences in Hungary, where their principal estates once lay. Despite the loss of roughly 500,000 hectares in Hungary, the current head of the clan, Dr Paul Esterhazy, still owns about 60,000 in Austria as well as the Schloss. Joseph Haydn was court musician here and his body lies in a dignified mausoleum a few hundred yards from the palace. The princely Esterhazys were not just outstanding patrons of the arts; they were also official purveyors of wines to the Imperial Household. Wines are still made at the Esterhazy'sche Schlosskellerei at the palace. The 43 hectares of vineyards are dispersed around the villages that line the slopes of the Leitha Gebirge: Rust, St Margarethen, St Georgen, and

Eisenstadt itself. 75% of the vineyards are planted with white grapes, and Welschriesling at 20% claims the greatest share, followed by Weissburgunder, Traminer, and Muskat-Ottonel (10% each).

Beneath the Schloss stretch long cavernous cellars lined with elaborately carved casks that mark the births of successive generations of the family. Dr Paul Esterhazy's barrel is likely to be the last, for he has no direct heirs. The burly and boisterous cellarmaster remarked testily to me that the romantic old cellars were lovely to look at but a pain to work in. He produces a full range of wines, from crisp Weissburgunders and sparkling wines to sumptuous TBAs. Even in the Burgenland, TBA cannot be produced annually, and the Esterhazy estate was typical of most in only producing them, in recent years, in 1969, 1973, 1979, and 1981. The top Prädikatsweine ferment slowly and are stored in 20- or 30-hectolitre vats for up to two years before being bottled. Relatively forward, the Esterhazy Beerenauslesen and TBAs are drinkable within five years and are at their best between ten and twenty years after the vintage.

The wines are of high quality, and the Schlosskellerei will occasionally downgrade a wine. The 1981 Ruster Traminer Auslese, for instance, had a must weight of 26 KMW, entitling it to a Beerenauslese rating. But it is sold as Auslese, because, the cellarmaster explained, he would rather market an outstanding Auslese than an undernourished Beerenauslese. Their top wine, a 1981 St Margarethen Jubiläum TBA, has an astonishingly high KMW reading of 40 and 212 g/l residual sugar, and it is certainly promising. It will undoubtedly improve as it ages, for it was a comparatively youthful five years old when I tasted it, still rather closed on the nose and lacking in depth and character.

Despite the dependable quality of the Esterhazy wines, they enjoy less of a reputation than they deserve. This is a classic case of a missed opportunity. The vast majority of Burgenland producers are small family businesses with fewer than 5 hectares of vineyards. In addition there are the large cooperatives and a handful of wholesalers, such as Sepp Hold and Alexander Unger. The Esterhazy estate has a pedigree unmatched by any other in the Burgenland. If, instead of operating as a sound if unadventurous small commercial winery, it were to concentrate on making and marketing the very finest wines that the region is capable of, it could surely establish itself as the flagship estate of the Burgenland. When wine drinkers dream of Bordeaux or Burgundy, such names as Lafite, Pétrus, Romanée-Conti, and Leflaive drift past. When, however, one speaks of Esterhazy one thinks of glorious Haydn string quartets more than of the fine wines of today. There is no name in the Burgenland that reverberates as magnificently as Esterhazy, but unfortunately Dr Esterhazy has no special interest in his winery and has not encouraged its development. It is surely significant that, even before the wine scandal, no more than 10% of its wine was exported.

It is of course mostly the larger firms that find exportation worthwhile. For a small producer with only a few hectares and a wide selection of wines in different styles, the whole procedure is simply more trouble than it is worth, especially now that bulk sales of Prädikatswein are not allowed. Thus any international reputation the wines have earned has been established by cooperatives and larger dealers. Many of these make wines of a very high standard. Nevertheless, with a very few exceptions, their wine rarely matches the very finest of which the Burgenland is capable. With technologically advanced equipment and scrupulous quality control, they release wines that are well made and reasonably priced, but often lack character. Prädikatsweine fail when they are packed with sugar and not much else. Acidity is as essential to successful Austrian sweet wines as to those of Germany, and so is character. This is achieved by the quality of the raw materials and by the skills of the individual winemaker. It is far harder for a cooperative or merchant who buys and blends grapes and wine from a variety of sources to achieve such character.

The principal cooperative is the Burgenlandische Winzerverband, which links twenty-six producers into what is primarily a marketing organisation. It produces about seven million litres each year and stocks two million bottles, since quality wines are usually kept in bottle for up to a year before being released. Its Beerenauslese and TBA are not single variety wines, but blends of any of six varieties. There is nothing wrong with that, but it suggests that the grapes have come from a variety of sources and that the resulting wine will lack complexity and character, as indeed it does. Both wines lacked acidity and were slightly sticky on the finish. Similar flaws marred the sweet wines marketed by Sepp Hold, a St Georgen winery with a cellar capacity of two million litres. There is very little wood-ageing undertaken here. Not all the grapes are bought in, for the estate owns 13 hectares of vineyards in St Georgen, half of which have recently been replanted with red grapes. The 1983 Bouvier Beerenauslese had sweetness and delicacy, but no real grip; it slipped pleasantly through the mouth and down the throat and, while well balanced, had little distinctiveness. The 1981 TBA (a blend, mostly Traminer) was surprisingly lively and elegant for a wine with 142 g/l residual sugar; though rich and sweet on the palate, the flavour lacked persistence.

One cooperative does seem to make significantly better wines than its rivals: the Winzergenossenschaft St Martinus of Donnerskirchen. Although its headquarters are in a fine old building that formerly belonged to the Esterhazys, the cooperative was only founded in 1953 and purchases grapes, usually the entire crop, from about 400 growers. Its cellars have a capacity of 6.5 million litres. Like all other Burgenland wineries, St Martinus is cutting back on the production of sweet wines. St Martinus claims that what may have been the world's first TBA was made in its cellars in 1526. Documents refer to this famous wine as Lutherwein, and the cooperative understandably generates as much favourable publicity as it can from this historical accident. There is a distinct style fashioned by the cellarmasters at St Martinus: they aim for low alcohol and high residual sugar. The Pradikatsweine are for the most part gentle, well-balanced flavoury wines. Among those I tasted the only failure was a 1978 Neuburger Eiswein. In that year there was little botrytis, so growers left the grapes unpicked longer than usual, and they were rewarded with an early December frost that made possible an Eiswein harvest. The 1976 and 1981 Beerenauslesen and TBAs, varietal wines made from either Müller-Thurgau or Welschriesling, were outstanding, with a full honeyed botrytis bouquet and excellent acidity to counteract the richness. The 1981 Welschriesling TBA, with about 250 g/l residual sugar, should develop into a superb wine in a few years' time, demonstrating just how good Austrian cooperative wine can be at its best.

Like the St Martinus cellars, the estate now owned by Alexander Unger at St Margarethen was purchased from the ubiquitous Esterhazys. Unger's operation is both a Weingut – making and selling wines from its own 20 hectares of vineyards at St Margarethen and Theresienfeld – and a Kellerei, buying in from other growers and making and marketing blended wines. Here too the Eiswein – a 1983 Rheinriesling – was disappointing; the nose was somewhat attenuated, and the lively acidity could not fully disguise a thinness and lack of body behind the sugar. If the 1983 Gewürztraminer Beerenauslese seemed insipid on the palate, I could not say the same about two of the TBAs, a 1979 Neuburger and a 1980 Bouvier. The Neuburger was particularly good, with just the concentration and roundness one looks for in a well-made wine of this richness. Although I always hesitate to hazard a guess at the grape variety from which any TBA is made – varietal characteristics tend to be smothered by the residual sugar – I did detect that whiff of tropical fruit that often gives Neuburger wines their character.

Predictably, the very finest Prädikatsweine come from individual producers who can control the entire process of winemaking, from the vineyard to the bottling line. Austria rejoices in the institutions of the Heurige and the Buschenschank. Although the terms are sometimes interchangeable, a Heurige is simply an inn where young local wines are sold, with or without simple food. A Buschenschank is often an extension of a Weingut where you can order a range of wines by the glass. The dates when a Buschenschank is open – usually during the spring and autumn – are regulated, so as to give each winemaker an equal crack at the market. It was at his Buschenschank in Rust that I encountered Peter Schandl. Rust, perhaps the best-known wine town of the Burgenland, is a charming place, filled with dignified seventeenth century houses, each with large carriage gates leading into long courtyards lined with winery outbuildings. Storks nest on the chimneytops, surveying the 480 hectares of vineyards within the community, which are divided between 120 growers. In great years up to 90% of the wines can be Prädikatsweine. Half the wine is sold to the cooperative, another 10% is sold as grapes, and of the remainder a third used to be sold in cask, though it seems certain that an ever-increasing proportion will be bottled. Schandl wears all possible hats: he sells grapes to the cooperative, wine to wholesalers, operates a Buschenschank, and bottles his own wines. Not surprisingly, the pick of the crop finds its way into his own bottles. Schandl is a burly man, red-faced, bearded, and ebullient, who resembles a prize-fighter. He is pugnacious in his attacks on the bureaucracy that impedes his commercial activities and opinionated on the subject of wine, as all good winemakers generally are.

His own property is relatively large, but of his 20 hectares only 13 are currently in production. Like most of the best vineyards at Rust, his enjoy a south-east exposure, and from their gentle slopes you can see the Neusiedler See drawing a grey line along the horizon. Only a third of his grapes are white; in descending order, Welschriesling, Rheinriesling, Weissburgunder, Rülander, Traminer, and Muskat-Ottonel are his most widely planted varieties. The grapes for Prädikatsweine are destalked and the must is left in contact with the skins for up to eighteen hours, depending on the soundness of the grapes. The must is then racked into casks, in which fermentation proceeds for two or three weeks. The wine is stored in vats of various sizes until April, when it is bottled. Schandl derides those who heat the wine before bottling to eliminate any possibility of secondary fermentation in bottle. He would rather take the slight risk than tamper with the wine more than is strictly necessary. 'I watch my wines constantly. You shouldn't rely on chemicals and other agents to do the work for you.' He prefers to age his wines in bottle rather than in cask, so as to preserve their freshness; the sweetest wines will stay in his cellars for up to eighteen months before being released.

For the sweeter styles he prefers Weissburgunder and the two Rieslings, because of their high acidity; he aims for at least 7 g/l.

Schandl also thinks well of Rülander, for its body more than its acidity, and they are among his best wines. He seeks to make wines that are capable of ageing, and maintains that a well-made Spätlese with good structure should last fifteen years, and that Ausbruch and TBAs can age for between twenty and thirty. 'But you can't make great wines in poor years. You need botrytis on grapes that are healthy and ripe. Sometimes noble rot arrives before the grapes are fully ripe, and that's a real problem. In 1980 I had to wait until the end of October before the grapes were sufficiently ripe, and even then the sugar content was low. We didn't stop picking till 15 November.'

His wines are outstanding, and are distinguished by their high acidity. His Spätlesen and Auslesen are rounded and complex and at 12–13% fairly high in alcohol. Those from the 1981 vintage were packed with fruit yet remarkably elegant. His 1981 Rülander TBA is a gorgeous wine, of a brilliant orange-amber colour and a lush marmalade nose; it is certainly not ready to drink. Despite its richness, it has 11% alcohol and 11.5 g/l acidity, which should ensure this beautifully concentrated wine a long life. Equally outstanding is his 1981 Rülander Ausbruch; at 29 KMW it approaches TBA quality. The wine had sweetness and richness, but it also had more elusive qualities; an appley freshness, superb balance, and excellent definition and grip; its acidity gave it very good length. His 1983 Eiswein was almost as fine, with intense barleysugar flavours, fresh lively acidity and excellent length. Schandl does not usually believe in leaving sound grapes on the vine in order to gamble on a frost, but in 1983 he did so. The frost came early, on 2 November, and he was able to make a Welschriesling Eiswein of Beerenauslese quality. Until 1982 Schandl made mostly Prädikatsweine, but doubts whether he will be able to continue to do on the same scale.

Johannes Holler's Weingut Elfenhof is tucked inconspicuously behind a modern house on the edge of the town. Holler, probably the most esteemed winemaker in Rust, has a 3000-hectolitre capacity at his cellars, so he undertakes bottling for other producers and also operates a small wholesale business. A self-possessed, reserved man, Holler consolidated his reputation by winning top prize out of 700 wines at the 1985 Bordeaux Vinexpo for his 1981 Weissburgunder TBA. While not wishing to deny Holler any credit for his success, it must be said that many Austrian wines are plastered with labels certifying their success at wine fairs, usually in Krems or Ljubljana. It sometimes seems that hardly a wine in Austria (or Germany, for that matter) has failed to pick up a medal somewhere along the way. Of course, many medal-winning wines are as good as their jewellery suggests, but it is wiser to trust one's own taste buds rather than the innumerable awards made by overwhelmed juries.

Holler aims for slightly lower alcohol levels than Schandl, and also practises cold sterile bottling. He maintains that the wines of Rust mature quite rapidly but can age well because of their high extract. I was disappointed by his Spätlesen and Auslesen, many of which had a mildness that was distinctly unexciting. In 1985 Holler made an Auslese for the first time from the new Goldburger grape (a crossing of Welschriesling and Orangetraube), which we tasted from the vat. Its spicy nose and fresh liveliness on the palate faded quite rapidly. Austrian growers have been encouraged to plant Goldburger, but on the evidence of this and other tastings it is hard to see why.

If the lower levels of Prädikatsweine were disappointing, the Beerenauslesen and TBAs were superb. The 1979 Rülander Beerenauslese was delicious, with a nose that was surprisingly racy given its rich aroma of honey and apricots; the wine did not follow through as powerfully as its initial attack promised, but it was marvellous while it lasted. A 1967 Weissburgunder TBA proved how well these wines can last, contradicting those who maintain that Austrian sweet wines are incapable of longevity. This 1967 TBA was

still very fresh on the nose, with aromas of apricots and botrytis; on the palate it was stylish and lively, had excellent length and was far from tired. And the World Champion? It was certainly a superb wine, brilliant yellow-gold in colour, and with a rich honeyed nose that was absolutely clean; the balance was perfect, and the acidity gave it elegance and length as well as great intensity. It seemed almost clinically perfect; I could not help longing for a flaw to show the wine was, well, human?

Another Rust winery, Weingut Hans Feiler, is well thought of and its wines were selected for the German president to taste during a recent visit to the town. The Feilers, who raise cattle as well as 17 hectares of vineyards, involve the entire family, in-laws included, in the business. Their wines are traditionally made and the sweeter styles can spend up to two years in cask before being bottled. Their reputation is sound, deservedly so, but I was struck by startling variations in quality when I tasted a full range of their wines. Part of the problem, of course, is that with so many grape varieties and styles available, even a medium-sized winery such as Feiler's offered simultaneously no fewer than thirty-two Prädikatsweine. Some, such as the 1981 Rülander TBA, are of excellent quality, while others, such as the 1983 Rülander Beerenauslese and the 1981 Weissburgunder Ausbruch, are flabby or dull. Such variations make life interesting but arduous for those who would seek out the best Prädikatsweine from the thousands available. A Bordeaux estate will offer one or two wines each year; would-be purchasers can consult wine merchants who pride themselves on their knowledge of that finite list of wines. Such expertise regarding Burgenland wines is hard to find in Austria, let alone outside the country, because good small producers rarely engage in wholesaling and export and instead rely heavily on over-the-counter sales. Reputations are established in part by the numerous wine fairs and their awards, and in part by word of mouth.

Visits to individual producers also enable you to unearth some curiosities. At Weingut Feiler I tasted an Ausbruch made from the red Zweigelt grape. With its bright brown onionskin colour and a curious bitterness behind the surprisingly unassertive sweetness, it was a curious wine, not to my taste. More enthralling was the 1981 Müller-Thurgau TBA Essenz. The must had a sugar content of 46 KMW and the wine had remained in cask for four years in an attempt to induce a bit of fermentation from time to time. Eventually the alcohol crawled up to 6.5%, leaving about 350 g/l residual sugar. Not surprisingly the wine was almost gluelike in its viscosity; it had an oxidised nose with caramel overtones quite reminiscent of Tokay, as was the intense marmalade flavour. The acidity (8.5 g/l) was firm and pronounced, and in a decade or so it should knit together into something quite remarkable. Essenz may not be wine, but it is an unforgettable experience to dip one's tongue into a thimbleful and count the minutes as the flavours waft around one's mouth.

From Rust you can head west to Siegendorf, home of the large Klosterkeller Siegendorf estate, which makes classy wines that range from bone-dry Weissburgunders to luscious TBAs. By heading south you will reach the dozy wine-growing border village of Morbisch. North of Rust are Oggau, Donnerskirchen, and Purbach, where private cellars tunnelled into the rock resemble ancient barrows. On the eastern side of the Neusiedler See, a region known as the Seewinkel, the landscape changes, for the terrain is utterly flat. From the villages raised lanes plunge through banks of reeds and water meadows towards the shore. In summer, thousands of tourists, mostly from Germany, descend on the Seewinkel, and the populations of Illmitz and Podersdorf jump tenfold. Until the wine scandal scared off some buyers, few BMWs would return to Germany without a few cases of Prädikatsweine stashed in the rear.

The Seewinkel vineyards are relatively recent. Thirty years ago near Podersdorf a certain Herr Gisch founded a chicken farm along the sandy lakeside terrain known as Hölle (hell) because the heat of the sun is more relentless here than in more verdant parts of the Burgenland. Herr Gisch's farm was not a success, so he planted a few vines to see what would happen. They flourished. While the sandy soil meant that the grapes developed lower acidity than their counterparts on the opposite shore, it also retained the summertime heat that battered the flat vineyards, and this helped the grapes to ripen early. Scattered around the vineyards are hundreds of ponds, some so shallow that they dry up in summer. Cumulatively, however, they add moisture to the autumn air, assisting the development of botrytis. The expansion of the Seewinkel vineyards has been rapid. In the 1950s there were about 300 hectares planted in Illmitz; now there are 1800, and in neighbouring Apetlon there are 1300 more, mostly smallholdings. The Lenz Moser firm owned a large estate near Apetlon, but that is an exception. The Illmitz vineyards, for instance, are divided among about 500 proprietors. There are no wholesalers here, and finding the best Seewinkel wines can be the task of a lifetime.

Many red wines are made on the western side of the lake, but 95% of Illmitz wines are white. Burly, reserved Johann Gartner is a typical grower, with 7.5 hectares of vineyards and a winery behind his house. In 1981 and 1983 70% of his crop was Prädikatswein. The hot climate ensures good yields most years – 60–70 hl/ha on average – though harvests for Prädikatswein tend to be about half that quantity. Seewinkel wines are said to lack acidity and the capacity to age as well as their counterparts from Rust or Eisenstadt. Herr Gartner was keen to demonstrate that this need not be so. We tasted three Neuburger Auslesen, from 1984, 1981, and 1978. All were attractive, with a flowery nose, and fruity and rounded on the palate. The oldest was easily the best, even though 1978 was far from a great year. The wine had a creaminess that the younger wines lacked, good balance, and better length. The same was true of two Bouvier TBAs, one from 1984 and the other from 1978. Both were, as TBAs go, lacking in body and complexity, but the 1978 was better balanced and more elegant. It seems likely that most soundly made sweet wines from the Burgenland will benefit from five or more years in bottle. Some Seewinkel wines have truly surprisingly longevity. Herr Gartner opened, with some trepidation, a dusty bottle of 1966 Sämmling (known in Germany as Scheurebe) of Auslese quality. His fears were groundless. It was by no means a great wine, but it had aged nobly and developed real finesse and character. I would expect a fine TBA to be alive and well after twenty years, but that a mere Auslese from a good winemaker of no pretensions should have survived so well did seem to confound those who argue that Seewinkel wines are inherently short-lived.

Another Illmitz proprietor demonstrated the hit-and-miss character of small-scale winemaking. Stefan Tschida was particularly distressed by the wine scandal, since one of the culprits shared his surname, and buyers unfamiliar with the family trees of the Seewinkel were shying away from his wines, even though he himself was in no way implicated in the scandal. In the meantime he is doubtless wondering what to do with the 5000 litres of TBA he made from his 9 hectares of vineyards in 1981. Easily the best of his Auslesen came from this vintage. A Welschriesling, it tasted more like Beerenauslese, and successfully combined high alcohol (13%) with a relatively high level of residual sugar (70 g/l). The result was soft and creamy, yet elegant and long in the mouth. In 1985 he made 1000 bottles of Auslese from Zweigelt. It was quite different in character from Feiler's rather attenuated Zweigelt Ausbruch. The young wine was deep purple in colour, and there was a whiff of cherries on the nose; the KMW reading of 21 made itself felt not so much in sweetness as in an intensity of flavour. Like many Seewinkel growers, Tschida cannot resist gambling on making Eiswein from time to time. In November one year the temperature obligingly dropped to −7 °C, so his pickers raced into the vineyards. They were only able to pick seven rows before the temperature began to rise; the must sugar content was 28 KMW. The following night registered −10 °C, so out they went again, and picked the remaining rows at 35 KMW. The 1984 Eiswein was equally high in sugar (210 g/l), and the grapes were picked on New Year's Day 1985. This Welschriesling lacked the feebleness of many other Burgenland Eisweine and had good length. The 1983 Welschriesling TBA was almost as good, and again its quality seemed directly related to its acidity level.

Herr Tschida is also cellarmaster of the Gemeindekeller, the municipal cellars. In many Burgenland villages the municipality itself owns vineyards (17 hectares in this case) and makes and sells its own wines. The Illmitz wines are mostly sold in the picturesque Heurige known as the Pusztascheune, a remarkable structure built of reeds and thatched, a splendid example of a vernacular style once common in the Seewinkel, where cattle-raising used to be the principal occupation. With the exception of a 1981 Welschriesling TBA (it seems hardly anyone could put a foot wrong with that grape variety in that year) that combined 11% alcohol with 200 g/l residual sugar and reasonable acidity (8.2 g/l), the Gemeindekeller wines were less impressive than those from Herr Tschida's own Weingut. They were, however, distinctly superior to the Gemeindekeller wines from Morbisch on the other side of the lake.

The most easterly village of the Seewinkel is Halbturn. It is dominated by the baroque Schloss, once the summer residence of Empress Maria Theresa, and now used for art exhibitions; it also houses the Schlosskellerei. Of the estate's 57 hectares in Halbturn and Jols 48 are planted with white grapes. Johann Beck, the cellar-master, has recently reduced his plantings of Traminer from 10 hectares to 2, reflecting changes in taste. Most of his wine is sold over the counter, enabling Herr Beck to monitor at first hand fluctuations in public demand. In 1980, he told me, a quarter of his production was Prädikatswein; now the figure is down to 6%. The Schlosskellerei enjoys great prestige in Germany, largely because of its good red wines. The white wines, however, were distinctly disappointing. There were some successes, such as a nicely balanced 1981 Traminer Auslese, broad but lively. Most of the wines, however, including a loosely-knit 1982 Jubiläum TBA, were flabby and had a slightly bitter aftertaste. Herr Beck heats the wine before bottling so as to avoid any possibility of secondary fermentation in bottle. It is hard to demonstrate that such radical treatments actually harm the wine, but they surely cannot do it any good.

Gols, on the north-eastern shore, is home to a number of energetic and innovative winemakers. The Weingut Achs is typical of the changes taking place. The traditional methods of the beaming elder Herr Achs have given way to the newer technology installed by his son Hans. Hans's wife comes from Rust, and grapes from her family's vineyards are also vinified here in Gols. Weingut Achs specialises in dry racy wines, but Prädikatsweine are not neglected. His 1984 Ruster Traminer Auslese, 1983 Traminer Beerenauslese, and 1981 Müller-Thurgau TBA were all well-balanced fruity wines, not in the very top rank but well-made and pleasing. A 1977 Ruster Neuburger Ausbruch was showing signs of its age; there were traces of oxidation on the nose and it was beginning to dry out.

Zweigelt is not the only grape used to make sweet red wines. Alexander Unger offers two sweet Blaufränkisch (Gamay) wines, a rather sickly 1983 Spätlese and a far better 1981 Auslese, though even this wine seemed to lack structure and balance. In 1979 the Weingut Achs made a Blaufränkisch Beerenauslese that proved remarkably good. With its deep colour, rich fruity nose, and sweet-ness on the palate followed by a dry, almost bitter finish, it was reminiscent of an Italian Recioto. While it lacked the depth of flavour of great Recioto, it was still an excellent wine. So too was a 1976 Blauer Burgunder Ausbruch, which showed what you can get up to with red grapes in certain wine regions. The wine had a deep cognac colour, and a lovely dried-fruit nose with an attractive touch of oxidation; though losing its fruit, it was still striking and stylish, and a few years earlier must have been splendid.

Curiously, the 1979 Blaufränkisch Beerenauslese made by Achs's neighbour Paul Allacher had an entirely different character. Orange-pink onionskin in colour, it had an earthier nose, good concentration on the palate and a touch of bitterness on the lingering aftertaste. Like many of Herr Allacher's wines it suffered from excessive alcohol. He aims for wines that are higher in alcohol at the expense of residual sugar. If not carefully balanced, such wines will have the hot, slightly burnt flavour that indeed marred many of the Allacher wines. In other respects they were very good, especially a 1979 Welschriesling Beerenauslese, though a mediocre 1981 Goldburger TBA confirmed yet again how very little character this new grape variety brings to the wine. Herr Allacher willingly joined in the burgeoning local sport of proving how well Seewinkel wines can age. He was unlucky with a 1969 Bouvier Beerenauslese, but a 1973 Traminer Beerenauslese was delicious, bright yellow-gold in colour, with a big lush botrytis nose that was surprisingly elegant, a stylish vanilla sweetness on the palate, and good length.

Both Hans Achs and Paul Allacher are progressive winemakers, representing new generations keen to shed the image of being *Bauernbetriebe*, peasant firms. One Gols winemaker, however, is streets ahead of all his competitors when it comes to innovation. This is Georg Stiegelmar, a small intense moustachioed man who is extremely vociferous on the subject of wine, especially his own. Considering that he owns no more than 6.5 hectares of vineyards, he makes an astonishing range of wines, from barrique-aged Sauvignon Blanc to amazingly concentrated Essenz. (He also charges the highest prices in the Burgenland.) One of Stiegelmar's innovations (or rather restorations) is a wine called Masslasch, which is, he says, made by the traditional Ausbruch methods. Shrunken overripe berries, in this case Gewürztraminer, are trodden by foot, and the mash is left for a few days before being added to new wine. As in Tokay, the addition of a mash made from grapes rich in sugar prompts a further fermentation that boosts the alcoholic level by about three degrees and adds sugar and extract. However, the two vintages of Masslasch that I tasted bore no relation to Tokay; indeed, they were positively feeble. (In 1839 John Paget wrote in *Hungary and Transylvania*: 'To produce the Máslás, a large quantity of less choice must is poured over the same berries, which are now pressed as in making common wine . . . [It] is a much thinner wine, rather sweet, with a preponderating flavour of the dried grape.')

More successful is Stiegelmar's Strohwein, a style he was the first in the Burgenland to revive. For this wine he selects overripe but healthy grapes, which are then hung from rafters or placed on mats beneath the roof from September until just before Christmas, when the grapes are pressed. His 1983 Bouvier Strohwein was an attractive wine, very sweet and with a marzipan undertone and good acidity. Whether it justifies its intimidating price is more questionable. Stiegelmar's 1979 Zweigelt Ausbruch was a good example of that style, with a caramel nose and good depth of flavour. A 1982 Muskat-Ottonel Beerenauslese retained a strong varietal character, while successfully avoiding the sickliness of poorly-made sweet Muscat. Two Ausbruch wines, however, a 1981 Bouvier and 1984 Gewürztraminer, were disappointing.

The great rarity on the list is Essenz. In a good year Stiegelmar obtains, from each suitable grape variety, between fifty and eighty litres of this nectar, which is sold in half-litre bottles at prices that range from 500 to 1100 Schillings. Because of the high sugar content of the must (38 KMW for Bouvier, and 46 KMW for Welschriesling, both in 1981), it is very difficult to initiate fermentation. Stiegelmar explained: 'The wine is kept in small casks – there is so little of it – and during the winter and spring nothing at all happens. Then in summer some fermentation starts up on the surface of the must. Four months later it grinds to a halt. The highest alcohol level is around 9%, and more usually it's about 7%.' The Bouvier had a very deep colour, and a thick honey and barleysugar nose; it tasted intensely sweet and remarkably fresh, with excellent acidity. The Welschriesling (at double the price) was even fatter and richer, positively syrupy; at five years old it was showing less well than the Bouvier, but these are early days and in a decade I suspect the Welschriesling will be showing its true form. Nevertheless it struck me that with alcohol levels of 8–9% and residual sugar levels of just over 200 g/l, these wines, even though made by the traditional Essenz method, were in analytical terms little more than very rich TBAs. The Welschriesling, with an estimated residual sugar level of over 300 g/l, was much closer to Tokay Essenz in concentration. While it did not seem quite the equal of aged Tokay Essenz itself, this is unquestionably a magnificent wine which, unlike Tokay Essenz, is at least commercially available – at a price.

A short drive takes one from the flat industrial suburbs south of Vienna to the charming main street of Gumpoldskirchen, lined on both sides with solid but attractively ornamented inns and wineries, many of which operate Buschenschenken. Up at the top of the street, just before the vineyards begin, are the large monastic wineries, including the Deutsch-Ordens Schlossweingut, now owned by Stift Klosterneuburg. The Schlossweingut has owned vineyards here since the thirteenth century, and many of the best sites still remain in ecclesiastical hands. Most proprietors, however, are smallholders, and 457 hectares in the demarcated area are divided between 248 owners. Since the monastic estates own 40 hectares or more, the average size of the family properties is small indeed. This used to be Austria's best-known wine internationally, and it became obvious some years ago that, as in the case of Beaujolais, there was far more Gumpoldskirchener on the market than was being produced in the district. New regulations tightened up the labelling laws and you can now be confident that bottled Gumpoldskirchener is what it claims to be.

A number of familiar white grapes are grown here – Weissburgunder, Neuburger, Gewürztraminer – but the most characteristic wines are made from two local varieties: Zierfandler (also known, to confuse you further, as Spätrot) and Rotgipfler. Both varieties ripen late and cannot be grown successfully in cooler regions; they also find congenial the calcium subsoil of Gumpoldskirchen and often share the same vineyard. Zierfandler is occasionally vinified on its own, but usually the two varieties are blended, with Rotgipfler usually dominant. Zierfandler in its guise as Spätrot is so called because late-developing berries are tinged with red; the name Rotgipfler also refers to a similar attribute. Harvests rarely begin before the end of October and continue into mid-November. Yields vary according to the vintage from 20 to 60 hl/ha. Both grapes tend to make wine high in alcohol, acidity, and, in the case of Prädikatswein, residual sugar. Although these wines are usually drunk within four to seven years of the vintage, they are capable of lasting up to twenty years. Botrytis is infrequent, and the right conditions for making Eiswein are very rare. Just as Burgenland winemakers look back in wonder at the *annus mirabilis* of 1969, so the producers of Gumpoldskirchen regard theirs as 1968. Other fine years included 1967, 1969, 1977, 1979, 1981, 1982, and 1983.

Some wines carry a special Königswein label, crude in design but of some significance. In the 1950s, when the reputation of Gumpoldskirchener wine was slipping, a committee was set up to blind-taste wines from various producers; the best would be entitled to the special Königswein label, which still seems a reasonably reliable indicator of quality. About 5% of the total production is thus designated. Only wines made from Zierfandler, Rotgipfler, Weissburgunder, and Neuburger may be submitted for consideration.

I found it hard to assess the general quality of Gumpoldskirchener wines. Many local producers proved less than welcoming – and a few downright rude – and wines tasted in Buschenschenken were adequate but far from impressive, with the exception of Alfred Freudorfer's. A 1979 Gewürztraminer Auslese from the Deutsch-Ordens-Schlossweingut was lacking in varietal character and flat in the mouth. Nor were the wines of another large monastic producer, Stift Heiligenkreutz, with estates and a winery at Freigut Thallern, a neighbouring hamlet, of the quality I had expected. Most of the estate's 80 hectares are in Gumpoldskirchen; others are in the Burgenland. Wood-ageing is common here, as among most Gumpoldskirchen producers, for these broad hefty wines often benefit from time in cask. (The new cellarmaster at Thallern observed that since the 1985 wine law has reduced the maximum levels of SO_2 that may be added from 300 g/l to 200, winemakers may have to reduce residual sugar levels so as to avoid possible secondary fermentation in bottle.) A 1983 Zierfandler Auslese from one of the best vineyards in Gumpoldskirchen, Ried Wiege, gave some indication of what this grape variety can do. Bright straw in colour, the wine had a distinctive rotting vegetable nose, less nasty than it sounds; on the palate it was quite sweet, rich and spicy, yet elegant and complex with good length. A Spätrot-Rotgipfler Beerenauslese of the same year showed the weaknesses of these varieties. The heavy flowery nose was attractive, but on the palate the wine was very sweet and broad, suggestive in flavour of banana and peach; a lack of acidity made it cloying on the finish. A rather unlovely, gawky wine.

The local wine school also owns vineyards and makes some wines of excellent quality. A 1979 Spätrot-Rotgipfler Auslese was soft and spicy on the nose, with a whiff of mango; on the palate it was creamy and fat, with plenty of fruit. With insufficient acidity, such a wine could easily be blowsy, but the 67 g/l residual sugar were nicely balanced by 9.8 g/l acidity. Even better was the same wine of the 1971 vintage, lower in residual sugar and acidity, but higher in extract; despite the age of the wine, it was still packed with flavour and had excellent length, and a certain aggressiveness that kept it from being cloying. The same fine qualities were exhibited in a 1981 Beerenauslese (a blend of Spätrot, Rotgipfler, and Weissburgunder): great extract (46.3 g/l), 10.2 g/l acidity to keep the wine lively, and a vigorous complexity. Even finer, though far too young to drink, was the 1981 TBA from the same three varieties. This wine had admirable concentration and structure, as well as good acidity on the finish and excellent length. Acidity levels are generally higher here than in the Burgenland, even though the climate is less generous to the would-be maker of Prädikatsweine.

No other wine regions of Austria enjoy a climate suitable for producing sweet wines. Nevertheless, a few such wines slip through the net in the Wachau. The major cooperative at Dürnstein, the Winzergenossenschaft Wachau, made wines up to Auslese quality in 1977 and 1979. The 1979 Dürnsteiner Müller-Thurgau Auslese was fat and voluptuous on the nose, and plump and creamy on the palate, though it lacked structure and length. At the distinguished Weingut Undhof at Stein, a suburb of Krems, Erich Salomon has also made occasional Auslesen. The 1983 Weissburgunder was full but fragrant on the nose, and full, rich, nutty, and well-balanced on the palate. A 1975 Riesling Auslese, which had a beautiful gold colour, a soft honeyed nose, and great delicacy, demonstrated that here too well-made Auslesen can age successfully. Another top estate of the Wachau, the Saass (also spelt Saahs – even family members cannot make up their minds) family's Weingut Nikolaihof, actually managed to make a TBA in 1983. They also achieved this in 1971 and 1975, and eked out a Beerenauslese in 1979. The wine was made mostly for the challenge of attempting to do so in a climate normally unfavourable to the style. By selecting in early November individual botrytised grapes from his best Ried (vineyard) in Mautern, across the Danube from Krems, Herr Saass attained a KMW level of 32.

Different grape varieties were used to balance the wine: Riesling, Grüner Veltliner, and Neuburger. After a whole year of fermentation, the grapes produced 400 litres of wine, with 7.7 g/l acidity and 152 g/l residual sugar. The result is certainly delicious, though the different elements of the wine are far from knit; it needs at least five years more in bottle. The enterprising Herr Saass is also making a Beerenauslese from Grüner Veltliner and Riesling; although the grapes were picked in 1979, the wine was still in cask seven years later, for he is attempting to make a *dry* Beerenauslese. A cask sample suggested the final wine will be not unlike a yeasty Amontillado, but only time will tell.

Just outside Krems in the village of Rohrendorf stands Austria's largest private winery, Lenz Moser, named after its founder, who also radically transformed Austrian viticulture by devising a system of training vines that is still widely used throughout the country. With exports at 40–50% before the wine scandal, Lenz Moser was so badly hurt by the subsequent collapse of export sales that the firm declared itself bankrupt in 1986. The firm will survive, but under new ownership. Although Lenz Moser own large vineyards at Rohrendorf, Retz, and in the Seewinkel, they also buy in grapes and wines from other sources, and the provenance of Prädikatsweine is not always stated on the label. In good years such wine is produced in substantial quantities: approximately 40,000 bottles of Beerenauslese, and half as much TBA. About 90% of such wines used to be exported, mostly to Germany. Inevitably the wines are fairly commercial. Both the 1982 Gewürztraminer Beerenauslese and the 1981

Nikolaihof
Ried Süssenberg
Wachau
1983 Trockenbeerenauslese

Gewürztraminer TBA were whisky-coloured, honeyed on the nose, and rich on the palate, with good length. The quality was more than acceptable, yet unexciting and unmemorable. A 1982 Ruster Weissburgunder Beerenauslese was bland, while a 1983 Grüner Veltliner Eiswein, though pretty, also lacked definition. No wood is used during the vinification and the wines are bottled and released relatively early.

Just north of Vienna, along the banks of the Danube, stands the large Augustinian abbey of Klosterneuburg. Founded in 1108, it took its present form in the 1730s when Emperor Karl VI initiated its reconstruction. More a palace than an abbey, Klosterneuburg is an impressive pile, though it was originally planned to be four times its present size. When the abbey was built, cellars four storeys deep were tunnelled beneath it; these too were intended to be four times the size, but with the present capacity of 3.5 million litres and a stock of 1.5 million bottles, the abbey has enough cellarage to be getting along with. The winery owns 120 hectares of vineyards, of which 60% are planted with white grapes. The winery also buys in grapes from smaller producers, including some in the Burgenland, and recently acquired the Deutsch-Ordens-Schlossweingut in Gumpolds-kirchen. Despite its size, the winery is traditional in its methods, and seeks to give its wines strong varietal character. Beerenauslese and TBA are fermented for three weeks or more, then left in cask until ready to be bottled. Wines are bottled early, but commendably, Klosterneuburg does not rush to put its wines on the market, and even dry Weissburgunder and Welschriesling are bottle-aged. Only 5% of the abbey's wines are Prädikatsweine. Beerenauslesen are made on average every other year, while TBAs were only made in 1968, 1969, and 1973.

There are no ancient bottles in the cellars. During and after World War II first German and then Russian soldiers occupied the abbey and helped themselves to its wines. A single bottle from the 1938 vintage is the oldest remaining in the cellars. A 1981 Weissburgunder Auslese, while pleasant enough, seemed bland and lacking in acidity; but the same wine from 1970 seemed better balanced, still very much alive, and the bouquet had developed remarkably: it was fat and aromatic, with suggestions of tropical fruit. The same grape variety produced an excellent Beerenauslese in 1976, still fruity and very fresh, with distinct botrytis on the nose. A 1981 Ausbruch (blending

Weissburgunder, Traminer, and Rheinriesling) was closed on the nose and aggressive on the palate – clearly too young to be showing well. A beautifully balanced 1971 Neuburger Beerenauslese displayed the lushness of which the variety is capable, as well as considerable complexity. An even older wine, the 1967 Neuburger TBA, was sumptuous on the nose, and although very attractive and pleasantly concentrated on the palate, did not seem to have sufficient acidity to sustain the wine much longer. Nevertheless it was impressive to note how well these essentially commercial wines are made, and how well they improve with age. Most consumers drink these wines far too young, for though temptingly delicious and fresh in their youth, they often need five or ten years before the bouquet in particular is unleashed in its full glory.

Austrians are no better and no worse at making sweet wines than anyone else, but the country is wonderfully blessed in its climate, especially in the Burgenland. Nowhere else in the world is botrytis so widespread and so dependable. Ironically, the very abundance of Prädikatsweine has worked against their reputation, for consumers, mindful of the costly rarities from Germany, cannot believe that comparable wines at a fraction of the price can be authentic. Sadly, such fears proved partly justified, and the Austrian wine industry as a whole is paying heavily for the turpitude of a few. It is all very well for innocent winemakers to lament that they should be suffering for the sins of a few, but it was long suspected in the Burgenland that some wines were being doctored. After all, 16,000 hectolitres were identified as contaminated – that is a lot of wine. Winemakers and merchants are no fools: they must have known that it was impossible for certain wines to be sold so cheaply if they were what they claimed to be. Had the authorities moved more swiftly to nip such adulteration in the bud – no easy task, admittedly, for it is often hard to analyse wines for illegal additives unless you know in advance what you are looking for – the scandal might have been avoided. The draconian new wine law is, on the whole, to be welcomed, though some regulations, hastily introduced, may have to be annulled because they conflict with EEC law; other regulations are clearly absurd, and will no doubt have to be revised. For instance, wines with more than 10 g/l residual sugar will have to be labelled Sweet. Since many wines that are almost entirely dry on the palate may contain, say, 12 or 15 g/l residual sugar, to label such wines as sweet is preposterous.

As in Germany, winemakers are tempted to follow the regulations to the letter and bottle wines of certain must weights as Auslese or TBA regardless of their quality and taste, and no doubt there is a great deal of surreptitious blending in order to upgrade Spätlesen to Auslesen. Nevertheless at their best the quality of Austrian sweet wines is such that any winelover who ventures into the Burgenland in search of glorious wines at reasonable cost should be richly rewarded.

15

Italy

Italy produces more wine than any other country in Europe, but what makes Italian wine difficult to discuss is not its profusion so much as its variety. It is not merely that each region has its own grape varieties, its own styles and traditions of winemaking, but that often within each region there are dozens of sub-regions with the same profusion of grapes and styles. Some excellent wines are made in a single village and not seen in neighbouring villages, let alone in the rest of the world. Some of the wines mentioned below are produced in such minute quantities that they will never, can never, be exported; but they are worth mentioning because they are great wines of enormous character and style. They expand our notions of what sweet wines can be.

Certain terms will be used frequently in the following chapters. *Passito* refers to wine made from grapes that have been dried, sometimes in racks (like French *vin de paille* or German and Austrian *Strohwein*) and sometimes in the sun. While the French and German styles are close to extinct, *passito* wines are very common throughout Italy, and the best of them are superb. The purpose of drying the grapes is to concentrate the sugar content to form wines high in alcohol and residual sugar. Often the same wine is made in different styles. The word *liquoroso* usually signifies that the wine has been fortified, and such wines are common in southern Italy. They are usually higher in alcohol than non-fortified styles, but minimum strength varies from wine to wine according to the relevant DOC (laws of name and origin). Terms such as *extra* and *superiore* do have defined meanings – usually indicating higher alcohol and richness – but, again, these will vary from wine to wine. Some Italian sweet wines arc lightly sparkling, and are known as *frizzante* to differentiate them from the more vigorously sparkling *spumante* style.

VALLE D'AOSTA

It seems impossible that any wine at all could be made in the Alpine valleys of this small region north of Turin. The few roads pass through valleys dramatically hemmed in by walls of rock. Here and there, where a slope faces towards the south, farmers have, over the centuries, terraced the steep mountainsides and planted the harsh earth with vines. Near the village of Chambave, Ezio Voyat has planted 1.7 hectares on south-facing slopes, and from his grapes he makes small quantities of red wine, dry Moscato, and a remarkable Passito, made from Moscato grapes, which he usually picks in early October, and then leaves to dry on metal racks laid within open boxes. Voyat tries to alternate this indoor drying with sun-drying outdoors. This process continues for ten to twenty days; then the grapes are pressed and fermented in steel tanks for two to three months. The wine is aged in tank for up to two years before being bottled. In certain years he will put the wine briefly into wooden casks. The wine is quite high in alcohol, between 14% and 15%, but Voyat does not record the sugar content. In its youth the wine is quite sweet, but as it ages, which it is capable of doing for twenty years, it loses some sweetness and becomes more rounded. The 1982 Passito di Chambave, sampled in 1986, was a lovely wine: deep amber-copper in colour, with a fresh Muscat perfume; in the mouth it was fresh and elegant, even charming, with excellent length. Since the total annual production is a mere 3000 bottles, older bottles are scarce, but Voyat tells me the best years for his Passito di Chambave have been 1961, 1971, 1978, 1981, and 1985.

It is no use for restaurateurs and sommeliers to try to add Malvoisie de Nus to their wine lists, because this other sweet wine of Aosta is virtually extinct. It sounds French because Nus is close to the French border and many of its inhabitants speak bad French as well as bad Italian. Malvoisie de Nus was revived by the village priest, Father Pramotton, but he died a few years ago. Although he restored its reputation, the wine was never made on a commercial basis. Felice Tassi, like many other inhabitants of Nus, owns a few rows of vines and makes wine for his own consumption. He has occasionally made Malvoisie (a misnomer, since the Aosta grape is in fact a variant of Pinot Gris), but the 1985 vintage will be his last. To make the wine, he told me, is simply too much trouble. The grapes must be dried for a month or more. Pressing them is hard work because the dried berries have become small and hard; three pressings are required. Fermentation takes place in a small oak barrel, which is sealed and left alone for four to five months. The wine is then racked every four months for two years. And all this labour produces, for Tassi, 80–100 bottles. We sampled the 1983 vintage, some of which he had stored in Campari Soda bottles – a very sensible size. The colour was unpromising, a rather dirty olive-copper. The nose was attractive and perfumed, and smelled of dried fruit. On the palate the wine was very sweet and intense, but had clean sharp acidity that kept the wine fresh and lively. Malvoisie de Nus supposedly tastes of cooked chestnuts, but this flavour eluded me. Sr Tassi will make no more sweet Malvoisie, but fortunately a new generation is prepared to do so. In 1982 Renato Roux made his first vintage, a wine of 16% alcohol.

Other rare sweet wines, such as the Réserve du Prieur and Malvoisie de Cossan, are made at the Ecole d'Agriculture Aoste.

PIEDMONT, LIGURIA, LOMBARDY

Caluso is an unprepossessing little hillside town north-east of Turin. On slopes that face south over the Po plain the Erbaluce grape is grown. Most Erbaluce is made into nondescript dry white wine, but some producers make an excellent Passito. The wine may be made in Caluso itself and in over thirty other communes, so the zone of production is fairly large. Nevertheless, production remains quite restricted. The wine is aged for four years or more before being bottled.

Vittorio Boratto takes the making of Caluso Passito seriously, and the results are very fine indeed. His 8 hectares of vineyards lie close to the village of Piverone on slopes overlooking Lake Viverone. Sometimes botrytis attacks the grapes, though the noble rot is not a prerequisite for making the wine. In 1985, for instance, there was no botrytis, but Boratto is very pleased with the quality of the wine. The climate does not permit the wine to be made every year, and in 1977 and 1981, for instance, there was none. Boratto harvests the Erbaluce grapes in early October and lays them in old fruit boxes in a well-ventilated area for five to six months. The grapes are usually pressed in March. Fermentation, which takes place in glass demi-johns, sometimes continues for years. After four years the wine is bottled; it is not filtered. Caluso Passito must have at least 13.5% alcohol, but Boratto's wine usually has closer to 15%. Production is tiny – no more than 2000 bottles a year – and prices are quite high. The best recent vintages were 1974, 1978, 1979, and 1980, and there has been a string of good vintages from 1982 to 1985. The 1980, tasted in 1986, is a beautiful wine, light copper in colour, and with a powerful raisiny nose, redolent of stewed fruits. On the palate the wine is medium-bodied, soft with a light caramel flavour; it is very well balanced and elegant. The finish is clean.

Another important producer of Caluso Passito is Corrado Gnavi, who has a fine line in vituperation. His opinion of some other prominent Italian wine producers is unprintable. His Passito is made from grapes grown on 2.5 hectares of sandy soil near Caluso itself; they are, he insisted, the best vineyards of the region, just as his Passito is the best. Instead of leaving the grapes on racks in an attic, as Boratto and other producers do, Gnavi speeds up the process by

blowing hot air at 28–30 °C over the grapes for three or four weeks. The grapes for the wine must be healthy, not botrytised, so by shortening the drying process he is less likely to expose the bunches to rot. Fermentation takes place in 25-hectolitre casks. There is no temperature control and the fermentation takes its own course, sometimes lasting four years. Gnavi insists that long barrel-ageing is the secret of good Passito, and his wines often spend eight or more years in wood before being filtered and bottled. His wine has 14.5% alcohol, about 7.5 g/l acidity, and at least 130 g/l residual sugar. He makes about 6000 bottles a year. Gnavi's 1974 Passito, from an exceptional vintage, bore very little resemblance to Boratto's. The colour was a brilliant orange-copper; the nose was soft and rich, with dried-fruit tones; in the mouth the wine was very concentrated and fruity, slighty cooked and marmaladey, and although very rich had good length. This wine had spent ten years in wood and had over 200 g/l residual sugar. I liked this old-fashioned hefty style, which was in striking contrast to Boratto's leaner, more elegant wine.

Piedmont's best-known sweet wine is Moscato d'Asti, which comes from a fairly large region south-east of Turin. This is a *frizzante* wine, less bubbly than the famous Asti Spumante, which in other ways the wine resembles. The region comprises 7462 hectares divided among as many proprietors, many of whom supply grapes to the larger producers such as Fontanafredda and Villa Banfi. Moscato d'Asti, which is made from the Moscato di Canelli grape, is extremely light, as fermentation is arrested by chilling when the wine has attained 7% alcohol, and some producers seek even lower alcohol levels. The sparkle in the wine is natural and no CO_2 or other gases are introduced. A greater contrast with the luscious Caluso Passito could hardly be imagined, for Moscato d'Asti at its best is delicate and scintillating. The wine must be drunk very young. After a year in bottle it can lose its aromatic grapy nose and some of its charm and freshness on the palate. If you want to drink wine for breakfast, Moscato d'Asti is the one to go for.

Less common but similar in style is the *frizzante* red wine called Brachetto d'Acqui. The low-yielding Brachetto grape was beginning to disappear but in recent years it has been revived by Giacomo Bologna, Villa Banfi, and other top producers. This wine also has only about 7% alcohol, though it can have as much as 150 g/l residual sugar. Like Moscato d'Asti it should be drunk as young as possible. It is a wine of striking individuality. A pale raspberry-red in colour, Brachetto when poured bubbles with bright pink foam. It is highly aromatic, with scents of roses and violets, and on the palate the wine is sweet and intense. In some versions there is a touch of bitterness on the finish, which is clean and bracing. Although the wine sounds frivolous (like an up-market Lambrusco), it is full of character and brilliance and well worth seeking out.

The coastal region of Liguria, just south of Piedmont, is known for one semi-sweet wine, Cinqueterre, made from Bosco grapes. It varies in style, and is *amabile* (medium sweet) rather than *dolce*. The large Piedmont region is not noted for sweet wines, though a good Moscato, not unlike that of Asti or Strevi in Piedmont, is made at Oltrepò Pavese.

VENETO

If I wished to illustrate the meaning of the word 'undistinguished' when applied to wine, I would probably uncork a bottle of Valpolicella or Soave. Greed, in the form of obtaining ever higher yields from the grape varieties grown in these two regions, has wrecked the reputation of the wines. Yet conscientious winemakers such as Anselmi and Masi have demonstrated that it is possible to make exceptionally fine wine from the very grape varieties that produce the

Brachetto d'Acqui

denominazione di origine controllata

—◦◦◦◦◦—

Imbottigliato all'origine
da'B R A I D A Giacomo Bologna
Rocchetta Tanaro (AT) - R. I. 501/AT

0,750 Litri   Alcole effettivo 7 % VOL.

insipid tanker-loads mass-marketed across the world. Soave and Valpolicella are also the source of Recioto, *passito* wines that, while not to everyone's taste, are among the great wines of the world.

Recioto di Soave is made from dried Garganega grapes. One of the best is made by Roberto Anselmi. Anselmi is widely regarded by his fellow winemakers in Soave as crazy. The firm he now runs at Monteforte was, in his father's day, a typical producer, churning out standardised, relatively inexpensive Soave in bulk. Roberto Anselmi has chucked out many of the huge stainless steel tanks in which the wines were made and stored, and replaced them with rows of casks that line his air-conditioned cellars. It would be tempting to dismiss Anselmi as yet another Italian succumbing to the fad of ageing anything and everything in *barrique*, but this would be an injustice. That Anselmi is a highly serious winemaker can be seen in his vineyards. He insists that viticulture is the basis of good wine-making; you can have the best equipped winery in the world, but it is no use unless you have grapes to match. He showed me a hillside that he is literally rebuilding. The topsoil has been scraped off to expose the chalky subsoil beneath. A thinner topsoil will be replaced so that the vines planted here will benefit more obviously from the limestone base and give better quality grapes. In Burgundian style, Anselmi is building a dry stone wall around the vineyard, which is officially called Capitel San Vincenzo, though Anselmi likes to think of it as Montrachet di Monteforte. He owns 10 hectares of vineyards in all, and rents 20 more. In certain spots he has planted Chardonnay and Sauvignon, to the horror of his neighbours. But, Anselmi insists, he is no revolutionary or iconoclast; he prefers to see himself as restoring traditions and standards in danger of extinction in Soave.

The hills of Soave rise roundly from the plains, and their contours give a variety of exposures to the sun. The best vineyards, such as Anselmi's Capitel Foscarin, are not necessarily the best for Recioto grapes. He limits yields – another sign of madness – and the harvest is staggered to ensure that the grapes are at their peak of ripeness when picked. The Recioto grapes are picked in October and carefully inspected to ensure that they are not too tightly bunched, for if the clusters are too tight, air cannot circulate properly and dry the berries evenly. Sometimes the grapes are botrytised, but this is not a prerequisite for Recioto, though it can give the wine additional richness of flavour. The grapes are left for four or five months before

being pressed. When I visited the winery on 26 February, the
Recioto grapes were just about to be pressed. The must is fermented
in steel for about a month, then put into *barriques* for a year. 80% of
the casks are new, and the remainder a year old or retoasted. After
bottling, the wine is aged for about two years before being released.
The wine has 14.5% alcohol and up to 8% (about 135 g/l) residual
sugar. Production is limited to about 2500 bottles (compared to
350,000 for his dry Soave). It is a difficult wine to assess. Anselmi's
first vintage was made in 1982, and is designed for long ageing. A
bottle of 1983 tasted in 1986 was bright pale gold in colour, but on
both nose and palate the oak was overwhelming the fruit. There was,
to be sure, plenty of appley fruit discernible and, equally important,
very high acidity and superb length, which should ensure the wine a
long life. My guess is that the structure is sufficiently tight to ensure
that Anselmi's Recioto will become a great and harmonious bottle of
wine.

Barrique-aged Recioto di Soave is a departure from the norm. A far
more characteristic Recioto is made by Leonildo Pieropan, another
top-quality producer. His 300-year-old cellars lie within the walled
town of Soave itself. Like Anselmi, Pieropan uses only Garganega
grapes, which are grown on 15 hectares of chalky soil with considerable clay content. He harvests the Recioto grapes about a week before
the rest of the Garganega, and selects clusters carefully to ensure they
are golden in colour and open-bunched. The grapes are dried on
bamboo racks for about three months, and before they are pressed a
further selection takes place to remove any mouldy berries. After a
gentle pressing, the must ferments in wood at 17–18 °C for forty to
sixty days. The wine is then refrigerated and left for ten days before
being racked and, a month later, filtered. It rests in old casks until
September when it is bottled. Pieropan's Recioto is less forceful than
Anselmi's. It usually has 12.5% alcohol and 60–70 g/l residual sugar.
Annual production amounts to about 8000 bottles. I tasted a range of
vintages from 1984 to 1969. All the wines were light gold in colour,
though the oldest had darkened beautifully. The nose was floral
rather than heavily fruity, though some vintages had suggestions of
apricots and honey. The general style was delicate and elegant rather
than rich and sweet. Most vintages had good acidity and balance
but did not, quite deliberately, have the kind of structure and
power that would guarantee them longevity. Pieropan thinks his

Recioto is best drunk after five years, and that exceptional vintages can still be good after ten, as the lovely and still very fresh 1969 demonstrated.

Sadly, most commercially available Recioto di Soave is not of this quality. In 1986 Anselmi's was priced at 11,000 lire, Pieropan's at 7500. On Italian supermarket shelves you can find Recioto di Soave at 3000 lire, but as Pieropan points out, you cannot make good or even adequate Recioto for that price, just as you cannot make cheap Sauternes. Another Veneto Recioto made from Garganega is produced at Gambellara. Recioto di Gambellara is not only lightly sweet (50–70 g/l residual sugar) but often *frizzante* or *spumante* too. At Zonin, a huge winery based at Gambellara, the grapes are picked early and dried for a month. The must is cool-fermented in steel for another month. A second fermentation is induced to provide the sparkle, and this is arrested by refrigeration. The finished wine has about 11.5% alcohol.

Excellent though Recioto di Soave can be, it pales in comparison with the great red Recioto from Valpolicella. The term Recioto is derived from the Italian for 'ear', and refers to the grapes at the top of the bunch that ripen most fully. It is a *passito* wine made from the same grape varieties as Valpolicella: Corvina, Rondinella, and Molinara. There are two basic styles. Recioto di Valpolicella is fermented to about 14–15% alcohol, leaving a small amount of residual sugar. Recioto Amarone di Valpolicella is fermented dry, and is exceedingly powerful. I shall use Recioto to refer to the sweeter style, and Amarone to denote the drier. Recioto is the traditional wine of the region, though Amarone has outstripped it in popularity, simply because many consumers do not find the idea of a sweet red wine alluring. Recioto is very much an after-dinner wine, whereas it is conceivable that drinkers of sound constitution could put away a bottle of Amarone with a meal, though I would not recommend it. It is for this reason that I include Amarone, which is not sweet at all, in this book, since it has in common with all great sweet wines that it is best drunk on its own.

Renzo Tedeschi owns a medium-sized winery in the village of Pedemonte not far from Verona, though his 21 hectares of vineyards are in the surrounding hills. Many discerning tasters consider his Recioto the finest of them all. Of a total production of 200,000 bottles, about 30,000 are Recioto or Amarone. Of those made from individual vineyards, such as Capitel Monte Fontana, only 2000–3000 bottles are produced each year. Tedeschi also makes about 1500 bottles of delicious white Recioto. The two styles require different kinds of grapes. Recioto grapes need sun early in the day; Amarone grapes need the late sunshine. Hence Tedeschi's grapes for the two styles come from different vineyards. The Recioto grapes are picked first, before all the other grapes, so as to preserve their acidity, while the Amarone grapes are left on the vine rather longer. Picking is usually completed by 25 September; the grapes are dried until late January, when they are pressed very gently. Tedeschi stresses that the first ten days of the drying process are crucial; the grapes must be kept well ventilated, especially if the weather is humid and there is a possibility that rot will attack the fruit.

Tedeschi encourages a long fermentation of up to sixty days and uses a kind of carbonic maceration method to extract good colour. The wine is matured in casks – the smaller the better for Recioto, says Tedeschi – for at least two years. Recioto is not especially long-lived and is often at its best five to six years after the vintage, though it can keep much longer; oxidation, however, may occur if the wines are kept too long. This is less of a danger with Amarone, which can keep for up to twenty years. Tedeschi's best vintages have been 1961, 1962, 1964, 1967, 1969, 1971, 1974, 1976, 1977, 1978, 1979, 1983, and 1985.

His top Recioto, Capitel Monte Fontana, has a very deep colour, and a soft and fruity nose with plenty of reserved power. What is so admirable about Recioto is that the attack of the wine is soft and sweet and intense; then a slight spiciness takes over, refreshing the palate. Tedeschi's wine was remarkable for its elegance; there was no trace on the palate of high alcohol, and the finish was dry and clean. I compared two Amarones of 1979, his standard bottling and a *cru* wine from Capitel Monte Olmi. The former was sombre in colour, the Monte Olmi a more limpid garnet. Both were reserved on the nose, but the richness and power lurking in the background would emerge more strongly after the wines had had more time to breathe. Amarone is more austere than Recioto: its concentration and richness fill the mouth, but then a very dry aftertaste takes over, and the standard bottling had just a hint of bitter almond on the finish – by no means unpleasant, though the *cru* wine had better length. There is no

DOC for Recioto Bianco in Valpolicella, so Tedeschi's white Recioto is sold as Vin de la Fabriseria di San Rocco. I found his 1983 absolutely ravishing, a glorious medium gold in colour, and with a lush yet elegant apricot nose. The wine is soft and stylish on the palate, utterly seductive, and has a somewhat nutty finish that eliminates any trace of sugar from the palate.

Recioto and Amarone may be the mainstay of Tedeschi's deservedly high reputation, but it only constitutes about 15% of his total production. The Allegrini family of Fumane, on the other hand, make half their wine in these styles. The grapes come from 35 hectares of top vineyards, and are picked in late September before they become overripe and lose acidity. The grapes are separated, cleaned, and left to dry on trays for four to six months. Amarone grapes are pressed first, usually in January, and Recioto grapes two months later. Fermentation takes thirty to forty days. The wine spends six months in casks, and a year and a half in tanks, since Franco Allegrini fears that too long a spell in wood can imperil the wine's freshness. He also makes a Recioto Bianco called Campogardane, made from 70% Garganega grapes and 30% Trebbiano Veronese; the vines are up to sixty years old. These grapes are not pressed until April. Allegrini maintains that the white Reciotos of Valpolicella are fatter and richer than those from Soave, and in my experience this is so. White Reciotos are rare in Valpolicella because the white grapes formerly grown in the region were not replanted, since it was the red varieties that made the more saleable basic Valpolicella. Allegrini also make two *cru* wines, Amarone Fieramonte and about 1200 bottles of Recioto Fiorgardane. The Reciotos from Allegrini are deeply coloured and complex on the nose, with more overt spiciness than Tedeschi's: there were aromas of musk and nutmeg as well as blackberries. On the palate they are lush and lively, more assertive and perhaps less elegant than Tedeschi's, though at this level of winemaking one is speaking of nuances rather than qualitative differences. Here too the white Recioto is ravishing: a fabulous medium gold in colour, and a complex nose of apricots, apples, and honey; on the palate the wine is sweet, rounded, and appley, with excellent depth and good length, and a hint of boiled sweets on the finish.

The great firm of Masi, with 75 hectares of vineyards, operates at a greater level of sophistication than most others in Valpolicella, and

even their standard wines are of a very high quality. Nino Franceschetti is the principal winemaker here, though the success of Masi is
very much a team effort. Dr Sandro Boscaini heads the firm, and one
of his brothers runs the local oenological school. Another partner in
the enterprise is Count Pieralvise Serègo Alighieri, a descendant of
Dante and the owner of a nearby estate at Gargagnago. As with the
other producers, the grapes for Recioto and Amarone come from
mostly old vines from different sides of the valley. Selection by
experienced pickers is crucial. Masi produce one Recioto called
Mezzanella, and three Amarones: one from the Serègo Alighieri
estate called Vaio Armaron; one from Campolongo di Torbe; and one
from Mazzano. The climatic conditions necessary for the production
of these wines do not occur every year. If during the drying process
the weather is too humid, the desiccation will not be satisfactory and
rot may occur. 1982, for instance, was disastrous for Masi, and in
1981 no Vaio Armaron was made. Their best vintages have been
1964, 1974, 1975, 1979, and 1983. The grapes are left on racks in an
open room for three months. By the time they are pressed in
mid-January, they will have lost 30% of their water content. For
Amarone, skins and stalks are left in the must during fermentation,
which can take fifty to sixty days. Franceschetti is not a believer in
lengthy cask fermentation, as he seeks great elegance as well as

SerègoAlighieri

VAIO ARMARON
Recioto Valpolicella (Denominazione Origine Controllata)
AMARONE
*Prodotto e vinificato nella possessione in Gargagnago
con l'assistenza tecnica della*
MASI
che ne cura l'imbottigliamento e la distribuzione.
*Conte di Serègo Alighieri agricoltore in Gargagnago di Valpolicella • Verona
Masi Agricola s.p.a. imbottigliatore in S. Ambrogio di Valpolicella • Italia*
75 cl. e Annata 1980 n.   *16,5% vol.*

structure and power. After fermentation the wine is racked every ten days, then put in 2000-litre barrels, where Recioto remains for up to two years, and Amarone for at least four.

The 1983 Mezzanella is a very elegant wine, but still being young, also aggressive and tarry. The 1977 was a good example of their mature Recioto, for the colour had taken on some brick hues, and the nose was far more developed, reeking of violets and nutmeg. There was still a tarry flavour, one of the hallmarks of Recioto, but the wine had become rich and fat and the tannins had softened. The finish was completely dry, and this is what Franceschetti aims for above all else; without it, the wine would be tiring rather than stimulating.

The Serègo Alighieri Recioto is classic wine: deep garnet in colour, and with lovely sweet fruit and nutmeg on the nose; in the mouth the wine begins sweetly before that peppery tannic attack fills the mouth with complex flavours before fading to a dry finish. Count Pieralvise took me into his cellars to taste a 1983 Recioto that he is vinifying dry. A beautiful orange-gold in colour, it had a yeasty flavour and was not unlike Almacenista sherry. I prefer the sweeter styles that are unique to the region. Masi also make a lovely white Recioto called Campo-ciesa, not especially sweet but fat, rich, and rounded, and enlivened by its finesse and dry finish. It is slow work tasting such wines, for they are complex and sophisticated. And that is as it should be. The Italians call them *vini di meditazione* – meditation wines to be gazed at, sniffed, sipped, and discussed at leisure.

Superb though the wines mentioned above are, the Master, surely, is Giuseppe Quintarelli, who makes a bewildering range of Reciotos and Amarones. He plays with the styles as though conducting an orchestra, drawing on his large and seemingly disorganised cellar full of old casks to create blends and single-vineyard wines of the highest distinction. A visit to Quintarelli cannot be lightly undertaken. He takes his wines very seriously, and expects visitors to do so too. However, since my tasting notes record no fewer than eighteen wines tasted (plus a few others I did not note down), each of which had at least 14.5% alcohol and some of which had 17%, the demands on the palate and concentration were extreme. Before lunch he brought up from the cellar a bottled labelled 1980 Recioto Bianco Extra Amabile. It was sensational: a beautiful orange-gold in colour, with rich glycerol streaking the sides of the glass; the wine was full and concentrated and tasted of stewed peaches, but was balanced by terrific fresh acidity. It was a brilliant piece of winemaking, with that rich fruit impeccably balanced to produce what the French call *nervosité*. The wine had beautiful length and a clean finish. (It was made from Garganega, the low-yielding local grape Saorin, and small amounts of Trebbiano, Malvasia, and Tocai. It was aged for two years in wood, and for a further three in demijohns.)

After lunch the serious tasting in the cellars began. It was snowing outside, and icily cold in the cellars. Quintarelli moved slowly from cask to cask, pausing as he wondered which lot to sample next. Sometimes there would be a longer gap as he fetched a stepladder in order to reach the bung, which had to be prised out of the sealing plaster with a knife. Every wine we tasted came from a cask or demijohn, not a bottle, for Quintarelli bottles when he feels the wine is ready. Were he to respond to demand alone, he could bottle the entire contents of his cellars immediately and retire, but he is, I suspect, something of a tease, taunting his clients with superlative cask samples and then declaring the wine not yet ready to be bottled.

Giuseppe Quintarelli owns about 15 hectares of vineyards near his hillside home in Negrar and around Verona. He picks the grapes for Recioto and Amarone relatively early, and dries them till late February. The must is fermented with skins and stalks, giving the wine its depth of colour. There is no temperature control at any stage. 'Si è caldo è caldo. Si è freddo è freddo,' he says with a shrug. After fermentation, which usually takes about three months, the wine is sealed in casks for about three years. Some Amarones had been in wood for nine years, and seemed none the worse for it. Apart from topping up occasionally, he leaves the wines alone. They are racked once before bottling, but not fined. Our tasting began with no fewer than four Amarones from 1979. As I sipped each, Quintarelli would gaze soberly at me awaiting my response. I did my best to characterise the virtues of the first three, but was thrown by the fourth, which, while very good, struck me as distinctly inferior. Finally I summoned up my courage and told him what I thought. Instead of throwing me out into the ice and snow, he beamed and said 'Bravo', adding that he had agreed and had omitted that cask from the blend released for sale.

From that moment on, it was plain-sailing, as though I had survived an initiation rite, and the tour of the casks continued. It would be pointless to describe each one. There is no way of knowing which cask will end up in which bottling; only Quintarelli knows that. In general, however, his Amarones are extremely deep in colour, almost opaque. Because of the cold in the cellars, the bouquets were closed in, but even so it was possible to discern their astonishing fruit and richness and spiciness. So rich in fruit are these Amarones that they seem almost sweet on the palate; but that seductiveness does not last long, for it is followed by a burst of pepperiness, not unlike the savage attack of vintage port. After that vinous aggression dies down, flavours of fruit, tannin, and tar linger in the mouth; the length is usually extraordinary, and the wine clean on the finish. The biggest wines, including his single-vineyard Riservas, have enormous weight and concentration; other lots have more charm and a more marked note of bitterness, a not undesirable quality in wines of such richness and power. The Reciotos were all voluptuous, but the greatest was the 1978 Riserva Vignetto di Tre Terre, sampled from a demijohn, since many of the wines are transferred to glass before being bottled. Although eight years old, the wine still showed a touch of youthful purple, and the nose was rich and deep and curranty. On the palate this Recioto was massive yet not overpowering, a soft complex wine with all its constituents in perfect harmony; it was supremely elegant, unimprovable, classic.

Because Quintarelli leaves his wines alone as much as possible, their eventual balance is not entirely predictable. Sometimes the wine lodges itself in a borderland between dry and sweet, and such wines he calls Amandorlato, which suggests a rare musical instrument depicted in Carpaccio paintings. I sampled two, the 1980 and the brilliant 1979, both splendid, tasting of Recioto at first, but then drying out on the aftertaste, and with a more peppery tone than Recioto. Another astonishing wine is still in its infancy. This is a blend of local grapes varieties with 50% Cabernet Franc, which had been dried in the same way. At three years old, this 1983 was still purplish in colour, and had an aromatic fruity nose, but seemed rather shorter on the finish than the straight Amarone. Two white Reciotos tasted from cask and demijohn were as sensational as the Extra Amabile. The star was his Bianco Bandito Amabile del Cere, so called because in 1969, when he first made the wine, he put the barrels outdoors in a sort of cage that, he fancied, resembled a bandit's hideout. Bandito was made from *fiore* (botrytised) grapes and kept in a sealed cask; in five years it has never been topped up, and has lost 40% of its volume. A number of merchants, says Quintarelli, will gladly buy up all his Bandito tomorrow, but, characteristically, he is letting them wait. When the wine does come on the market, it will cost, he says with satisfaction, at least 30,000 lire per bottle ex-cellars. Worth it too, to judge by the sample I tasted. It is a brilliant copper-amber and the nose is rich, honeyed and peachy. The wine's incredible intensity is balanced by acidity; it ought to be overpowering, but it is not, for the balance gives it elegance and class, lovely length and a clean finish. It seemed odd that a wine made by a method similar to that used for Vin Santo (see p. 276) bore few obvious traces of oxidation. Perhaps I was less diligent than usual in taking notes, for we had now been in the cellars for four hours. In France, it is all right to spit out the wine. Less so in Italy, and although I occasionally snuck behind a cask for a surreptitious spit, I was certainly not invited to do so.

Giuseppe Quintarelli is a great winemaker but probably one of a dying breed. His reputation is extraordinary and his prices high, so he can afford to keep his wines in cask until he feels they are ready to be bottled, but few of his colleagues could afford that luxury. He nurses each of his wines because he knows that each has a different personality. And he can leave his wines untreated for as long as he does because of the amazing quality of the fruit and the care with which it is harvested. Quintarelli himself gives the credit to the soil rather than to his own skills: 'Terreno è primo.' And of course he is a perfectionist. While I was there, his wife and daughter were bottling (by hand, needless to say) a small consignment. I examined the corks; they were thick and dense and cost as much as the bottle itself – another sign of his perfectionism. His scrupulousness and unerring instincts as a winemaker are easily put to the test. Taste a bottle of Recioto or Amarone from any large producer side by side with a bottle from Tedeschi or Quintarelli and the difference will be obvious: power, concentration, intensity of flavour, voluptuousness. Old vintages are hard to find, but in recent years the greatest have been: 1961, 1964, 1966, 1969, 1970, 1971, 1974, 1975, 1977, 1978, 1979, and 1983.

Breganze, some distance north-east of Soave, is the home of a rare wine called Torcolato. The principal grape variety used for this wine is Vespaiolo, which is blended with a few other local varieties.

For centuries Torcolato, being high in sugar content, doubled as a medicine, and ailing folk would call for a glass to aid their recovery. The local firm of Maculan, the north Italian equivalent of a Californian boutique winery, has since 1971 made and marketed the wine on a commercial basis. The Maculans own no vineyards but buy their grapes from contracted growers whose vines are planted on the south-facing slopes behind Breganze. Botrytis does occur but is not common. The grapes are carefully selected and any with broken skins that would encourage oxidation are rejected. The bunches are tied to strings and suspended from roof beams; no grapes touch the ground, so the air can circulate around them. They are pressed in January. Fermentation takes place over about twenty days at cool temperatures in steel tanks, and then the wine is put into barrels, of which a high proportion are of new oak. The result bears some resemblance to Anselmi's Recioto di Soave. In both wines the influence of new oak is profound. Maculan's Torcolato, of which about 10,000 bottles are made each year, has about 15% alcohol and 6–10% residual sugar. The wine certainly does not taste that sweet and is balanced by good acidity that keeps it fresh and gives it good length. Torcolato has great refinement and style, and is far from overblown. Pale gold in colour, it is oaky on the nose when young, though with some bottle-age the rich fruity aromas of the wine begin to develop. With its appley elegance and lively acidity, Torcolato is not unlike Barsac. Generally lean in style, the wine can in certain years such as 1978 acquire considerable complexity. Since this oak-aged Torcolato is a relatively recent invention, it is hard to say how well the wine will age. A string of recent vintages seemed to have

sufficient acidity and alcohol to sustain the wine for a decade or more, though a bottle of 1981 was beginning to dry out in 1986.

TRENTINO – ALTO ADIGE

Like the Valle d'Aosta, this northerly region nestles against the Alps. The Alpine part, the Alto Adige, is almost indistinguishable from the Austrian Tyrol, and its inhabitants speak German and exhibit Teutonic sobriety rather than Italian flamboyance. Almost all the sweet wines made here are Muscats, with the exception of the Vin Santo of Trentino. This *passito* wine is only found in the area near Lake Garda, for here the winds coming off the water are sufficiently strong to dry the grapes. The firm of Pisoni makes an outstanding example from old vines of Nosiola. The grapes are left on racks till late March before being pressed, then fermented in 500- or 800-litre casks, in which the wine remains for up to five years. It is wonderfully intense, a clear light brown in colour, raisiny, rounded, and elegant. This rich wine, with 12% alcohol and 8% residual sugar, is hard to find, since only about 9000 bottles are made annually, of which 1500 are made by Pisoni. Most of it is consumed locally.

A Moscato is produced in the region, but examples I have tasted cannot compare with those from Asti and Strevi, and tend to be flabby and lacking in pep. A more liquorous Moscato del Trentino is said to exist but I have never encountered it.

Further north, in the Alto Adige, two varieties of Muscat are the mainstay of sweet wine production: Moscato Giallo and Moscato Rosa, or, to give them their more commonly used German names, Goldenmuskateller and Rosenmuskateller. Only 6 hectares of vineyards are registered as DOC Goldenmuskateller, yet large quantities are sold locally as table wine. For this there are two reasons: the DOC regulations limit yields to 56 hl/ha, and stipulate that the wines must contain residual sugar; but because of the fashion for drier wines, many producers, such as Tieffenbrunner, ferment to complete dryness to make a strong aromatic wine designed to accompany food. Tieffenbrunner makes a Rosenmuskateller also sold as Vino da Tavola, because his version contains no residual sugar and thus flouts DOC rules. 'Authentic' Goldenmuskateller is never particularly sweet. That made by Alois Lageder, for instance, has only 12–13 g/l residual sugar. A pretty yellow-straw in colour, the wine is delicate and flowery on the nose, much fatter than, say, Asti; on the palate it is quite full, lightly sweet, and has prominent acidity and a dry finish. Other producers make a richer, spicier style of wine, which I find too sticky; they lack either the raciness of the Piedmont Muscats or the opulence of the southern Italian Muscats.

Rosenmuskateller is another matter entirely. Nicolas Belfrage in *Life Beyond Lambrusco* rightly calls it 'one of the world's greatest sweet wines'. It is, in its authentic forms, very rare, for the vine gives extremely low yields. It originated in Sicily and was brought to the Alto Adige towards the end of the century. The finest Rosenmuskateller is made at Schloss Sallegg, owned by Graf Eberhard Kuenburg. Of this 25-hectare estate above Lake Caldaro, only 0.7 hectares are planted with Rosenmuskateller. The winemaker here, Walter Tapfer, has to attend to those few vines constantly, for they are temperamental and require constant pruning. Those presently in the ground are between twenty and fifty years old and their yields average 9 hl/ha, about the same as for Yquem and a third of the maximum permitted yield. When the weather is fine, Tapfer leaves the grapes on the vines to shrivel and concentrate their juices to the maximum extent. Botrytis is rare. In fine weather he can delay the harvest until mid-October; in less good years he picks in mid-September. Some years, about one in four, he can make no Rosenmuskateller at all.

This is a prodigious grape, for when picked late it has such high sugar content that it will ferment to 16% alcohol and 4% residual sugar. You can find on the market Rosenmuskateller that is relatively inexpensive (a bottle from Schloss Sallegg, if you can find it, will set you back 35,000 lire) but much lower in alcohol. These wines may have their qualities, but they cannot be authentic. Some producers have planted better-yielding clones and treat the vines with hormones to boost their productivity; others chaptalise, though this is illegal in Italy. Tapfer strongly disapproves of such manipulations. His wine is entirely natural, but of course it is also superbly made. The must is fermented for up to six months in small casks; it is then filtered and returned to cask for about four months, or as long as he considers necessary. It is, he says, a 'Gefühlsache', a matter of intuition. The wine must be watched constantly, for its high sugar content makes it hard to control. Tapfer thinks the wine should be given about five years' bottle-age before it is drunk, though the wine can age for fifty or sixty years.

I tasted four vintages, and was the first visitor to taste the 1985 from cask. In colour, the wine was deep pink, not unlike Pinot Noir, with beautiful garnet glints. And then the nose, for it is the bouquet that bowls over anyone who has ever tasted this stupendous wine, does truly smell like roses – not only like roses, for there are obvious traces of Muscat too. To look into this luminous deep pink liquid and sniff what seems to be a distillation of rose petals was a quite extraordinary experience. This particular vintage has very high extract, and when tasted from the cask it was still closed and tough and almost bitter. Tapfer said the grapes had been fantastic, and he had every confidence that the wine would develop beautifully. The 1984 was sweeter and even tasted rosy, but it is the 1983 that is especially ravishing. The colour was quite brilliant, a wonderful deep garnet-pink, and the nose equally extraordinary, with aromas of roses, marzipan, herbs and spice; on the palate it was rich and soft and intense. The colour of the 1973 had matured to a kind of onionskin pink, just as lovely as the more youthful pink-garnet, but graceful rather than brilliant. On the nose some of that specifically rosy aroma had been replaced with the most perfumed bouquet I have ever encountered. In the mouth the wine was mellow and elegant, completely harmonious. The length was terrific, the finish lingering but clean. It seemed impossible that a wine so velvety and refined had 16% alcohol, for there was no trace of it on the nose or palate.

Sadly the wine may soon be no more than a museum piece. The total annual production is never more than 700 bottles. It horrifies me to think that having drunk two bottles of the 1973, I have personally consumed 0.3% of the vintage. The production is so limited not only because the vines are old and exceptionally low-yielding, but because Tapfer is prepared to wait until late in the season to obtain the ripest grapes, and thus, like the Sauternes grower, he risks losing the entire crop. Moreover the present Graf Kuenburg, a teetotaler, is not especially interested in wine and may soon replant many of his vineyards with more profitable orchards. Tapfer has long wanted to plant a total of 2 hectares with Rosenmus-kateller, but has not yet succeeded. After thirty-five years as wine-maker, he is about to retire, and it is unlikely that his successor will be able to succeed where the almost legendary Walter Tapfer failed.

The only other Rosenmuskateller that even approaches Schloss Sallegg's in quality is made by the Istituto Agrario Provinciale at S. Michele all'Adige. The 1981 had 15.5% alcohol, and though slightly hot on the palate, did not taste chaptalised. The colour and aroma were superb, and it was only on the palate that the wine, which was still young in 1986, was less harmonious than Tapfer's. A quite well-known producer told me that he does not leave the grapes on the vine for nearly as long as Tapfer; sometimes he chaptalises to bring the alcoholic strength up to 13% and there is usually about 18 g/l residual sugar. His wine will keep for a few years but is not designed for long ageing. It was pleasant enough, with an attractive colour and bouquet, but the flavour was a dim reflection of the authentic wine; it was lively, almost peppery, but lacked concentration and was slightly bitter on the finish, which was short. Another producer, Roberto Zeni at Grumo, macerates his Rosenmuskateller grapes for three days and ferments in steel and bottles very young; the result is thin and rather bitter.

FRIULI

North-east from Venice lies the lovely region of Friuli–Venezia Giulia, and east of Udine, close to the Yugoslav border, is the district known as Colli Orientali del Friuli, from which most of the best wines come. It is here that two remarkable grape varieties, Verduzzo and Picolit, are grown, and both can make exceptional sweet wines. Verduzzo is grown throughout the region, but it is around the mountainous village of Ramandolo that it produces the finest fruit. There are no more than 30 hectares of vineyards, south-facing, in Ramandolo, and these are the most northerly vines in Friuli. The microclimate is special here too, for this is the rainiest spot in Italy, and the harvest is twenty days later than in Collio around Gorizia. Yields are low and variable. Ramandolo as a whole produces 1000 hectolitres annually, and its most notable winemaker is Giovanni Dri.

The grapes are picked very late, from mid-October to early November. Ramandolo, as Dri refers to Verduzzo di Ramandolo, is

not made from dried grapes. The must is fermented in steel throughout the winter, which is cold enough to make temperature control
unnecessary. In exceptional years, certain lots may spend a month or
two in new French oak. There are indeed discernible differences
between lots, some being more fragrant, others more delicate.
After bottling, the wine is aged for six months before being released.
Dri is an admirer of *barrique*-ageing, but feels that new wood must be
used with the greatest of care: 'Barrique non fa miracoli.' In 1984 he
used no wood, but in 1985, a very fine year, he did. His Ramandolo is
balanced with 12–13% alcohol and 5–6% (80–90 g/l) residual sugar.
Verduzzo resembles Riesling in one important respect: it is a high-
acidity variety that can succeed in off-years, if you have the patience
to wait for the wine to mature. Verduzzo is obviously at its fruitiest in
good years, but in a mediocre year such as 1984, the wine will
probably age, according to Dri, twice as long, on account of its high
acidity and natural tannin. The flowery fragrance of his 1985, tasted
just before bottling, reminded me of young Chenin Blanc, but on the
palate the wine was sweet and balanced and had that peculiarly
Italian quality of a slight almondy bitterness to balance the fruit; a
barrique sample was fatter and more rounded, though less fresh, and

the flavours of the wood were not too pronounced. The 1984 is leaner, more lemony and subtle; its marked acidity promises a good future for the wine.

Walter Filiputti is another important winemaker in the region. His winery adjoins the eleventh-century Augustinian abbey at Corno di Rosazzo, and the monastic cellars are still in use. The 15 hectares of vineyards surround the hilltop abbey. Filiputti is a stylish and confident man. He has firm views about viticulture as well as winemaking, and has spaced his vines less generously than most growers do, because he wants the vines to fight for the nutrients in the soil; they will bear less fruit, but the quality of each grape will be higher as a consequence. Close planting also encourages the roots to descend deep into the earth in search of nourishment rather than spread horizontally across the less nutritionally complex surface of the soil. Filiputti picks his Verduzzo comparatively late and ferments the must for two to three months at 18 °C. Half the wine is fermented in steel, the other half in wood. After fermentation the wine is put into new *barriques* for four to twelve months. After bottling (about 3600 bottles per year) the wine is given five to six months more ageing before being released. His wines tend to have slightly less alcohol and residual sugar than Dri's. The 1985, tasted from cask, was very good indeed, rich and nutty on the nose, with obvious woody overtones; but on the palate it was quite rich and complex, not especially sweet, and had a touch of tannin. Filiputti thinks that while most Verduzzo should be drunk within three or four years, certain vintages are capable of lasting up to fifteen years.

Filiputti also makes the wine at other estates in the area, such as Ronchi di Fornaz and Vigne dal Leon. The Fornaz wine is also aged in *barrique* for four to five months, and a cask sample of the 1985 was astonishingly good: fresh, fruity, delicious, with good acidity and an almondy aftertaste; the wine did not seem unbalanced by the oak, demonstrating just how sturdy the Verduzzo grape can be. Other excellent Verduzzos are made by Volpe Pasini at Togliano and Graziano Specogna of Rocca Bernarda. Specogna ferments his Verduzzo Friulano in steel at 18 °C and bottles in April; his wines are delicate and subtle, though austerity and lack of fruit marred the 1984. The large firm of Collavini, based at Corno di Rosazzo, makes about 10,000 bottles of Ramandolo each year from bought-in grapes. Collavini aim for 12.5% alcohol, and 55 g/l residual sugar. The 1984 seemed balanced on the dry side and was not showing well because of sulphur on the nose and some bitterness on the palate. Like all good Verduzzo, it finished dry.

The other sweet wine of Friuli is Picolit. This highly-strung vine suffers from something called 'floral abortion', a failure of pollination that often prevents the grapes from materialising at all. A large bunch of grapes would normally bear about 150 berries; but Picolit rarely bears more than twenty-five. Although yields are consequently very low, the concentration of flavour and extract can be correspondingly high. To add to its problems, Picolit is prone to fungal attack. (Botrytis is not considered desirable.) For these reasons production costs are high, and Picolit is extremely expensive. Friuli, which produces an average of 4000 hectolitres, is the major producer, though the grape grows fitfully elsewhere in northern Italy. For all the difficulties associated with Picolit, even a large high-quality producer such as Zonin at Gambellara manages to produce 6–7000 bottles each year from grapes grown on volcanic soil near Udine and Gorizia. At up to 30,000 lire per bottle, it is almost as costly as Schloss Sallegg's prized Rosenmuskateller. Collavini also make a small quantity (1000 bottles) of well-regarded Picolit each year at comparable prices.

Walter Filiputti's Picolit receives the same *élevage* as his Verduzzo, and he produces about 1500 bottles annually. His wines tend to have 12–13% alcohol and 7–8% (115–130 g/l) residual sugar. The 1985, tasted from cask, had sufficient fruit to balance the oakiness,

though in lesser years the wood can be obtrusive. The qualities I enjoy in Picolit, an intense sweetness checked by wonderful delicacy and an almondy piquancy, were certainly present. In the mouth Picolit is a small wine, though I do not use the word pejoratively; anything less like Sauternes, to which it is sometimes compared, it is hard to imagine, for the wine succeeds by virtue of intensity and finesse.

Giovanni Dri ferments his Picolit very slowly in steel tanks and racks frequently, since the lees of Picolit have a peculiarly unpleasant flavour. He likes to bottle early, towards the end of March; to delay the bottling is to jeopardise delicacy. Unlike his gutsier Ramandolo, Dri's Picolit should be drunk within two years. He makes only 700 bottles a year and the wine is exorbitantly priced, though such is its reputation that he has no difficulty disposing of his stock. Dri's wines are a touch higher in alcohol and lower in residual sugar than Filiputti's from the Abbazia di Rosazzo. A cask sample of the 1985 had a wonderfully floral nose, and a sweet marzipan flavour, and despite its frailty tasted rounded and balanced.

I have encountered exquisite Picolit not only from the Abbazia and Dri, but from other producers such as Graziano Specogna. He reports that his vines rarely produce more than eight berries on each bunch, and yields from 1400 vines vary from 1 to 4 hectolitres. The must is left on the skins for twenty-four hours, then fermented in demijohns. Specogna does not bottle until about a year after the harvest, as in his view the aromas do not develop until the summer. His wines are quite high in alcohol and residual sugar; on the nose his 1985 (from demijohn) was tremendously delicate and floral; on the palate it was very sweet, pretty, and rather light, though Specogna felt it would fill out after malolactic fermentation had taken place. The Volpe Pasini Picolit, made from seventy-year-old vines, is fermented in steel and bottled in September. A sample of the still unbottled 1985 vintage struck me as too pretty and lacy; it had delicacy and refinement, but lacked concentration and depth of flavour. The 1984, admittedly a poorer vintage than the exceptional 1985, seems distinctly dull and pallid. Possibly the loveliest Picolit I have encountered came from Ronchi di Fornaz and was made by the ubiquitous Walter Filiputti. Here the must is fermented without the skins in steel tanks, then transferred to *barriques* for four to five months and bottled in the spring. Compared to some other

Picolits, this is, at 11.5% alcohol and 3.5% (about 55 g/l) residual sugar, a lightweight; but the bouquet of a cask sample of the 1985 was utterly charming, and on the palate the wine was absolutely delicious and impeccably balanced. Without losing any delicacy, the wine was lissom and seductive.

Is Picolit worth between 15,000 and 50,000 lire a bottle? Paulo and Dina Rapuzzi, who own the Ronchi di Cialla estate in the beautifully situated hillside hamlet of Cialla, agreed to put this matter to a practical test. Rapuzzi makes two great red wines, both from indigenous varieties, Refosco and Schioppettino, as well as Verduzzo and Picolit, and was one of the first Italian winemakers to mature wines in new oak. He finds Verduzzo well suited to oak-ageing, because the wine is naturally tannic. He prefers to pick early to preserve acidity, though in 1984, for example, he was still picking in mid-November because he found it necessary to make three passages through the vineyards to select the best grapes. Since the 8 hectares surround the winery, he can usually press the grapes within thirty minutes of picking them.

PICOLIT

1985

COLLI ORIENTALI DEL FRIULI

denominazione di origine controllata

PRODOTTO ED IMBOTTIGLIATO ALL'ORIGINE DALLA AZIENDA AGRICOLA
RAMANDOLO GIOVANNI DRI ITALIA

0,75 l e   13% VOL

With Verduzzo the must is given twelve hours of skin contact to extract aromas and yeasts. The juice is then racked, very slowly fermented in steel at no more than 18–20 °C, then racked again before being put into lightly-toasted Burgundian *barriques*, half of which are new. Verduzzo spends seven to nine months in cask, while the less robust Picolit stays only three to four months. Rapuzzi admits that a slight oxidation occurs in cask, but is untroubled by it. After blending, the wine rests in tank for a few months before being filtered, bottled, and aged one year before being released. Like Quintarelli, he uses only top-quality Sardinian corks, despite the expense. Verduzzo is sweeter than Picolit and can age for up to ten years, though the Italian wine authority Veronelli thinks Rapuzzi's wines can age even longer. Picolit is so delicate that Rapuzzi is opposed to decanting the wine on the grounds that rapid exposure to the air could bring about undesirable changes.

We tasted three Verduzzos, 1983, 1982, and 1977; and two Picolits from 1983 and 1979. The younger Verduzzos were very distinguished, especially the 1983: medium gold in colour, delicate on the nose, and fresh and nutty and lively on the palate. The tannin masks the sweetness and I would not have guessed that the 1982 has about 75 g/l residual sugar. The 1977 was a revelation. The nose had become fat and buttery, and the wine was rich and supple on the palate, with splendid acidity and great length. The balance was quite superb. The 1983 Picolit was certainly a wonderful wine, very pretty, highly-strung, with a great deal of *nervosité*, and a surprising dryness at the back of the palate. Picolit is not supposed to age well, so uncorking the 1979 was a bit of a gamble. It was green-gold in colour, like a fine Mosel of the same age, and very lovely on the nose: delicate but perfumed. On the palate it disappointed; it had lost some of its sweetness, though not its concentration, and was rather austere, as though it did not have sufficient fruit to give the wine firmness and body after the sweetness had diminished. It was still perfectly drinkable, but clearly past its best. Rapuzzi's wine, aged in wood, has probably survived better than most, but even his lacked complexity and backbone. These comparisons confirmed my view that for all the charms of Picolit, and they are genuine and delightful, Verduzzo is the serious sweet wine of Friuli. It has weight and vigour and complexity and, unlike Picolit, develops in bottle. It is also about a third of the price. Picolit's scarcity has inflated its cost and the wine is clearly overvalued. Good Verduzzo, on the other hand, is worth every penny.

EMILIA-ROMAGNA

This large region, stretched like a choker across the throat of Italy, produces more wine than all of Germany, most of it quaffable unpretentious stuff that washes down the admirable cuisine of the area. Lambrusco is the best-known wine, though whether it is the best is doubtful. There are *amabile* Lambruscos, nearly always *frizzante*, and the best of these come from Sorbara, Modena, and Reggio Emilia. Each district has its own variation of the grape variety; since Sorbara has lower-yielding vines than other Lambruscos, the quality is likely to be somewhat higher. I am no admirer of Lambrusco, though I do not doubt that when drunk properly chilled under pleasurable circumstances in this delectable part of Italy, it can be thoroughly enjoyable.

A curiosity called Cagnina has recently been revived by one or two producers, such as Fattoria Paradiso. It is made from the Canaiolo Nero grape, widely-grown in central and southern Italy. The most remarkable thing about it is its colour, a bright purple-violet. Cagnina, the sweet version, is, at 9%, low in alcohol and has about 50 g/l residual sugar. It is not to my taste, to put it mildly, though Nicolas Belfrage considers it 'bizarre but delicious'. Bizarre, certainly.

Perhaps the most serious sweet wine of the region is made from Albana di Romagna, a prolific variety found throughout the region. I have not been impressed by its sweeter manifestations, though it has an attractive herby nose that is quite aromatic, and considering that the wine usually has no more than 10% alcohol, it is remarkably mouth-filling and can have good clean acidity. Some Albanas have a slightly resinous flavour that some may find unappealing.

TUSCANY

The great sweet wine of Tuscany is Vin Santo. The only other important sweet wine of the region is the charming Moscadello di

Montalcino, a frothy delicate Muscat. Villa Banfi make a very good example, marginally fuller in flavour than their Moscato di Strevi. Vin Santo, however, is at the opposite end of the taste spectrum, for it is a rich, concentrated and alcoholic wine. It is found in two styles, sweet and dry, and, as in the case of Recioto and Amarone, the sweet style is more traditional, though the dry wine conforms more to modern tastes. No one is quite sure how Vin Santo got its name, but the most likely explanation is that, being an oxidised wine that will not deteriorate rapidly after being opened, it is ideally suited for sacramental purposes. The wine is made from Malvasia, Grechetto and Trebbiano grapes, though not necessarily all three. Red Vin Santo is also made but I have never encountered it. The grapes are usually picked early to ensure that they are sound and healthy. They are then either laid on straw mats or suspended on strings from the rafters of a well-ventilated attic. The longer they are left to dry, the higher the concentration of sugar and the sweeter the finished wine is likely to be. Before the grapes are pressed, any rotten berries are weeded out. After pressing, the must is placed into 50-litre oak barrels called *caratelli*, which are then sealed and usually left untouched for up to six years, during which the must ferments and a gentle oxidation takes places within the cask. The final results are not always predictable, since the fermentation takes place at its own pace, without manipulations of temperature or other treatments.

It does not sound like a reliable formula for great winemaking, for summer temperatures in a Tuscan attic can be formidable, and so can the frosts in winter. Yet such dramatic fluctuations aid the vinification process. The expansion and contraction of the wood encourages the oxidation that gives Vin Santo its character. The artisanal producer, with a cask or two in his attic, will simply wait until he considers the wine ready, and then unseal the *caratelli* and hope the results are satisfactory. The more commercial producer may have to blend various *caratelli*, which may have fermented to varying degrees of alcohol and residual sugar, in order to maintain consistency. Intensity of flavour, as well as consistency, are aided by the practice of leaving about one eighth of the wine in the cask after the remainder is bottled; the pressed juice of the next vintage is then added to this *madre*, as the old wine is known. This is not unlike the solera system of Spain. Not surprisingly, Vin Santo is a formidable wine, often with 16–17% alcohol. It is a strong medium gold in colour, and the aromas are very aggressive, suggesting dried fruits, iodine, and sherry. The taste will vary considerably: it can be raisiny and almost gummy in texture, or starkly dry and powerful. The sweeter style is usually more harmonious, and a fully fermented Vin Santo, such as the stern 1978 from Tenuta di Capezzana, can be highly pugnacious.

With such methods of vinification, it is not surprising that Vin Santo can, like Tokay, age almost indefinitely, since there is no risk of oxidation. An example from Antinori, tasted after sixteen years, was magnificent; bright orange-amber in colour, with butterscotch on the nose; and on the palate medium sweet, intense and rich, elegant and lively, and with a touch of bitterness in the background that gave the wine grip and interest. Standards vary, and it is important to buy only from reputable producers, such as Tenuta di Capezzana, Avignonesi, Antinori, Badia e Coltibuono, and Frescobaldi. Like all *passito* wines, the best can only be made in small quantities, and is correspondingly expensive, though in Italy older vintages of good Vin Santo can still be found at reasonable prices.

THE MARCHES AND UMBRIA

The only sweet wine produced in the Marches is Vernaccia di Serrapetrona, a sparkling red wine made from Vernaccia Nera and Sangiovese. I have not tasted it. The range is somewhat wider in Umbria. Some Vin Santo is made here, and that produced by Lungarotti has, predictably, a high reputation. A rare red *passito* called Sagrantino di Montefalco is also made here. That made by Arnaldo Caprai is highly regarded. A bottle of his 1982 tasted in 1986 was an almost opaque brick-red, and had a forceful and earthy nose that while dry was quite heady. On the palate this still young wine was sweet at first, though there was plenty of tannin to follow; the flavour was concentrated and intense, though this particular example seemed to lack length. At 15.5% alcohol it was a formidable glassful.

One of the loveliest white wines of Italy is Orvieto Abboccato, mild and succulent and gently honeyed. It is not really a sweet wine and goes well with food, but it can be drunk as an aperitif. Botrytis is not uncommon in Orvieto, and this can give the wine considerable richness and style. Decucgnano dei Barbi have made an Orvieto from botrytised grapes. The 1983 vintage, of which 1623 bottles were made, was expensive but disappointing: it was dull in colour, and there was a curious petillance on the palate; quite rich and supple in the mouth, the wine lacked definition and assertiveness. It may well improve after a few years.

LATIUM, ABRUZZI, MOLISE, CAMPANIA, BASILICATA

The region of Latium, around Rome, is not known for any out-standing sweet wines, though many wines, including the abundant Frascati and the less common Cesanese, are often made in *amabile* styles. A little Muscat is made in Abruzzi and Molise. Another wine better known in its dry forms, Lacryma Christi del Vesuvio from Campania, is also occasionally made in an *amabile* style. Apart from an unusual sparkling red Aglianico made by Fratelli d'Angelo and a Muscat called Moscato del Vulture, Basilicata is also not known for sweet wines.

APULIA AND CALABRIA

Here, in the sprawling province of Apulia along the southern Adriatic coast, we are truly in the southern Italian wineland, home of rich Muscats and dark intense sweet red wines. One of the most notable is Aleatico di Puglia. The Aleatico grape is thought to be related to Muscat, but no one seems certain. It is made in two styles: *dolce naturale* (which must have at least 13% alcohol and 2% residual sugar) and the fortified *liquoroso* (16% + 2.5%). Hugh Johnson is somewhat dismissive of this wine, but the one example I have encountered (a *liquoroso* from Achille of Conversano) was splendid. The colour was an extremely deep but limpid ruby-red, and the nose smelt of blackberries (not at all like Muscat); on the palate the wine was very sweet and intense, peppery and hot, but with a dry finish; formidable, perhaps not very subtle, but rich and supple.

Apulia's leading Muscat is Moscato di Trani, made from Moscato Reale. The specifications for *dolce naturale* and *liquoroso* are the same as for Aleatico. The region's other sweet wine of special interest is Primitivo di Manduria, which many viticulturalists maintain is identical to the versatile Zinfandel so widely grown in California.

This wine too is made in a variety of styles: *dolce naturale* (13% + 3%), *liquoroso* (15% + 2.5%), and the dry *liquoroso secco* (16.5% + 1.5%). A *liquoroso* from Vinicola Amanda tasted capable of reviving the dead. A deep red-garnet in colour, it has a heady port-like nose, rather too alcoholic; on the palate the wine seems strikingly harmonious at first, soft and sweet, but then the alcohol marches up and delivers a hefty kick in the throat. A wine for winter warming, but rather too big and clumsy to give continuing pleasure after many sips.

The outstanding wine of Calabria is the rare Greco di Bianco. Unusually for southern Italy, this is a white wine, and is distinguished by its orange scent; it usually has 14% alcohol and 3% residual sugar. I have not tasted it, but it is said to be quite superb, sweet in its youth, and drying as it ages.

SICILY

Sicily's best-known dessert wine is surely Marsala. Since the great majority of Marsala is fortified, we cannot give the wine much attention here. Non-fortified Marsalas of high quality are produced, but they are rare and costly. The DOC regulations require Marsala to have 18% alcohol, and this can only be achieved by fortification. The principal producer of non-fortified Marsala, Marco De Bartoli, cannot achieve such a level naturally, so he sells his wine as Vino da Tavola under the name of Vecchio Samperi. The best grapes for Marsala, and those used by De Bartoli, are the relatively low-yielding Inzolia and Grillo, though it is also permitted to use the more prolific Cataratto and Trebbiano. Only Inzolia and Grillo, however, will give high potential alcohol in the grapes, and wines made from higher-yielding grapes must not only be fortified but sweetened with cooked or concentrated musts. De Bartoli is able to achieve a natural alcoholic content of 16.5%. He uses a solera system to offer his Vecchio Samperi in varying styles. The ten-year-old wine has enormous character: caramelised-orange in colour, it has a delicate yeasty nose easily mistaken for sherry; on the palate it is dry, demanding, full-bodied, and powerful, with great style, considerable austerity, and excellent length.

Of the other styles of Marsala, the finest is Marsala Vergine, which, like Vecchio Samperi, tends to be bone-dry, since it is not permitted to sweeten this wine. The solera method is common, and the wine must have a minimum of five years' barrel-age. This differentiates it from the often acceptable Marsala Superiore, a lesser grade which is also made in dry as well as sweet styles. The best examples of Vergine and Superiore have beautiful colours and heady aromatic bouquets of refinement and complexity; and are dry, powerful, and subtle on the palate.

Another Sicilian wine found in both fortified and unfortified styles is Moscato di Pantelleria, from a volcanic island between Sicily and Tunisia. The African influence is apparent in the name of the grape, Zibbibo, a clone of Muscat. The cooperative, the Cantina Sociale, makes a *liquoroso* version called Tanit. This is aged for three years in wood and fortified with 2% of alcohol. It's an excellent *passito* wine, deep amber-brown and with a sweet, burnt-caramel nose; on the palate it is very sweet, almost syrupy, intense and caramelised, and a bit overpowering.

By far the best Moscato di Pantelleria, good though Tanit is, is produced by the same perfectionist who produces Vecchio Samperi: Marco De Bartoli. The grapes come from the estate of Salvatore Casano, who also buys in fruit from trusted neighbours in his village of Bukkuram, after which the wine is named. The grapes here are of

particularly high quality, and the policy agreed by Casano and De Bartoli is to pick as early as August to ensure high acidity. Very high sugar content is less important, since the *passito* process will concentrate the sweetness in any case. Even so, with the North African heat, the grapes attain high must weights. Instead of drying the grapes on racks or suspending them from rafters, they are laid on nylon mesh mats to dry in the sun; they are turned by hand to make sure they get evenly tanned. After two to three weeks, the grapes are crushed, pressed and fermented at cool temperatures for six days before being transferred to large casks, where the fermentation continues more slowly until the desired balance is attained, at which point the wine is filtered. It is then placed in large old casks for about a year before being shipped to the De Bartoli cellars in Marsala. A proportion of the wine is retained in cask and used as *madre*, as is done with Vin Santo. The wine itself is fabulous: deep copper in colour, with a velvety nose suggestive of dried apricots and raisins. Moreover, it does have Muscat aromas, which are less prominent in the fortified Tanit. On the palate the wine is big, rich, and rounded, but with excellent acidity. The balance is remarkable. With 14.5% alcohol and 11%

(185 g/l residual sugar), it could so easily be cloying. To make a rich sweet Muscat is not difficult; to make one with real finesse and style is miraculous.

There are other Sicilian Muscats, such as the almost extinct Moscato di Siracusa, and those of Noto and Villa Fontane, and a Passito called Solicchiato Bianco di Villa Fontane. There is one other remarkable wine, which, like Moscato di Pantelleria, owes its renown to the dedication of a single producer. This is Malvasia di Lipari, another island wine. The basic wine must have 8% alcohol and 3.5% residual sugar; the Passito must have a total alcohol of 18%, and the *liquoroso* 20%. They are lower in residual sugar than the Muscats. Most of these Malvasias are not exceptional, but that made by a Swiss expatriate called Carlo Hauner is remarkable. It has a fabulous orange-gold colour, quite ravishing, and an aromatic nose suggestive of both stewed apricots and rose petals; the wine, which has only 40 g/l residual sugar, is distinguished by its elegance and a touch of bitterness that keeps it from being cloying. The length is exemplary.

SARDINIA

Malvasia is also widely grown on Sardinia, and the best is Malvasia di Bosa from the western part of the island. It is made in three styles, *dolce* (13% alcohol + 2% residual sugar), *liquoroso* (15% + 2.5%), and *liquoroso secco* (16.5% + 1%). For the more plentiful Malvasia di Cagliari, the total alcohol requirements are slightly lower. The Monica grape forms the base of naturally sweet and fortified red wines, and throughout the province of Cagliari the Nasco grape makes a sweet wine said by some to resemble Tokay. The only example of the *dolce naturale* (13% + 2.5%) that has come my way was a 1980 tasted in 1986 that was, I hope, a dud bottle, for it was resinous on the nose, oxidised on the palate, and generally nasty. Muscats are common, and are usually found in both fortified and non-fortified styles. The Moscato di Sorso-Sennori has the best reputation, though the Moscato di Cagliari, a thicker style, is also quite well regarded. Giro is an increasingly rare grape variety on the island, and it too makes a potent wine in styles from naturally sweet to fortified and dry. Again, I seem to have been unlucky with this wine, for a seven-year-old bottle was definitely drying out, though its potent cooked-fruit and caramel nose, and its austere raisiny flavours gave some indication of its character.

The leading firm of Sella & Mosca make a very dependable and rich sweet wine called Anghelu Ruju from *passito* Cannonau grapes, a variant of Grenache. With 18% alcohol, it is fortified and has about 80 g/l residual sugar. A twenty-year-old bottle proved superb, like a cross between Recioto and vintage port. Other sweet Cannonau wines are made throughout the island, in the usual range of styles, fortified and not fortified, sweet and dry.

16

The Rest of Europe

HUNGARY

The histories of sweet wine production in France and Germany are
ancient but patchy, while the wines of Tokay have been in con-
tinuous production since the seventeenth century. These wines are
made by a special process that will be explained below, and while that
process has been modified by technological developments, its essential characteristics, including very long barrel-ageing, have scarcely
altered in centuries. The Tokaj-Hegyalja region (which I shall
abbreviate to plain Tokay) is, even in terms of Hungarian geography,
remote. It lies in the north-eastern corner of the country, close to the
Czech and Russian borders and far from the cosmopolitan delights of
Budapest. The floodplain of the River Bodrog is overlooked by a
range of south-east-facing slopes, and it is here, and along the side
valleys that poke into the hills, that the Tokay vineyards lie. 90% of
them enjoy this near perfect exposure to the sun. Sheltered by the
Carpathian Mountains behind them, they bask in the warm air that
blows off the Great Plains each summer. The demarcated region,
which includes twenty-four villages and four small towns, is quite
large: it is shaped like a crocodile's snout, with Sátoraljaújhely,
where the state wine farm's head office is based, at its tip, and the
villages of Tokay and Tállya about twenty-five miles to the south-
west. Tokay itself is a lovely town of about 5000 inhabitants, and the
storks perched on the chimneypots and the dignified façades of
the houses along the main street remind me of the villages of the
Burgenland in present-day Austria.

The vineyards themselves occupy about 7000 hectares, of which

1400 are owned by the state wine farm. The remainder are divided between cooperatives and private owners. These private growers supply grapes, must and wine to the cooperatives, and also sell to private clients. Very few, if any, have bottling facilities, so these private sales to individuals are on a modest scale. Before phylloxera eradicated 95% of the vineyards, there were about one hundred and thirty grape varieties grown in Tokay. Now there are no more than three, all of which are used to make the sweet wine. The most important is Furmint (55%), which also makes superb, fiery, dry white wine, followed by Hárslevelü (40%) and Muskat Lunel (5%). This last variety rarely succumbs to botrytis, unlike the other two, and is not blended into the sweet wine. Instead, it is either made into a light white wine or, when conditions are appropriate, into Tokay Muskotály, a 100% Muscat wine vinified in the same way as the traditional Tokay Aszú.

The local method for making sweet wine from botrytised grapes – the aszú method – became established in the seventeenth century, but the history of winemaking in Tokay is far more ancient. As long ago as the thirteenth century, winemakers were imported from Italy to practise their skills here. But with its Aszú, Tokay found a unique product that soon came into international demand. Before that time the wines of the region were not regarded as superior to those from elsewhere in Eastern Europe. Aszú was a great favourite of Peter the Great and the Russian Tsars, who installed a garrison in Hungary until 1798 to safeguard the quality and integrity of wines made from

PRODUCE OF HUNGARY   50 cl

TOKAJI ASZÚ

BOTTLED BY TOKAJHEGYALJA STATE WINERY, TOLCSVA

EXPORT   IMPORTED BY   MONIMPEX
Colman's
CARROW   NORWICH

vineyards the Tsars had leased. Louis XIV of France did wonders for the reputation of Tokay by allegedly declaring it to be 'Vinum regum, rex vinorum' (the wine of kings, the king of wines). Greek and Polish merchants were also active in marketing the wine, and many settled in the region; indeed, the new wine museum in Tokay is located in a charming Greek merchant's house. Tokay was popular throughout Europe not only because of its rich flavour and high quality, but because of curative properties that supposedly alleviated all manner of ailments, from lack of virility to anaemia. It is certainly probable that a wine so rich in sugar, minerals, and extract should have beneficial properties. In the nineteenth century these merchants began to withdraw from the wine trade and were replaced by Jewish merchants. Nowadays, of course, the making and selling of the wine is, with the exception of small-scale private dealing, in the hands of the state wine farm.

The soil is volcanic and very stony over a layer of loess; this rough texture helps to retain the daytime heat during the cool autumn nights and mornings. The climate is quite harsh, with fierce winter gales, though frost is rarely a problem before December. Birds, especially starlings, like to feast off the ripening grapes, and apparently they are still warned off by the whirling of rattles. Since autumns tend to be dry and sunny, the vintage is delayed as long as possible in order to give the grapes the maximum opportunity both to ripen and to succumb to botrytis, which is nurtured by the mists rising off the Bodrog to the east and the River Szerencs to the west. The aszú (botrytised and raisined) grapes are picked by hand, cluster by cluster, a long and arduous process lasting from early November, when the harvest usually begins, and continuing for twenty to thirty days. Average yields are 50 hl/ha, though they are much lower for aszú grapes.

The harvest differs little from that in any other traditional wine-growing region of the world. Where the Tokay method comes into play is after the aszú grapes reach the press house. They are carried in baskets or tubs known as *puttony*. Each *putton* holds about twenty-five kilos of grapes. These are carefully crushed into a mash; this eliminates the skins (which have already been shrivelled by botrytis) but keeps the seeds intact. The pulped contents of one or more *puttonyos* are added to a cask of top-quality must or wine. This must or wine, made from healthy grapes picked earlier in the harvest, often rests in casks known as *gönci*, and each *gönc* holds 136 litres. There is no special significance to this; it just happens to be the traditional size of cask found here, and its volume is used to measure the ratio of aszú mash added to fermented wine. The mash and wine are stirred together for twenty-four to thirty-six hours, so as to elicit as much tannin and extract as possible, not to mention aromatic and other compounds such as glycerol, from the botrytised grapes. The mixture is then racked into either *gönci* or 200-litre *szerednye*. Because of the additional sugar added by the mash to the fermented wine, a further fermentation takes place, very slowly over three to six months. This boosts the alcohol level by 1–2%, and the sugar that has not fermented remains in the wine in residual form.

Aszú wine is graded according to the number of *puttony* added to the fermented dry wine. Clearly, the more *puttony* added, the more sweet and rich the wine will be. The lowest grade is three *puttonyos*; four and five are common in good years; and in exceptional years a six-*puttonyos* wine may be made. The *puttony* as a physical object is now little used, but the principles of Aszú winemaking remain the same. Thus to make a five-*puttonyos* wine, 125 kilos of mashed aszú berries must be added to 136 litres of dry wine. Instead of counting *puttony*-loads individually, the winemakers at the state wine farm measure the must weight of the mash in order to ensure that the correct proportion of mash is added to the wine to make whichever grade of Aszú is desired. It is their ratio which is crucial for determining the style of the finished wine.

When the wine has completed its secondary fermentation, it is racked, fined, filtered, then aged for a minimum of five years. It is this long ageing, as well as the distinctive vinification, that give Tokay such individuality. The formula for ageing is as follows: to the number of *puttony* used, add two. Thus a three-*puttonyos* wine is aged for five years, a five-*puttonyos* wine is aged for seven. Regulations specify the amount of residual sugar and sugar-free extract that must be present in each wine. Three-*puttonyos* wine must have at least 60 g/l residual sugar and 30 g/l extract; four-*puttonyos* 90 g/l and 35 g/l; five-*puttonyos* 120 g/l and 40 g/l; and the rare six-*puttonyos* 150 g/l residual sugar. When the wine is ready to be bottled, it is transferred into tanks. With such a long ageing process, there may be slight variations between the wines of different villages, and to ensure a uniform product some blending may take place at this stage. All Aszú is bottled in Hungary. Bottled wine receives a further few months of ageing before it is released. About three-quarters of the production is exported. The distinctive fifty-centilitre bottles that contain the wine were first devised especially for the Great Exhibition at the Crystal Palace in London in 1851.

Aszú wines cannot be made every year. Moisture, even rain, is required as well as hot sunshine. On average, conditions permit good Aszú wines to be made three years out of ten; unexceptional Aszú to be made four or five years out of ten; and no Aszú at all in two years out of ten. In most years some aszú berries are not separated from healthy grapes, but pressed and fermented together with the healthy grapes. The resulting wine is called Szamorodni (a Polish word meaning 'as it comes' or 'self-made'). Sometimes Szamorodni can be dry, at other times sweet, depending on the amount of aszú grapes present in the must, though it is less sweet than Tokay Aszú itself. Even Szamorodni receives long barrel-ageing for between two and four years.

The casks are stored in over two hundred ancient cellars, some of which have been in existence since the thirteenth century. Forty are still privately owned. These cellars are tunnelled for miles into the hills, and the total storage capacity is about 500,000 hectolitres. The temperature is a reasonably constant 8–12 °C, and the maturing wines also benefit from a mould (*clodosporium cellare*), thick, black, and spongy, that covers not only the walls and ceilings of the tunnels, but casks and bottles too. This mould probably contributes to the flavour of the maturing wine and it definitely helps to maintain an average humidity level of 85% that rises to 98% in certain cellars; consequently there is no danger of corks drying out, and bottles can be stored vertically, which cannot be done in any other cellars in the world. Nevertheless, the corks of so-called museum wines are changed every thirty years to ensure that when the wine is eventually put on the market (usually at auction houses, where it sells for very high prices) it will be in sound condition. Because of this high humidity, the loss by evaporation from casks is minimal, and wines need to be topped up only once a year; sometimes, indeed, cellar-masters have to aid the maturation process by not filling the casks completely and by leaving a large surface area of wine exposed to the air. When oxidation is sufficiently advanced, the casks will be topped up. Exposure to air is important, for the style of Tokay Aszú requires it to be partially oxidised.

It does seem that the bottled wine can age almost indefinitely. The oldest bottle in the museum at Tolcsva dates from 1670 and came from the Imperial Cellars in Berlin. It was bought at auction in London by a British business man, who presented it to the museum. That is a unique rarity, but the cellars still contain good stocks of wines from 1922 and 1936. Here too, among the museum wines, are the bottles known as Aszú Essencia. The term means that the wine contains more aszú paste than is required for six-*puttonyos* wine. Such a wine can only be made in the greatest years, when the grapes have been intensely botrytised and shrivelled. The aszú grapes are individually selected from bunches brought to the presshouse. Their residual sugar levels can be from 150 to 250 g/l. In recent decades Aszú Essencia has only been made in 1945, 1952, 1955, 1962, 1964, 1967, 1968, 1972, 1975, 1982, and 1983. (Good years for Tokay in general were 1945, 1947, 1956, 1963, 1966, 1969, 1975, 1976 (Szamorodni), 1978, 1981, and 1983; and great years were 1957, 1959 (Szamorodni), 1962, 1964, 1967, 1968, 1972 and 1973.) These ultra-rich Tokays are left in cask for between ten and fifteen years, and then aged in bottle for perhaps six more before they even begin to be cautiously released onto the market.

Tokay produces an even more rare nectar known simply as Essencia – and not to be confused with Aszú Essencia. This is simply the juice that falls to the bottom of the *puttony* because of the sheer weight of the grapes pressing down. One *puttony* will produce a quarter pint of Essencia. This juice is so rich in sugar that fermentation only takes place on its surface; after about a month that fermentation slows down considerably, but simmers on for years. So unctuous is this Essencia that sometimes it can attain no more than 3% alcohol (some examples have less than 1%). It is not truly wine at all, but, as the name suggests, a quintessence of the grape. Essencia is never sold, and most of it is used to add richness to other grades of Tokay. I have only tasted true Essencia once, and count myself lucky to have had that opportunity. This particular sample was probably made in 1975 and taken from a cask in the cellars at Tolcsva. In colour it was a murky brown, thick and heavy and far from pleasing to the eye. The wine even felt heavy as I swirled it in the glass, so viscous was its texture. The aromas were of honey and caramel, but again there was a strange almost palpable thickness to the aroma. In the mouth the texture was quite extraordinary, as if the wine were aspiring to become honey. It was oily, velvety, and intensely sweet (it had about 300 g/l residual sugar and a trifling 3.4% alcohol), and yet there was a remarkable acidity (17 g/l) that kept it from being cloying. It was still thick and clinging, and its flavour and texture coated my mouth for a long time. Without that acidity the sensation of tasting Essencia would have been interesting but not wholly pleasurable. Yet it was actually palatable, though a thimble-full will go a long way. Essencia cannot be judged as a wine. It is an almost unique concentration of all the constituents of great sweet wine: the sweetness, aromatic energy, viscosity, and intensity that botrytis brings to the grapes it attacks and transforms. I experimented by adding a couple of drops to a glass of 5-*puttonyos* Aszú. The change was remarkable: both the aroma and the taste became richer and sweeter, seemingly out of all proportion to the tiny drops of Essencia I had added.

In 1986 I tasted a range of wines, from cask and bottle, in the No. 1 Cellars at Tolcsva, where hundreds of small oak casks are stored on three levels. The tunnels plunge through the rock for two miles, and there are forty-three side wings. The electricity had failed that day, so the cellarmaster and I tramped through the dark mouldy tunnels with flashlights in our hands and candles in our pockets. We tasted by candlelight, supremely romantic in these thirteenth-century cellars, though I did not consider shivering in the damp wholly ideal conditions for comparing wines. The cask wines did not show well. All the most assertive qualities of Tokay were present – its oxidised Christmas pudding nose, its aggression and spiciness on the palate – but the more seductive properties of roundness and voluptuousness had not yet developed. All these wines had at least 14% alcohol, and this too was over-prominent on the palate.

Tokay begins to show its true class after the wine has had some bottle age. The 1976 five-*puttonyos* Tokay, which I have often tasted, has struck me as a copybook example: a burnished brown-amber in colour, heavily oxidised on the nose yet soft and rich, and on the palate very sweet and rounded and buttery and suggestive of toffee, yet packed with extract and glycerol and acidity. The wine is very well-balanced, with 13.4% alcohol, over 10 g/l acidity, and 122 g/l residual sugar. The 1975 wines (three-, four-, and five-*puttonyos*) were less rich, medium-bodied and more appley in flavour, very attractive wines without the sumptuousness of the 1976, though they are likely to be greater in the long run. A five-*puttonyos* wine from 1937 also had this appley quality, especially on the nose; unfortunately this particular bottle was beginning to dry out, though it still had a crisp acidity that kept the wine lively and interesting. It should not be assumed that the higher the *puttonyos* grade, the better the wine. Richer, yes, but sometimes the lesser wines may have greater elegance.

Of the two six-*puttonyos* wines that have come my way, the 1972 (sampled from cask) was arguably better than the 1964 (sampled from bottle), though both were very great years in Tokay. Both had a lovely, almost toasted Cognac nose, and were rich, sweet, and sumptuous. The 1972 particularly impressed me with its concentration of flavour and richness in extract (47 g/l sugar free). Good acidity (8.5 g/l) kept the 155 g/l residual sugar from overpowering the palate, and the wine was wonderfully harmonious. A 1969 Aszú Essencia was impressive in much the same way.

Szamorodni can also be a very fine wine, though it varies from year to year more than Tokay Aszú. I find dry Szamorodni excessively aggressive, almost harsh, but a wine from the excellent 1983 vintage with 50 g/l residual sugar was excellent: only slightly sweet, but with flavours quite similar to those of Tokay Aszu. Szamorodni should not be thought of as a weaker brother of Tokay Aszú; it is just as alcoholic.

Sweet wines are found in other regions of Hungary, such as Badacsony and Villány, and many of them are Muscatels. Muskat Lunel (yellow Muscat) and Muskat Ottonel are widely planted. A three-year-old non-vintage Muskat from the Tokay region was an excellent wine, though not especially sweet. On the nose oxidised aromas almost overpowered the characteristic Muscat aroma, and on the palate spice and extract were more noticeable than residual sugar. Since the wine had 13% alcohol, I doubt that the residual sugar content was especially high. Muscats from other regions often contain 50 g/l of residual sugar. Grapes more familiar in Austria such as Traminer (Tramini) and Zierfandler (Cirfandli) are also found in Hungary but are rarely made in very sweet styles. Sweetish Leányka is found around Gyöngyös in northern Hungary. Some of these wines are sweetened with the equivalent of Süssreserve, which is permitted in Hungary. Late-picked Olasz Riesling from Badacsony occasionally attains high residual sugar content and is sold as Szemelt Rizling. Curiously, the area around Sopron close to the Neusiedler See is best known for red wines, rather than the rich botrytised wines found just across the border in the Burgenland.

BULGARIA

The majority of Bulgarian sweet wines are fortified and made in a slightly oxidised style, and do not concern us here. Non-fortified sweet wines are made mostly from two white grapes, Rikat and Tamianka (a native of Romania, where it is known as Tamiioasa), and from two red grapes, Mavrud and Cabernet Sauvignon. These wines range in sweetness from 40–70 g/l residual sugar. They are not much prized in Bulgaria itself and are made principally for export to the Soviet Union. Quite recently a mildly sweet white wine, part of the Mehana range, has been imported into Britain, but it has been made especially for this market and is atypical of indigenous Bulgarian sweet wine production. Sweet Mehana is a blend of Ugni Blanc, Muskat Ottonel, and Rikat, and is made by adding unfermented grape juice to fully fermented white wine – the Süssreserve method. Though fairly insipid stuff, it does have the merit of being extremely cheap.

YUGOSLAVIA

Yugoslavia's best known sweet wine is Tiger Milk, a mild and bland concoction from Radgona, which sells in vast quantities in Britain but has few redeeming features as wine. It is made from the Ranina grape, which is identical to Austria's Bouvier. Far more interesting is Prosek, from the region around Split along the Dalmatian coast. The grape variety is primarily Marastina, which is blended with other local varieties. This is a vigorous dessert wine of high alcohol, often 15% or more. With its brilliant copper-amber colour, it is stunning to look at, and has a sweet toffee-like aroma. The wine tastes sweet and a touch oxidised, and is obviously alcoholic. Other sweet wines, such as the oak-aged red Postup and Dingac from the Plavac Mali grape, are also made in modest quantities along the Dalmatian coast. I once encountered a curious 1971 Sauvignon Blanc from Maribor just south of the Austrian border. It was a promising bright light gold in colour, but distinctly catty on the nose. However, it was better on the palate, sweet and soft and remarkably fresh and of medium length. I detected no botrytis.

GREECE AND CYPRUS

It is arguable that Greece produces (or certainly exports) the worst wines in Europe. Of course there are honourable exceptions, such as Ch Carras, but all too few of them. The probable explanation is that many Greek wineries are still not equipped with cool fermentation facilities. This does not affect the production of dessert wines, though some of these are also of indifferent quality. Many are made from Muscat grapes. Muscat Hamburg is the base for Amandia from Rhodes, and Fivos from Tyrnavos. It is hard to say which is less unpalatable. The sweet aromatic aromas and sturdy red and orange-red colours of the wines are promising, and their crudity emerges on the palate. Both are bland and taste not unlike cheap port. Amandia with 16.5% alcohol and 6% (about 100 g/l residual sugar) is surely fortified, as, I suspect, is the less powerful Fivos. Limnos Muscat, made from Muscat of Alexandria, is marginally better, a firm deep gold in colour, and intense and syrupy in the mouth; examples that have come my way have been marred by unbalanced sweetness and too much alcohol. The same is true of the Muscat of Patras, which has a good reputation but which in my experience lacks acidity and freshness. The best Greek Muscats I have tasted are from Samos, where 2300 hectares are planted with the grape. The wine is made from bunches that have been dried after picking. They attain very high must weights, and the resulting wine is both high in alcohol (about 15%) and residual sugar. Samos is usually, but not always, unfortified. The Samos cooperative exports two sweet Muscats. That labelled Sweet Muscat has a lovely fresh Muscat nose, and on the palate is unctuous, richly sweet, rounded, and well balanced. Even better is the ten-year-old Muscat marketed as Nectar. Despite the presumptuous name, this is excellent wine, slightly less sweet than the Sweet Muscat (no bad thing) but with better depth of flavour and terrific length. The colour, a bright copper-amber, is also sensational.

It should be stressed that all the wines mentioned here are made by the cooperatives that dominate the Greek wine industry. Growers from any country are tempted to hang on to some of their best grapes and make wine for family consumption, and no doubt fine sweet wines are still made on an artisanal basis. Sadly those that are commercially available are mostly of indifferent quality. Another famous Greek sweet wine, Mavrodaphne from Patras, has also struck me as disappointing, though examples that justify its reputation must surely exist. Made from Mavrodaphne and Korintiak grapes, this sturdy red wine, lightly fortified, can have up to 15.5% alcohol; it reminds Hugh Johnson and others of Italian Recioto, but examples I have tasted have been marred by a hot syrupy finish unacceptable in Recioto. Of the medium sweet concoctions known as Madonna (from Lefkas, and made from the Vertzami grape), Kadmos and Ino (from Thebes), and Lais (from Nenea), I think it prudent to remain silent.

Cypriot wine production is dominated by four huge companies, all equipped with technologically sophisticated wineries. The wines are frankly commercial and designed to appeal, it would seem, to the lowest common denominator in terms of taste. KEO's St Panteleimon, with its pallid resinous nose that reminds me of fixative, is in my view positively unpleasant, and the Muscat of Alexandria marketed by SODAP is exactly the kind of thick cloying syrup that has given the grape a bad name. Cyprus, is, however, famous for one great sweet wine: Commandaria. Its history is ancient, and it owes its name to the Knights Templar in the twelfth century. It is produced in eleven villages in the Troodos Mountains, the source of Cyprus's best wines. Local grape varieties are used to make this wine: Xynisteri (white), and Mavron and Ophthalmo (both red). After the harvest the grapes are dried for up to two weeks before being pressed and fermented. The wine gains much richness from the solera system, known as Mana in Cyprus, and younger wines top up older wines in the maturation tanks. Village wines are often made in earthenware jugs, just as they would have been in the Middle Ages. The wine, supposedly unfortified, can reach 16% alcohol plus 8% (135 g/l) of residual sugar. How authentic the commercially available St John Commanderie from KEO is I cannot say, but it is a more than acceptable wine, a forbidding copper-brown in colour, and rich, raisiny, and caramelised on the nose; velvety and alcoholic, it tastes like liquid toffee, but is quite well balanced.

SPAIN AND PORTUGAL

Nearly all the magnificent sweet wines of Spain, those of Jerez and Malaga and the *rancios* of Penedes, are fortified. However, there are one or two wines to which alcohol is not added. The best known is Extrísimo from Masia Bach in the Penedes region. This is not a botrytis wine, but is made from overripe grapes and fermentation is arrested before all the sugar is converted into alcohol. The wine spends five years in old oak casks. It can only appeal to those who like a heavily oaked style. The nose is woody, oily, resinous, and the same is true on the palate. The wine is capable of long ageing, and a 1970 Reserva was much better balanced.

López de Heredia also make a sweet white wine known as Zaconia Bianco from healthy Malvasia as well as Viura grapes. It too spends over five years in oak, and has a lovely nose of pears and marzipan; but on the palate the 1978 wine was insipid and surprisingly lacking in fruit.

Portugal's great sweet wines, Port and Madeira, are clearly beyond the scope of this book, as are the delicious and aromatic Muscats of Setúbal. Joao Pires, who makes stylish dry wines, occasionally produces a plump Sauternes-style wine from botrytised grapes (mostly Fernão Pires) charmingly acclaimed on the capsule for its 'Noble Rottenness'.

17

California

While it is a myth that botrytis was 'discovered' at various spots across Europe, such an act of discovery was much closer to the Californian experience, although in the early 1960s the winemaker Myron Nightingale had experimented with the artificial inducement of botrytis spores on Sémillon grapes (a method we shall discuss later in more detail). Other winemakers encountered botrytis almost by chance. Karl Wente, whose winery was based in Livermore, bought additional vineyards in the Arroyo Seco area of Monterey which, he discovered when it first occurred to his grapes in 1969, was prone to attacks of noble rot. In 1972 and 1973 he again made sweet wines from botrytised grapes. Such wines were virtually unknown in the California vineyards, which in those days were less cluttered with small boutique wineries than they are today. In his book *The Wines of California*, Roy Andries de Groot tells how in 1967 federal inspectors found Louis Martini, a respected Napa Valley producer, processing botrytised grapes at his winery and promptly had them destroyed as unfit to be made into wine. Twenty years later, such idiocies are, fortunately, no longer imaginable.

RIESLING

Most top-quality Californian sweet wines are made from Riesling (known in California as either Johannisberg Riesling or White Riesling – anything labelled solely as Riesling should be regarded with suspicion), and thus the preponderant style is German rather than French. Although it would have been possible to devise category and quality levels based on the German model, this has not been done. 'Late Harvest', the generic term for all wines made from overripe or botrytised grapes, indicates a sweeter style but no more than that. There are Late Harvest Rieslings equivalent to Spätlesen, and others closer to Beerenauslesen. Naturally, conscientious producers try to give more specific information on the label. Château St Jean has at various times released Rieslings labelled as: Select Late Harvest, Special Select Late Harvest, and Individual Dried Bunch Late Harvest. These different gradations clearly refer to the degree of selectivity practised at the harvest, and a rough rule of thumb is that the more words on the label, the more residual sugar in the wine. Unfortunately, there is still no codification of labelling. To know exactly what you are buying, you will have to read the back label (where there is one). Château St Jean, for instance, is very specific about harvest dates, must weight, acidity, residual sugar, bottling dates. The Californians convey this information using their own method, which is unlike that used in Europe. Must weight is measured in Brix, a hydrometer scale (see Glossary and the comparative table on p. 333). 29° Brix is the same as 125° Oechsle (Beerenauslese level), while 34° Brix is equivalent to 150° Oechsle (TBA level). Residual sugar and acidity are both expressed in terms of percentage by weight. As the Californian formula of 0.9% acidity is roughly equivalent to the European 9.0 g/l, for the sake of clarity I shall retain the European figuration here.* As in Germany, the numbers game is popular and winemakers vie with each other to produce the most extravagantly rich wine. Chateau St Jean is probably in the lead with a dazzling Riesling that has 37.5% residual sugar.†

Once you have mastered the significance of all this information, a rapid glance down the back label will tell you a great deal about the style of the wine, though clearly nothing about its quality or flavour. Of course it would be much more sensible for there to be an agreed common labelling policy for Late Harvest wines. The California Wine Institute has approved the following code, but it is not legally binding: Late Harvest should be equivalent to Auslese (minimum

* According to Richard Arrowood of Chateau St Jean, Europeans express total acidity as a sulphuric acid equivalent, while Americans express it as a tartaric acid equivalent. The systems are thus only approximately equivalent.

† Residual sugar, expressed in percentage by weight, can be converted into European measurements (grams per litre) by multiplying by ten.

24° Brix); Select Late Harvest signifies Beerenauslese (minimum 28° Brix); and Special Select Late Harvest is equivalent to TBA (minimum 35° Brix). Phelps has adopted this system, but many other wineries still use their own, more idiosyncratic labelling. Chateau St Jean has also accepted it, but vintages prior to 1981 displayed a different system: Selected Late Harvest (24.5°+ Brix) meant Auslese; Individual Bunch Selected Late Harvest (30°+ Brix) meant Beerenauslese; and Individual Dried Bunch Selected Late Harvest (40°+ Brix) meant TBA.

Some producers use proprietary names, such as Freemark Abbey's Edelwein, which is a heavily botrytised Riesling. In richness it is equivalent to a Beerenauslese, while their Edelwein Gold is comparable to a TBA. Edelwein, the first commercially available naturally botrytised wine from California, was first made in 1973, and then again in 1976, 1978, and 1982. Edelwein Gold has only been made in 1976 and 1982. Out of Freemark's total production of about 30,000 cases, 900 are of Edelwein. The vines are quite young (most were planted in the 1970s, but a few remain from the late 1960s), though yields are low at about one ton per acre.

The winemaker who made the first Edelwein was Jerry Luper. Botrytis was infrequent in the Napa Valley, where many of the top-quality Californian vineyards were planted. When, however, in 1973 Freemark's Riesling vineyards at Rutherford were attacked by botrytis in late September, Luper was not slow to exploit the situation. Luper has moved on and been replaced at Freemark Abbey by a series of other winemakers, and they have continued the tradition he founded. They aim for a must weight of at least 30° Brix and cool-ferment the must in steel for as long as it takes. In 1973 fermentation continued until Christmas Eve, when it was arrested by chilling, but in 1982 it was all over in two weeks. The wine is fined twice and bottled young, usually in January, but given at least three months' bottle-age before release. (The 1973 was not bottled until a year after the harvest, and then given a further year's bottle-age before being released.) A common complaint voiced in Europe is that Californian Rieslings lack acidity and thus the potential longevity of a high-acidity German Riesling. This can certainly be true of ordinary bottlings of Riesling, which tend to be higher in alcohol and lower in acidity than their German counterparts. It is less true of the sweet styles. In 1976 the Edelwein, for instance, had 8.4 g/l acidity, and the Edelwein Gold had, at 9.3, even higher acidity, as it should. A significant difference of styles between German and Californian stems from alcohol levels. These two wines had 10.3% and 10.5% respectively, rather higher than one would find in Germany.

The 1978 Edelwein, with 10.2% alcohol, 11.4 g/l acidity, and 15.5% residual sugar, was an exemplary piece of winemaking: a lovely bright copper colour, and with a beautiful raisiny nose that had elegance as well as good botrytis; in the mouth the wine was very stylish if not complex, with a crisp barleysugar flavour and excellent balance. It was very long on the finish. The 1982 Edelwein Gold, picked at 39° Brix and with 21.9% residual sugar, was deep yellow-gold in colour, had a rich peachy botrytis nose, with a trace of volatile acidity; orangey in flavour, it had fine richness and acidity, though less crisp on the finish than the 1978.

Another Napa Valley winery that has made Late Harvest Rieslings regularly is Raymond, a family firm founded in the early 1970s, though the Raymonds have been involved in California winemaking for half a century. The eighty-acre vineyard was planted in 1971, and the first wine made in 1974. The styles of their Late Harvest wines vary greatly. The 1982 wine, picked at 26.5° Brix, has 11.1% alcohol but only 7.5% residual sugar. It is an attractive wine, quite intense and fresh, but a lightweight with a rather short finish. In contrast, the 1978 was picked at 44° Brix, has 10.5% alcohol but 25% residual sugar. A splendid wine, but very forward. Deep copper in colour, it had a butterscotch nose, suggesting oxidation; yet on the palate the wine was rich and creamy, with honeyed toffee and apricot flavours, and good length. This wine, eight years old when tasted, seems unlikely to improve but, equally, shows no sign of tiredness. Similarly, the 1975, picked at 39° Brix, and with 12.8% alcohol and 13% residual sugar, seemed at or slightly past its best in 1986: it had good depth of flavour, but the high alcohol was all too apparent. It remains something of a mystery how wines with such high must weights can ferment through to such alcoholic strength, while a German wine of TBA richness would have difficulty creeping past 8%. The 1979, with a similar must weight, is better balanced with 10% alcohol and 19% residual sugar, and this was the loveliest and most stylish of the Raymond Rieslings: it had real concentration of flavour and an elegance not always found in these sumptuous

Californian Rieslings. The latest vintage, 1985, was disappointing, and I could detect no botrytis.

For the Raymonds, even though they make these wines whenever the climate allows, Late Harvest Rieslings are a diversion from their principal activity of making excellent Chardonnay. Joseph Phelps, at St Helena, specialises in such wines, which used to be made here by the revered Walter Schug, who came to Napa from his native Germany. Phelps began making Late Harvest wines in 1976 and has done so every year since then except 1984. Both the winery and vineyards occupy a stunning hillside site, just above the valley floor; 175 acres are under vine, and Phelps owns an additional 125 acres along the valley floor. The Riesling is grown on the west side of the valley between Yountville and Napa. More recently, Phelps has made sweet wines from that very German grape variety, Scheurebe, of which 5 acres were planted close to the winery in 1974, though the first to be marketed was the 1979 vintage. They have been pleasantly surprised by the success of their Scheurebe, despite the unfamiliar name.

When the grapes are heavily botrytised, the crusher can get jammed with the dense sticky mush, and in such vintages the grapes are pressed immediately. As at many other California wineries, the must is usually centrifuged before fermentation, so as to remove from it any solids that might detract from the purity of the eventual wine. It is often very difficult to induce fermentation when the must is high in sugar, so it is first clarified, then deodorised to get rid of mouldy smells (odd that such a procedure should be required), racked, and then inoculated with yeasts; the acidity is adjusted if necessary. Both grape varieties are cool-fermented for two to four weeks at 55 °F, sometimes a touch higher, since Schug and his successor Craig Williams argue that slightly higher temperatures help to get rid of undesirable esters and volatile elements in the must. To arrest fermentation, the wine is chilled, sulphured, and centrifuged. To those familiar with the European tendency, at least at high-quality wineries, to treat sweet wines as little as possible, such methods suggest the proverbial sledgehammer and the nut. Nor do the treatments stop here. The wine is left to settle for a week or two, then fined, filtered, and bottled in January or February. Phelps used to age the sweet wines in bottle up to a year, but the demand for them is now so great that they have been releasing them much sooner.

Freemark Abbey will sometimes make an Edelwein and an Edelwein Gold from different pickings, depending on the must weights, but at Phelps only one of the two styles is ever made in a single vintage: Select or Special Select, equivalent to Beerenauslese and TBA.

The wines are more Germanic in style than, say, Raymond's, but that is to be expected. The richest Phelps Riesling I have tasted, the 1983 Special Select, of which the winery is especially proud, was picked at 37° Brix. Fermentation was not pushed, for the wine has only 8% alcohol, and it has a hefty 23.6% residual sugar. It is exceedingly delicious, quite developed in colour but after three years still closed on the nose, though the botrytis was evident; on the palate it was extremely sweet, quite appley and enticing, with good length. Acidity was more prominent on the less sweet 1985, picked at 29° Brix and with only 11.2% residual sugar. The wine seemed very much more obviously Riesling: it had a greenish tinge, and a distinct Riesling nose overlaid with honeysuckle aromas; on the palate it was soft yet spicy, and while less rich than some other Phelps wines, it has excellent acidity and should have quite a long life. Certainly the lush

but fresh 1979 wine, harvested at 34.5° Brix and with 16.8% residual sugar, is still going strong, though it is very developed.

Of the two Phelps Late Harvest Scheurebes I have tasted, the richer was the better. The 1985, harvested at 31° Brix and with 12.5% residual sugar, was rather broad and melony. California Rieslings are not usually as racy as their German counterparts, so I did not expect that style, especially from Scheurebe, but this wine seemed flabby. Not so the 1982 Special Select, harvested at 35.3° Brix and with 18% residual sugar. This wine was a beautiful orange-gold, and the nose showed botrytis and was nicely complex, with aromas of barleysugar and honey. It tasted rich and intense, with a flavour of mandarins, viscous and concentrated, slightly lacking in acidity, perhaps, but not tired. And although it tasted delicious at four years old, I could not help wondering how well it would keep. It is worth noting that Phelps, in common with most other Californian specialists in sweet styles, bottles them in halves only (at $25 in 1986 for Special Select wines).

Other wineries, while not specialising in such wines, do produce them on occasion. Even Christian Brothers, the largest grower in Napa Valley (not to mention its leased acreage in the Central Valley to the south-east), has made Rieslings. Most have been in an Auslese style, picked at 23–26° Brix. The 1980 was attractive, though slightly thick, and of two 1981 bottlings (one with 8.5% residual sugar, the other with 13%) the lighter, with its fresh flavours of apricot and pineapple, was preferable. Pleasant though these wines were, they all lacked weight and depth of flavour. But in 1982 they produced a Very Late Harvest, picked at 42° Brix and with 26% residual sugar, that was perfection: magnificent rich wine, impeccably balanced. Franciscan Vineyards made a very good Riesling from grapes harvested at 35° Brix in early October 1982. Botrytis was evident on the nose, and the wine was concentrated and quite spicy; though lively and attractive at three years old, it may not be long-lived. Mike Grgich, of Grgich Hills Cellars, who makes some of the best Chardonnay in California, made Late Harvest Riesling in 1977, 1982, and 1985. The 1982, the only example I have tasted, was a severe disappointment. Although deliberately quite low in residual sugar (8%), it was not recognisable on the nose as Riesling, and was flabby on the finish. Caymus Vineyards, a Napa winery celebrated for its Cabernet, also seems to go adrift when it comes to Riesling. A 1983 wine, made from grapes picked at 31° Brix and with 17% residual sugar, was better on the nose than Grgich's, but lacked body and character on the palate; and there was a disconcerting bitterness on the finish.

Although the great firm of Robert Mondavi has made sweet Rieslings, they are a minor part of its operations. Mondavi has always been technologically sophisticated, and centrifuges and pasteurising equipment (used before rather than after fermentation) are routinely employed in conjunction with the most scrupulous use of traditional vinification and maturation practices. Late Harvest Rieslings spend up to two years in German oak. Mondavi first made such a wine in 1977, and did so again in 1978, 1981, and 1985. The 1981, a good if not great wine, was made in trifling quantities, a mere 1200 bottles. In 1986 it tasted well-balanced (9% alcohol and 15% residual sugar); there was obvious botrytis on the nose, and the wine, though somewhat light and lacking in concentration, was very sweet, lively, and clean.

Chateau Montelena is another Napa winery associated less with sweet Riesling than with fabulous Cabernet and Chardonnay. The winemaker, Bo Barrett, told me they did once make a Late Harvest wine. In 1983 they discovered that botrytis had attacked some of the Riesling grapes, which they picked at 27.5° Brix in late October. Unfortunately he used what he described as a 'killer yeast' and the wine went soaring up to an absurd 13.8% alcohol, leaving only 3–4% residual sugar. Only twenty cases of this monstrosity were made, and just for the hell of it Bo opened a bottle for me. It looked beautiful – a glistening medium gold – and smelt even better, full of plump Riesling fruit. It was only on the palate that the wine was a disaster:

1983
Napa Valley
JOHANNISBERG RIESLING
ALCOHOL 10% BY VOLUME
PRODUCED AND BOTTLED BY
ROBERT MONDAVI WINERY
OAKVILLE, CALIFORNIA

fruity, to be sure, and quite rich, but also oily and hot. As Bo Barrett would, I am sure, be the first to admit, this was an object lesson in how not to make Late Harvest Riesling.

Another winery that found itself making sweet Riesling almost by accident is Stag's Leap, also better known for its wonderfully elegant Cabernet. Their Riesling grapes come from the Birkmyer Vineyard in Wild Horse Canyon, 1200 feet up and far cooler than the valley floor. In 1983 there was some rain in September, which is not unusual, but it lasted longer than usual. Botrytis set in, and at the end of the month, after the healthy grapes had been picked, the botry-tised grapes were harvested at 31° Brix. This was a challenge to Warren Winiarski, the owner and winemaker at Stag's Leap. He destemmed and crushed the grapes lightly, pressed them, let the must settle before racking it into steel and inoculating with yeasts. The wine fermented at 48–50 °F for three weeks. It was then centrifuged and filtered, and bottled in January. The 5400 bottles were released six months later. Despite the fierce treatments entailed in the vinification, the wine is superb: a deep yellow-gold, and with a classic botrytis nose, racy and clean. The wine, which has 13.4% residual sugar and 9.8 g/l acidity, triumphs because of its balance, which compensates for its lack of weight. Sadly, Winiarski found making the wine so troublesome that he has said it is unlikely he will want to repeat the experience.

Beringer Vineyards have long made Late Harvest Rieslings, but because they are primarily known for their botrytised Sémillon wines, their Rieslings will be mentioned in the following section.

Many consider that the best California sweet Rieslings are made by Joseph Phelps Vineyards, though a rival school gives the honours to Chateau St Jean, based north-west of Napa Valley in Sonoma Valley. Richard Arrowood is the brilliant winemaker here. Although the winery owns 75 acres of vineyards, most of the grapes are bought in from trusted growers. For Late Harvest Riesling, the grapes usually come from the Robert Young or Belle Terre vineyards in the cool Russian River Valley. The grapes are not harvested at once, but picked selectively by a system akin to the French *triage*. The grapes are pressed in a pneumatic bladder press and the must inoculated with Steinberg yeasts and fermented at 55–60 °F for three to ten weeks. Sometimes the must has to be warmed to prevent the fermentation from sticking. To arrest fermentation, the wine is chilled and centrifuged, then returned to the tank for two weeks before being racked, clarified, cold-stabilised, and then bottled. The Riesling never sees wood. After listening to the cellarmaster, Don Van Staaveren, describing what Californians call the crush, I could see why Winiarski never wanted to see another botrytised grape: 'Handling the fruity is sticky, sloppy work. The must is the consistency of chocolate syrup and sticks in the press and the tanks. Usually our crusher can handle forty tons of grapes each hour. But with botrytised grapes it's down to five or ten. We have to be careful about not diluting the wine when we clean out the must lines going in and out of the tanks, so we clean them out with medium-sweet wine, not with water.' They try to use as little sulphur dioxide as possible, but without high alcohol levels to preserve the wine, they cannot dispense with it as much as they would wish.

The Chateau St Jean winemakers admit that they do not expect most of their Rieslings to last more than a decade, though Late Harvest Sémillon and Sauvignon should have greater longevity. I suspect that the richest wines may last longer than a decade. The 1984 Select, picked at 34° Brix and with 18.4% residual sugar (a lightweight by Chateau St Jean standards), exemplifies the quality of this winery. The balance was perfect, and there were strong aromas and flavours of dried apricots, velvety richness of flavour, and great length. The 1983, also from the Robert Young Vineyards, was marginally richer, and more developed. It actually tasted like a Riesling TBA and the balance was quite brilliant, so that the richness and concentration of fruit were matched by acidity and excellent length. Almost too much of a good thing is a wine made in 1982 with the grandiloquent title of Individual Dried Bunch Late Harvest Johannisberg Riesling (Robert Young Vineyards). The grapes were picked at an astounding 46° Brix; fermentation crept up to 7.4% alcohol, leaving 29% residual sugar. The wine shouted fat and richness on the nose as well as on the palate, which was voluptuous and chewy, and with that essential acidity in abundance. Glycerol oozed down the side of the glass. Will it keep? I do not know. It is already forward, but it is hard to imagine this stupendous wine tiring in a hurry.

In Russian River Valley itself a few wineries occasionally produce sweet Rieslings. It is surprising that there are not more, since the relatively cool climate here is better suited to characteristic Riesling than the hotter Napa Valley. Mark West Vineyards 1983 Riesling, harvested at 33.5° Brix, has almost too much acidity (10 g/l) – too much because there does not seem to be sufficiently rich fruit to balance that acidity. The wine is a beautiful amber-gold, and the nose, while raisiny, has good varietal definition, yet I have twice found it disappointing on the palate. Another Russian River winery that makes botrytised Riesling is Clos du Bois in Healdsburg. They do not make these wines every year. In 1984 there was no botrytis and in 1985 fermentation continued longer than expected and reached an unacceptable 14% alcohol, so it had to be used for blending. None of their Late Harvest wines receives barrel-ageing. The 1981 and 1982 are both in a Beerenauslese style and have good acidity (8.6 and 8.9 g/l respectively) to balance the residual sugar of just below 14%. The 1981 is less good than the 1982 and unlikely to improve, but the 1982, with its full ripe apricot nose and good fruit and intensity on the palate, should do so. From a vineyard neighbouring the Belle Terre Vineyards that supply Chateau St Jean, Johnson's Alexander Valley Vineyards made a small quantity of Riesling harvested in 1983 at over 40° Brix. Unfortunately this wine, which has 12.5% alcohol and 18% residual sugar, is weighty and oily in texture.

All the vineyards mentioned above are north of San Francisco, but there are some important wine-growing regions to the south, including the Santa Cruz Mountains near San Jose. Felton-Empire Vineyards is one of the oldest properties in this region. Its precious 5 acres of vines are dry-farmed (i.e. no irrigation) and yields are extremely low. Botrytised grapes for Felton-Empire's highly regarded Late Harvest wines come from the Tepusquet Vineyard far further south near Santa Barbara. The Rieslings are excellent, with clear, botrytis characteristics and a raisiny flavour. The acidity is good, though some vintages lack weight. The 1983 is outstanding, better than a slightly feeble 1984 Late Harvest. Although a 1979 tasted in 1986 was showing no signs of fading, I doubt that these wines will live indefinitely; the best vintages would be at their most satisfactory after five or ten years. The 1985, which will not be released until mid-1987, should be interesting: the grapes had very high must weights, since the harvest was only completed on 23 December and fermentation took ninety days.

The giant Almaden Vineyards are also based near San Jose. As at Phelps, the winemaker is a German immigrant. Klaus Mathes made a number of Rieslings from botrytised grapes between 1975 and 1979. They were grown in San Benito County, halfway between San Jose and Santa Barbara. The only one I have tasted, bottled under the Charles Lefranc label, bore out the worst fears of those who find Californian botrytis wines inferior to their European counterparts. At seven years old, the wine was already a deep copper-amber, not what one would expect from Riesling picked at 32.5° Brix. The wine was sweet and luscious, but decline seemed just around the corner. The problem, of course, is acidity; 6.6 g/l is simply insufficient for a wine of this richness if it is to be properly balanced.

Monterey County is also the home of the Jekel winery. Bill Jekel's vineyards are in the Arroyo Seco area of the Salinas Valley, the same area where Karl Wente found his grapes being attacked by botrytis in the 1960s. The 40 acres planted with Riesling are particularly susceptible to botrytis, since right through the summer cool damp air is sucked inland from off the ocean. This leaves overnight fog that slowly burns off the next morning. Even Jekel's 'ordinary' Riesling usually contains up to 10% botrytised grapes, which give the wine greater complexity. Since the area is an arid one with only eight inches of annual rainfall, Jekel can supplement the moisture level by turning on overhead sprinklers, which also encourage the development of botrytis. In dry years he must wait until November before picking, though when September proves cool and moist and noble rot develops fast, he finds he must pick the botrytised grapes first. Sometimes repeated pickings are required, though he would rather avoid this. The must weights range from 30° to 40° Brix.

Jekel gives the must skin contact for twenty-four hours to extract some tannin. After pressing, the grapes are cold-fermented for up to forty days. He aims for a balance of not more than 10% alcohol and of about 19% residual sugar. Once this balance is achieved, the wine is chilled to arrest fermentation and the yeasts are filtered out. The wine remains in tank at very low temperatures in order to stabilise it, and it is bottled by April. Admirably, Jekel gives the wine three years' bottle-age before releasing it, and during that period it gains in richness and viscosity. On average about 3500 bottles are produced annually in those years, such as 1978, 1979, 1980, 1981, 1982, and 1985, when such a wine was feasible. It is not only a question of climate; if the botrytis arrives at the wrong time, the winery may be too preoccupied with other vintages to devote the care and attention that botrytised wines demand.

The 1979 Riesling grapes were hand-picked on 1 December at 29° Brix. Fermentation lasted eighty days, and residual sugar was a modest 10%. The result, while more lean and citric than some of the Napa and Sonoma blockbusters, is very appealing: botrytis was very evident on the nose, which was lush and peachy and supple; on the palate the wine was fresh, with a touch of CO_2, although it was seven years old when tasted. There was a hint of bitter orange on the finish, and though the wine did lack depth and concentration, it was undoubtedly stylish, a welcome example of a California botrytised Riesling that should keep for well over a decade.

Even further south than the Salinas Valley is the Santa Ynez Valley, close to Santa Barbara. Here the Firestone Vineyard is situated. The climate is surprisingly cool, and since fog is quite common, botrytised grapes are not unusual. Excellent conditions prevailed in 1982, and 80% of the Riesling grapes picked at 31° Brix on 11 October were botrytised. The must was given fourteen hours' skin contact before a long, slow pressing began. After settling, the

THE
FIRESTONE
VINEYARD

Santa Ynez Valley, California
JOHANNISBERG RIESLING
The Ambassador's Vineyard
Selected 1982 Harvest

RESIDUAL SUGAR 12.2° BRIX   HARVEST SUGAR 31.0° BRIX
GROWN, PRODUCED & BOTTLED BY THE FIRESTONE VINEYARD
LOS OLIVOS, CALIFORNIA. BW4720 · ALCOHOL 10.5% BY VOLUME

juice was inoculated with Steinberg yeast and fermented for five weeks at 50 °F. Unusually for a California Late Harvest Riesling, the wine spent a month in French oak. The resulting wine was deep gold, showed clear botrytis on the nose, and was ripe and forward on the palate. Despite fairly high acidity, the wine did not seem built for long ageing. The 1985, which I have not tasted, promises to be a richer and bigger wine. The fully botrytised grapes were harvested at 40° Brix, spent four months in French oak, and gave a wine of 22.5% residual sugar. The Firestone wines have the additional merit of being very reasonably priced.

SÉMILLON AND SAUVIGNON

California's emergence onto the international wine market as a leading producer of top-quality wines encouraged many wineries to plant ever increasing acreage of classic grape varieties. Within a few years, even Cabernets and Chardonnays from young vines were scoring exceedingly well in blind tastings against their models from Bordeaux and Burgundy. Inevitably, some winemakers also sought to pit their skills against those exhibited by the top Sauternes properties. It was Myron Nightingale and his wife Alice who pioneered the making of botrytised Sémillon in California. What makes their work interesting is that they were probably the first winemakers anywhere to induce botrytis artificially. They devised the method in the 1950s, and are still at it thirty years later under the auspices of Beringer Vineyards. In the early days they were convinced that the Californian climate could not regularly provide the alternations of humidity and dryness necessary for botrytis to take hold without giving way to *pourriture grise*, and this is why they brought the grapes indoors and induced the infection artificially.

It was not, in retrospect, the wisest of choices to select Sémillon for their experiments, for Californian Sémillon is not especially susceptible to the fungus, which is more likely to attack Riesling or Chenin Blanc or even Zinfandel. On the other hand, it was the basis of Sauternes, and that was the model for the Nightingales' experiments. In the laboratory, Alice Nightingale pored through botrytis cultures to isolate fertile spores that, when sprayed on grapes, would infect them thoroughly. Entirely healthy Sémillon bunches are selected in the vineyard (usually Knights Valley grapes from Sonoma) at roughly 23° Brix. These bunches are laid on chicken-wire trays inside the temperature-controlled winery and the next day the spores are sprayed on. The grapes are wrapped in plastic for thirty hours to ensure 100% humidity, and then alternating cool and warm air is blown over the grapes to simulate ideal conditions in the field. After two weeks the grapes shrivel and Brix readings almost double. They are now ready to be pressed. The juice is inoculated with Champagne yeasts and fermented at 55 °F for up to thirty days until arrested by chilling. The wine, after settling for three days, is racked off the lees, rested for another month, then racked again or filtered, and finally clarified and put in Limousin oak barrels for a month or two. The wine is bottled in May and aged for six months before release.

Although artificially induced botrytis should allow comparatively large quantities of wine to be made, the first commercially available botrytised Sémillon made by the Nightingales and marketed by Beringer, the 1980 vintage, was limited to fewer than 2000 bottles. It had 15% residual sugar (the following year's wine had 21%) and 8.0 g/l acidity. In 1982 the grapes picked at 22° Brix increased their sugar content to 36° after infection, leaving 10.3% residual sugar, 12% alcohol, and 8.0 g/l acidity. It was a curious wine, rather oily on the nose, and quite rich, rounded, and complex. It will certainly improve, but it seemed a charmless wine, lacking in verve. The 1985 Sauvignon Blanc (the grapes came from Yountville near Napa) registered 40° Brix after infection, and had 11.2% residual sugar. Not surprisingly it was closed on the palate, but young Sauvignon· is usually quite fruity and aggressive on the nose, whereas this one was grassy and even suggested peanuts. The structure seemed sound, but the wine lacked zip and vigour. The Beringer Late Harvest Rieslings, on the other hand, can be first-rate. The 1982 is superb wine, very rich yet clean and perfectly balanced by acidity, and the 1985 is almost as good. An Auslese-style 1978 is, however, beginning to tire.

Robert Mondavi has also tried his hand at botrytised Sauvignon Blanc, a style, incidentally, alien to Sauternes, where this grape would always be blended with Sémillon. In 1981 he made 2400 bottles, but it is not a complete success. The nose is fine and lush, with aromas of melon and banana, and though the wine attacks the palate nicely and is quite fat and rounded, it is hot and slightly bitter on the finish. Monticello Cellars began making this style of wine the following year (with 6% Sémillon blended in), and rather pretentiously call it Chateau M. The botrytised grapes were harvested at 36° Brix, and vinification followed French models: the must was partially barrel-fermented and then aged for seventeen months in Limousin oak barrels. 1200 bottles were made. The balance, with 14.2% alcohol and 10% residual sugar, echoes the 1981 Mondavi wine, but it is fresher, more charming, leaner. The botrytis is most pronounced on the nose, and the wine is well-balanced, lively, and has very good length. Far richer than either of these wines is Cakebread Cellars' Rutherford Gold made in 1982 from botrytised Sauvignon Blanc picked at 48° Brix; the wine is high in acidity and has 27.9% residual sugar. I have not tasted this very expensive wine (released at $35 per half), but it must be curious indeed, for with only 7.7% alcohol and high residual sugar it must be Germanic in style if not in flavour. Other California wineries that made botrytised Sauvignon wines in 1982 include Almaden, who produced one under their Charles Lefranc label from partially botrytised Monterey County grapes. It is a melony wine, quite sweet with reasonable acidity, though not especially appealing. (A 1984 Late Harvest Sémillon from Caymus was similar in style, though more flabby.) The 1982 from Christian Brothers, from grapes picked at 28° Brix and thus with only 8.3% residual sugar, was vegetal on the nose and palate, with a strong whiff of asparagus; it was dilute and lacked acidity.

The Late Harvest Riesling champions have also begun to take an interest in the French varieties, and in 1985 Phelps barrel-fermented a Late Harvest Sémillon (with 5% Sauvignon Blanc). This is quite a hefty wine, with 13.8% alcohol and 11.5% residual sugar. The oak is certainly discernible on the nose, though it does not mask the fruit; on the palate the wine suggests tropical fruits. Lush and intense and with good acidity, it should develop well. Chateau St Jean are pleased with their 1984 Sémillon d'Or, which blends 62% Sémillon with 38% Sauvignon, harvested with an average of 32° Brix. This wine also has 13.8% alcohol but a modest 8.2% residual sugar. It had been in bottle for less than a year when I tasted it, and it was very closed, especially on the nose. Both alcohol and acidity were dominating the wine, and the balance seemed suspect, though it was probably going through a spell of hibernation. Chateau St Jean expect this wine to outlast most of their Rieslings.

GEWÜRZTRAMINER

Chateau St Jean have also made Late Harvest Gewürztraminer from grapes picked at the Belle Terre vineyard in Alexander Valley at 27° Brix. The varietal character is strongly present on the nose, which is broad and spicy; it is a gentle wine on the palate, ample and soft, and while it has good acidity, it still lacks verve and raciness. But that is a lot to ask of any Gewürztraminer, and within its own terms this is a good and successful wine.

Mark West Vineyards in Russian River Valley have built up a sound reputation for their Gewürztraminers. In 1984 the crop was enormous, so they left some fruit on the vine and made two Late Harvest wines, one from grapes picked at 27° Brix, and the other from grapes picked at 31.5°. In 1986 the lighter wine was showing better; the varietal character was pronounced and the wine had a vivacity unusual for Gewürztraminer. The sweeter wine, still with only 9.7% residual sugar, conveyed mixed messages, tasting both sweet and aggressive and not very pleasant. Whether it will pull itself together in the next few years is questionable.

Also in Sonoma County, the Field Stone Winery made 1200 bottles of delicious lush Gewürztraminer from grapes picked at 31° Brix in 1984; the bouquet, broad and floral, was especially delightful. Unusually, the wine had spent four months in oak. It is immediately appealing, though it would be surprising if it retained its charm for many years. Even richer, and more obviously botrytised on nose and palate, was a 1981 Late Harvest Gewürztraminer from Clos du Bois, also in Sonoma. The grapes were picked at 41° Brix and fermented to 10.7% alcohol and 19.5% residual sugar. The wine's sweet creamy intensity and rich tones of apricot and honey were nicely cut by very good acidity. This wine does seem to have a future, though sadly only 1200 bottles were made.

Gewürztraminers, dry or sweet, are less common in Napa Valley. Monticello, who succeeded admirably with their botrytised Sauvignon, picked botrytised Gewürztraminer at 29° Brix in 1983, and made a reasonably stylish wine with 11% alcohol and 7% residual sugar; though a touch dilute in flavour, it does have good length. It was aged in old French oak for ten months.

Felton-Empire in the Santa Cruz region has made Late Harvest Gewürztraminers as well as its more famous Rieslings. Both the 1979 and 1981 were very good, quite classic in style and not at all overblown. There was sufficient acidity to keep the wines lively in the mouth and on the finish, though neither had great length. It is their balance and structure that give them grace and charm, and it is regrettable that the winemaker, Leo McCloskey, has decided to discontinue making Gewürztraminer.

CHENIN BLANC AND CHARDONNAY

Callaway Vineyards, located in the hills 90 miles south-east of Los Angeles, first invented and then cornered the market for Late Harvest wines made from these two varieties. Callaway consider both soil conditions and microclimate ideal for white grapes, and produce nothing else. Their botrytised Chenin Blanc is labelled Sweet Nancy, but fortunately the wine's reputation is better than its name. The 1982 vintage was typical. On 27 October grapes were harvested at 39° Brix. The must was fermented at a very low temperature (38 °F), which is why it took sixteen months to complete fermentation. The resulting wine had 16% residual sugar and 9.5 g/l acidity. The following year a combination of summer showers and a mild autumn provoked botrytis to attack not the Chenin Blanc but some Chardonnay vineyards. The grapes were harvested on 31 October and cold-fermented for over ten months, resulting in a wine very similar in balance to Sweet Nancy's. And in 1984 Callaway moved to a third grape variety and produced a Late Harvest Sauvignon Blanc. All these wines are fermented very slowly, then racked, cold-stabilised, bottled, and given three months' bottle-age before being released. Even though the acidity levels are quite high, Callaway does not expect the wines to gain in complexity with age, and recommends they be consumed within about three years of release.

MUSCATS

All the grapes varieties previously discussed are, in terms of California's heritage as a wine-producing state, relative newcomers. Muscats of various varieties, however, have been around for a long time, and many are still very popular. Their grapiness and lovely fragrance give them an immediate appeal. Most Californian sweet Muscats strike me as unsubtle wines, brazen, obvious, tiring. Beaulieu Vineyard's Muscat de Frontignan is typical: bright orange-gold in colour, hefty and hot on the nose, and sweet, grapy, and direct on the palate. Simi's Muscat Canelli is made from the same variety; it is well-made, more sophisticated than Beaulieu's, fresh and sweet and direct, but nonetheless vapid. The huge Papagni winery in the Central Valley, the hottest of California's many wine regions, produces a non-vintage Muscat of Alexandria called Moscato d'Angelo. The grapes are hand-harvested – unusual in the highly mechanised Central Valley vineyards – and cold-fermented at 36 °F for six months. Fermentation is arrested by chilling when the wine reaches 12% residual sugar and the yeasts are filtered out. Such vinification certainly preserves the fresh floral aromas of the grape, but the high sugar content throttles any potential delicacy and crispness, and the result is rich and blowsy and unctuous. Moscato d'Angelo does have a strong following, however, as does the Spumante made from the same must. In the Napa Valley, Sutter Home Vineyards also make a Muscat of Alexandria called Muscat Amabile. It is less sweet than Moscato d'Angelo, but less well-made, flabby and short.

Christian Brothers' Ch La Salle is also produced in the Central Valley, and this is a much less fatiguing wine. The nose is grapy and fresh, and there is a hint of *pétillance* on the palate, which is pert and attractive. Although not low in alcohol, the wine does bear some resemblance to the Muscats of Piedmont, and does not betray the low acidity one associates with high-yielding grapes from the hot Central Valley. Rather lighter in style is Mondavi's Moscato d'Oro, a medium sweet wine, also slightly *pétillant*; but its pleasures are fleeting and it has never managed to engage my interest beyond the initial grapy attack on the palate.

One of the most persuasive of Californian Muscats is that labelled, rather grandly, as Essensia by Andrew Quady, a Central Valley winemaker. As a fortified wine, much like a French Vin Doux Naturel, it should be beyond the scope of this book. But it is such an engaging wine that it would be a pity not to mention it. He has planted 10 acres with Orange Muscat vines (the Italian Moscato Fior d'Arancio) and picks early, in mid-August, when the flavours of this relatively low-yielding variety are at their peak. The wine is very appealing, concentrated in aroma and flavour, with a distinctive orange tone. However it does have 15% alcohol, and the wine is rather fierce. Quady has also begun to make a fortified Black Muscat labelled, with typical attention-grabbing overstatement, as Elysium. This is a most striking wine: light purple magenta in colour, with an enchantingly rosy and perfumed nose. The alcohol does tend to mask the fruit, but the wine is otherwise well made and has a fairly dry finish. Philip Togni has also used this grape (more commonly known as Muscat Hamburg) to produce a stunningly aromatic and intensely concentrated wine he labels, unappetizingly, as Black Hamburger.

ZINFANDEL

I used to think Chenin Blanc was versatile until I encountered Zinfandel. Indeed, its versatility partially explains its decline in popularity in recent years; consumers never quite know what to expect when they buy it from an unfamiliar producer. In its basic form it is a gutsy red wine with some affinity to, say, Syrah, but while it is inconceivable that some dashing Rhône winemaker would produce a white Syrah, there is no shortage of White Zinfandel in California. Sutter Home, one of the Napa wineries that pioneered this style, have sold millions of bottles of this innocuous pale pink fluid. At the other extreme are the Late Harvest Zinfandels, a style that Mayacamas Vineyards, a spectacular mountain winery high up between Napa and Sonoma counties, was one of the first to exploit.

The wines are not unlike Italian Amarone, though they are made from overripe rather than dried grapes. Fermentation often sails along to 16% or 17% alcohol, and even at that fearsome level there is usually a touch of unfermented sugar left in the wine to give it a hint of sweetness. In general the wines have less than 1% residual sugar, yet most taste sweeter than their analyses would suggest. What gives a good Late Harvest Zinfandel its distinction is less its sweetness than its intensity and concentration of flavour. The soil in the Mayacamas vineyards, which are dry-farmed, is volcanic and rough. There are a number of old vines, and yields never exceed 1.5 tons per acre. (Mike Grgich, who is Croatian by birth, once told me: 'Where I come from, we say old chicken makes good soup. The same applies to old vines.')

Soon after Mayacamas's Late Harvest Zinfandels appeared on the market, they were acclaimed. Michael Broadbent, who tasted the 1968 in 1972, compared it to 'a big young Latour in cask' and the 1972, tasted in 1979, had, he considered, 'decades of life ahead'. Both wines received five stars in his *Great Vintage Wine Book*. However, I have tasted two vintages of this wine in the mid-1980s, and while they are undoubtedly extraordinary, their longevity must now be in question. The 1974, a massive, hot, peppery wine of great concentration and power, is definitely beginning to dry out. And the 1978, sweet, rich, and intensely fruity in 1985, seemed at the summit of its excellence. When I compared my own tasting notes with those made by the winery staff at a vertical tasting some months before, there was considerable disagreement even among the winemakers. Linn Brinner, the assistant winemaker, agreed the 1978 was at its best, and the 1976 was not much liked. But the 1974, which I have tasted twice and found in decline, is the favourite vintage of Bob Travers, the owner and winemaker, and his least favourite is the excellent 1978! The 1984, which was not released when I visited Mayacamas, is said to be exceptionally good, and, unusually, it has 4.6% residual sugar.

It is said that the first Late Harvest Zinfandels were made by accident; the grapes were left on the vine longer than intended, and had alarmingly high must weights when harvested. This was certainly the case at Mount Veeder, another Mayacamas Mountains winery. Stuck with overripe grapes picked at 29° Brix, the winery had no choice but to ferment them and see what happened. The result was a wine of 15.3% alcohol and 0.45% residual sugar. Marketed as a Late Harvest wine, it was not a commercial success. Opaque ruby in colour, it shows extreme ripeness on the nose, with masses of fruit, yet an over-intense, almost medicinal quality that is somewhat off-putting; on the palate the wine is fairly sweet, then hot and peppery. The balance, or lack of it, betrays the wine, and though it would provide a very welcome glass after a trek to the South Pole, it is too overwhelming to give very profound pleasure. Nor does it appear to have much future.

In 1980 Johnson's Alexander Valley winery produced a Late Harvest Zinfandel of rather ordinary quality, sweet and soapy on the nose, and intense, concentrated, grapy, yet one-dimensional, and short. The grapes were picked at 35° Brix, and the wine has 15.8% alcohol and 2.1% residual sugar. Zinfandel is also the basis for some

California ports, some of which are vivid and highly drinkable. Sutter Home produce a fortified 'Dessert' Zinfandel, which has 18% alcohol and 9.4% residual sugar – a fiery drink, yet lively and with good fruit.

The most striking Late Harvest Zinfandel I have ever encountered was made by the Calera Wine Company, based 1300 feet up in remote hill country near Hollister, between San Jose and the Central Valley. Calera is best known for its remarkable Pinot Noir, but in 1976, a year after the first Pinot vines were planted, wine was made from bought-in botrytised Zinfandel picked at 38° Brix. Ten years later, when I tasted the wine, it was quite brown at the edges and not very alluring, but the nose was extraordinary, since it reeked of botrytis. So much so that with my eyes closed I would not have been able to say that the wine I was sniffing was red. It bore little resemblance to the Beerenauslesen made from Pinot variants and other red grapes in Germany and Austria, simply because the Zinfandel has so much body and extract. On the palate this wine was very sweet and concentrated and had good depth of flavour, though slightly musty; moreover, it showed no signs of fading and had excellent length. In contrast, a 1978 Late Harvest Zinfandel picked at 39° Brix but made from healthy grapes was less satisfactory. This truly is a sweet wine, for despite the 13.9% alcohol, it has 12% residual sugar. Inky purple-red in colour, it has a sweet porty nose also reminiscent of nail polish; on the palate it is extremely sweet, intense and grapy, still a bit tannic, and with a slight stickiness out of harmony with the essentially dry finish. Though initially splendid, it would surely have tired the palate more rapidly than the eccentric 1976.

Probably the greatest exponent of Zinfandel in California is Paul Draper of Ridge Vineyards in the Santa Cruz Mountains. His wines are remarkable for their finesse – high alcohol and intensity of fruit that manage not to be fatiguing – and he has occasionally made Late Harvest wines. Much as I admire Ridge's Cabernets and 'ordinary' Zinfandels, I have not been overwhelmed by the Late Harvest wines. The 1978, picked at 40.5° Brix, had 10.5% residual sugar, and a sweet intensity and silkiness in the mouth nicely allied to a dry finish. Yet it lacked spiciness and conspicuous length. Draper's 1981 wine is far less formidable (the grapes were picked at 26° Brix and left 2% residual sugar). This wine spent a year in wood and like its predecessor has great richness on the palate and a sweet portiness on the nose. Though admirable in its way, it lacks complexity, and is not a wine I would care to drink very often.

Late Harvest Zinfandels do not, in my experience, live up to their promise. Whether this is a consequence of their harvesting and vinification, or an intrinsic attribute of the grape variety, it is difficult to say. It is significant that in the Veneto, the grapes for Recioto and Amarone are grown and harvested and dried with immense care and selectivity. The best winemakers seek not only intensity of flavour but good acidity, and top Recioto has an elegance that Late Harvest Zinfandel, for all its power and magnificence, rarely attains.

It is, in my view, idle to make qualitative comparisons between the sweet wines of California and their European models. The very finest Californian Late Harvest Rieslings can easily hold their own with many a German Beerenauslese, and even a well-made Mosel can seem pallid next to a sumptuous Chateau St Jean or Phelps wine. Californian sweet wines ought to be accepted on their own terms. With the exception of some Sémillon and Sauvignon, they are immediate wines, rich and generous on the nose and palate, that hold little back in reserve. As in Austria or some parts of Germany since the wine law of 1971, too much emphasis may be placed on must weights and residual sugar at the expense of other constituents, of which acidity is the most important. Californian vines tend to be younger and higher-yielding than their European counterparts, though these are not especially significant factors in the production of sweet wines. The technological sophistication of most wineries' vinification procedures preserves the fruitiness and immediate allure of the wines – and such features are certainly important – but the tendency to bottle early may result in a lack of structure. The winemakers of the Mosel and the Loire may bottle just as early, but their wines have a striking acidity that will keep the wine alive in the bottle for a decade or more and influence its development. Many Californian wines do not have that high acidity, and although it is legal for winemakers to adjust acidity, it is uncommon to find wines of such exemplary structure and balance that one feels certain they will keep for decades. Another important problem with Californian wines is a tendency to push the fermentation too far, which can result in wines uncomfortably high both in alcohol and volatile acidity.

Despite these reservations, one has to applaud the general quality of these wines, especially when one bears in mind that Californians have only been experimenting with their production for just over a decade. It is entirely conceivable, given the willingness and eagerness of Californians to adjust and experiment and think again when required, that in another ten years there will be wines that can challenge the best of Germany and France not only in terms of their immediate impression but in terms of their staying power and finesse. Chateau St Jean and Phelps are certainly well along that path.

Australia and South Africa

AUSTRALIA

Until a few years ago Australia's best known dessert wines were magnificent Liqueur Muscats and Tokays, many of which came from north-east Victoria. These wines, the result of careful blending, long wood-ageing, and a solera system, are all fortified, and it is only recently that Australian winemakers have turned their skilled hands to unfortified styles. Unlike those of California, the botrytised wines of Australia are made as often from Sémillon and Sauvignon as from Riesling.

The De Bortoli winery at Griffith, New South Wales, had long been interested in trying its hand at such wines. In 1958 the McWilliams company had made a wine from botrytised Pedro Ximenes grapes, of all things, so Deen De Bortoli and his son Darren knew that botrytis did occur in the region. An attempt at such a wine made in 1981 failed because of lack of humidity, but in 1982 the De Bortolis reaped a large crop of botrytised Sémillon, picked at 22° Baumé. The harvest was supplemented by crops from neighbouring growers, who on the brink of despair at seeing the grapes attacked by rot, were soothed by the knowledge that the De Bortolis were prepared to take the botrytised grapes off their hands and even pay them for the rotten fruit. (Ten years ago, most Australian growers would simply have thrown away any botrytised grapes.) After crushing – a slow and laborious business – the must was pumped into steel tanks and allowed to settle. Pressing took place in old-fashioned hydraulic basket presses, and after clarification, the must was fermented in temperature-controlled stainless steel tanks for almost twelve weeks. The wine was aged for almost a year in French oak.

That year also enabled the De Bortolis to repeat the experiment of the McWilliams' winery many years before, since they also picked a small quantity of botrytised Pedro Ximenes at 26° Baumé, which produced a wine with 165 g/l residual sugar and an astonishing 13.1% alcohol. The following year De Bortoli produced a slightly less rich botrytised Sémillon, which was blended with 20% Sauvignon Blanc. Alerted to the possibility of imminent rains, the De Bortolis harvested earlier than they had intended and picked the grapes at 18–20° Baumé. Fermentation took four weeks less than in 1982, and most of the wine was aged in French oak for between six and twelve months. The 1983 has 112 g/l residual sugar, compared to 129 g/l in the 1982. Both wines are extremely good, and I particularly liked the more aromatic, if less sumptuous, nose of the 1983. The following year, botrytised grapes were being picked at 24° Baumé and the wine was as lush as the 1982, and the 1985 was even richer, with 145 g/l residual sugar. Botrytis attacked the grapes yet again in 1986, and they were picked at 23° Baumé; this wine will not be released until 1988. Acidity levels in all these wines are very good, ranging from 9 to 10.5 g/l.

De Bortoli have also made sweet wines, in styles ranging from Spätlese to Beerenauslese, from botrytised Traminer and Riesling. Botrytised Rieslings are also a speciality of the Hill-Smith Estates, though they have also marketed Botrytised Sémillon. These wines are also very good, perhaps not as sumptuous as the De Bortoli range and with more obvious volatile acidity, but nonetheless wines of great style and balance. A 1984 Botrytis Riesling from Petaluma had excellent varietal character and good balance between the fruit and a nutty appley acidity on the finish. More disappointing are the sweet wines from Brown Brothers of Milawa, Victoria. Their Noble Riesling is very sweet and intense but fades rapidly in the mouth; enjoyable while it lasts on the palate, the wine simply does not have enough acidity to keep it going. Nor have I been greatly excited by Brown Brothers' blend of Orange Muscat and Flora (a crossing of Sémillon and Gewürztraminer), both late harvested. The grapes ensure that the nose is penetrating and grapy, but the wine lacks weight and is short; a pleasant enough apertif, but little more.

A very different style of wine is made at Primo Estates by Joe Grilli

by artificially injecting grapes with botrytis in controlled conditions.
His methods are not dissimilar to those pioneered by Myron and
Alice Nightingale in California, and subsequently pursued in Australia by Tim Knappstein of Enterprise Wines in Clare. Primo Estates is
based in South Australia, just outside Adelaide, not a region conducive to botrytis attacks. Botrytis cultures are assembled in Grilli's
laboratory before the harvest, which usually begins in March.
Healthy bunches of Riesling are laid on raised trays, and then
sprayed with a solution containing the botrytis spores. The room in
which the grapes are laid is then flooded with a couple of inches of
water and the grapes covered with plastic sheets to ensure very high
humidity. After botrytis has taken hold, the grapes are subjected to
blasts of cool air for two weeks so as to shrivel further before being
pressed and fermented. While the grapes are shrivelling, they must
be carefully watched and any fruit that attracts unwanted moulds or
infections has to be weeded out. The grapes' must weight has usually
risen by the time they are pressed to an average of 23. The result is a
series of vintages, beginning in 1981, of what Grilli calls Auslese and
Beerenauslese wines. Riesling is the grape he uses most, though in
1983 he blended 90% Sémillon and 10% Sauvignon Blanc. Acidity
levels are adjusted to over 10 g/l, and alcohol is also fairly high at
10.5% to 11.5%. The principal reason why such methods are not

more widespread is that they are costly and labour-intensive. I have only tasted one of Grilli's sweet wines – his very rich 1984 Botrytis Riesling Beerenauslese, and none of those made by similar methods by Neil Jericho at Woorinen Estate, but I found it impossible to distinguish the wine made by artificially inducing botrytis from others made from naturally botrytised grapes.

Despite the successes among Australian sweet wines – and the De Bortoli Sémillons can stand comparison with Sauternes – many are still clumsily made, and fail to take best advantage of good fruit. Seppelt's Ausleses and Orlando's 1980 Late Harvest Sémillon suffer from oiliness and a lack of acidity that leaves them blowsy, while Norman's Rieslings are over-alcoholic, aggressive, and disjointed. Curiously the 1985 Norman's Beerenauslese was much superior to their TBA of that year, which was made from selected grapes picked from the same bunches used for Beerenauslese. A similar fierceness flawed the otherwise delicate 1985 Crawford River Beerenauslese.

SOUTH AFRICA

Two centuries ago South Africa was internationally renowned for a rich dessert wine called Constantia that has been extinct for decades. (A detailed historical account of Constantia is given by André P. Brink in his *Dessert Wine in South Africa*.) The practice of making wines from botrytised grapes was revived at Nederburg in the Cape by Gunter Brozel, who came to South Africa from Germany. In 1969 he made a wine called Edelkeur that has since become celebrated as the country's finest sweet wine. The grape varieties most commonly used to make botrytised wines are Chenin Blanc (called Steen in South Africa) and Riesling. Edelkeur is a Steen wine, but Brozel has also made botrytised wines from Riesling and Bukettraube, an obscure import from Germany. Since 1975 the Edelkeur wines have only been sold at auction, where they fetch very high prices. The only vintage I have tasted was the 1978, which was certainly very good, with a sweet appley nose, also suggestive of dried fruits, while on the palate it was intensely sweet and orangey but a bit cloying and lacking in acidity and length. The 1979 is said to be even better, and in 1983 Edelkeur won top prize for a botrytised wine at the Bristol Wine Fair.

Following Gunter Brozel's example, other South African wine-makers, including some cooperatives, have taken to making wines from late-picked or botrytised grapes, and the wine authorities have recently devised a labelling system for categorising the various styles. Late Harvest need have no more than 30 g/l residual sugar, may contain concentrated must, and is roughly equivalent to German Spätlese; Special Late Harvest and Noble Late Harvest must contain no Süssreserve. Special Late Harvest must have 20–50 g/l residual sugar, and Noble Late Harvest, which must contain a proportion of botrytised grapes, must have at least 50 g/l residual sugar.

Other Cape wineries that make Noble Late Harvest wines include Bergsig, Delheim (theirs is called Edelspatz), Groot Constantia, Saxonburg, Simonsig, Spier, Wetevrede, and De Wetshof, whose Edeloes is a pretty, well-balanced wine made from a blend of grape varieties. Other wineries produce Muscats of Alexandria that can be quite sweet.

Sweet Wine and Food

Although there are a few combinations of food and sweet wine that complement one another – such as *foie gras* with Sauternes – it is my stern belief that sweet wines of high quality (and there is no point drinking any other kind) are best enjoyed on their own. While it is certainly true that strong swaggering sweet wines, such as Anghelu Ruju or Amarone, will not be overpowered by even the richest desserts, I see little point in struggling to accommodate two elements that are best enjoyed separately. Certain cheeses can be nibbled very happily to the accompaniment of Sauternes or Tokay, but I usually prefer to consume them with the red wine left over from the main course. At Brook Towers, sweet wines are served in one of two ways. A light sweet wine – certain Barsacs, German Auslese, Coteaux du Layon – will provide a delectable aperitif, while richer wines are only brought onto the table after all the food has either been eaten or cleared away. There are those who say that after a satisfying meal it is difficult to appreciate a sweet wine and that the palate is numbed. That has not been my experience. On the contrary, the palate is stimulated by the mild shock to the tastebuds that a sweet wine invariably provides. With no sticky puddings to distract the attention, it is possible under such circumstances to treat the wine with the respect it ought to deserve. I see no point in making it fight for its integrity in the face of gustatory challenges from fruit tarts, rice puddings, ice creams, or, heaven forbid, chocolate mousse.

Those who feel it is somehow wasteful to drink wine on its own without propping it up with food should consult Richard Olney's book on *Yquem*, which contains an exhaustive and, it must be admitted, intriguing and stimulating chapter on dishes either made with or designed to accompany Sauternes and other sweet wines.

Glossary

acidity There are two kinds of acidity in wine: fixed, which is derived from the various acids (malic, tartaric, citric) in the grape juice, and volatile, which is generated during vinification. Acidity levels mentioned in the text refer to total acidity, a combination of fixed and volatile. Acidity is an essential component of sweet wines, providing balance and ensuring longevity.

amabile (It) A medium sweet wine.

appellation contrôlée (Fr) The system regulating which grapes may be grown where and which styles of wine may be made from them. Usually abbreviated to AC or AOC. In Italy, the comparable system is known as DOC.

assemblage (Fr) The blending of barrels or lots from different vineyards or grape varieties to give a uniform single wine.

Aszú The distinctive method, used in Tokay in Hungary, of adding a paste made from botrytised grapes to must or wine.

barrique (Fr) 225-litre barrel, usually of oak.

Baumé (Fr) Sugar content of grapes is expressed in terms of their Baumé reading on a hydrometer scale, which is close to the readings for potential alcohol. For instance, a Baumé reading of 17.9° is equivalent to 17.5% potential alcohol. Thus grapes picked at 18° Baumé will, if fermentation ceases at 13%, give a wine with roughly 5° Baumé left in the form of residual sugar. Nowadays many French winemakers use potential alcohol rather than Baumé to measure must weights, though residual sugar is still often expressed in Baumé. 1° Baumé is roughly equivalent to 18 g/l residual sugar.

Bereich (G) A large sub-region within one of the eleven German wine regions.

Botrytis A fungus that attacks certain grape varieties under certain climatic conditions. It is an essential condition for the production of most sweet wines of the finest quality. For a full discussion of botrytis and its actions, see Chapter 1.

Brix (US) A hydrometer scale that measures the sugar content of grape juice. The scale indicates percentage by weight of sucrose when immersed in sucrose solutions at 20 °C.

centrifuge A machine that employs centrifugal force to eliminate solid particles in must or wine.

cépage (Fr) Grape variety.

chaptalization The addition of sugar to must before or during fermentation as a means of increasing alcohol levels in the finished wine. Practised, under controlled circumstances, in France and Germany, but forbidden in Italy.

débourbage (Fr) The practice of allowing newly-pressed juice to settle before fermentation begins. This allows solid particles to fall to the bottom of a vat or tank and be removed, though many New World wineries use a centrifuge to achieve the same end. Fermentation is delayed either by chilling or by the addition of sulphur dioxide.

Einzellage (G) A single vineyard.

élevage (Fr) The process by which a wine is matured and treated between fermentation and bottling.

encépagement (Fr) The proportion of grape varieties planted at any one estate.

extract Non-sugar solids that give a wine substance, character, and body.

fermentation The conversion of grape sugar into alcohol and carbon dioxide. This chemical process is promoted by the action of yeasts that may be naturally present on the grapeskins or may be inoculated.

filtration A method of clarifying wine by passing it through various kinds of filter. The finer the filtration, the more particles are removed and the cleaner the final wine, and, in the view of some winemakers, the more characterless.

fining A method of clarifying wine by adding agents such as bentonite, egg white, or isinglass (purified fish glue) to the wine, causing suspended particles to coagulate and fall as sediment to the bottom of the cask or tank.

foudre (Fr)   A barrel.

frizzante (It)   Lightly sparkling.

Fuder (G)   Cask used in the Mosel in Germany, holding about 1000 litres.

fût (Fr)   A barrel, usually larger than a *barrique*.

Gemeinde   A village or commune.

Grosslage   A group of vineyards often extending over a number of villages and communes.

hectare   2.471 acres.

lees   A deposit of dead yeasts and bacteria that sinks after fermentation or during maturation to the bottom of a barrel or tank.

liquoreux (Fr)   Rich sweet white wine.

maceration   A method of vinification by which skins are kept in contact with the fermenting must. This extracts the maximum colour and aroma from the grapes.

maître de chai   Cellarmaster.

moelleux (Fr)   Sweet white wine.

must   Unfermented grape juice.

must weight   The sugar content of grapes or must.

mutage (Fr)   The addition of pure alcohol, usually grape spirit, to wine to arrest fermentation.

négociant (Fr)   A wine merchant who acts as a middleman between producer and retailer.

noble rot   See Botrytis cinerea.

Oechsle (G)   A measurement of must weight directly related to the specific gravity of the must. Oechsle indicates by how many grams a litre of must is heavier than water. Thus 100 litres with an Oechsle reading of 100° contains roughly 25 kilograms of sugar. In terms of specific gravity, an Oechsle degree of 100° means the must's specific gravity is 1100; 105° Oechsle is equivalent to a specific gravity of 1105, and so forth. The higher the Oechsle calibration, the higher the degree of potential alcohol.

Ortsteil (G)   A vineyard of such quality that it is entitled to bear its own name or that of its sole proprietor rather than be identified by its locality. Steinberg and Schloss Vollrads are well-known examples.

oxidation   The exposure of wine to air during fermentation and/or maturation. Oxidation darkens the colour and alters the taste of the wine. Desirable in certain sweet wines and inevitable after prolonged ageing in cask or bottle, excessive oxidation can be a fault in a young wine.

passage (Fr) A foray into a vineyard to pick only those grapes in prime condition.

Passito (It) Wine made from grapes that have been dried for weeks or months either on racks in a ventilated attic or for a briefer period in the sun. The drying process concentrates the sugar content of the fruit.

potential alcohol A calculation of the alcohol that would be attained were grapes of a certain must weight fermented until no sugar remained.

pourriture grise (Fr) Grey rot, usually brought about by heavy rain and very destructive.

pourriture noble (Fr) See Botrytis cinerea.

Prädikatswein (G) In Germany and Austria, categories of wine as determined by the sugar content of the grapes.

presses For an explanation of different kinds of wine press in common use, see p. 24.

racking Drawing off clear wine from the lees or other sediments found at the bottom of barrels and tanks.

rancio (Fr) A style of fortified wine made by deliberately exposing the wine to air in order to oxidise it.

régisseur (Fr) The principal winemaker and/or administrator at a large estate.

residual sugar Any grape sugar not converted by yeasts into alcohol remains in the wine in the form of residual sugar, which gives sweet wine its flavour. It is measured in grams per litre (g/l). 17 g/l are roughly equivalent to 1% alcohol.

Strohwein (G) See Passito.

Süssreserve (G) Concentrated musts prevented, usually by chilling or sterilisation, from fermenting, in order that they can be added to finished wines to increase the sugar content. The addition of such juice, its provenance and quality, are strictly controlled in Germany, where its use is most widely practised.

tonneau (Fr) A wholesale measurement equivalent to 1152 bottles.

triage (Fr) A harvesting system whereby pickers return repeatedly to the same vineyards in order to pick the grapes as selectively as possible rather than all at once.

vin de paille (Fr)   See Passito.

viticulteur (Fr)   Wine-grower.

yield   The amount of wine that can be made from a vineyard. Usually measured in hectolitres per hectare (hl/ha), yields are strictly regulated in France.

Table of Correspondences

The following table is not to be interpreted too strictly. The proportion of sugar converted into alcohol during fermentation is variable, only by a small degree, to be sure, but enough to provide some latitude in establishing correspondences. I have not included Klosterneuburger Mostwaage, the scale employed in Austria for measuring must weights, as it is simple to keep in mind the approximate formula for relating KMW to Oechsle. To convert KMW to Oechsle, simply multiply by 5. It is also possible to convert Brix measurements into approximate potential alcohol equivalents by multiplying by 0.55.

Oechsle	Baumé	Brix	Alcohol
65	8.8	15.8	8.1
70	9.4	17.0	8.8
75	10.1	18.1	9.4
80	10.7	19.3	10.0
85	11.3	20.4	10.6
90	11.9	21.5	11.3
95	12.5	22.5	11.9
100	13.1	23.7	12.5
105	13.7	24.8	13.1
110	14.3	25.8	13.8
115	14.9	26.9	14.4
120	15.5	28.0	15.0
125	16.1	29.1	15.6
130	16.6	30.1	16.2

135	17.3	31.2	16.8
140	17.9	32.3	17.5
145	18.7	33.4	18.1
150	19.3	34.5	18.7

Index